MAPPING FEMINIST ANTHROPOLOGY IN THE TWENTY-FIRST CENTURY

MAPPING FEMINIST ANTHROPOLOGY IN THE TWENTY-FIRST CENTURY

EDITED BY ELLEN LEWIN
AND LENI M. SILVERSTEIN

RUTGERS UNIVERSITY PRESS
New Brunswick, New Jersey and London

Library of Congress Cataloging-in-Publication Data
Names: Lewin, Ellen, editor. | Silverstein, Leni M., 1947– editor.
Title: Mapping feminist anthropology in the twenty-first century / edited by Ellen Lewin and Leni M. Silverstein.
Description: New Brunswick, New Jersey : Rutgers University Press, [2016] | Includes bibliographical references and index.
Identifiers: LCCN 2015037350| ISBN 9780813574295 (hardcover : alk. paper) | ISBN 9780813574288 (pbk. : alk. paper) | ISBN 9780813574301 (epub) | ISBN 9780813574318 (web pdf)
Subjects: LCSH: Feminist anthropology.
Classification: LCC GN33.8 .M36 2016 | DDC 305.42—dc23
LC record available at http://lccn.loc.gov/2015037350

A British Cataloging-in-Publication record for this book is available from the British Library.

Visit our website: http://rutgerspress.rutgers.edu

Manufactured in the United States of America

Leni dedicates this book to Manuela and Leonora Silverstein Zoninsein, the next generation, with pride and hope.

Ellen dedicates this book to Liz Goodman, my companion through the twenty-first century.

CONTENTS

ACKNOWLEDGMENTS

Assembling this volume has been an ambitious but extremely satisfying project. But, as is the case with all such ventures, its completion depended on the support and counsel of people from many parts of our lives. The editors first became friends in the early 1960s, when we were undergraduates at the University of Chicago, the place where we both fell in love with anthropology. And we mean "fell in love." Anthropology offered a way to understand the lives of others in a manner that seemed to us (then) to be uniquely respectful, an approach to the world in which every person held a place of honor—as an actor in cultural dramas and as the bearer of viewpoints that were inherently valuable. As women who often felt like outsiders, it also afforded us a way to situate ourselves within a global setting. Although in those prefeminist days, women had yet to be "discovered" and difference in general was deemphasized, anthropology already contained the tools that would enable it (and us) to illuminate these issues—they had only to be unveiled.

After our Chicago years, we both became immersed in the early feminist movement and, as graduate students in anthropology, were both committed to the business of helping the discipline to stretch in order to incorporate questions about gender and sexuality being raised by the movement. Each of us has had a different sort of career in anthropology. For both of us, the question of how to make our anthropological training relevant and responsive to the pressing issues of the modern world was answered clearly by the demands of the feminist movement: to understand the inequities associated with gender and sexuality as they present themselves in many different socioeconomic and historical contexts and to perhaps offer some avenues for their redress.

Our shared history means that our first acknowledgment must be to each other: for the friendship, respect, and support we have shared throughout these years and during the creation of this project, even when we disputed the right way to approach the task of editing this volume. We have (mostly) been patient with one another, and working together has taught us both more than we could have imagined when we launched this undertaking. We discovered that, fortunately, our writing styles were quite similar and that our editorial preferences complemented each other's, producing a more cohesive and thorough book. Co-editing is not an easy job and the fact that our friendship survived is a testament to both the strength of our relationship and the importance we attributed to birthing this volume.

We want to thank everyone who participated in the two sessions at the 2013 American Anthropological Association Chicago meetings that inspired us to edit this volume. Each presenter challenged us to rethink what we thought we knew about the contours of feminist anthropology.

Marlie Wasserman of Rutgers University Press has been every author's dream editor. She has been enthusiastic about the project since we first accosted her at the AAA book exhibit in 2013 and has shepherded us through the various stages of the process with patience and precision. Marlie "gets" feminist anthropology in a way that makes her advice uniquely appropriate. We couldn't have completed the volume without her wisdom—and her insistence on staying on schedule.

All the contributors to the volume have worked diligently to produce the best chapters possible. They accepted our comments, whether they were substantive or seemingly trivial matters of grammar or format, with grace; even those who were asked to produce multiple drafts did so without complaint and adhered to the deadlines we asked them to meet. We are grateful that we were able to assemble such a stellar group of scholars in this volume.

We owe special thanks to anonymous reviewers who evaluated the book proposal and to Claire Wendland, who carried out the review of the completed manuscript. Her comments were substantive and thoughtful, and led us to careful reassessments of parts of the volume. Her attention to the details of arguments was particularly meticulous, and was enormously helpful as we crafted the final version of the introduction. Rayna Rapp and Tom Boellstorff also contributed their critical insight and editorial acumen in vastly sharpening our introductory argument.

Finally, we wish to acknowledge the endless support of our friends and family who accepted numerous pauses, interruptions, and detours in their schedules as we strove to complete this manuscript.

MAPPING FEMINIST ANTHROPOLOGY IN THE TWENTY-FIRST CENTURY

PROLOGUE

RAYNA RAPP

Social movements always recast contested pasts as they stake their claims on a more just future. Recently, much anthropological discussion has been devoted to futurity.[1] Whether traveling under labels like anticipation (Adams et al. 2009), potentiality (Taussig et al. 2013), digital futures (Pels et al. 2010), Afrofuturism (Nelson 2002), or the politics of hope (Miyazaki 2004), these intersecting theoretical discussions broadly concern what Arjun Appadurai calls *The Future as Cultural Fact* (2013). By this title, Appadurai intends to highlight the tensions between risk-saturated probabilities that face escalating numbers of human communities living under conditions of extreme precarity, and more hopeful if fragile possibilities for collective action that might help to shape newly inclusive prospects. Future-oriented writings are highly diverse, focusing on intersecting topics currently of great interest to anthropologists. These range from the globalization of chronic disease and epidemics, and the highly stratified benefits of biomedical and pharmaceutical interventions to the escalation of precarious labor and labor migration. Such writings also focus on growing threats of and responses to climate change and food insecurity as well as the present-day impact of chronic warfare, violations of human rights, and the upending of vulnerable refugee populations, and much more. All involve escalating inequalities and all highlight the impact of social injustice on future generations, as well as our own. These discussions combine a widespread commitment to rethinking anthropological objects/subjects so that retellings of the past in the present will help to construct a future that might thus "be otherwise," to use Elizabeth Povinelli's construction (2012). Yet such disparate literatures cannot simply or easily be lumped together. I bring them briefly into this conversation for a reason: anthropologists and the people among whom we work all hold stakes in imagining futures beyond present-day exclusionary practices that separate out certain groups of people from the conditions of survival, mute their aspirations, and mark their legibility or invisibility. Gender, of course, is interwoven with varying degrees of explicitness into all of these analyses. Likewise, the presence of a gender dimension to any and all forms of rising inequality and future aspirations indexes the kinds of mapping projects undertaken in the chapters in this volume.

Long before the present interest in future imaginaries, feminists in our field developed potent fusions of anthropological theory and practice to scrutinize, critique, and ally with social movements. These projects bore their own utopian/dystopian risks and limitations, as Robyn Wiegman (2000) reminded us. Many of the chapters in *Mapping Feminist Anthropology* provide genealogies of gender-sensitive pasts in order to influence potential futures through present research, writing, and teaching. Some authors document the emergence of gender and sexual critiques and practices designed to heighten theoretical and practical interventions into the heart of the anthropological enterprise (Bolles, Weiss). The book's introductory textual map and eleven chapters offer many rich, lively, open-ended, contentious, and—above all—hopeful readings of hitherto neglected or untheorized lineages. A substantial subset of authors describe current projects to institutionalize or transcend where or how gender in its many intersectionalities reproduces the marks of inferiority, and in turn marks rifts in social life. Collectively, these chapters illustrate how feminisms in all their diversity can articulate continuous critique of present inequality in the service of imaging how more just futures might emerge.

Mapping Feminist Anthropology morphed and developed from conference panels intended to celebrate and assess the twenty-fifth anniversary of the founding of the Association for Feminist Anthropology within the American Anthropological Association. At the time of AFA's founding, most of us whose lives were touched by various versions of what was then called the women's liberation movement understood that we were charged with the seemingly impossible task of transforming the subjects, objects, methods, and theories of our entire field. Naively utopian as this vision seemed then and now, its futurity was focused on addressing gender inequalities and their many forms of intersecting injustice both in our home societies and the ones whose stratifications we often studied.

Improbably enough, feminist interventions succeeded beyond what many of us anticipated; some iterations of gender relations were rapidly embraced as objects of anthropological investigation. Yet I might argue that the very success of institutionalizing the study of gender in intersectional perspectives not only mirrored the unruly heterogeneity and dividing practices of anthropology itself; it also created present-day tensions and barriers to the project of retelling our diverse histories in the service of imagining sufficiently transformational futures. Most who participated in new visions of anthropology dreamed of an "otherwise" future for our field.

Now that some of us dwell in various academic, governmental, nongovernmental, and corporate worlds, how might these modicums of our own inclusion limit our ability to imagine a continuous and always unreachable horizon of social justice?

All the chapters in *Mapping Feminist Anthropology* explore those tensions between institutionalization—securing a home for gender-sensitive intersectional understandings of power, oppression, subjectivity, and mobilization (Kramer)—and continued theoretical, empirical, and practical commitments to building future imaginaries that supersede current understandings of what continual social transformations might look like. Whether discussing widespread violence against Peruvian *indígenas* viewed as an artifact of civil war rather than more accurately and capaciously the subject of multiple, ongoing forms of racialized oppression (Theidon), or the role of women's labor in global climate change and the brutal market opportunities it enforces (Khandelwal), these chapters aim to mobilize ethnographic insight in pursuit of a more just future. To do so, they collectively address many intersecting themes. Here I suggest just three.

First, many chapters unearth hidden and not-so-hidden institutional histories of discrimination and activism. Some focus on tangential connections in and out of our academic homes while others index the heterogeneous relations between feminist anthropologists and burgeoning social movements at home and internationally (Lamphere). As Lynn Bolles tells us, the profound political value of ethnographically derived partial truths should not be underestimated. She thus highlights the productive complexities and built-in uncertainties that we as scholars, as well as advocates, located in our own diverse perspectives and genealogies of experience and activism, bring to institutionalizing gender projects. Second, some authors highlight the importance of reflexivity, situating our own intellectual and political stakes in the questions, methods, and findings of our work (Mascia-Lees). They ask how we perhaps inadvertently other Others, reproducing the boundaries of our own knowledge, and often in that process disabling the usefulness of our findings for intervention (Weiss). The goal of such reflection is, of course, to transform the future of anthropology as a discipline, a lens, a habitus for contributing to a potentially alternative world. Third, these chapters critique what Elizabeth Roberts identifies as "legacies of essentialism." By this, she means attribution of the root cause of suffering and resistance to a naturalized embodiment. Other authors offer similar critiques of identities putatively based on religion, sexuality, and kinship as if any or all predetermine present and therefore future forms of social life. The process of engendering cannot be reduced to reproduction or racialized ethnicity or labor or national/migrational status or religion or sexuality. Indeed, attempts to essentialize gender, making women or men the naturalized victims or agents of their own oppression, misapprehends historical contingency and deep legacies of an overdetermined and hence virtually immutable identity. Identifying iterations of essentialism holds the potential to contribute to future imaginaries, but at the same time it may also entrap us in reflexive halls of mirrors.

Where next? Many of these chapters are frank in their ambition to lay a road map for ongoing transformations, whether in the work of human rights NGOs or the analysis of local, national, and international forces as they redefine domestic violence (Kwiatkowski); the parsing of neoliberal strategies for removal of highly gendered state services to woman-headed families in need (Kingfisher); the importance of recognizing multiple forms of masculinity in indigenous communities, where legacies of military slaughter remain an active presence shaping the lives of men and women traumatized by this violence (Dudgeon). The tensions, constraints, contradictions, small victories, and immense challenges that feminist anthropologists identify and sometimes help to address place us under a collective obligation to continually engage the object and subject of our risk-laden desires and aspirations. The heterogeneous non-synchrony of the social movements, geopolitical forces, and sheer political–economic power relations addressed in these chapters unearth one certainty: whatever the surprises, feminists are obligated, indeed, overdetermined to "write beyond the ending," as feminist poet and literary theorist Rachel DuPlessis (1985) long ago dubbed our messy dilemma in making narratives of new futures possible. And as Alondra Nelson entitled her interview with the Afrofuturist novelist Nalo Hopkinson (2002), "making the impossible possible" is the challenge that we continually glimpse in much of our collective work. By venturing this far and beyond into *Mapping Feminist Anthropology in the Twenty-First Century*, you, too, Dear Reader, are invited and implicated in using the fantastically rich feminist pasts provided to us in the present by this valuable book, so that collectively we might participate in making an otherwise future.

NOTE

1. My understanding of futurity as an aspect of theory/method has been developed in long-standing conversations and writings with Faye Ginsburg. As ever, I thank her for our vibrant anthropological friendship.

REFERENCES

Adams, Vincanne, Michelle Murphy, and Adele E. Clarke. 2009. "Anticipation: Technoscience, Life, Affect, Temporality." *Subjectivity* 28: 246–265.

Appadurai, Arjun. 2013. *The Future as Cultural Fact: Essays on the Global Condition.* London: Verso.

Du Plessis, Rachel. 1985. *Writing Beyond the Ending: Narrative Strategies of Twentieth-Century Women Writers.* Bloomington: Indiana University Press.

Hopkinson, Nalo. 2002. "'Making the Impossible Possible': An Interview with Nalo Hopkinson by Alondra Nelson." *Social Text* 71 (2): 98–113.

Miyazaki, Hirokazu. 2004. *The Method of Hope: Anthropology, Philosophy, and Fijian Knowledge.* Stanford, CA: Stanford University Press.

Nelson, Alondra. 2002. "Future Texts." *Social Text* 71 (2): 1–15.

Pels, Peter, et al. 2010. "The Future Is Elsewhere: Towards a Comparative History of Digital Futurities." http://futurities.info/about/, accessed March 3, 2015.

Povinelli, Elizabeth. 2012. "The Will to Be Otherwise/The Effort of Endurance." *South Atlantic Quarterly* 111 (3): 453–475.

Taussig, Karen-Sue, Klaus Hoyer, and Stefan Helmreich. 2013. "The Anthropology of Potentiality in Biomedicine: An Introduction to Supplement 7." *Current Anthropology* 54 (S7): S3–S14.

Wiegman, Robyn. 2000. "Feminism's Apocalyptic Futures." *New Literary History* 31 (4): 805–825.

INTRODUCTION

Anthropologies and Feminisms: Mapping Our Intellectual Journey

LENI M. SILVERSTEIN AND ELLEN LEWIN

Try to imagine what it was like to study anthropology during the 1960s. First, the profession was predominantly male and androcentric. Second, objectivity or taking a neutral stance in our research was valorized and the notion that politics could influence our investigations was strictly eschewed. And, third, not coincidentally, anthropological research in all four fields was concentrated (albeit unconsciously) on reifying patterns of culture that mirrored conventional elements of contemporary life in the West. Women were viewed as the lesser partners of men. For example, most reconstructions of the life of ancient hominids started with the chase, the public imagination stoked with stories of hunting, aggression, and sex: "me Tarzan, you Jane" evokes the image.

A brief excerpt taken from Frances Dahlberg's edited volume *Woman the Gatherer* offers an account of ancient hunters that illustrates the problems this kind of story provided for scholars or members of the public who had begun to wonder about women's roles in evolution.

> Imagine a group of people walking beside a lake in East Africa two million years ago: five thin, wiry men who carry spears for throwing at game or enemies walk rapidly away from the group. These hunters will search for bushbuck and may be gone for several days while the women and children stay behind. The women move slowly; they are pregnant, carrying toddlers, and besides, they are not going anywhere that day.
>
> They will stay close to the edge of the lake, cooking the remnants of the meat the men brought several days before, maybe looking for snails or gathering some

> squalid roots from the rather sparse vegetation. They will wait patiently until their men return with meat. Each woman was chosen by her husband, so the legend continues, on the basis of her loveliness, especially her prominent breasts and buttocks. Her father or brother gave her to her husband on the basis of his hunting skills and fierceness. Other men will not seduce her because they fear her husband's anger. (Dahlberg 1981, 1)

In this story, Dahlberg was reflecting on the shape of anthropology before serious thought about women and gender transformed the discipline. Her parodic characterization of the "man the hunter" formulation emphasized the pervasive view that human evolution, social organization, culture, and language were all rooted in the centrality of men's activities. The essays included in her edited volume all took aim at the inadequacies of this formulation, setting the stage for the dramatic changes that feminist anthropology would bring to the discipline, as the long-accepted story of the preeminence of hunters collapsed under the persuasive weight of new inquiry.

In this introductory chapter, we propose to map the most salient lines of analysis that led to the disruptive and transformative new field that came to be known as feminist anthropology. These new perspectives constituted a dramatic paradigm shift that today seems mundane. But at the time it began, it represented a bold challenge and rethinking of the entire discipline of anthropology. In bringing this book to fruition, we intend to demonstrate that feminist scholarship continues to breathe new life into anthropology broadly conceived and to generate theoretical innovations. We also will delineate how anthropological studies of women evolved from a unified focus on females (Quinn 1977) to broad lines of inquiry impossible to imagine when the field first made its appearance. This analysis will also lead us to note how the feminist challenge to anthropology both influenced and expanded the changing interests and persuasions of the field itself, helping to legitimize anthropological research not only in exotic locales but at home as well. This was part of a much larger postcolonial transformation of reflexivity, not a concept available to us at the time, but already described by anthropologists working in many locations such as South Africa, India, and parts of Latin America. Thus we will recognize, as well, how our political engagements kept pace while also becoming transformed with the greater inclusion of people of color and gays and lesbians in the discipline; analyses of colonialism and postcolonialism; and the evolving challenges of globalization.

This volume underscores the productive tension between advocacy and theory that has been characteristic of feminist anthropology since its beginnings. The chapters move between a focus on non-Western ethnographic research and engagements with the United States and the West, highlighting shifts in method and writing, as well as topics of research, that have been the trademark of feminist critiques of anthropology. Much of the work in this volume, then, reflects the persistent struggles between academic rigor and public engagement (Lamphere), a movement that continues to challenge and drive our future investigations.

A BIT OF HISTORY

Beginning in the late 1960s, critiques of British structural functionalism and American cultural anthropology began to open up new spaces for understanding cultures as more dynamic than envisioned by the static models that had long dominated the field. Responding to an earlier linear evolutionary focus (Harris 1969; Sahlins and Service 1960; Steward 1955), this shift returned anthropology to thinking about history and change over time, but in a different manner than in nineteenth-century Darwinian models. Questions of boundaries were raised in new ways (Barth 1969; Leach 1967) as were assumptions about the links between biology and kinship systems (Schneider 1968). At the same time, the work of the French structural anthropologists, preeminently that of Claude Lévi-Strauss (1969), showed us how to discover deeper meaning in myths, symbols, and ritual structures. Marxist theory also generated new questions about social change and its material foundations, mirroring the political turmoil of the 1960s (Engels 1902; Marx 1932). These new perspectives enabled us to imagine that women and men might not operate within the strictures of unitary cultural forms, and that their divergent positions in societies might, in fact, produce different ways of conceiving and pursuing their interests.

This intellectual ferment paralleled the upheaval in the United States—the civil rights movement, opposition to the Vietnam War, the emergence of second-wave feminism—which all resonated with and inspired our intellectual journey. In a particularly audacious paper, "Woman the Gatherer," Sally Slocum (1975) exposed the pervasive male bias in anthropology and offered an alternative account of human development to that presumed by the ubiquitous "Man the Hunter" narrative. Other anthropologists soon followed Slocum's lead in deploring the absence of data and theories specific to women. In another key contribution, Sherry Ortner's article "Is Female to Male as Nature Is to Culture?" (1974) began the task of deconstructing women's subordination to men in the realm of representation. Gayle Rubin's theoretical tour de force, "The Traffic in Women" (1975), used Freud, Marx, Lacan, and preeminently Lévi-Strauss to locate what she saw as the universal secondary status of women in the arrangements of exchange that characterized kinship systems. Other feminists (Conkey and Gero 1991; Wylie 1992) noted that male archaeologists had paid virtually no attention to material remains that could inform our understandings of prehistoric gender patterns.

Thus, feminism found its way into anthropology through the same processes that brought it into other disciplines in the humanities and social sciences in the United States, through the second wave of feminism that emerged in the late 1960s and 1970s. Among this new generation of feminist activists were anthropology students and relatively marginalized female academic anthropologists (see Lamphere, this volume). How unprepared we were to provide answers to many pressing questions that the new focus on women's oppression presented and that our (non-anthropologist) sisters in the women's movement raised: was female subordination universal? Were there cultures, either contemporary or ancient, in which women had achieved higher status? What factors contributed to the relatively low status of women across cultures?

As we struggled to answer these questions, we were amazed to discover that few useful materials were available in the anthropological literature. Despite the looming presence of figures such as Ruth Benedict and Margaret Mead in the English-speaking canon, "women" had no more than an incidental place in the history of the discipline. They seemed to have only supporting (or cameo) roles in many ethnographies, mentioned when reproduction or childrearing was discussed and appearing in (typically) non-speaking parts when marriage exchanges were transacted. Women were assumed to passively cooperate with men's desires and to have little independent social existence or agency of their own. We also discovered that the earlier work of female scholars tended to be ignored in the academic canon, largely through lack of citation. Men cited each other, but women's contributions were effectively erased from the anthropological intellectual genealogy (Lutz 1990). The situation was even more egregious when examining the work of anthropologists of color (Bolles 2013).

THE IMPACT ON THE PROFESSION

For the emerging first generation of active feminist academic anthropologists, issues of discrimination addressed in the US Civil Rights Act (1965) and other legislation also applied to the institutions where they worked and studied. Since there were almost no senior faculty, not to mention junior colleagues, who were women, female graduate students faced discouraging prospects on the job market. Their efforts to introduce materials about women into the curricula of their departments were too frequently greeted with derision, understood by established (male) anthropologists to be a passing fad. They were often subject to sexual harassment and suffered the tenured male faculty's tendency to discourage their efforts, based on the assumption that marriage and family would cause them to abandon their anthropological careers. These experiences, along with the activism of the times, motivated them to consider the disadvantages facing women in anthropology and to conclude that they had the right to demand redress. A group of activists in the American Anthropological Association (AAA) began investigating the status of women in the profession and produced important surveys that documented the prevalent inequities (Sanjek 1982). This work led to the formation of a permanent committee on the status of women, now called the Committee on Gender Equity in Anthropology, and in 1988 to the organization of the Association for Feminist Anthropology (AFA) to spotlight and legitimate the work of scholars who focused on gender.

HOW THE "DISCOVERY" OF WOMEN CHANGED ANTHROPOLOGY

Did women really need to be discovered? Apparently so. As subject matter for the discipline, their beginnings recall Mel Brooks's startled announcement in the comedy skit "The Two-Thousand-Year-Old Man" that "there are ladies here." An early acknowledgment of the invisibility of women in sociocultural anthropology appeared in Edwin Ardener's famous article, "Belief and the Problem of Women" (1975), in which he argued that women (and other subordinated groups) are culturally "muted." They are not literally mute, of course, but what they say doesn't find its way into anthropological analyses because their contributions are irrelevant to understanding "culture." In other words, women's accounts of their culture fail to reproduce the normative systems that men are more likely to report; their views appear more localized and personal, and therefore, less valid and inclusive. When added to the restrictions in many cultures regarding extensive contact between male researchers and female "informants," most anthropologists (females included) came home from the field with little data about women, particularly in their own words.

These lacunae in the ethnographic record inspired women anthropologists to return to sites of earlier research to launch studies that would take women's voices and concerns into account. Jane Goodale's *Tiwi Wives* (1971), for example, documented the ways in which Tiwi women understood their marriage system that an earlier account (Hart and Pilling 1960) had represented as completely male-dominated. However, rather than being mere pawns in a manipulative system that exchanged women even before they were born, Goodale learned that Tiwi women understood themselves as powerful arbiters, able also to pursue romantic bonds despite how they were situated in marriages. Other important restudies followed, including Marilyn Strathern's *Women In Between* (1972), Annette Weiner's *Women of Value, Men of Renown* (1976), and research undertaken jointly by Yolanda and Robert Murphy, *Women of the Forest* (1974), reexamining work done earlier (under Robert Murphy's name) among the Munduruku of the Amazonian rain forest (Murphy 1960).

Beyond merely documenting that women were present and were important, the pioneering feminist anthropologists of the 1960s and 1970s had to define what it was that they should be studying. Debates ensued between those who argued that the subordination of women was a universal feature of all cultures and those who traced such status differentiation to particular socioeconomic configurations beginning with the classic Marxist focus on the advent of private property. These inquiries reflected our determination to generate a grand theory of gender inequality that would have explanatory power across all cultural boundaries. How we wished that a feminist theoretician could supplant Marx, Freud, or Lévi-Strauss in the anthropological canon (with acknowledgment to Gayle Rubin [1975]).

At the same time, feminist anthropologists also were called upon to engage with writers outside the discipline who devoted themselves to documenting the existence of purported ancient matriarchies. In *The First Sex*, for example, librarian Elizabeth Gould Davis (1971) mined anthropological and archaeological data to support her assertion that matriarchies had once been ubiquitous until overthrown by patriarchal forces. One academic archaeologist, Marija Gimbutas, argued that matriarchies and goddess worship were evidenced in the archaeological record (Gimbutas 1982, 1989, 1991), while other popular writings influential in feminist circles crafted wistful scenarios of a "golden age" in which goddess worship demonstrated the ancient power held by women (see Diner 1973; Eisler 1987; Eller 2001; Morgan 1972; Spretnak 1981; Starhawk 1979; Stone 1978; cf. Webster 1975).

Feminist anthropologists busily debunked these fanciful scenarios, while also weighing the intense internal debates between those who argued that the subordination of women was a universal feature of all cultures (Ortner 1974; Rosaldo 1974) and those who traced such differentiation to particular socioeconomic (capitalist) configurations (Etienne and Leacock 1980). These latter scholars called attention to the colonial impact on sexually stratified societies, arguing that such influences masked the "pristine" egalitarian conditions that must have been characteristic before contact (Leacock and Nash 1977). In their assessment, female subordination could not have existed in societies that otherwise appeared to be egalitarian (Leacock 1983). Drawing on these perspectives, some anthropologists considering relations between the sexes questioned how to refine concepts of hierarchy generated from our own society to understand gender relations in non-Western cultures (Sacks 1979). Still, the proponents of Marxist and other approaches that traced gender inequality to private property were criticized for failing to appreciate instances of marked asymmetry, even sexual violence, in small-scale foraging societies (Begler 1978). At the same time, those who argued for universal gender asymmetry had to contend with accusations that they were unduly influenced by experiences in their own culture (Rosaldo 1980) or obsessed with developing a meta-theory of gender.

As we continued to bring women to the foreground of ethnographic investigation, we also rediscovered the work of anthropologists who aptly could be called our foremothers. We celebrated such important (mainly US-based) figures as Elsie Clews Parsons, Margaret Mead, Ruth Benedict, Ruth Landes, and Phyllis Kaberry, who had been largely ignored in the anthropology of the postwar period. Zora Neale Hurston and Katherine Dunham, remembered for their accomplishments in literature and dance, were rediscovered as anthropologists, as were American Indians like Mourning Dove and Ella Cara Deloria (Finn 1995). The marginalization of these figures reflected both the colonial and racist temperament of the anthropology of their time; they were seen more as "informants" than as full-fledged anthropologists, receiving minimal opportunities to move ahead in their careers—or even to complete their PhDs.

At the same time, feminist activists used emergent ideas about the importance of positionality and standpoint theory (see, for example, Harding 1986; Hartsock 1983) to demand that scholars account for themselves—where they came from and what connected them to particular research topics—to make such reflexivity a prominent part of their scholarship. These approaches achieved particular centrality in the work of black feminists like Patricia Hill Collins (1990), who argued that black women's experience produced a distinctive set of feminist (or womanist) positions. Feminists also wanted to know how anthropologists intended to improve the lives of those with whom they worked, reinforcing the original, but now reconfigured, activist strain always present in our work. In this volume, Louise Lamphere examines the impact of political activism, in particular, on the development of feminist anthropology in the United States.

METHODOLOGICAL AND REPRESENTATIONAL INNOVATIONS

In a related move, feminist anthropologists also pioneered new forms of representation and a range of experimental ethnographic forms, paying close attention to issues of affect, sexuality, and the body (see Mascia-Lees, this volume). Ruth Behar and Deborah Gordon's influential collection, *Women Writing Culture* (1995), presented a wide range of textual innovations, including the use of fiction and drama to present ethnographic analyses, and contained essays that highlighted the work of many foremothers, including women of color who had been especially ignored. Their volume was assembled largely in response to the prominent collection *Writing Culture* (Clifford and Marcus 1986), in which

James Clifford claimed, in his introduction, that the work of feminist anthropologists would not be included in the volume because their writings had introduced neither innovation nor experimentation to ethnographic representation, failing, in his terms, to produce either "unconventional forms of writing or a developed reflection on ethnographic textuality" (Clifford 1986, 21; see also Abu-Lughod 1991). *Women Writing Culture* was followed a few years later by *Black Feminist Anthropology* (McClaurin 2001) that expanded the mandate to take special note of the accomplishments of colleagues who had been doubly devalued by the intersection of racism and sexism in the academy.

These strategies had methodological implications that have had far-reaching effects on ethnographic research methods. Feminists pioneered the centrality of *reflexivity*, sought out and acknowledged collaboration with interlocutors, including participatory action research (Olesen 2011), and emphasized personal narratives and storytelling both to highlight women's voices and to mount a vigorous challenge to "top-down" knowledge production. Feminist methods challenged and, consciously muted, the ubiquitous "God voice" that previously had characterized canonical ethnographic writing. That is, feminist ethnographers tended to locate themselves within the ethnographic project while also striving to represent the voices of the people they studied. These challenges have led to profound changes in the generation and shape of ethnographic writing in general: ethnographies now normatively include personal statements by researchers, along with more attention to evidence and historical and social context.

Among the salient issues that feminist scholars reconsidered was the strict distinction long made between "insider/outsider" or informant/anthropologist in ethnographic research. The relevance of personal commitments and the intensified attention given to issues of reflexivity meant that the boundaries between insiders and outsiders became more vexed and fluid, leaving researchers to confront ever more difficult ethical dilemmas that defined or threatened "belonging." Anthropologist Lila Abu-Lughod coined the concept of the "halfie" to describe the researcher who both shared fundamental identity markers with her informants and also found herself distanced from their priorities (Abu-Lughod 1991; see also Narayan 1993). Questions of loyalty and the mandate to activism could make this position particularly uncomfortable (Lewin 1995). No matter how "inside" an ethnographer might be, she always had the privilege of movement or departure, and multiple choices for defining her identity.

Discussions across the humanities and social sciences offering critiques of the "exotic" and how Western political agendas shaped scholarly inquiries also were central to reframing studies of women in non-Western cultures, particularly in Islamic societies. Edward Said's persuasive work, *Orientalism* (1979), put anthropologists on notice that their location in the Euro-American milieu made them likely to be under the sway of biases deeply entrenched in Western colonial sensibilities. This has nowhere been more prominent than in feminist anthropological research in the Middle East. Beginning with an early focus on the veil and female seclusion (Fernea 1965; Mernissi 1975), which reflected and struggled with the Orientalist perspective of much work in the area, some feminist anthropologists have critiqued scholars for an overemphasis on Islam as the key force shaping gender relations in this region (Abu-Lughod 2013).

At the same time, world events, particularly political upheavals in the Middle East and elsewhere, heralded an increased interest in new forms of women's agency, much of it challenging Western notions of female liberation (Abu-Lughod 2013; Mahmood 2011). "Studies of the relationship of piety to subjectivity, activism, and participation in Islamic movements also challenge notions of an emancipated female subject" (Deeb and Winegar 2012, 544) (see, for example, Deeb 2006; Hafez 2011). While this body of work has produced a substantial literature on women and Islam, it is worth noting that there has been less systematic attention to the articulation of gender with other religious affililations and movements. In other words, although feminist anthropologists have been eager to document resistance among women, we have been less successful at revealing the complex ways that agency and subordination intersect in a variety of locations and institutions, including religions.

In parallel reflections, anthropologists confronted the implications of relativism for addressing cultural forms that are deeply disturbing to Western sensibilities (e.g., veiling, female genital surgeries, female seclusion, polygamy). While some feminist activists embraced the cause of eliminating these practices, particularly female genital surgeries, others pointed to the ways in which discourse on this topic had been shaped by the exoticization of those engaged in these customs and by obsessions with sexual pleasure that arguably have their roots in particular Western sensibilities (Walley 1997). As Christine Walley pointedly asked: is clitoridectomy a more alarming issue than malnutrition and lack of access to potable water in various developing countries? At the same time, feminist health activists were concerned with the adverse effects of such practices on maternal morbidity and mortality. How can feminists address the negative health consequences of clitoridectomy and infibulation without slipping into a discourse that portrays women as passive and victimized, as utterly without their own agendas and agency? When does feminist activism veer into a colonial domination that suppresses local cultural sensibilities both at home and abroad? (See Gruenbaum 2001 for an overview of these issues.)

Examinations of both specific forms of religious discipline and body alterations, then, asked feminists, within and outside of anthropology, to interrogate what they meant by "oppression." Must women recognize customs as restrictive and seek to resist them for the practices to be defined as oppressive? What about conventions that women in specific locations welcomed, but that Western women, including anthropologists, understood as harmful? Should the goal of feminist social justice campaigns be the establishment of women as autonomous decision makers whose assessment of their own welfare corresponds to that of Western women? Could women who embrace seemingly repressive forms of regulation be defined as having false consciousness or as colluding with forces of patriarchy? These questions compel us to reevaluate such cherished anthropological assumptions as cultural and methodological relativity and demand that we specify the meaning and impact of particular customs and expectations before we judge them negatively. They also point to ways in which we need to consider the stated preferences of women rather than automatically labeling their behaviors as unthinking conformity within a social system in which such practices are upheld (Davidman 1991; Griffith 1997; Stacey and Gerard 1990).

REFRAMING GENDER

The shift from assuming that "woman" is a singular unified category of study, properly the focus of the new field within anthropology, to a framework of gender as relational, revised our inquiry to underscore questions of agency, power, and identity. Studies of language and gender have done much to shed light on the nature of language as a social, as well as communicative tool, and demonstrate how it shapes people's perceptions and lived experience (see Kramer, this volume). In some instances, the understanding that reductive definitions of "woman" (and "man") needed to be jettisoned also grew out of the growing assertiveness of women from developing countries. Many critics argued that early formulations of "woman" depended on essentialized conceptualizations, masking the complexity subsumed within the category. Such approaches implied that there could be a single response to Freud's famous question, "What do women want?"

Work undertaken in the wider, interdisciplinary field of gender studies also interrogated reductive definitions and urged scholars to adopt concepts of *intersectionality* (Crenshaw 1991), arguing that no single identity category could be deployed without considering others that might inflect its expression—race, class, sexuality, gender—categories that were now understood to be mutually constitutive. Interdisciplinarity also characterized feminist anthropology's contributions in the parallel field of women's/gender studies, though the two areas increasingly diverged over the decades (see Bolles, this volume).

New research on the powerful impact of postcolonial and transnational conditions on gender was inspired by and built upon parallel developments in other disciplines, especially literary theory and cultural studies. Gayatri Spivak, Chandra Mohanty, and Uma Narayan, along with other scholars from outside anthropology, urged Western scholars, in particular, to fully engage with the legacy of colonialism (Alexander and Mohanty 1997; Narayan 1997; Spivak 1988a); at the same time, these new directions demanded that we imbed our analyses in deep historical contexts (Gailey 1987; Roseberry 1989; Silverblatt 1987; Stoler 1991).

Even as these discussions were unfolding, controversies over the stability of the category of sex, as opposed to gender (Kessler and McKenna 1985), forced us to develop new ways of thinking about gender and sexuality as performative and strategic (Morris 1995). For example, Esther Newton's (1972) pioneering work on drag queens elucidated the ways in which performance revealed individual understandings of identity and personal value. This work opened anthropology to the legitimation of sexuality as a focus of ethnographic attention (Blackwood 1986; Blackwood and Wieringa 1999; Rubin 1984) but always in relation to other dimensions of identity such as race, class, nationality, and so on. This move also validated the possibility of working with stigmatized populations close at hand (Kennedy and Davis 1993; Leap 1996; Lewin 1993, 1998; Newton 1972, 1993; Weston 1991). Until this time, most anthropologists defined their research arena as non-US-based, especially non-Western, but scholars of sexuality, in particular, embraced the opportunity to interrogate Western "exotica" (Read 1980), as well as same-sex related behaviors in non-Western societies (Herdt 1981). This trend is reflected elsewhere in feminist anthropology as revealed in this volume (see Weiss). This work reinforced the importance of more explicit attention to *positionality*, even exposing sexual connections with informants (Blackwood 2010; Wekker 2006; Williams 1986). Elizabeth Lapovsky Kennedy and Madeline D. Davis, drawing on approaches from John D'Emilio (1983) and Eric Hobsbawm (1965), used ethnohistorical methods to delve into the preconditions for revolutionary action they found in working class lesbian bars in the decades before the gay rights movement surfaced in the United States. These new approaches to sexuality, like parallel work on poverty and female-headed households in African American communities, focused on rediscovering the past of stigmatized groups and legitimating their cultures (Kennedy 2002; see also Valentine 1968; Williams 1992) and on repudiating Oscar Lewis's theories of the "culture of poverty" (Leacock 1971), as well as responses to the infamous "Moynihan report" (1965).[1]

Social phenomena that were considered deviant in the United States—such as the female-headed black family (Stack 1974) and drag performance (Newton 1972)—were instead revealed to have their own rules. That is, the new emphasis on positionality demanded that anthropological symmetry be applied at home, just as it enriched analyses of distant cultures. Indeed, scholars whose personal identifications overlapped with the groups they studied were empowered to offer new perspectives on blacks, Chicanos, Indians, and other marginalized populations (see, for example, Altorki and El-Sohl 1988; Limón 1991). In the same vein, queer theory emerged, largely driven by work in cultural, literary, and cinema studies, challenging conventional binary definitions of sexuality and identity, of maleness and femaleness (de Lauretis 1991). Gayle Rubin's "Thinking Sex" (1984), for example, proposed that the study of gender and sexuality be understood as separate intellectual and ethnographic domains. Queer theory allowed us to conceptualize sexuality and sexual identity as fluid and site-specific. This opened an ethnographic window to problematize sexuality and the social units it generates, stimulating innovative interrogations of formerly rigid categories (Valentine 2007). At the same time, scholars intensified their investigations of sexual minorities in other cultures, reconsidering interpretations from earlier studies and wresting research from the grip of psychological anthropology. For example, *berdache,* once considered a psychological oddity, emerged in work, much of it by self-identified two-spirit people, as a coherent aspect of particular cultures (Jacobs et al. 1997). Similarly, Indian *hijras* were reexamined from a feminist perspective (Reddy 2005) along with other "gender-deviant" populations (Kulick 1998).

All of this work expanded our understanding of gender and sexuality as culturally and historically constructed, and countered the tendency to equate non-Western sexual/gender variations with contemporary Western gay and lesbian cultures. Thus, new generations of feminist anthropologists have been increasingly receptive to incorporating theoretical perspectives from other disciplines as can be seen in the growing importance of queer theory for reconceptualizing sexuality, family formation, and transgender identities (see Weiss, this volume).

GLOBAL PERSPECTIVES ON THE BODY

Unsurprisingly, women's reproductive capacities and experiences quickly became central to the unfolding field of feminist anthropology. Feminist theory had long placed women's biological and domestic obligations at the center of their social devaluation, and the burgeoning women's health movement (Boston Women's Health Book Collective 1973; Ehrenreich and English 1972; Morgen 2002) also emphasized the ways in which women's reproductive experiences were shaped by their social status. Brigitte Jordan's (1978) path-breaking comparative study of childbirth in Mayan Yucatan, the United States, Sweden, and the Netherlands definitively collapsed universalizing notions of women's reproductive experience. Her work demonstrated that many of the cross-cultural differences in childbirth practices were reflections of *authoritative knowledge,* highlighting the various degrees to which women's experiences were subordinated to health care practitioners' preferences in medical settings, particularly in the United States (Davis-Floyd 1992; Davis-Floyd and Sargent 1997). Such cross-cultural studies confirmed feminists' suspicions that US medical practice devalued women's embodied knowledge and empowered medical professionals (predominantly male at the time) to dictate the terms of health care and research. Some feminist anthropologists undertook detailed ethnographic studies of childbirth and reproductive health practices in various non-Western cultural settings (Sargent 1981; Van Hollen 2003), while others used these comparative perspectives to mount powerful critiques of the medicalization of childbirth and the spread of new reproductive technologies (Davis-Floyd 1992; Fraser 1998; Martin 1989; Rapp 1999).

Central to these developments was the important work done by Nancy Scheper-Hughes and Margaret Lock (1987) that called for new ways to conceptualize the body as a culturally constructed set of meanings. In particular, Margaret Lock's (1993) comparative research on menopause in the United States and Japan offered new ways to understand cultural difference in relation to presumably stable physiological realities and introduced the notion of *localized biologies* that could unfold in distinctive ways in various material-cultural contexts. Lock's work effectively challenged the modernist assumption of a universal material body, instead arguing that interactions among bodies, environments (historical and local), and social/political variables shape biological processes (Lock 1993; Lock and Nguyen 2010).

As these developments continued to transform the field, feminist anthropological studies of reproductive health and women's bodies focused on specific health practices in relation to larger cultural realities, looked carefully at childbirth technologies, and, harkening back to our activist roots, often proposed ways in which these procedures could be made more responsive to women's expressed needs, more respectful of their autonomy and the validity of their experience. Robbie Davis-Floyd and associates (Davis-Floyd and Johnson 2006; Davis-Floyd et al. 2009) have been especially active in this area, proposing ways to make midwifery and home birth more accessible to women in the West (see also Craven 2010). Sparked by the women's health movement, anthropologists forged connections among the production of new knowledge, applied anthropology and feminist activism.[2]

In the same period, feminist medical anthropology flourished and engaged with the political roots of reproductive policy in various Western and non-Western locations. Some of this work focused on China's one-child policy (e.g., Anagnost 1995; Greenhalgh 2008; Handwerker 1995), and on pronatalist policies elsewhere (e.g., Gal and Kligman 2000; Inhorn 1994, 1996; Kahn 2000). This body of work also examined how social conditions, particularly those created or exacerbated by inequality, shape reproductive choice and experience. Shellee Colen's (1995) classic article on *stratified reproduction* catapulted reproduction into the arena of globalization. The 1995 volume edited by Faye

Ginsburg and Rayna Rapp, *Conceiving the New World Order*, set the agenda for much of this scholarship, linking reproductive issues, broadly conceptualized, to the political and economic realities that impinge upon them.

The study of stratified reproduction, following changes in reproductive health care, also turned its focus to ARTs (assisted reproductive technologies), especially the proliferation of technologies affecting how conception, pregnancy, and birth unfold and are managed. Further, the social context in which reproduction occurs has changed dramatically as these new technologies have become normalized and ideas about all aspects of reproduction are increasingly biomedicalized throughout the world (Becker 2000; Clarke 1998; Mamo 2007). Recently, feminist medical anthropology has focused on assisted reproductive technologies including ultrasound and other diagnostic technologies, in particular, tracing the movement of specific technological procedures from the West to developing nations (Gammeltoft 2014; Inhorn 2003; Roberts 2012). Rayna Rapp's (1999) examination of amniocentesis in the United States, for example, highlighted how technology's reception and interpretation depends on the social position of patients and their interactions with health care providers. Similarly, anthropologists have examined US clinical settings for both provision of care and articulation of systems of racial and class hierarchies (Bridges 2011). Studies of assisted reproductive technologies, both in the West (Taylor 2008) and cross-culturally (e.g., Inhorn 2003; Roberts 2012) have shown their mutable reception and re/interpretation when embedded within particular individual, social, cultural, and national agendas, such as those dictating sex and racial selection. Medical anthropologists analyzing reproduction and technology in Israel, for instance, have produced a complex picture of how the intertwining of state and religion create a unique environment in which technology can be consumed (Ivry 2009; Kahn 2000; Kanaaneh 2002; Teman 2010). Other scholars have begun to pay careful attention to unforeseen or undesirable aspects of reproduction, looking at what Marcia Inhorn (2007) has called "reproductive disruptions." Linda Layne (2002), for example, focused her work on pregnancy loss and Gail Landsman (2008) studied mothers of disabled babies, both thoughtfully placing these outcomes in the context of consumption patterns in the United States.

This engagement with technologies has led directly to another strand of feminist medical anthropological research: science and technology studies (STS). Feminist involvement in this area is a natural extension of our commitment to challenge received knowledge and entrenched authority. In moving to question science as a source of cultural values, anthropology joins postcolonial critiques of hegemonic Eurocentric explanatory systems, building on feminist challenges to patriarchal power. As Sarah Franklin has noted, it is no surprise that "feminist anthropology was a critical testing ground for biologisms from the mid-1970s onward, and it is no coincidence that many leading feminist scholars are now engaged in the anthropology of science" (Franklin 1995, 170). As we have seen, some scholars have focused on reproductive health, while others have expanded into areas of health care provision, for example, HIV/AIDS services (Susser 2009), immunology (Martin 1995), mental health (Martin 2009), and disability (Ginsburg and Rapp 2013; Rapp and Ginsburg 2001, 2011). This body of work represents a coming together of intellectual and activist agendas, often sparked as well by the personal experience of the scholars. Although not solely concerned with gender, these fields have been shaped profoundly by the reflexive attention of researchers who are also mothers and caregivers; their intimate understandings of medical and disease processes have problematized the cultural features of biology (see Roberts, this volume).

A FOCUS ON HUMAN RIGHTS

Global recognition of the importance of women's issues, buttressed by increasingly visible feminist political engagement and scholarship was reflected by the United Nations' expanded definition of human rights and rape (see Theidon, this volume). Previously defined as a domestic issue, the United Nations was compelled at the 1993 Vienna Conference on Human Rights, in response to the Bosnian conflict, to recognize rape as a weapon of war, perpetrated by government as well as opposition forces (Bunch 1994). Thus, along with the United Nations Conference on Environment and Development (UNCED; also known as the Rio Summit, Rio Conference, and Earth Summit) in Rio de Janeiro in 1992, the 1994 UN International Conference on Population and Development (ICPD) in Cairo, and the 1995 Fourth World Conference on Women in Beijing, the UN meetings all contributed to the organization of a global network of scholars and activists, constructing a common basic agenda on women's rights in the broadest sense, and reproductive rights in particular. These activists redefined environmental degradations, climate change, violence, human rights, and reproductive rights in a comprehensive manner, and called attention to their specific impacts on women (see Khandelwal, this volume).

This uneasy coalition effectively expanded as each UN Conference offered opportunities for women to convene and broaden the reach of feminist political concerns. Areas such as sexual identity and abortion, previously seen as outside the purview of feminist scholarship and activism (Friedlander 2013) began to be included in a broadening international feminist agenda. The conflicts that emerged over these years challenged feminists and anthropologists to grapple with the political ramifications of research and action, competition for philanthropic funding, bourgeoning non-governmental organizations, and the identity politics enveloping religion and sexuality. These experiences also grounded research on questions of violence and the centrality of a rights-based perspective in discussing these issues, approaches that meshed with feminist anthropologists' emphasis both on local conditions and on the role of the state and organized religion in shaping these domains (see Kwiatkowski, this volume). Simultaneously, as neoliberalism and structural adjustment programs have become widespread globally, feminist anthropologists have also devoted research to their impact on gender systems and their ramifications for the challenges facing women and men in many different settings (see Kingfisher, this volume).

Currently, many in this field are collecting data on the intensifying world movement of populations, including both relocations within states and international migration as people seek to escape deepening poverty and ethnic/religious conflict. Feminists have also focused on the "trafficking" or the forced transfer of women and men for sexual and other forms of labor exploitation. Once again, applying a gender lens to these social phenomena offers a more nuanced basis for analysis and a foundation for influencing public policy (see, for example, Constable 2014; Segura and Zavella 2007).

More recently, feminist anthropology has been energized by what might be called "the discovery of men," with studies of gender expanding to examine the cultural imperatives framing men's lives. Matthew Gutmann (1996, 2007) has made major contributions to this area, much of it overlapping with feminist medical anthropology. Marcia Inhorn (2012) has queried the involvement of Egyptian men in ARTs; Emily A. Wentzell (2013) the attitudes of aging Mexican men toward erectile dysfunction treatment; and Tony O. Pomales (2013) how Costa Rican men have come to accept vasectomy, thus correcting narrowly female-centric understandings of reproductive health care (see Dudgeon, this volume). This body of work continues to demonstrate the resilience of reproduction and the fertility of the feminist imagination as we interrogate what has become a rapidly changing landscape.

THE GENESIS OF THIS VOLUME

Stimulated by the changed consciousness inspired by the women's movement, anthropologists in the 1970s began collecting new information, studying new issues, and asking new questions of the existing data. Back in the early 1970s, it was easy to locate the small number of "key" articles that spoke to these issues (e.g., Ardener 1975; Brown 1970) and feminist anthropologists of that era all read the same few books about women's roles in society and looked to the two collections, *Woman, Culture, and Society* (Rosaldo and Lamphere 1974) and *Toward an Anthropology of Women* (Reiter [now Rapp] 1975), to help them define the issues.[3] But once the lid on the Pandora's box of gender had been lifted, it became less and less viable to speak of "women" as the object of our concern, as research proliferated in economic, ecological, political, psychological, medical, and legal anthropology, as well as in mythology and folklore, religious and symbolic studies, phenomenology, structuralism, Marxism, and area studies—to mention just a few.

This evolution is revealed in the progression of articles about gender that have appeared in the *Annual Review of Anthropology* beginning in the 1970s, a formal recognition that the field had arrived and was incorporated into the mainstream. As one historical indicator, these articles reflect the changing scope of feminist anthropology (Ginsburg and Rapp 1991; Morris 1995; Mukhopadhyay and Higgins 1988; Quinn 1977; Silverblatt 1988; Visweswaran 1997). During the years that these expanding treatments of gender and feminism were making their way into the *Annual Review*, other new concerns also emerged. These areas—sexuality, disability, globalization and race, colonial and postcolonial studies, peace and conflict studies, migration studies in many different guises, structural adjustment, credit and debt, sustainability, resistance, Internet-mediated social relations, to mention only some—reflect a growing diversification of what are considered "anthropological" topics as well as the expanded willingness of anthropologists to engage with the intellectual agendas of other disciplines. In addition, feminist anthropologists found their work on Western societies, including their own, to elicit more widespread interest and acceptance in the field at large than in the past. Recent contributions to the *Annual Review* indicate a broader conceptualization of topics that once were narrowly construed as being about women (see, for example, Baxi 2014; Mills 2003; Van Esterik 2002) and an extension of insights from feminist anthropology into new areas of inquiry that don't seem to be about gender per se yet use feminist theoretical insights to situate new foci at their own intersections (see, for example, Constable 2009 on the commodification of intimacy; Gammeltoft and Wahlberg 2014 on selective reproductive technologies; Moran 2010 on gender and militarism; Morgen and Maskovsky 2003 on welfare reform; Taylor 2005 on medical imaging).

A constant conceptual theme in this emerging research agenda is the questioning of binary oppositions as feminist anthropologists continue to interrogate both spatial and disciplinary boundaries. The field has thus shifted from a concern with women, narrowly defined, to one that depends on contextualized conceptualizations of gender and that, in fact, rigorously questions inflexible or conventional notions of genders or sexes: pried loose from their earlier foundational status, these concepts are now viewed as unstable and intersectional. Feminist anthropology's commitment to projects that intersect with social justice agendas and activism has also been a constant theme in our research, both at home and abroad (see Lamphere, this volume).

In 2013, the editors organized two double sessions at the American Anthropological Association annual meeting in Chicago, to mark the twenty-fifth anniversary of the Association for Feminist Anthropology, and to offer, in part, an overview of the research that has taken place across the breadth of anthropology since the 1960s. Twenty-two papers were delivered in the two sessions with Rayna Rapp and Tom Boellstorff, who now "bookend" our book's many chapters, serving as discussants. The sessions highlighted the early contexts in which feminism began to impact anthropology; the paths that emerged in the four fields over the years; and then moved to a detailed examination of many of the most compelling new directions that have emerged in cultural anthropology in the twenty-first century.

This latter direction provides the impetus for this volume, which we conceive of as an intellectual genealogy, a mapping exercise that takes stock of the ideas and questions that spawned new and unexpected directions in feminist anthropology. As feminist anthropology gained a foothold in the discipline, many scholars found themselves moved from the margins to the center of the field. Some who once constituted an insurgency, fighting for the rights of women in the discipline and for the legitimacy of research on women and gender, (finally) obtained secure employment; many became celebrated scholars, several came to occupy prominent positions in our professional organizations, while others choose to influence policy and political agendas. These latter have nudged the field of applied anthropology forward, committed to introducing gender at every possible opportunity to affect policy and programs. In a parallel development, since the 1970s the rate of scholarly publications in feminist anthropology has increased exponentially, including monographs, articles appearing in selective journals, and edited volumes issued by respected academic publishers. The vast quantity of new work has meant that feminist anthropologists no longer share a single frame of reference, with feminist scholarship present in many necessarily specialized discursive communities. This phenomenon is reflected by the fact that the field has now become highly specialized, as amply demonstrated in this volume.

Furthermore, the success that some have achieved may indicate that our activist agenda (but presumably not our political principles) has become a more diluted or fluid aspect of the original feminist anthropological project. Becoming an academic feminist anthropologist can now lead a scholar to a solid career. How is such professional security, which often depends on producing a substantial corpus of theoretically innovative scholarship, compatible with maintaining an activist agenda as historically conceived? Have new activist projects involving feminist anthropologists evolved? Do these successes demand that we redefine activism and its relationship to the academy?

How might we conceive of activism inside and outside the academy in the face of an ever-expanding field of research and practice as well as the changing landscape within the academy? Many scholars have focused their energies on addressing issues of social justice and equality through applied work that makes direct efforts to understand and analyze pressing problems facing women and disenfranchised populations. As we complete this volume, there seems to be room for both emphases—academic and applied—in the more capacious field that feminist anthropology has become. But we also recognize the complications that accompany our continuing desire to contribute to meaningful social change through feminist activism. Perhaps most troublesome is that we don't all share the same definition of "feminism," nor do we agree on what constitutes "activism" or its expression in ethnographic research and writing. In *Feminist Activist Ethnography* (Craven and Davis 2013), essays point to some of the ambiguities in our deployment of terms like "feminist" and "activist." Does attending to issues that involve or affect women, particularly disadvantaged women, constitute activist anthropology? Can an examination of institutions that are connected to gender, but extend their reach far beyond it, like the United Nations, be readily understood to be feminist? Does calling oneself a feminist mean attending not only to the institutional and cultural arrangements that encompass gender, but caring enough about the intersecting inequities we encounter to address (and perhaps contribute to changing) them? Recent research raises even more unsettling questions about "activism" in ethnography, possibly because anthropological knowledge per se is less likely to produce the kinds of liberatory social change for which we hope. What are our obligations when our informants ask us to breach confidentiality because of their (possibly mistaken) assumptions about what we can achieve by telling their stories? Such dilemmas persist no matter how much effort we put into trying to minimize the inequalities between researcher and informant (Davis 2013; Stacey 1991).

While storytelling may call attention to local problems, as feminist anthropologists we have yet to figure out how to link the local with the global in a politically efficacious way.[4] In other words, we face continuous and contentious issues of how to define the domain within which we work and also how to understand when we are contributing to activist objectives. Does "activist" amount to a kind of identity based on intentions and principles that de facto saturate anything an activist does? Does something actually have to change as a result of feminist activism, in our ethnographic practice and in the larger world, for us to regard it as legitimate? And how do we assess the impact of such change? Such questions resemble the dilemmas we face in attempts to recognize resistance in the people with whom we work. We valorize subordinated people's resistance and agency and we may "see" these forces in the smallest gestures, regardless of what our interlocutors actually tell us (Abu-Lughod 1990). In what ways is identifying patriarchal oppression opposite or parallel to identifying resistance? How might we address the dilemmas of trying to evaluate both intention and efficacy in both cases? We often find ourselves parsing matters of intention and consciousness as we try to decide whether activism—or resistance—needs to be intentional or efficacious to matter.

Further, in the current climate, analyzing the effects of major transnational forces such as neoliberalism often lies at the heart of our activist agendas. Indeed, "neoliberalism" seems to have taken the role once played by "patriarchy" as the bad guy we all hope to defeat. Like patriarchy, neoliberalism is everywhere; like patriarchy it is difficult to outmaneuver. As with the struggle against patriarchy, some effective lines of attack involve the strategic use of what Audre Lorde eloquently labeled "the master's tools" (Lorde 1984). As she rightly observed, the master's tools will never dismantle the master's house, but in the short term, they may gain activists some time, open up space and grant temporary relief from pressure (see also Spivak 1988b).

One of anthropology's strengths has always been to provide a vocabulary for understanding and recognizing the meaning of small-scale, local actions that reveal the impact of global forces on individual lives. We record how seemingly modest responses to oppression bring with them real benefits, even if they don't amount to a total overthrow of the system. Such forms of agency exist, even in the face of tremendous opposition. As anthropologists, one of our most effective responses to these dilemmas resides in our commitment to avoiding reductive interpretations, whether they invoke culture, patriarchy, neoliberalism, or any other seemingly immovable force as a totalizing explanation. In *Mapping Feminist Anthropology in the Twenty-First Century*, the reader will be exposed to contributions that—while modest—are essential to identifying what qualitative social researchers bring to the social justice table, including patience!

And how do these goals play out in the current US academic environment in which corporate forces are increasingly undermining and delegitimizing the kind of in-depth intellectual projects that have long been the foundation of anthropology? Among other effects, these conditions are gutting the professoriate in US universities (in favor of contingent labor and Internet learning) while simultaneously valorizing economic rewards as the measure of educational success. Will future citizens exemplify Oscar Wilde's description of the cynic as someone *"who knows the price of everything and the value of nothing"* (Wilde 1985, 88)?

THE ORGANIZATION OF THIS VOLUME

We have gathered together in this volume many current lines of inquiry that have transformed and expanded feminist cultural anthropology. We concentrate on areas that have matured within the last fifteen to twenty years, pointing to some of the relatively new directions the field has explored in the twenty-first century. Among these has been the meteoric growth of anthropological research in the West and particularly in the United States. Much of this research is directly inspired by the earlier questions asked in feminist anthropology but reflects a change in the scope of our inquiry, and the necessity to address the complexity of power relations "at home." Other efforts emerged out of areas of concern that have increasingly assumed a more central space in our discourse—neoliberalism, transnationalism, ecological sustainability, human rights, social studies of medicine, science and technology, and masculinity, for example. And of course, many of these are intertwined, as our earlier commitments to intersectional theory and methodology revealed. Our contributors challenge us to engage with interdisciplinary and applied ventures. The writings as a whole stimulate us to step outside our disciplinary "comfort zone" and generate responses to compelling questions that will inform our discipline in the future and affect our lives. Since venturing into unknown territory is a vital part of any new exploration, intellectual or otherwise, we conceive of this account as a kind of "mapping," not only of the home territories from which we come, but the relatively unknown terrains into which feminist anthropologists now venture. We aim to reveal the sites where our field originated and to locate the twists and turns—the routes—that have led us to the various locations that now constitute feminist anthropology. These maps demonstrate that this journey has not been a linear one; on the contrary, it has been characterized by many unanticipated detours and surprising points of arrival.

We have organized the chapters in three sections that provide a context for understanding many of these directions.

Foundations: Problematizing Feminist Anthropology

This section provides an historical, intellectual, and theoretical overview of the concerns that shaped the emerging contours of feminist anthropology, with an emphasis on examples from the United States. Although the research that followed over decades spanned many Western and non-Western sites, the debates that are reflected in these three chapters generated what would come to be understood as feminist anthropology in the United States. Louise Lamphere and Elise Kramer each consider the ways in which cultural and linguistic anthropology respectively have evolved from their foci in the early days of the field, including a consideration of the place of activism in these formative periods. A. Lynn Bolles analyzes the evolving relationship between feminist anthropology and women's studies, two fields that emerged in the same time period and which overlapped in varying measures with each other.

Expansions: Confronting Universals

Chapters in this section refute abstract, universalizing models and ideologies, interrogate loci of power, and identify possibilities for agency and political change. Both theoretically and in specific ethnographic contexts, these inquiries continue to expand our understanding of lived experience. Elizabeth F. S. Roberts explores how feminist medical anthropologists have drawn on science and technology studies, philosophy of science, and queer theory to interrogate assumptions about a universal and fixed biology. Matthew R. Dudgeon considers the ways in which questions about men and masculinity have offered valuable new perspectives on reproduction, long a central topic in feminist anthropology. Frances E. Mascia-Lees follows the history of the body as a topic in feminist anthropology, exploring its current use both to refute binary sex and gender oppositions and to understand the significance of emotions for examining gendered experience. Margot Weiss examines intersections between queer studies and queer anthropology, particularly focusing on how such approaches unsettle the boundaries between human and animal, or human and non-human.

Reverberations: Transnational Encounters

Chapters in this section address situations in which feminist anthropologists reflect directly on questions of human rights, domestic abuse, environmental pressures, and the globalization of neoliberal adjustments, salient new lines of inquiry within the expanding research agenda. Feminist anthropologists clarify the stakes in particular ethnographic situations, paving the way for possible interventions that may contribute to meaningful change. For example, Kimberly Theidon elucidates the role that gender played in Peru's transitional justice process. She examines how the priorities of survivors of gender-based harm challenge liberal notions of justice and suggests a more robust theorization of collective rights and redress. Meena Khandelwal turns our gaze to India, tracing how cultural anthropology and transnational feminism contribute distinct, if equally important, perspectives for understanding the relationship among deforestation, women's seemingly local food preparation practices, and changing global patterns of food consumption. Lynn Kwiatkowski illuminates the ways in which intersecting local, state, and transnational cultural and religious discourses, along with continuing gender and economic inequalities, contribute to the persistence of husbands' abuse of their wives in Vietnam. Finally, Catherine Kingfisher shows how neoliberal models of welfare state restructuring in New Zealand made their way to Canada, and how poor mothers in each setting have coped with these adjustments.

Throughout our engagement with all of these challenging issues, we advocate an emphasis on accountability and reflexivity, on understanding how our work as feminist anthropologists is always inflected by who we are and where we stand. To maintain a focus on this vital epistemological insight, we have persevered in imagining new ways to represent our interlocutors and new ways to enhance social justice while aiming to decrease gender-based inequalities everywhere. We are no longer introducing women into the cultural and societal record (*Woman, Culture, and Society*), nor are we initiating a field (*Toward an Anthropology of Women*). As evidenced in this volume, just as the rise of feminist anthropology some forty years ago has brought us further than we ever could have imagined, so forces underway in the twenty-first century will lead us to destinations—conceptual and political—beyond those we are able to envision but are amply prepared to tackle.

NOTES

1. *The Negro Family: The Case for National Action.* Office of Policy Planning and Research United States Department of Labor, March 1965, www.blackpast.org/primary/moynihan-report-1965.
2. Another expression of the links between research and activism on health, particularly reproductive health, was inspired by the United Nations (UN) World Conferences on Women held over several decades (1975–1995). After the 1975 Mexico City Conference, feminist anthropologists were active in documenting the emerging power of non-governmental organizations (NGOs) to affect UN policy. They also helped to enable grassroots women's voices to be heard in the organization's policy-making process. Identifying their mutual interests, a fledging international women's health movement was born, propelling Third World and First World feminists to recognize common ground on issues of reproductive freedom.
3. Other books feminists read in this period included *The Second Sex* by Simone de Beauvoir, *A Room of One's Own* by Virginia Woolf, *The Feminine Mystique* by Betty Friedan, *Sisterhood Is Powerful* edited by Robin Morgan, *Sexual Politics* by Kate Millett, *The Dialectic of Sex* by Shulamith Firestone, *Century of Struggle* by Eleanor Flexner, and fiction by such authors as Doris Lessing, Marge Piercy, Toni Cade Bambara, Kate Chopin, Tillie Olsen, Marilyn French, and many others who were "rediscovered" by the activists of the second wave.
4. A notable exception is the recent initiative by the American Anthropological Association (2014) to actively harness the expertise of anthropologists to advise WHO, NIH, and other international agencies to combat the spread of Ebola. Anthropologists who have studied local cultures in Liberia and Sierra Leone are contributing directly to shaping health policies by demonstrating how the spread of Ebola is linked to local cultural practices (e.g., burial rites) and population dislocations (e.g., increased cross-border transit during the dry season). See the recent AAA publication, "Strengthening West African Health Care Systems to Stop Ebola," a 2014 pamphlet to which feminist anthropologist Mary Moran contributed, for further documentation of this example of engaged or activist anthropology within the discipline.

REFERENCES

Abu-Lughod, Lila. 1990. "The Romance of Resistance: Tracing Transformations of Power through Bedouin Women." *American Ethnologist* 17 (1): 41–55.

———. 1991. "Writing Against Culture." In *Recapturing Anthropology: Working in the Present*, ed. Richard G. Fox, 137–162. Santa Fe, NM: SAR Press.

———. 2013. *Do Muslim Women Need Saving?* Cambridge, MA: Harvard University Press.

Alexander, M. Jacqui, and Chandra Mohanty. 1997. *Feminist Genealogies, Colonial Legacies, Democratic Futures.* New York: Routledge.

Altorki, Soraya, and Camillia Fawzi El-Solh, eds. 1988. Arab Women in the Field: Studying Your Own Society. Syracuse, NY: Syracuse University Press.

Anagnost, Ann. 1995. "A Surfeit of Bodies: Population and the Rationality of the State in Post-Mao China." In *Conceiving the New World Order: The Global Politics of Reproduction,* ed. Faye D. Ginsburg and Rayna Rapp, 22–41. Berkeley: University of California Press.

Ardener, Edwin. 1975. "Belief and the Problem of Women." In *Perceiving Women,* ed. Shirley Ardener, 1–27. London: Malaby Press.

Barth, Fredrik. 1969. *Ethnic Groups and Boundaries: The Social Organization of Culture Difference.* Boston: Little, Brown.

Baxi, Pratiksha. 2014. "Sexual Violence and Its Discontents." *Annual Review of Anthropology* 43: 139–154.

Becker, Gay. 2000. *The Elusive Embryo: How Men and Women Approach New Reproductive Technologies.* Berkeley: University of California Press.

Begler, Elsie B. 1978. "Sex, Status, and Authority in Egalitarian Society." *American Anthropologist* 80 (3): 571–588.

Behar, Ruth, and Deborah A. Gordon, eds. 1995. *Women Writing Culture.* Berkeley: University of California Press.

Blackwood, Evelyn, ed. 1986. *The Many Faces of Homosexuality: Anthropological Approaches to Homosexual Behavior.* Binghamton, NY: Hayworth Press.

———. 2010. *Falling Into the Lesbi World: Desire and Difference in Indonesia.* Honolulu: University of Hawaii Press.

Blackwood, Evelyn, and Saskia E. Wieringa, eds. 1999. *Female Desires: Same-Sex Relations and Transgender Practices Across Cultures.* New York: Columbia University Press.

Bolles, A. Lynn. 2013. "Telling the Story Straight: Black Feminist Intellectual Thought in Anthropology." *Transforming Anthropology* 21 (1): 57–71.

Boston Women's Health Book Collective. 1973. *Women Unite: Our Bodies, Ourselves: A Book by and for Women.* New York: Simon and Schuster.

Bridges, Khiara M. 2011. *Reproducing Race: An Ethnography of Pregnancy as a Site of Racialization.* Berkeley: University of California Press.

Brown, Judith K. 1970. "A Note on the Division of Labor by Sex." *American Anthropologist* 72 (5): 1073–1078.

Bunch, Charlotte. 1994. "Transforming Human Rights from a Feminist Perspective." In *Women's Rights, Human Rights: International Feminist Perspectives,* ed. Julie S. Peters and Andrea Wolper, 11–17. New York: Routledge.

Clarke, Adele E. 1998. *Disciplining Reproduction: Modernity, American Life Sciences, and the Problems of Sex.* Berkeley: University of California Press.

Clifford, James. 1986. "Introduction: Partial Truths." In *Writing Culture: The Poetics and Politics of Ethnography,* ed. James Clifford and George E. Marcus, 1–26. Berkeley: University of California Press.

Clifford, James, and George E. Marcus, eds. 1986. *Writing Culture: The Poetics and Politics of Ethnography.* Berkeley: University of California Press.

Colen, Shellee. 1995. "'Like a Mother to Them': Stratified Reproduction and West Indian Childcare Workers and Employers in New York." In *Conceiving the New World Order: The Global Politics of Reproduction,* ed. Faye D. Ginsburg and Rayna Rapp, 78–102. Berkeley: University of California Press.

Collins, Patricia Hill. 1990. *Black Feminist Thought: Knowledge, Consciousness, and the Politics of Empowerment.* New York: Routledge.

Conkey, Margaret, and Joan Gero, eds. 1991. *Engendering Archaeology: Women and Prehistory.* Malden, MA: Wiley-Blackwell.

Constable, Nicole. 2009. "The Commodification of Intimacy: Marriage, Sex, and Reproductive Labor." *Annual Review of Anthropology* 38: 49–64.

———. 2014. *Born Out of Place: Migrant Mothers and the Politics of International Labor.* Berkeley: University of California Press.

Craven, Christa. 2010. *Pushing for Midwives: Homebirth Mothers and the Reproductive Rights Movement.* Philadelphia: Temple University Press.

Craven, Christa, and Dána-Ain Davis, eds. 2013. *Feminist Activist Ethnography: Counterpoints to Neoliberalism in North America.* Lanham, MD: Lexington Books.

Crenshaw, Kimberlé. 1991. "Mapping the Margins: Intersectionality, Identity Politics, and Violence Against Women of Color." *Stanford Law Review* 43 (6): 1241–1299.

Dahlberg, Frances. 1981. "Introduction." In *Woman the Gatherer,* ed. F. Dahlberg, 1–33. New Haven, CT: Yale University Press.

Davidman, Lynn. 1991. *Tradition in a Rootless World: Women Turn to Orthodox Judaism.* Berkeley: University of California Press.

Davis, Dána-Ain. 2013. "Border Crossings: Intimacy and Feminist Activist Ethnography in the Age of Neoliberalism." In *Feminist Activist Ethnography: Counterpoints to Neoliberalism in North America,* ed. Christa Craven and Dána-Ain Davis, 23–38. Lanham, MD: Lexington Books.

Davis, Elizabeth Gould. 1971. *The First Sex.* Baltimore: Penguin Books.

Davis-Floyd, Robbie. 1992. *Birth as an American Rite of Passage.* Berkeley: University of California Press.

Davis-Floyd, Robbie, Lesley Barclay, Jan Tritten, and Betty-Anne Daviss, eds. 2009. *Birth Models That Work.* Berkeley: University of California Press.

Davis-Floyd, Robbie, and Christine Barbara Johnson, eds. 2006. *Mainstreaming Midwives: The Politics of Change.* New York: Routledge.

Davis-Floyd, Robbie, and Carolyn Fishel Sargent, eds. 1997. *Childbirth and Authoritative Knowledge: Cross-Cultural Perspectives.* Berkeley: University of California Press.

Deeb, Lara. 2006. *An Enchanted Modern: Gender and Public Piety in Shi'i Lebanon.* Princeton, NJ: Princeton University Press.

Deeb, Lara, and Jessica Winegar. 2012. "Anthropologies of Arab-Majority Societies." *Annual of Anthropology* 41: 537–558.

de Lauretis, Teresa. 1991. "Queer Theory: Lesbian and Gay Sexualities." *differences: A Journal of Feminist Cultural Studies* 3 (2): iii–xviii.

D'Emilio, John. 1983. *Sexual Politics, Sexual Communities.* Chicago: University of Chicago Press.

Diner, Helen. 1973. *Mothers and Amazons: The First Feminine History of Culture.* New York: Doubleday.

Ehrenreich, Barbara, and Deirdre English. 1972. *Witches, Midwives, and Nurses: A History of Women Healers.* New York: Feminist Press.

Eisler, Riane. 1987. *The Chalice and the Blade: Our History, Our Future.* New York: HarperCollins.

Eller, Cynthia, 2001. *The Myth of Matriarchal Prehistory: Why an Invented Past Won't Give Women a Future.* Boston: Beacon Press.

Engels, Friedrich. 1902. *The Origin of the Family, Private Property, and the State*. Chicago: Ernest Untermann.

Etienne, Mona, and Eleanor Leacock. 1980. *Women and Colonization: Anthropological Perspectives*. New York: Praeger.

Fernea, Elizabeth Warnock. 1965. *Guests of the Sheik: An Ethnography of an Iraqi Village*. Garden City, NY: Doubleday.

Finn, Janet L. 1995. "Ella Cara Deloria and Mourning Dove: Writing for Cultures, Writing Against the Grain." In *Women Writing Culture*, ed. Ruth Behar and Deborah A. Gordon, 131–147. Berkeley: University of California Press.

Franklin, Sarah. 1995. "Science as Culture, Cultures of Science." *Annual Review of Anthropology* 24: 163–184.

Fraser, Gertrude Jacinta. 1998. *African American Midwifery in the South: Dialogues of Birth, Race, and Memory*. Cambridge, MA: Harvard University Press.

Friedlander, Eva. 2013. "IWAC at the Scholar/Activist Interface: Lessons and Challenges for the Future." Paper presented at annual meeting of American Anthropological Association. Chicago, November.

Gailey, Christine Ward. 1987. *From Kinship to Kingship: Gender Hierarchy and State Formation in the Tongan Islands*. Austin: University of Texas Press.

Gal, Susan, and Gail Kligman. 2000. *The Politics of Gender after Socialism*. Princeton, NJ: Princeton University Press.

Gammeltoft, Tine M. 2014. *Haunting Images: A Cultural Account of Selective Reproduction in Vietnam*. Berkeley: University of California Press.

Gammeltoft, Tine M., and Ayo Wahlberg. 2014. "Selective Reproductive Technologies." *Annual Review of Anthropology* 43: 201–216.

Gimbutas, Marija. 1982. *The Goddesses and Gods of Old Europe, 6500–3500 B.C., Myths and Cult Images*. Berkeley: University of California Press.

———. 1989. *The Language of the Goddess: Unearthing the Hidden Symbols of Western Civilization*. New York: Harper & Row.

———. 1991. *The Civilization of the Goddess: The World of Old Europe*. San Francisco: Harper & Row.

Ginsburg, Faye D., and Rayna Rapp. 1991. "The Politics of Reproduction." *Annual Review of Anthropology* 20: 311–343.

———, eds. 1995. *Conceiving the New World Order: The Global Politics of Reproduction*. Berkeley: University of California Press.

———. 2013. "Disability Worlds." *Annual Review of Anthropology* 42: 53–68.

Goodale, Jane C. 1971. *Tiwi Wives: A Study of the Women of Melville Island, North Australia*. Seattle: University of Washington Press.

Greenhalgh, Susan. 2008. *Just One Child: Science and Policy in Deng's China*. Berkeley: University of California Press.

Griffith, R. Marie. 1997. *God's Daughters: Evangelical Women and the Power of Submission*. Berkeley: University of California Press.

Gruenbaum, Ellen. 2001. *The Female Circumcision Controversy*. Philadelphia: University of Pennsylvania Press.

Gutmann, Matthew C. 1996. *The Meanings of Macho: Being a Man in Mexico City*. Berkeley: University of California Press.

———. 2007. *Fixing Men: Sex, Birth Control, and AIDS in Mexico*. Berkeley: University of California Press.

Hafez, Sherine. 2011. *An Islam of Her Own: Reconsidering Religion and Secularism in Women's Islamic Movements.* New York: New York University Press.

Handwerker, Lisa. 1995. "The Hen That Can't Lay an Egg (Bu Xia Dan de Mu Ji): Conceptions of Female Infertility in Modern China." In *Deviant Bodies,* ed. Jennifer Terry and Jacqueline Urla, 358–386. Bloomington: Indiana University Press.

Harding, Sandra. 1986. *The Science Question in Feminism.* Ithaca, NY: Cornell University Press.

Harris, Marvin. 1969. *The Rise of Anthropological Theory: A History of Theories of Culture.* New York: Thomas Y. Crowell.

Hart, Charles William Merton, and Arnold R. Pilling. 1960. *The Tiwi of North Australia.* New York: Holt.

Hartsock, Nancy. 1983. "The Feminist Standpoint: Developing the Ground for a Specifically Feminist Historical Materialism." In *Discovering Reality: Feminist Perspectives on Epistemology, Metaphysics, Methodology, and Philosophy of Science,* ed. Sandra Harding and Merrill B. Hintikka, 283–310. Dordrecht: D. Reidel Publishing.

Herdt, Gilbert H. 1981. *Guardians of the Flutes: Idioms of Masculinity.* New York: McGraw-Hill.

Hobsbawm, Eric. J. 1965. *Primitive Rebels.* New York: W. W. Norton.

Inhorn, Marcia C. 1994. *Quest for Conception: Gender, Infertility, and Egyptian Medical Traditions.* Philadelphia: University of Pennsylvania Press.

———. 1996. *Infertility and Patriarchy: The Cultural Politics of Gender and Family Life in Egypt.* Philadelphia: University of Pennsylvania Press.

———. 2003. *Local Babies, Global Science: Gender, Religion, and In Vitro Fertilization in Egypt.* New York: Routledge.

———, ed. 2007. *Reproductive Disruptions: Gender, Technology, and Biopolitics in the New Millennium.* New York: Berghahn Books.

———. 2012. *The New Arab Man: Emergent Masculinities, Technologies, and Islam in the Middle East.* Princeton: Princeton University Press.

Ivry, Tsipy. 2009. *Embodying Culture: Pregnancy in Japan and Israel.* New Brunswick, NJ: Rutgers University Press.

Jacobs, Sue-Ellen, Wesley Thomas, and Sabine Lang, eds. 1997. *Two-Spirit People: Native American Gender Identity, Sexuality, and Spirituality.* Urbana: University of Illinois Press.

Jordan, Brigitte. 1978. *Birth in Four Cultures: A Crosscultural Investigation of Childbirth in Yucatan, Holland, Sweden, and the United States.* Montreal: Eden Press Women's Publications.

Kahn, Susan Martha. 2000. *Reproducing Jews: A Cultural Account of Assisted Conception in Israel.* Durham, NC: Duke University Press.

Kanaaneh, Rhoda Ann. 2002. *Birthing the Nation: Strategies of Palestinian Women in Israel.* Berkeley: University of California Press.

Kennedy, Elizabeth Lapovsky. 2002. "'These Natives Can Speak for Themselves': The Development of Gay and Lesbian Community Studies in Anthropology." In *Out in Theory: The Emergence of Lesbian and Gay Anthropology,* ed. Ellen Lewin and William L. Leap, 93–109. Urbana: University of Illinois Press.

Kennedy, Elizabeth Lapovsky, and Madeline D. Davis. 1993. *Boots of Leather, Slippers of Gold: The History of a Lesbian Community.* New York: Routledge.

Kessler, Suzanne, and Wendy McKenna. 1985. *Gender: An Ethnomethodological Approach.* Chicago: University of Chicago Press.

Kulick, Don. 1998. *Travesti: Sex, Gender, and Culture among Brazilian Transgendered Prostitutes.* Chicago: University of Chicago Press.

Landsman, Gail. 2008. *Reconstructing Motherhood and Disability in the Age of "Perfect" Babies.* New York: Routledge.
Layne, Linda L. 2002. *Motherhood Lost: A Feminist Account of Pregnancy Loss in America.* New York: Routledge.
Leach, Edmund R. 1967. *Political Systems of Highland Burma: A Study of Kachin Social Structure.* Boston: Beacon Press.
Leacock, Eleanor, ed. 1971. *The Culture of Poverty: A Critique.* New York: Simon and Schuster.
———. 1983. "Interpreting the Origins of Gender Inequality: Conceptual and Historical Problems." *Dialectical Anthropology* 7 (4): 263–284.
Leacock, Eleanor, and June Nash. 1977. "Ideologies of Sex: Archetypes and Stereotypes." *Annals of the New York Academy of Sciences* 285: 618–645.
Leap, William L. 1996. *Word's Out: Gay Men's English.* Minneapolis: University of Minnesota Press.
Lévi-Strauss, Claude. 1969. *The Elementary Structures of Kinship.* Boston: Beacon Press.
Lewin, Ellen. 1993. *Lesbian Mothers: Accounts of Gender in American Culture.* Ithaca, NY: Cornell University Press.
———. 1995. "Writing Lesbian Ethnography." In *Women Writing Culture,* ed. Ruth Behar and Deborah A. Gordon, 322–335. Berkeley: University of California Press.
———. 1998. *Recognizing Ourselves: Ceremonies of Lesbian and Gay Commitment.* New York: Columbia University Press.
Limón, José. 1991. "Representation, Ethnicity, and the Precursory Ethnography: Notes of a Native Anthropologist." In *Recapturing Anthropology: Working in the Present,* ed. Richard G. Fox, 115–135. Santa Fe, NM: School of American Research.
Lock, Margaret. 1993. *Encounters with Aging: Mythologies of Menopause in Japan and North America.* Berkeley: University of California Press.
Lock, Margaret, and Vinh-Kim Nguyen. 2010. *An Anthropology of Biomedicine.* Malden, MA: Wiley-Blackwell.
Lorde, Audre. 1984. "The Master's Tools Will Never Dismantle the Master's House." In *Sister Outsider: Essays and Speeches,* 110–113. Berkeley, CA: Crossing Press.
Lutz, Catherine. 1990. "The Erasure of Women's Writing in Sociocultural Anthropology." *American Ethnologist* 17 (4): 611.
Mahmood, Saba. 2011. *Politics of Piety: The Islamic Revival and the Feminist Subject.* Princeton, NJ: Princeton University Press.
Mamo, Laura. 2007. *Queering Reproduction: Achieving Pregnancy in the Age of Technoscience.* Durham, NC: Duke University Press.
Martin, Emily. 1989. *The Woman in the Body: A Cultural Analysis of Reproduction.* Boston: Beacon Press.
———. 1995. *Flexible Bodies: The Role of Community in American Culture from the Days of Polio to the Age of AIDS.* Boston: Beacon Press.
———. 2009. *Bipolar Expeditions: Mania and Depression in American Culture.* Princeton: Princeton University Press.
Marx, Karl. 1932. *Capital, the Communist Manifesto, and Other Writings.* New York: Modern Library.
Mascia-Lees, Frances E., Patricia Sharpe, and Colleen Ballerino Cohen. 1989. "The Postmodernist Turn in Anthropology: Cautions from a Feminist Perspective." *Signs* 15 (1): 7–33.
McClaurin, Irma, ed. 2001. *Black Feminist Anthropology: Theory, Politics, Praxis, and Poetics.* New Brunswick, NJ: Rutgers University Press.

Mernissi, Fatima. 1975. *Beyond the Veil: Male–Female Dynamics in a Modern Muslim Society.* New York: John Wiley and Sons.
Mills, Mary Beth. 2003. "Gender and Inequality in the Global Labor Force." *Annual Review of Anthropology* 32: 41–62.
Moran, Mary H. 2010. "Gender, Militarism, and Peace-Building: Projects of the Postconflict Moment." *Annual Review of Anthropology* 39: 261–274.
Morgan, Elaine. 1972. *The Descent of Woman: The Classic Study of Evolution.* London: Souvenir Books.
Morgen, Sandra. 2002. *Into Our Own Hands: The Women's Health Movement in the United States, 1969–1990.* New Brunswick, NJ: Rutgers University Press.
Morgen, Sandra, and Jeff Maskovsky. 2003. "The Anthropology of Welfare 'Reform': New Perspectives on U.S. Urban Poverty in the Post-Welfare Era." *Annual Review of Anthropology* 32: 315–338.
Morris, Rosalind C. 1995. "All Made Up: Performance Theory and the New Anthropology of Sex and Gender." *Annual Review of Anthropology* 24: 567–592.
Moynihan, Daniel. 1965. *The Negro Family: The Case for National Action.* Washington, DC: Office of Policy Planning and Research, US Department of Labor.
Mukhopadhyay, Carol C., and Patricia J. Higgins. 1988. "Anthropological Studies of Women's Status Revisited: 1977–1987." *Annual Review of Anthropology* 17: 461–495.
Murphy, Robert. 1960. *Headhunter's Revenge.* Berkeley: University of California Press.
Murphy, Yolanda, and Robert F. Murphy. 1974. *Women of the Forest.* New York: Columbia University Press.
Narayan, Kirin. 1993. "How Native Is a 'Native' Anthropologist?" *American Anthropologist* 95 (3): 671–686.
Narayan, Uma. 1997. *Dislocating Cultures: Identities, Traditions, and Third World Feminism.* New York: Routledge.
Newton, Esther. 1972. *Mother Camp: Female Impersonators in America.* Englewood Cliffs, NJ: Prentice-Hall.
———. 1993. *Cherry Grove, Fire Island: Sixty Years in America's First Lesbian and Gay Town.* Boston: Beacon Press.
Olesen, Virginia. 2011. "Feminist Qualitative Research in the Millennium's First Decade: Developments, Challenges, Prospects." In *The SAGE Handbook of Qualitative Research,* ed. Norman K. Denzin and Yvonna S. Lincoln, 129–145. Thousand Oaks, CA: Sage.
Ortner, Sherry B. 1974. "Is Female to Male as Nature is to Culture?" In *Woman, Culture, and Society,* ed. Michelle Z. Rosaldo and Louise Lamphere, 67–87. Stanford, CA: Stanford University Press.
Pomales, Tony O. 2013. "Men's Narratives of Vasectomy: Rearticulating Masculinity and Contraceptive Responsibility in San José, Costa Rica." *Medical Anthropology Quarterly* 27 (1): 23–42.
Quinn, Naomi. 1977. "Anthropological Studies on Women's Status." *Annual Review of Anthropology* 6: 181–225.
Rapp, Rayna. 1999. *Testing Women, Testing the Fetus: The Social Impact of Amniocentesis in America.* New York: Routledge.
Rapp, Rayna, and Faye D. Ginsburg. 2001. "Enabling Disability: Rewriting Kinship, Reimagining Citizenship." *Public Culture* 13 (3): 533–556.
———. 2011. "Reverberations: Disability and the New Kinship Imaginary." *Anthropological Quarterly* 84 (2): 379–410.
Read, Kenneth E. 1980. *Other Voices: The Style of a Male Homosexual Tavern.* Novato, CA: Chandler and Sharp.

Reddy, Gayatri. 2005. *With Respect to Sex: Negotiating Hijra Identity in South India.* Chicago: University of Chicago Press.

Reiter (Rapp), Rayna. 1975. *Toward an Anthropology of Women.* New York: Monthly Review Press.

Roberts, Elizabeth F. S. 2012. *God's Laboratory: Assisted Reproduction in the Andes.* Berkeley: University of California Press.

Rosaldo, Michelle Zimbalist. 1974. "Woman, Culture, and Society: A Theoretical Overview." In *Woman, Culture, and Society,* ed. Michelle Z. Rosaldo and Louise Lamphere, 17–41. Stanford, CA: Stanford University Press.

———. 1980. "The Use and Abuse of Anthropology: Reflections on Feminism and Cross-Cultural Understanding." *Signs* 5 (3): 389–417.

Rosaldo, Michelle Zimbalist, and Louise Lamphere, eds. 1974. *Woman, Culture, and Society.* Stanford, CA: Stanford University Press.

Roseberry, William. 1989. *Anthropologies and Histories: Essays in Culture, History, and Political Economy.* New Brunswick, NJ: Rutgers University Press.

Rubin, Gayle. 1975. "The Traffic in Women: Notes on the 'Political Economy' of Sex." In *Toward an Anthropology of Women,* ed. Rayna Reiter (Rapp), 157–210. New York: Monthly Review Press.

———. 1984. "Thinking Sex: Notes for a Radical Theory of the Politics of Sexuality." In *Pleasure and Danger: Exploring Female Sexuality,* ed. Carole S. Vance, 267–319. New York: Routledge.

Sacks, Karen. 1979. *Sisters and Wives: The Past and Future of Sexual Equality.* Westport, CT: Greenwood Press.

Sahlins, Marshall D., and Elman R. Service. 1960. *Evolution and Culture.* Ann Arbor: University of Michigan Press.

Said, Edward W. 1979. *Orientalism.* New York: Vintage Books.

Sanjek, Roger. 1982. "The American Anthropological Association Resolution on the Employment of Women: Genesis, Implementation, Disavowal, and Resurrection." *Signs* 7 (4): 845–868.

Sargent, Carolyn Fishel. 1981. *The Cultural Context of Therapeutic Choice: Obstetrical Care Decisions among the Bariba of Benin.* Dordrecht: Reidel.

Scheper-Hughes, Nancy, and Margaret Lock. 1987. "The Mindful Body: A Prolegomenon to Future Work in Medical Anthropology." *Medical Anthropology Quarterly* 1 (1): 6–41.

Schneider, David M. 1968. *American Kinship: A Cultural Account.* Englewood Cliffs, NJ: Prentice-Hall.

Segura, Denise A., and Patricia Zavella, eds. 2007. *Women and Migration in the U.S.–Mexico Borderlands: A Reader.* Durham, NC: Duke University Press.

Silverblatt, Irene. 1987. *Moon, Sun, and Witches: Gender Ideologies and Class in Inca and Colonial Peru.* Princeton, NJ: Princeton University Press.

———. 1988. "Women in States." *Annual Review of Anthropology* 17: 427–460.

Slocum, Sally. 1975. "Woman the Gatherer: Male Bias in Anthropology." In *Toward an Anthropology of Women,* ed. Rayna Reiter (Rapp), 36–50. New York: Monthly Review Press.

Spivak, Gayatri Chakravorty. 1988a. "Can the Subaltern Speak?" In *Marxism and the Interpretation of Culture,* ed. Cary Nelson and Lawrence Grossberg, 271–313. Urbana: University of Illinois Press.

———. 1988b. *In Other Worlds: Essays in Cultural Politics.* New York: Routledge.

Spretnak, Charlene, ed. 1981. *The Politics of Women's Spirituality: Essays by Founding Mothers of the Movement.* New York: Anchor Books.

Stacey, Judith. 1991. "Can There Be a Feminist Ethnography?" In *Women's Words: The Feminist Practice of Oral History*, ed. Sherna B. Gluck and Daphne Patai, 111–119. New York: Routledge Chapman and Hall.

Stacey, Judith, and Susan Elizabeth Gerard. 1990. "'We Are Not Doormats': The Influence of Feminism on Contemporary Evangelicals in the United States." In *Uncertain Terms: Negotiating Gender in American Culture*, ed. Faye Ginsburg and Anna L. Tsing, 98–117. Boston: Beacon Press.

Stack, Carol B. 1974. *All Our Kin: Strategies for Survival in a Black Community*. New York: Harper & Row.

Starhawk. 1979. *The Spiral Dance: A Rebirth of the Ancient Religion of the Goddess*. New York: HarperCollins.

Steward, Julian H. 1955. *Theory of Culture Change: The Methodology of Multilinear Evolution.* Urbana: University of Illinois Press.

Stoler, Ann Laura. 1991. "Carnal Knowledge and Imperial Power: Gender, Race, and Morality in Colonial Asia." In *Gender at the Crossroads of Knowledge: Feminist Anthropology in the Postmodern Era*, ed. Micaela di Leonardo, 51–101. Berkeley: University of California Press.

Stone, Merlin. 1978. *When God Was a Woman*. New York: Harcourt Brace.

Strathern, Marilyn. 1972. *Women In Between: Female Roles in a Male World: Mount Hagen, New Guinea*. London: Seminar Press.

Susser, Ida. 2009. *AIDS, Sex, and Culture: Global Politics and Survival in Southern Africa.* Malden, MA: Wiley-Blackwell.

Taylor, Janelle S. 2005. "Surfacing the Body Interior." *Annual Review of Anthropology* 34: 741–756.

———. 2008. *The Public Life of the Fetal Sonogram: Technology, Consumption, and the Politics of Reproduction*. New Brunswick, NJ: Rutgers University Press.

Teman, Elly. 2010. *Birthing a Mother: The Surrogate Body and the Pregnant Self.* Berkeley: University of California Press.

Valentine, Charles A. 1968. *Culture and Poverty.* Chicago: University of Chicago Press.

Valentine, David. 2007. *Imagining Transgender: An Ethnography of a Category*. Durham, NC: Duke University Press.

Van Esterik, Penny. 2002. "Contemporary Trends in Infant Feeding Research." *Annual Review of Anthropology* 31: 257–278.

Van Hollen, Cecilia. 2003. *Birth on the Threshold: Childbirth and Modernity in South India.* Berkeley: University of California Press.

Visweswaran, Kamala. 1997. "Histories of Feminist Ethnography." *Annual Review of Anthropology* 26: 591–621.

Walley, Christine J. 1997. "Searching for 'Voices': Feminism, Anthropology, and the Global Debate over Female Genital Operations." *Cultural Anthropology* 12 (3): 405–438.

Webster, Paula. 1975. "Matriarchy: A Vision of Power." In *Toward an Anthropology of Women*, ed. Rayna Reiter (Rapp), 141–156. New York: Monthly Review Press.

Weiner, Annette B. 1976. *Women of Value, Men of Renown: New Perspectives in Trobriand Exchange*. Austin: University of Texas Press.

Wekker, Gloria. 2006. *The Politics of Passion: Women's Sexual Culture in the Afro-Surinamese Diaspora*. New York: Columbia University Press.

Wentzell, Emily A. 2013. *Maturing Masculinities: Aging, Chronic Illness, and Viagra in Mexico.* Durham, NC: Duke University Press.

Weston, Kath. 1991. *Families We Choose: Lesbians, Gays, Kinship.* New York: Columbia University Press.

Wilde, Oscar. 1985. *Lady Windermere's Fan.* In *The Importance of Being Earnest and Other Plays,* 37–105. New York: Signet Classics.

Williams, Brett. 1992. "Poverty among African Americans in the Urban United States." *Human Organization* 51 (2): 164–174.

Williams, Walter L. 1986. *The Spirit and the Flesh: Sexual Diversity in American Indian Culture.* Boston: Beacon Press.

Wylie, Alison. 1992. "The Interplay of Evidential Constraints and Political Interests: Recent Archaeological Research on Gender." *American Antiquity* 57 (1): 15–35.

PART I FOUNDATIONS

Problematizing Feminist Anthropology

FEMINIST ANTHROPOLOGY ENGAGES SOCIAL MOVEMENTS

Theory, Ethnography, and Activism

LOUISE LAMPHERE

Social movements have been a critical component of the emergence, growth, and current research agenda of US feminist anthropology. Feminist anthropology officially emerged in 1974–1975 with the publication of *Woman, Culture, and Society* edited by Michelle Zimbalist Rosaldo and Louise Lamphere (1974) and *Toward an Anthropology of Women* edited by Rayna Reiter (now Rapp) (1975). As women anthropologists, many of us, already active in the civil rights and anti-war movements, became involved in the 1970s women's movement in the United States. Through participating in demonstrations for women's liberation, legislative hearings on abortion rights, and especially consciousness-raising (CR) groups, women anthropologists learned that "the personal is political" and began to bring a feminist sensibility to their research and teaching as well as to their own personal lives. At this stage, activism in the public sphere brought changes to anthropology, but feminist advocacy on issues of importance to women (abortion rights, child care, job discrimination, etc.) tended to be segregated from anthropological endeavors.

In the late 1970s and the early 1980s, our theoretical framework expanded to emphasize the category "gender" rather than solely women. Many younger graduate students and new PhDs who defined themselves as feminists also participated in other movements including the emerging gay and lesbian movement. African American, Chicana/Latina, and lesbian anthropologists brought new voices and concerns as well to feminist anthropology. Anthropological research itself began to expand to include not only women but also how rural and tribal societies around the world, as well as urban populations, were grappling with the impact of a globalizing economy, issues of health care and reproduction, environmental degradation, and migration, among others. In studying such matters, feminist anthropologists pioneered gender research in these growing subfields within anthropology and brought methodologies emphasizing collaboration, positionality, and personal narratives to their new research (see Silverstein and Lewin, this volume).[1]

Since 2000, a third generation of young feminist anthropologists, along with some senior scholars, has continued the engagement with social movements in the United States and in other parts of the globe but in a very different way. Feminist anthropologists have examined women's roles in these movements, how they intersect with local issues and populations, and what strategies are necessary to bring about change. In this approach, many feminists are attempting to balance their roles as researchers, critics, and activists, a stance enabled by both theoretical and methodological changes in the way anthropology is practiced.

This chapter focuses specifically on the development of feminist anthropology in the United States beginning in the early 1970s and extending through the transformations of feminist theory, ethnography, and activism that occurred in the next four decades.

First, feminist theory has evolved from a focus on women's status and a search for universal explanatory systems to studies that pay greater attention to history, local context, and the particular political economies in which our research subjects live. Sophisticated analyses of power, influenced particularly by the work of Michel Foucault (1977), and agency, as defined by Judith Butler (1993), emerged between 1980 and 1995 and have continued to the present. These evolving theoretical concepts (power and agency) allowed feminists to see women as having an active hand in forging their own fate.

Second, feminists have transformed ethnographic fieldwork and writing, paying more attention to the power dynamics between anthropologists and their subjects, resulting in increased collaboration. In ethnographic writing, feminists have assumed a more dialogical approach to highlight the voices of women more clearly in our research and publications.

These changes in theory and ethnographic practice set the stage for more attention to my third topic: activism. Since 2000 there have been increasing calls for an engaged or activist feminist anthropology, one where carefully conducted ethnographic research can be more directly relevant to social movements, to educating the public, and to efforts to bring about changes in public policy. With the exception of Karen Brodkin Sacks's and Ann Bookman's labor research (Bookman and Morgen 1988; Sacks 1988a), Sandra Morgen's study of the women's health movement (Morgen 2002), and Ida Susser's study of a New York working-class community (1982), participation in social movements was something that feminists engaged in outside of their anthropological research and writing, or at least "off stage."

Now, as in the 1970s, some feminist anthropologists might define their activism in terms of creating courses on women, building stronger women's studies programs, or teaching their students to take a gendered perspective. Here, I focus on activism off campus, particularly in bringing those we study into full collaborative partnerships at all stages of research. Activism, as Ida Susser insists, always involves an intervention and usually includes a social justice stance on the part of the feminist researcher (Susser 2009, 15). This is a definition I find helpful in analyzing current forms of feminist activist anthropology.

FEMINIST ANTHROPOLOGY AND THE WOMEN'S MOVEMENT

The 1970s saw the blossoming of feminist anthropology. The women who contributed to the earliest collections—*Woman, Culture, and Society* (1974) and *Toward an Anthropology of Women* (1975)—were all marginal to the anthropology departments where we were affiliated as graduate students, new faculty, or faculty wives. We were profoundly influenced by the women's liberation movement that emerged from both the civil rights and anti-war movements (Evans 1979). A number of centers of non-academic feminist activism appeared during the period between 1967 and 1969. Some (e.g., Chicago, Washington, DC) were more oriented to working within the anti-war movement while combating male domination, and others (e.g., New York) promoted an autonomous women's movement, emphasizing the oppression of women (rather than race, class, or capitalist forms of domination) as the central issue to combat (Echols 1989; Evans 1979). This split between the "politicos" and the "radical feminists" was less salient to those who became involved later in the 1970s. As young feminists, we read widely and became connected to feminism through myriad different local groups and activities.

Redstockings, a radical feminist organization, was a center of the movement in New York City. Their "Notes from the Second Year" (1969) was one of the first publications we all passed around and devoured because it called for personal relationships between men and women to be revolutionized. Rejecting male-dominated notions of leadership and forming solidary relationships with "our sisters" found broad appeal. One of the most important aspects of the women's movement was the consciousness-raising group started by Redstockings and the New York Radical Feminists,[2] a group that continued the women's liberation movement in New York as Redstockings began to fall apart (Echols 1989; Rosen

2000). The foundational principle of these small CR groups of five to ten women was "the personal is political," based on the idea that by talking about our personal lives, we would begin to understand the more systemic characteristics of our oppression. Usually the groups met weekly and often posed a general question that each woman addressed, mining her own experience. Marriage, money, housework, educational goals, standards of beauty, self-confidence, and sexual relationships were all grist for the mill.

In Boston, Bread and Roses, a socialist-feminist "politico" organization, advocated for a broad range of changes in women's lives from equality in the workplace, to control over their bodies, to free child care.[3] Michelle Rosaldo, for example, joined a Bread and Roses CR group composed of Radcliffe graduates in October 1969. She later participated in another group at Stanford, of which Ellen Lewin was also a member. I joined a small group at Brown University that emerged from our chapter of the New University Conference (NUC), a university- and college-based anti-war organization, and from activities that grew out of the Brown campus-wide May 1970 strike. We shared an interest in addressing our personal concerns in relation to men and to the larger power structure; these CR groups offered us a safe environment for exploring such issues.

Female anthropologists elsewhere also joined similar CR groups. In Michigan, Rayna Rapp and Gayle Rubin joined a consciousness-raising group that had spun off from Resistance, the draft resistance and anti-war movement group active on the University of Michigan campus. In New York, the Ruth Benedict Collective (RBC) brought together senior anthropologists (June Nash, Eleanor [Happy] Leacock, and Ruby Rohrlich-Leavitt), recent PhDs, and graduate students, including Leni Silverstein. In its early years (1969–1971), some of the twenty-five or more anthropologists in the RBC also met in small consciousness-raising groups that provided personal, intellectual, and professional support (Chernela 2013). Subsequently, members of the group began writing papers about women to explore the extent of discrimination among female anthropologists in universities, and to engage with the larger questions the women's movement was raising about women's roles and status cross-culturally (Leni Silverstein, personal communication 2014). An offshoot of this larger group initiated the New York Women's Anthropology Caucus (NYWAC) whose senior founders included Happy Leacock, Ruby Rohrlich-Leavitt, and Constance (Connie) Sutton (Friedlander 2013).

We discovered that—despite being mostly white and middle class—our feelings of subordination and inadequacy were widely shared by others. We also were united in the belief that we could change family and social structures that created women's second-class status through our academic work. We were involved not only in protest marches and organizing efforts, but also brought our new sense of the multiple meanings of women's position into our teaching and academic writing.

Given the interest in cross-cultural information among women in the movement, feminist anthropologists started putting together comparative ethnographic material on women's lives and teaching courses focusing on what little we could find in the existing literature. Between 1970 and 1973 courses on women were taught in anthropology departments at Stanford, Brown, the University of Michigan, New York University, the New School, and other campuses. Michigan students, in particular, were fortunate that, unlike most departments at the time, two women, Norma Diamond and Niara Sudarkasa, were faculty members in the Anthropology Department. Norma Diamond taught an initial course on women called "Second Sex/Third World" that Rayna Rapp took over during its second year in 1971 (Lamphere, Rapp, and Rubin 2007).

About the same time, in the spring of 1971, Shelly Rosaldo and Jane Collier (both faculty wives at Stanford) and four graduate students (Ellen Lewin, Janet Fjellman, Julia Howell, and Kim Kramer) taught a class at Stanford entitled "Women in Cross-Cultural Perspective." Looking back, it is hard to recall how audacious these efforts were; we never imagined at the time that we were launching a new subfield in anthropology. We just felt compelled to bring our new interest in analyzing women's lives into the classroom in order to explore how our own situation compared to that of women in other cultures.

These two courses (Stanford and Michigan) served as the impetus for *Woman, Culture, and Society* and *Towards an Anthropology of Women*, the first edited volumes to take up the status of women as a focal concern. Both collections acknowledged their relationship to the women's movement and to the questions that feminists looked to anthropology to answer. In our introduction, Shelly and I wrote, "Along with many women today, we are trying to understand our position and to change it. We have become increasingly aware of sexual inequities in economic, social, and political institutions and are seeking ways to fight them" (Rosaldo and Lamphere 1974, 2).

Rayna's comments were in a similar vein: "This book has its roots in the women's movement. To explain and describe equality and inequality between the sexes, contemporary feminism has turned to anthropology with many questions in its search for a theory and a body of information. These questions are more than academic: the answers will help feminists in the struggle against sexism in our own society" (Reiter 1975, 11).

The introductory essays by Rosaldo, Ortner, and Chodorow in *Woman, Culture, and Society* offered an integrated set of explanations, each at a different level of analysis, for the universal subordination of women: that is, respectively, through social structural arrangements, cultural ideas and values, and the psychological foundations of gender. The conclusion that women were universally subordinated not only made sense of the ethnographic examples we then knew, but fit well in a discipline that already emphasized universals like human language, marriage, incest taboos, and the family.

But the articles in both collections also attested to the variety of positions women held in cultures throughout the world. Authors offered examples where women held power or positions of great influence (McCormack, Brown) on the one hand, and demonstrated how women strategized to achieve their own goals even though men held power in patrilineal descent groups (Wolf, Collier, Silverman, Lamphere). Still other chapters sought to discover historical and cultural situations where relationships between men and women could be considered equal (Sacks, Gough, Draper). As Gayle Rubin put it, "So they [the books] were locally inflected [structural and cultural versus materialist and evolutionary], but the project was a common one, and it was one of those historical tectonic shifts where you don't understand the forces that are impinging on all these different people in different places but they clearly were." As Rapp said, "we and our whole generation were reconfiguring the field" (Lamphere, Rapp, Rubin 2007, 416–417).

EVOLVING FEMINIST ANTHROPOLOGICAL THEORY: THE TURN TO GENDER

In the late 1970s and early 1980s, as the women's movement in the United States focused on passing the ERA and fighting the backlash against its early accomplishments, feminist anthropologists turned toward the academy as well, expanding the number of courses on women, solidifying women's studies programs, recruiting and training new female graduate students, and building a feminist presence in academic professional associations including the American Anthropological Association (AAA). During this period, many took on new projects focused on women and encouraged our students to do the same. The ethnographic record that many of us found so untrustworthy and male-centered, often glossing over or marginalizing women (Reiter 1975, 2–14), became more nuanced over this period as new accounts appeared. Many studies were historical and examined women's relationship to the state or to colonialism (Gailey 1987; Sacks 1979; Silverblatt 1987, 1991; Stoler 2002), while others sought to firmly document women's participation in their society's economic, familial, and cultural life, and place these into the ethnographic record (Abu-Lughod 1987; Shostak 1981; Wolf 1968).

In general, the emphasis on universals and broad generalizations about "all women" began to fade as the complexity of women's actual strategies, actions, views, and values was analyzed in their appropriate historical and local contexts. The "turn to gender" was a large part of this trend and signaled a major theoretical shift. In addition, building on some of the insights of the Reiter 1975 volume, feminist anthropologists began to pay more attention to critiquing how our own conceptual frameworks were not only male-biased but based on thoroughly Western assumptions. Much of this new work was influenced by Marxist and political economy approaches, and by what became known as *social constructionism*, the idea that social hierarchies, gender roles, and ideologies are historically and socially constructed and dynamic rather than "given" (Ortner and Whitehead 1981).

Rosaldo's article, "The Use and Abuse of Anthropology: Reflections on Feminism and Cross-Cultural Understanding" (1980), provided an initial step in charting this emerging intellectual terrain. Deconstructing the categories of "female" and "male," she emphasized that even in simple societies women occupy a variety of roles as do men (wives, husbands, fathers, mothers, warriors, healers, marriageable women, etc.). Working with Jane Collier, she noted that "we are concerned to stress not the activities of women—or of men—alone; instead we are attempting to convey the ways in which a sexual division of labor in all human social groups is bound up with extremely complex forms of interdependence, politics, and hierarchy" (Rosaldo 1980, 412).

Both Weberian and Marxist feminists contributed to this discussion, as exemplified by Sherry Ortner and Harriet Whitehead's collection *Sexual Meanings* (1981) (from the Weberian perspective), and Michaela di Leonardo's collection *Gender at the Crossroads of Knowledge* (1991), which focused on political economy and culture. Thus, the work produced from the late 1970s through the 1980s yielded richer and more nuanced descriptions of women's lives and more sophisticated theoretical frameworks. Gender replaced women as the key concept and more careful attention was given to historical trajectories, social context, and political economy.

During this time, calls for a critical reappraisal of the fieldwork enterprise itself emerged from women, minority, and non-Western scholars and from the peoples we studied as well (Abu-Lughod 1987; Stacey 1988). Feminist anthropologists began to question their methodologies and how to best represent the voices of women. These efforts were stimulated by the recruitment to anthropology of more minority women who raised distinct research questions stemming from their own experiences in the United States. Scholars, especially those of their own ethnic and/or cultural background, established different kinds of relationships with the communities they studied.

INSIGHTS FROM AFRICAN AMERICAN AND CHICANA FEMINIST ANTHROPOLOGISTS

Minority voices were present in the women's movement from its inception (for example, Audre Lorde and Tony Cade Bambara), but it was the publication of Cherríe Moraga and Gloria Anzaldúa's *This Bridge Called My Back* (1981) and Gloria Hull, Patricia Bell Scott, and Barbara Smith's *All the Women Are White, All the Blacks Are Men but Some of Us Are Brave* (1982) that solidified a critique of the white women's movement and argued for a variety of feminisms rooted in women's identities as both women *and* members of racial minorities. It is important to note that before 1970 very few African American women had graduate training in anthropology or had earned PhDs. Irma McClaurin lists only seven women, including Zora Neale Hurston and Katherine Dunham, long recognized more for their artistic achievements than for their contributions to anthropology (McClaurin 2001, 6). Over the next two decades, twenty more black women were added to the list (McClaurin 2001, 6–8), but there were still very few Chicana and Latina feminist anthropologists.

In the 1970s and early 1980s, African American and Chicana anthropology graduate students often found themselves relatively isolated in anthropology departments. For example, Leith Mullings reports that while at the University of Chicago during the height of the Vietnam War, "As graduate students, we decoded symbols while Chicago burned." In 1968, in the wake of Martin Luther King's death, fires and the National Guard occupation of the black neighborhoods adjacent to the university were followed that summer by police beatings of protesting students at the Democratic National Convention. By then, the three African American graduate students in the department concluded that "what passed for objective knowledge was at best inadequate and distorted and at worse racist, oppressive, and false" (Mullings 1997, xiv–xv).

Many early African American feminist anthropologists conducted their first field research in the Caribbean (Vera Green, Lynn Bolles, Yolanda Moses, Faye Harrison), in black communities in South America (Brackette Williams, Angela Gilliam), or in Africa (Niara Sudarkasa, Johnetta Cole, Leith Mullings, Sheila Walker, Gwendolyn Mikell, Filomena Chicoma-Steady). Seeking to enhance the anthropological record on women of color and to reflect on their own experiences, most focused on women for their dissertations. The work of Lynn Bolles and Faye Harrison is particularly important in this analysis since they were among the first to analyze the impact of neoliberal economic policies (orchestrated by the World Bank and the International Monetary Fund) on poor black women's lives as well as on their activism (Bolles 1983, 1996; Harrison 1997). Bolles focused on union struggles and how factory women "make do" in a declining economy, while Harrison examined how women organized against violence.

As some African American feminists gained academic positions, many in the generation that earned degrees in the 1970s and 1980s turned to conducting research and writing about African American communities in the United States. The forging of black feminist anthropology is well-documented in the personal statements and research accounts contained in *Black Feminist Anthropology* (McClaurin 2001). These essays offer insights into these anthropologists' concern with *positionality* during field research and their evolving identity as women, anthropologists, and African Americans. McClaurin suggests the deployment of the concept of "*auto-ethnography*," that is, the use of insights into one's identity and individual social status to engage with subjects in the community under study. White and "*halfie*" (Abu-Lughod 1993) feminists may have been writing more dialogical texts, positioning themselves in relation to their subjects, but few were as clear as African American anthropologists about the simultaneous roles of race, class, and gender in configuring their own fieldwork and analyses.

At the same time, Chicanas and Latinas were exploring feminism and incorporating its approaches to study women and women's issues in Puerto Rican, Mexican American, and Mexican settings (Roth 2003). Chicana feminist anthropologists, working with sociologists, historians, and literary critics, debated what ethnic labels to use (e.g., Chicana, Mexicana, Mexican American, Hispanic, Latina) and how to portray women's agency while paying attention to both economic constraints and assumptions about the dominant role of Latino men in family and community life. These anthropologists emphasized women's work, family, and issues of reproduction. Patricia Zavella, for example, problematized her feminist field research by analyzing her "*social location*" in relation to that of her interviewees. Her book, *Women's Work and Chicano Families: Cannery Workers in the Santa Clara Valley* (1987), and María Patricia Fernández-Kelly's study of women *maquiladora* workers in Cuidad Juarez, *For We Are Sold, I and My People* (Fernández-Kelly 1983), took the lead in emphasizing the significance of women's work in the constitution of the family.

Ruth Behar's *Translated Woman: Crossing the Border with Esperanza's Story* (1993) was one of the first feminist life histories to use a dialogical approach to show how she elicited and interacted with the narrator while composing the latter's story. She also directly addresses her own shifting identity, incorporating the irony of being regarded as a "*gringa*" by her Mexican interlocutor despite being a Cuban immigrant to the United States.

African American and Chicana/Latina feminists were crucial in bringing the issue of difference to the forefront of feminist anthropology in the late 1970s and early 1980s and in deconstructing the emphasis on the commonalities among women assumed by early US feminism. Because race and ethnicity were so salient in shaping their own lives, these anthropologists were drawn toward research on African American and Chicana/Latina women to articulate the intersection of race and gender in individual lives.

CONTRIBUTIONS FROM LESBIAN AND GAY ANTHROPOLOGISTS

Gay and lesbian anthropology also emerged during this period. Many lesbians who were in graduate school or received their PhDs in the 1970s, like heterosexual women, came to feminism through the women's liberation movement. Some lesbian academics of that generation were able to find an institutional home in women's studies programs, often the first to offer courses in lesbian culture and politics. Lesbian anthropologists, especially those who studied sexuality and lesbian communities, had difficulty gaining acceptance in anthropology departments particularly in elite universities and large public institutions.

Feminist anthropologists had conducted little research on sexuality and sexual variation during the 1960s and 1970s. But Esther Newton's *Mother Camp*, based on her dissertation research in the 1960s, created the foundation for an emergent lesbian and gay anthropology (Newton 1972). Her research, based on interviews and fieldwork with drag performers in Chicago and Kansas City, was one of the first ethnographic accounts of a gay subculture. Using social science theory, principally Erving Goffman's concept of stigma (1963), she sought to understand the dynamics and inner workings of drag and camp as performances.

Three studies, two of which began in the late 1970s (Kennedy and Davis 1993; Lewin 1993) and one a decade later (Weston 1991), focused on how race, class, and/or sexual orientation shaped consciousness, identity, and community. The authors were motivated by their political commitment to feminism and their desire to provide accounts that would deconstruct stereotypes. As Elizabeth Kennedy remarked, "I was hoping to correct the assumption of my students that lesbian history consists of Sappho, Gertrude Stein, and gay liberation" (Kennedy and Davis 1993, xv). Their book documented the lives of butch-fem lesbians in the working-class bar culture of Buffalo, NY. With regard to her book *Lesbian Mothers: Accounts of Gender in American Culture*, Ellen Lewin wrote, "I felt I should generate knowledge that would help to eradicate sexism and patriarchal domination. . . . Further, as a lesbian, I felt a special obligation to focus my energies on a 'lesbian project'" (1993, xv). These authors clearly were motivated by their political commitment to feminism and their desire to provide accounts that could break down stereotypes that fueled discrimination.

Almost a decade later (1985–1986), Kath Weston conducted her research on lesbian and gay residents in San Francisco, focusing on how they built families from close friendships. Her book, *Families We Choose* (1991), contains accounts of "coming out" and addresses issues of estrangement from families of origin.

Theoretically, Weston, through her description and analysis of "new" and "flexible" families, helped to revive anthropological interest in kinship and to expand notions of what constitutes a family.

FEMINIST CONNECTIONS TO THE LABOR MOVEMENT

During the late 1970s and 1980s, a significant body of feminist research was dedicated to the labor movement and labor activism as historians rediscovered women's roles in the American labor movement and in union struggles. A number of feminist anthropologists, inspired by this work and by issues raised by women's participation in the labor movement, began to examine women's work and its intersection with the family, including their relationships with husbands and male partners.

For example, in our book *Sunbelt Working Mothers* (Lamphere, Zavella, Gonzales, with Evans 1987), we focused on unraveling the complexities of the Albuquerque working class to show how class, ethnicity, gender, and marital status come together to shape women's lives. Anglo and Hispano women formed two very different sectors of the working class, but the impact of marital status and family income cut across both groups. Like the majority of other feminists who studied working-class women, we emphasized an understanding of women's experiences in the workplace and family, rather than their relationship to labor activism.

An important contribution is Ann Bookman and Sandra Morgen's collection, *Women and the Politics of Empowerment* (1988), that brought together white, African American, and Chicana anthropologists to write about women's work in manufacturing, the insurance industry, domestic work, and health care, producing early examples of what we now call *feminist activist ethnography*. In their preface, Bookman and Morgen, broadening the concerns of the labor movement beyond union organizing, stressed women's leadership, community organizing, and workplace struggles. "We, like many other women in this country, have worked towards two visions—a feminist movement that represents women of all races and class backgrounds and a progressive popular movement rooted in the working class that takes seriously the needs, the leadership, and the ideas of women" (Bookman and Morgen 1988, vii).

The collection includes three contributions by anthropologists that are early examples of activist feminist ethnography, characterized by a commitment to social justice issues, as these authors took on volunteer roles in order to provide a more "inside" view and to help achieve local movement goals. During her research on the Duke University Hospital strike (1988a, 1988b), Karen Brodkin Sacks worked as a volunteer on the union organizing committee while pursing the first phase of her research. Likewise, Ann Bookman was a worker and union organizer in the factory about which she wrote (Bookman 1988), and Sandra Morgen was a participant-observer at a feminist health clinic and a representative to a community coalition she studied (Morgen 1988; Morgen 2002). These feminists were among the very few who in the 1970s and 1980s intervened as activists and advocates while also carrying out academic work on the labor and health movements they were studying. The full repertoire of activist strategies, including collaborative research subjects, would only become more widespread with changes in anthropological theory and ethnographic practice along with greater acceptance of engaged and public anthropology in mainstream departments and within the discipline as a whole.

KEY TRANSFORMATIONS IN THEORY AND RESEARCH

The theoretical trends that emerged in the late 1980s and continue into the second decade of the twenty-first century, along with gender and intersectionality, include an emphasis on redefinitions of power and a focus on agency. The work of Foucault revolutionized the ways in which feminists thought about power. We began viewing power as productive and capillary while always also entailing resistance.[4] Power through Foucauldian notions of the panopticon effectively shapes the self and inscribes habits of self-policing and states of subjugation, thereby forming "docile bodies" (Foucault 1977).[5] Butler used Foucault's perspective to argue that gender is performative and that constant iterative performance allows for failure, questioning, and subversion, and hence change (Butler 1993; Mahmood 2005). One can see this possibility for transformation in the analyses of agency that seeks out the everyday resistances and creativity that women engage as they struggle to make ends meet (e.g., Page-Reeves 2014).

Even more transformative have been the changes in field research and ethnographic writing. As feminist anthropologists, we began rethinking our relationship to our subjects and examining the ways in which our writing reflects the power relationships embedded within the research setting. Several essays began to examine the divide between the investigator/author and the women she studied (the division between Self and Other). Some concluded that the divide could not be bridged (Stacey 1988; Strathern 1987). Others felt that, despite the kind of class and national privilege that US middle class (white) women carried with them, feminist anthropology could disrupt differences and bring to light a grounded sense of commonalities and variances (Abu-Lughod 1992). Coming from a more privileged class background, some anthropologists who shared the same ethnic and cultural heritage as their subjects, thought of themselves as being partial "insiders," or as Lila Abu-Lughod put it, "halfies" when they entered the field (1992). Yet, without an intimate knowledge of the local culture and even language of the community they proposed to study, they were forced to acknowledge their partial "outsider" status. These differences had to be recognized, described, and then understood through careful attention to the way they shaped interactions and what subjects were willing to reveal (Narayan 1996; Zavella 1993). Such awareness opened the way for developing methodologies that increased partnerships and collaboration in the field.

Feminist evaluations of these power dynamics also led to innovative strategies for ethnographic writing. These include presenting women's voices in detail, paying attention to the variety among women's situations (rather than portraying a single universal experience), and historically contextualizing ethnographic material. Such writing strategies, along with including the ethnographer within the narrative and analyzing her position, moved anthropology toward creating more dialogic rather than objectifying accounts. Lila Abu-Lughod's ethnography of Bedouin women's lives, *Writing Women's Worlds: Bedouin Stories* (1993), along with Ruth Behar's life history, *Translated Woman* (1993) (mentioned earlier), are among the feminist contributions to the adoption of these new writing strategies. Marjory Wolf's *A Thrice-Told Tale: Feminism, Postmodernism, and Ethnographic Responsibility* (1992) discusses these strategies and calls attention to the various ways that ethnographic representation can be achieved. Foregrounding their subjects' voices and presenting narratives that include both the anthropologist and her interviewees created the possibility of women subjects having a say in how the texts were written, shaping conclusions, and even writing their own narratives and analyses.

The New Engagement with Social Movements

Since 2000, a new generation of young scholars has joined some senior feminist anthropologists in "Feminist Activist Ethnography" (Craven and Davis 2013). In this neoliberal era in which government is shrinking and safety net programs are being cut, the role of non-governmental organizations (NGOs) has grown to both provide and advocate for services.[6] Thus, it is not surprising that much of feminist anthropology's recent engagement with social movements entails working with NGOs and activists as well as the women they serve. An analysis of how neoliberal ideologies, assumptions, and policies operate in the areas of social movement activity is critical for understanding the possibilities and limits of contemporary research coupled with organizing.

Feminist activist anthropology may take several forms that entail more or less collaboration with activists or the staff of NGOs, and demands diverse research methodologies that may lead to foregrounding the voices of women. Drawing on recent feminist collections and ethnographies, I have identified six different ways in which feminist anthropologists may implement their engagement. Their research covers a broad range of movements that includes gender violence, immigration, food security, and marriage equality, among others. They all also involve various degrees of intervention (Susser 2009) and commitment to the goals of social justice advanced by the particular social movement.

Personal Intervention

Feminists who use this first approach to feminist activist anthropology try to help subjects or interviewees negotiate their personal situation, for example, by advocating with power brokers, spending time with subjects explaining policies or giving advice, or helping women get access to services such as health care. Much of this kind of personal activism is rarely written about or analyzed. Dana-Ain Davis, however, has provided a trenchant analysis of her experience working with women living in a battered women's shelter in upstate New York. Although anthropologists have attempted this kind of personal mediation for decades, since it is the nature of the fieldwork experience to create particular ties, it has been, however, rarely reported as part of the research process, much less analyzed for what these kinds of personal interventions mean for activism (and ethnography). Davis cautions that such interventions may effect change on an individual level but generally do not achieve systemic transformation (Davis 2013).

Telling Counter Stories

In a second approach, anthropologists use personal narratives to counter the widespread invisibility or stigmatization of a population of marginalized women. Although placing women's voices and experiences at the center of a text has been the goal of feminist ethnographers for the last thirty years, counter stories play an important role in legitimizing the demands and goals of women in contemporary social movements as well. Janet Page-Reeves's edited volume of research on women and food insecurity (2014) contains a number of articles that focus on the personal narratives of women as they negotiate the low-income food system (grocery stores with low food prices, school breakfast and lunch programs, food pantries, SNAP/food stamps). These counter narratives not only give us a sense of women's agency, but also salute their creativity and knowledge about food and provisioning a family with healthy food under real budgetary constraints.

Lynn Stephen's book, *We Are the Face of Oaxaca: Testimony and Social Movements* (2013), centers on women's narratives (presented in separate italicized sections of the book) concerning the events of a 2006 teacher's strike that lead to the formation of a coalition of popular and indigenous groups, a massive rebellion, and a violent backlash during 2006–2007. The book is accompanied by a website (http://faceofoaxaca.uoregon.edu) that contains the complete video testimonies of each narrator, expanding these "counter stories" from the flat printed page to a vivid "real time" witnessing of events. Stephen's research and teaching also involves collaboration with her research subjects at several levels (see the section on collaboration later). For example, the video narratives for this book and other projects were approved by each narrator before they were published as CDs or DVDs with subtitles in English (see, for example, their Latino Roots Video and the website for *We Are the Face of Oaxaca*). This process grants authorship to the subjects of the research and makes them visible throughout the dissemination process.

Critiquing Neoliberalism

The critique of neoliberalism is a third thread that runs through at least two recent collections (Bernal and Grewal 2014, and Craven and Davis 2013). For example, the appearance of professionalization in the NGO sector is directly related to the spread of neoliberal policies. The Victoria Bernal and Inderpal Grewal collection, *Theorizing NGOs: States, Feminisms, Neoliberalism* (2014), provides an analysis of why this has been the case and why there has been an explosion of NGOs since the 1990s. First, as a result of neoliberal policies, many public services have been dismantled. Although NGOs have stepped into the breach, many have become increasingly professionalized and subordinate to either the state (through government incorporation rules and tax regulations) or the market (through their financial survival in competition with other NGOs, both non-profit and for-profit). Second, several articles in this collection are critical of neoliberal agendas that emphasize personal responsibility and an ethic of self-help to clients, reinforcing neoliberal ideals about the rational, autonomous, independent consumer, along with a corporate vision about how service organizations should operate (Lang 2014). A few authors, however, are more hopeful that those NGOs that evolve from the cultural setting of the women's movement are more dedicated to meeting women's needs (Alvarez 2014; Hodžić 2014).

While these first three types of new engagement in social movements, personal interventions, telling counter stories, and offering critiques of neoliberalism, have been part of research and writing that is only tangentially activist, the following three strategies focus more directly on interventions and actions that involve research collaboration and advocate for concrete policy changes.

Working Inside NGOs and Social Movements as Activists and Researchers

In recent years, using this fourth approach to feminist activist ethnography, feminist anthropologists have often volunteered or have held paid positions analyzing data, teaching workshops, organizing public events, or making outreach phone calls for NGOs or other activist organizations. Some have also engaged in direct action. Mary Anglin (2013) was involved in an action jamming the phone lines of doctors conducting clinical trials in order to get women diagnosed with stage-four breast cancer access to new treatments on the basis of "compassionate use." Anglin's activism signifies a relatively new level of intervention, one beyond the usual stance of feminist anthropologists who engaged primarily in research and writing.

Four authors in *Anthropology at the Front Lines of Gender-Based Violence* (GBV) (Wies and Haldane 2011) provide accounts of their roles as activists. Roxane Richter (2011) describes her position as an emergency medical technician (EMT) during Hurricane Katrina. Jamilla Bargash (2011) offers an account of her volunteer role in creating and opening a domestic violence center in Morocco. Sharmon Babior's (2011) description of living in a Japanese shelter as a volunteer focuses on her gradual shift from observer to participant and the difficulties she faced in doing so. A similar theme is struck by Uwe Jacobs (2011) who worked for Survival International assisting survivors of gender-based violence who had immigrated to the United States and sought asylum. These accounts clarify that the role of volunteer may allow feminist anthropologists a number of different opportunities: (1) to make a positive effort to forward the goals of a social movement; (2) to provide access to a location for field work; (3) to gain knowledge of and entrée to the personal stories and everyday struggles of the women clients; and (4) to see firsthand how professionalization and bureaucratization shape the relationship that staff and other volunteers have with their clients.

Strategies of Collaboration

In this fifth approach, the anthropologist aims to form a collaborative relationship with the subjects of research (leaders, members of social movements, NGOs). The feminist anthropologist does not determine the research questions or agenda, but works with the leadership of the organization or a network of activists to formulate a project that meets their needs. Such research uses the tenets of Community Based Participatory Research (CBPR) (Minkler and Wallerstein 2003), primarily associated with medical anthropology or Participatory Action Research (PAR), an approach widely accepted within applied anthropology. The subjects in the research (or at least the leadership team) act as equal partners with the anthropologist, at each stage identifying a topic or research questions, putting together a proposal or research plan, carrying out the research, and disseminating the results. Although there are relatively few examples of this approach in recent feminist anthropological literature, such methodologies offer models for research with community organizations, NGOs, and activists in social movements.

In one example, Patricia Williams (2014) outlines the impact of using a PAR framework for researching food insecurity in Nova Scotia. The government-funded long-term project she was part of hired and trained female food "costers" from among those who had themselves experienced food insecurity. In her analysis, Williams shows how these women gained greater knowledge and awareness of food insecurity, increased their ability to take action, and acquired a feeling of belonging to a community.

Collaboration with research subjects in terms of publication and dissemination is even rarer. In one case, Christine Porter teamed up with LaDonna Redmond, a food justice writer and activist, to co-author an analysis of men's leadership dominance in the food movement (2014). It is much easier, of course, to incorporate middle-class activists as co-authors of publications than working-class, minority, and indigenous women, especially those who speak languages other than English. Nevertheless, Lynn Stephen (mentioned earlier) has designed several techniques for Oaxacan participants to be recognized as authors of their published narratives, a model others will hopefully follow. Certainly, co-publication is an important future step for feminist anthropologists to consider.

Collaborative research does present ethical dilemmas for feminist activist ethnographers. Since the 1980s we have written about the power differential that is common between feminists and their subjects, and some have taken steps to mitigate the researcher's power (through personal intervention on behalf of subjects, bringing subjects into the planning and carrying out of research, and reporting results to communities and subjects). But in recent research with NGOs and in projects that involve several "stakeholders" with different goals, interests, and economic or political resources, conflicts can arise over interpreting the data or analyzing policy decisions. Leaders or those in power can be reluctant to hear an analysis that is critical of their past decisions, strategies, or programs. For example, in our research on Behavioral Health Reform in New Mexico between 2006 and 2010, my colleague Cathleen Willging and our team found that changes made during the first two years of transforming the Behavioral Health system were poorly implemented. Also, the new billing procedures were very costly for clinics, but when state officials were presented with these findings, they felt the research was biased. In contrast, behavioral health clinic administrators and staff and Native American respondents (both providers and clients) welcomed the findings since they fit their own experiences during the first year of the reform. We learned that getting those who can change the course of a program to heed policy recommendations is difficult at best (Willging et al. 2012; Willging and Semansky 2010). How to handle such conflicts needs much more discussion among feminist researchers.

Research to Advocate for Policy Changes

In the sixth and final approach, feminist activist anthropologists have worked to make their research accessible in the public domain, writing op-ed pieces, presenting in public and community settings, working on reports or summaries for legislators, members of state or local government agencies, or directly lobbying for legislative change. No longer need there be a solid boundary between one's participation in feminist activity and one's academic work. Increasingly, within the academy, there is greater acknowledgment of the value of public engagement and some institutions are beginning to accept activist anthropological research and writing as part of a faculty member's tenure or promotion dossier. One feminist model for influencing policy is that followed by anthropologist Sandra Morgen and sociologists Joan Acker and Jill Weigt in their research on welfare reform. In the wake of the 1996 US government's welfare reform legislation, they conducted surveys and intensive interviews with women who had found employment under the new Temporary Assistance for Needy Families (TANF) welfare regulations. After obtaining employment they no longer received TANF payments, although most were still eligible for reduced child care assistance, health insurance, transportation, or housing subsidies. The researchers found that the employed former TANF recipients still struggled to make ends meet, and many often lost their jobs due to transportation difficulties or child care responsibilities (Morgen, Acker, and Weigt 2010).

In addition to presenting their report on the deleterious effects of the loss of TANF support to the state agency that funded their research, they wrote brief "cameo" reports on issues to legislators, widely publicized their results in the local press, and testified at legislative hearings. Morgen makes it clear that such work is not a "one shot" effort and that change comes only with painstaking lobbying efforts, work with friendly legislators, and collaboration with community groups. In 2004, Morgan's team's research helped change Oregon state policy so that some TANF recipients could count postsecondary education as part of their work requirements, thus allowing women to get the training that would help them qualify for higher-paying jobs and perhaps leave poverty behind.

CONCLUSION

This chapter has focused on the connections between feminist anthropology and social movements, examining the transformation of these relationships over the past forty years. Social movements and political activism have been intrinsically linked to feminist anthropology since its inception in the early 1970s. But there has been a distinct evolution in how feminists have engaged with them. During the 1970s through the mid-1980s there was a fairly clear distinction between feminist activism in the community and anthropological research and teaching. We focused primarily on bringing women's lives into the ethnographic record, and theorizing about women's positions in other cultures. We continued to use the standard methodologies of participant observation and in-depth interviewing to produce ethnographic writing. The first two forms of feminist activism I identified—personal intervention to support the needs of individuals in our research sites and telling "counter stories" to undercut stereotypes and include women's voices in our texts—were activist strategies present but not emphasized in the 1970s. In the 1980s African American, Latino, and lesbian anthropologists made much greater use of such counter narratives.

The critique of anthropological methodology and the evolving transformation of ethnographic writing, along with new approaches to analyzing power and women's agency, opened the door to a different kind of feminist research. This new approach encourages more participatory and collaborative research, prioritizes inquiry on critical social issues that women face, validates dialogical ethnographic writing that places both author and subject in the text, and emphasizes women's own voices, opinions, and agency. At the same time, the discipline as a whole has evolved, becoming more open to engaged or activist anthropology. Applied anthropology (itself transformed by PAR as a collaborative form of research) has also gained greater acceptance in most anthropology departments, signaling a de facto acceptance of feminist activist ethnography with its emphasis on intervention, advocacy, and policy change.

Nevertheless, feminist anthropology faces a number of challenges in the twenty-first century. It is essential that we increase our efforts to support collaborative and participatory research where subjects can have a greater impact on research questions and research procedures, and to bring our work to broader audiences. More effort is needed to translate analyses appropriate for academic publications and university courses into language that can better serve women and other disadvantaged populations. In order to effect change feminist anthropologists need to work collaboratively with social movements and NGOs that are struggling to transform the political process at local, state, and national levels.

NOTES

1. Although many feminists in this period were brought to their research through a personal connection (e.g., participation in the lesbian/gay rights movement, experience with a major health or reproductive issue), most of the published research remained in the objective mode and participation in a relevant social movement occurred "off stage" as it had in the 1970s.

2. Even in 1969 Redstockings was beginning to split into two factions, one interested in action and the other more dedicated to consciousness-raising. In the fall of 1969 Shulamith Firestone, a member of Redstockings, and Anne Koedt, who had just left The Feminists, another early New York group, decided to form New York Radical Feminists (NYRF) as a way to create a mass movement. (Echols 1989, 186). Redstockings dissolved in the fall of 1970, with most members leaving to found other groups. NYRF took over many of the functions of Redstockings including an analysis of women's oppression and the organization of women into small groups or brigades.

3. Bread and Roses in their outreach leaflet argued for "women being ourselves and believing in ourselves. Women find the strength to live how we feel, powerful women can lead the way to create a new kind of politics, a new life" (Baxendall and Gordon 2000, 35). Their Declaration of Independence outlined women's demands for equality in the work place, control of their bodies, alternatives to the nuclear family, free child care, and affordable housing, as well as equal access to education (Baxendall and Gordon 2000, 45–47).

4. The idea that power is capillary suggests that power not only emanates from the top of a hierarchy, but is produced and spread throughout institutions and networks (i.e., it sometimes comes from below).

5. Foucault's concept of the panopticon derives from the design of early French prisons that were constructed with an observation station in the center and prisoners occupying cells on the periphery of a round building so that their behavior was always on view to guards. Knowledge of this surveillance led prisoners to monitor themselves and become "docile bodies."

6. It is important to distinguish between neoliberalism as (1) an economic theory (originally promulgated by University of Chicago economists); (2) an economic ideology that foregrounds the importance of the market and calls for shrinking the role of the state in creating a social safety net; and (3) actual policies, for example cutting the food stamp program or privatizing social security. An important part of neoliberal ideology is the reification of the rational individual or "consumer" who makes choices and bears the responsibility for his or her own success or failure (see Evans and Sewell 2013). Some feminist analysis is concerned more with the impact of neoliberal ideology while others focus on concrete policies and laws that regulate or deregulate economic markets, erode or expand the role of the state, or push more responsibilities onto "consumers" or the general public (see Kingfisher, this volume).

REFERENCES

Abu-Lughod, Lila. 1987. *Veiled Sentiments: Honor and Poetry in a Bedouin Society.* Berkeley: University of California Press.

———. 1992. "Can There Be a Feminist Ethnography?" *Women and Performance: A Journal of Feminist Theory* 5: 7–27.

———. 1993. *Writing Women's Worlds: Bedouin Stories.* Berkeley: University California Press.

Alvarez, Sonia E. 2014. "Beyond NGOization? Reflections from Latin America." In *Theorizing NGOs: States, Feminisms, and Neoliberalism*, ed. Victoria Bernal and Inderpal Grewal, 285–300. Durham, NC: Duke University Press.

Anglin, Mary K. 2013. "Learning Social Justice and Activist Ethnography from Women with Breast Cancer." In *Feminist Activist Ethnography: Counterpoints to Neoliberalism in North America*, ed. Christa Craven and Dana-Ain Davis, 39–52. Lanham, MD: Lexington Books.

Babior, Roxane. 2011. "Participant and Observer: Reflections on Fieldwork in a Women's Shelter in Tokyo, Japan." In *Anthropology at the Front Lines of Gender-Based Violence*, ed. Jennifer R. Wies and Hillary J. Haldane, 20–49. Nashville, TN: Vanderbilt University Press.

Bargash, Jamila. 2011. "Laliti, Compassionate Savior: The Hidden Archaeology of Founding a Shelter." In *Anthropology at the Front Lines of Gender-Based Violence*, ed. Jennifer R. Wies and Hillary J. Haldane, 211–222. Nashville, TN: Vanderbilt University Press.

Baxendall, Rosalyn, and Linda Gordon, eds. 2000. *Dear Sisters: Dispatches from the Women's Liberation Movement.* New York: Basic Books.

Behar, Ruth. 1993. *Translated Woman: Crossing the Border with Esperanza's Story.* Boston: Beacon Press.

Bernal, Victoria, and Inderpal Grewal, eds. 2014. *Theorizing NGOs: States, Feminisms, and Neoliberalism.* Durham, NC: Duke University Press.

Bolles, A. Lynn. 1983. "Kitchens Hit by Priorities: Employed Working Class Jamaican Women Confront the IMF." In *Women, Men, and the International Division of Labor*, ed. June Nash and Maria Patricia Fernandez-Kelly, 138–160. Albany: State University of New York Press.

———. 1996. *Sister Jamaica: A Study of Women, Work, and Household in Kingston.* Lanham, MD: University Press of America.

Bookman, Ann. 1988. "Unionization in an Electronics Factory: The Interplay of Gender, Ethnicity, and Class." In *Women and the Politics of Empowerment*, ed. Ann Bookman and Sandra Morgen, 159–179. Philadelphia: Temple University Press.

Bookman, Ann, and Sandra Morgen, eds. 1988. *Women and the Politics of Empowerment.* Philadelphia: Temple University Press.

Butler, Judith. 1993. *Bodies That Matter: On the Discursive Limits of "Sex."* New York and London: Routledge.

Chernela, Janet. 2013. "Making Waves: The Role of the Ruth Benedict Collective in the Development of a Feminist Anthropology." Paper presented at Anthropologies and Feminisms: Our History, Our Present, Our Future panel, American Anthropological Association Meeting, Chicago, November.

Craven, Christa, and Dana-Ain Davis, eds. 2013. *Feminist Activist Ethnography: Counterpoints to Neoliberalism in North America.* Lanham, MD: Lexington Books of Rowman & Littlefield.

Davis, Dana-Ain. 2013. "Border Crossings: Intimacy and Feminist Ethnography in the Age of Neoliberalism." In *Feminist Activist Ethnography: Counterpoints to Neoliberalism in North America*, ed. Christa Craven and Dana-Ain Davis, 23–38. Lanham, MD: Lexington Books of Rowman & Littlefield.

di Leonardo, Micaela, ed. 1991. *Gender at the Crossroads of Knowledge: Feminist Anthropology in the Postmodern Era.* Berkeley: University of California Press.

Echols, Alice. 1989. *Daring to Be Bad: Radical Feminism in America 1967–75.* Minneapolis: University of Minnesota Press.

Evans, Peter, and William Sewell. 2013. "Neoliberalism: Policy Regimes, International Regimes, and Social Effects." In *Social Resilience in the Neoliberal Era*, ed. Peter Hall and Michèle Lamont, 35–68. Cambridge: Cambridge University Press.

Evans, Sara. 1979. *Personal Politics: The Roots of Women's Liberation in the Civil Rights Movement and the New Left.* New York: Vintage Books.

Fernández-Kelly, María Patricia. 1983. *For We Are Sold I and My People: Women and Industry in Mexico's Frontier.* Albany: State University of New York Press.

Foucault, Michel. 1977. *Discipline and Punish: The Birth of the Prison.* New York: Pantheon.

Friedlander, Eva. 2013. "IWAC at the Scholar/Activist Interface: Lessons and Challenges for the Future." Paper presented at Anthropologies and Feminisms: Our History, Our Present, Our Future panel, American Anthropological Association Meeting, Chicago, November.

Gailey, Christine. 1987. *Kinship to Kingship: Gender Hierarchy and State Formation in the Tongan Islands.* Austin: University of Texas Press.

Goffman, Erving. 1963. *Stigma: Notes on the Management of Spoiled Identity.* New York: Prentice-Hall.

Harrison, Faye. 1997. "The Gendered Politics and Violence of Structural Violence: A View from Jamaica." In *Situated Lives: Gender and Culture in Everyday Life*, ed. Louise Lamphere, Helena Ragone, and Patricia Zavella, 451–568. New York: Routledge.

Hodžić, Saida. 2014. "Feminist Bastards: Toward a Post-Humanistic Critique." In *Theorizing NGOs: States, Feminisms, and Neoliberalism*, 221–247. Durham, NC: Duke University Press.

Hull, Gloria T., Patricia Bell Scott, and Barbara Smith. 1982. *All the Women Are White, All the Blacks Are Men but Some of Us Are Brave*. Old Westbury, NY: Feminist Press.

Jacobs, Uwe. 2011. "Gender-Based Violence: Perspectives from the Male European Front Line." In *Anthropology at the Front Lines of Gender-Based Violence*, ed. Jennifer R. Wies and Hillary J. Haldane, 129–138. Nashville, TN: Vanderbilt University Press.

Kennedy, Elizabeth Lapovsky, and Madeline D. Davis. 1993. *Boots of Leather, Slippers of Gold: The History of a Lesbian Community*. New York: Routledge.

Lamphere, Louise, Rayna Rapp, and Gayle Rubin. 2007. "Anthropologists Are Talking: About Feminist Anthropology." *Ethnos* 72 (3): 408–426.

Lamphere, Louise, Patricia Zavella, Felipe Gonzales, with Peter Evans. 1987. *Sunbelt Working Mothers: Reconciling Factory and Family*. Ithaca, NY: Cornell University Press.

Lang, Sabine. 2014. "Women's Advocacy Networks. The European Union, Women's NGOs, and the Velvet Triangle." In *Theorizing NGOs: States, Feminisms, and Neoliberalism*, ed. Victoria Bernal and Inderpal Grewal, 266–284. Durham, NC: Duke University Press.

Lewin, Ellen. 1993. *Lesbian Mothers: Accounts of Gender in American Culture*. Ithaca, NY: Cornell University Press.

Mahmood, Saba. 2005. *Politics of Piety: The Islamic Revival and the Feminist Subject*. Princeton, NJ: Princeton University Press.

McClaurin, Irma. 2001. *Black Feminist Anthropology: Theory, Politics, Praxis, and Poetics*. New Brunswick, NJ: Rutgers University Press.

Minkler, Meridith, and Nina Wallerstein, eds. 2003. *Community-Based Participatory Research for Health*. San Francisco: John Wiley and Sons.

Moraga, Cherríe, and Gloria Anzaldúa. 1981. *This Bridge Called My Back: Writings by Radical Women of Color*. Watertown, MA: Persephone Press.

Morgen, Sandra. 1988. "'It's the Whole Power of the City Against Us!': The Development of Political Consciousness in a Women's Healthcare Coalition." In *Women and the Politics of Empowerment*, ed. Ann Bookman and Sandra Morgen, 97–114. Philadelphia: Temple University Press.

———. 2002. *Into Our Own Hands: The Women's Health Movement in the US 1969–90*. New Brunswick, NJ: Rutgers University Press.

Morgen, Sandra, Joan Acker, and Jill Weigt. 2010. *Stretched Thin: Poor Families, Welfare Work, and Welfare Reform*. Ithaca, NY: Cornell University Press.

Mullings, Leith. 1997. *In Our Own Terms: Race, Class, and Gender in the Lives of African American Women*. New York: Routledge.

Narayan, Kirin. 1993. "How Native Is a 'Native' Anthropologist?" *American Anthropologist* 95 (3): 671–686.

Newton, Esther. 1972. *Mother Camp: Female Impersonators in America*. Chicago: University of Chicago Press.

Ortner, Sherry B., and Harriet Whitehead, eds. 1981. *Sexual Meanings: The Cultural Construction of Gender and Sexuality*. Cambridge: Cambridge University Press.

Page-Reeves, Janet, ed. 2014. *Women Redefining the Experience of Food Insecurity: Life off the Edge of the Table*. Lanham, MD: Lexington Books.

Porter, Christine, and LaDonna Redmond. 2014. "Labor and Leadership: Women in U.S. Community Food Organizing." In *Women Redefining the Experience of Food Insecurity: Life off the Edge of the Table*, ed. Janet Page-Reeves, 261–273. Lanham, MD: Lexington Books.

Reiter (Rapp), Rayna, ed. 1975. *Toward an Anthropology of Women*. New York: Monthly Review Press.

Richter, Roxanne. 2011. "Disparity in Disasters: A Frontline View of Gender-Based Inequities in Emergency Aid and Health Care." In *Anthropology at the Front Lines of Gender-Based Violence*, ed. Jennifer R. Wies and Hillary J. Haldane, 19–28. Nashville, TN: Vanderbilt University Press.

Rosaldo, Michelle Zimbalist. 1980. "The Use and Abuse of Anthropology: Reflections on Feminism and Cross-Cultural Understanding." *Signs: A Journal of Women, Culture, and Society* 5: 389–417.

Rosaldo, Michelle Zimbalist, and Louise Lamphere, eds. 1974. *Woman, Culture, and Society*. Palo Alto, CA: Stanford University Press.

Rosen, Ruth. 2000. *The World Split Open: How the Modern Women's Movement Changed America*. New York: Viking Penguin Books.

Roth, Benita. 2003. *Separate Roads to Feminism: Black, Chicana, and White Feminist Movements in America's Second Wave*. Cambridge: Cambridge University Press.

Sacks, Karen Brodkin. 1979. *Sisters and Wives: The Past and the Future of Sexual Equality*. Westport, CT: Greenwood Press.

———. 1988a. *Caring by the Hour: Women, Work, and Organizing at Duke Medical Center*. Urbana: University of Illinois Press.

———. 1988b. "Gender and Grassroots Leadership." In *Women and the Politics of Empowerment*, ed. Ann Bookman and Sandra Morgen, 77–94. Philadelphia: Temple University Press.

Shostak, Marjorie. 1981. *Nisa: The Life and Words of a !Kung Woman*. Cambridge, MA: Harvard University Press.

Silverblatt, Irene. 1987. *Sun, Moon, and Witches: Gender Ideologies and Class in Inca and Colonial Peru*. Princeton, NJ: Princeton University Press.

———. 1991. "Interpreting Women in States: New Feminist Ethnohistories." In *Gender at the Crossroads of Knowledge: Feminist Anthropology in the Postmodern Era*, ed. Micaela di Leonardo, 140–172. Berkeley: University of California Press.

Stacey, Judith. 1988. "Can There Be a Feminist Ethnography?" *Women Studies International Forum* 11 (1): 20–27.

Strathern, Marilyn. 1987. "An Awkward Relationship: The Case of Feminism and Anthropology." *Signs* 12 (2): 276–292.

Stephen, Lynn. 2013. *We Are the Face of Oaxaca: Testimony and Social Movements*. Durham, NC: Duke University Press.

Stoler, Ann. 2002. *Carnal Knowledge and Imperial Power: Race and the Intimate in Colonial Rule*. Berkeley: University of California Press.

Susser, Ida. 1982. *Norman Street: Poverty and Politics in an Urban Neighborhood*. New York: Oxford University Press.

———. 2009. *AIDS, Sex, and Culture: Global Politics and Survival in South Africa*. Oxford: Wiley-Blackwell Publications.

Weston, Kath. 1991. *Families We Choose: Lesbians, Gays, Kinship*. New York: Columbia University Press.

Wies, Jennifer R., and Hillary J. Haldane, eds. 2011. *Anthropology at the Front Lines of Gender-Based Violence*. Nashville, TN: Vanderbilt University Press.

Willging, Cathleen E., Jessica Goodkind, Louise Lamphere, Gwendolyn Saul, Shannon Fluder, and Paula Seanez. 2012. "The Impact of State Behavioral Health Reform on Native American Individuals, Families, and Communities." *Qualitative Health Research* 22 (7): 880–896.

Willging, Cathleen E., and Richard M. Semansky. 2010. "'It's Never Too Late to Do It Right': Lessons from Behavioral Health Reform in New Mexico." *Psychiatric Services* 61 (1): 646–648.

Williams, Patricia L. 2014. "Women's Agency for Food Security through Participatory Action Research." In *Women Redefining the Experience of Food Insecurity: Life off the Edge of the Table*, ed. Janet Page-Reeves, 275–313. Lanham, MD: Lexington Books.

Wolf, Margery. 1968. *The House of Lim: A Study of a Chinese Farm Family*. New York: Appleton-Century-Crofts.

———. 1992. *A Thrice-Told Tale: Feminism, Postmodernism, and Ethnographic Responsibility*. Palo Alto, CA: Stanford University Press.

Zavella, Patricia. 1987. *Women's Work and Chicano Families: Cannery Workers of the Santa Clara Valley*. Ithaca, NY: Cornell University Press.

———. 1993. "Feminist Insider Dilemmas: Constructing Ethnic Identity with 'Chicana' Informants." *Frontiers: A Journal of Women Studies* 13 (3): 53–76.

FEMINIST LINGUISTICS AND LINGUISTIC FEMINISMS

ELISE KRAMER

Some of the most salient inroads made by American second-wave feminists revolved around language. The 1970s saw changes in the lexicon to accommodate and promote gender equality: from the invention and mainstreaming of "Ms." to the promotion of gender-neutral vocational terminology such as "flight attendant" and "postal worker." Perhaps even more significantly, second-wave feminists worked to call attention to and stigmatize harmful patterns of linguistic interaction: "sexual harassment" became a problematic category of behavior rather than a diffuse set of playful practices; sexist jokes, and especially rape jokes, took on a timbre of seriousness that counteracted their seeming frivolity (Gavey 2005). Second-wave feminists argued and convincingly demonstrated that language was important, both as a mechanism of sexism and as a tool for combatting it.

Of course, these instances of linguistic activism were also among the feminist movement's most contentious efforts, engendering a particularly vicious and enduring hostility whose legacy persists in the commonly held linkages between feminism, political correctness, and censorship (Cameron 1995; Faludi 1991; Kramer 2011; Lakoff 2000). Feminists are often accused of "language policing," an act that is somehow simultaneously frivolous (why waste your time playing around with mere semantics?) and threatening (it's like Newspeak all over again!). For better or worse, language is one of the primary fronts of the feminist battle, and feminist anthropologists have been particularly attuned to matters of language.

Meanwhile, gender has been an incredibly productive topic for linguistic anthropologists and sociolinguists: studies of language and gender have done much to shed light on the nature of language as a social as well as a communicative tool (e.g., Eckert and McConnell-Ginet 2013; Hall and Bucholtz 1995). Looking at the ways that men and women use language differently (or don't) has been a crucial part of the study of language and identity; looking at the ways that men and women *are talked about* differently has yielded an especially compelling demonstration of how language shapes people's lives; and putting those two topics together—looking at the ways people talk about the ways men and women use language—has highlighted the importance of language ideologies as cultural phenomena and as objects of study.

In this chapter, I suggest that the linkages between feminism and the study of language are not merely historical happenstance; rather, the two share key methodological and theoretical underpinnings, and each enriches the other in different and productive ways. From their shared emphasis on performativity, to their mutual concern with narrative and cultural representations, to their common understanding of meaning that marks the unmarked by highlighting the necessity of contrast, both feminist anthropology and linguistic anthropology take seemingly straightforward, natural concepts and reveal them as incredibly complex and culturally specific. Together, the disciplines show that language *is* an important front in the battle for gender equality, and that language change (whether it happens organically or not) may be a necessary component of social change. In some ways, linguistic anthropology is inherently a feminist anthropology, and feminist anthropology is inherently linguistic. And, as I will suggest, linguistic anthropology's importance to the feminist project will only increase as the twenty-first century unfolds.

GENDERED LANGUAGE

Performativity

Just as linguistic anthropologists have emphasized that language in action is never reducible merely to what is literally said, feminist anthropologists have strived to show that gender is not reducible to a set of anatomical or behavioral differences. One of the most powerful links between linguistic anthropology and gender studies has been their shared emphasis on performativity. When Judith Butler (1990, 25) famously described gender as "performative," she was not simply asserting that having a gendered identity required the active inhabiting of a role: this was, of course, an essential component of her argument, but in fact the term "performative" was doing much more work for her. In using the term, Butler was drawing on the realm of speech act theory, in particular the works of philosopher John L. Austin.

Austin (1975) discusses a subset of utterances that he refers to as "explicit primary performatives": utterances that simultaneously perform an act and describe the performing of that act. For example, the utterance "I promise I will call you tomorrow" simultaneously *makes* a promise and *describes* the making of that promise. Indeed, the only way "felicitously" to make a promise is to engage in this small verbal ritual whereby one tells a story about one's own making of a promise; a promise can only be made through the narration of the process of making it. "Performativity" is the simultaneous describing-of and committing-of an action, a sort of verbal Möbius strip that presumes the very fact that it calls into existence.

Performativity in this sense is much of what characterizes "ritual"—which linguistic anthropologists often define as an event that is particularly semiotically "dense" (and thus efficacious) due to its enactment of a change through the describing of that very change. From the US Declaration of Independence, a document that simultaneously established the colonies as sovereign and narrated the process of declaring sovereignty (Lee 2001); to Tzotzil marital mediation, which resolves conflicts between husbands and wives by transforming disorderly debates into metrically and socially ordered discourses (Haviland 1996); to that great classic of American oratory, the Gettysburg Address, which brought a fractured nation together by describing a process of unification from the shattered past to the gathered here-and-now to the collective future (Silverstein 2003), ritual speech has served as a powerful example of the ways that discourse creates meaning by drawing upon it.

So, too, Butler (1990, 25) argues, does gender performatively constitute itself. Discourses about gender don't just constrain behavior to certain extant categories, but actively *create* the categories in the first place. Moreover, they ultimately disguise this process of production by treating the categories as always already there. In other words, when you perform gender (which is to say, all of the time), you are not merely "describing" your gender but enacting it, and not merely enacting it but (re)creating the category of "gender" to begin with, and not merely creating the category but covering your tracks by treating it as unproblematically present and natural.

The linguistic anthropological notion of "performativity" encapsulates this dialogic process of presupposition and entailment. You cannot promise except through saying "I promise"; you cannot be gendered except through performing the seemingly infinite number of personal and social rituals that create gender (Goffman 1979). Some of these rituals are linguistic; all of them have the self-reinforcing efficacy of ritual language.

Gender Rituals

The linguistic rituals of gender performance have been a popular topic among feminist and linguistic anthropologists alike. Some of the earliest and most prominent feminist sociolinguistic work compared men's and women's ways of speaking—kicked off, of course, by the 1975 publication of Robin Lakoff's groundbreaking book *Language and Woman's Place,* and echoed in later popular works such as Dale Spender's (1980) *Man Made Language* and Deborah Tannen's (1990) *You Just Don't Understand: Women and Men in Conversation.* These and other popular books made headlines by suggesting that men and women speak differently, and that the linguistic gulf between the sexes is responsible for everything from marital misunderstandings to pay inequality to patriarchy. Women, it is often said, are more collaborative, ask more questions, use more hedges ("I think that . . ." "It might be that . . ."), and use "we" and "you" more frequently. Men, in contrast, are said to be more competitive, to direct the flow of conversation by introducing topics, to interrupt more often, and to phrase claims as bald declaratives without qualifiers (Maltz and Borker 1982). Attempts to mitigate the effects of these ostensible linguistic differences have included, on the one hand, teaching women how to speak more "assertively," and on the other hand, revaluing "women's language" as equal to or better than "men's language."

Although this body of work has proven popular among both scholars and science journalists, it is also highly contested, serving as the focus of a great deal of methodological and theoretical debate. Some of the controversy has surrounded the utility of conceiving of "men's speech" and "women's speech" as discrete categories. *Do* men and women actually speak differently, or is this merely a stereotype without empirical grounding? Deborah Cameron's (2009) book *The Myth of Mars and Venus* is one recent work that takes this skeptical stance. Certainly at the very least we can say that (at least in the Western cultures with which we are most familiar) not all men speak one way and not all women speak another way, but rather there are differences within gender categories and similarities across categories. Gender is cross-cut by other categories—race, class, age, and so forth—that may correlate with language use at least as much as gender does. Even those scholars who do argue that *on average* there are differences between men's and women's speech would likely agree that these differences are not nearly so dramatic as people tend to perceive.

And the cross-cultural perspective that feminist anthropologists provide has shown that what is considered "women's language" in one culture may be considered "men's language" in another. Although indirectness is considered a feminine quality in American culture, in the Malagasy community where Elinor Ochs worked, women were known for being blunt and straightforward (Keenan 1989). When it comes to language change, women are sometimes the engines for innovation and sometimes the conservative force resisting change. In an industrializing Austrian village, women were more likely than men to adopt German, the "modern," "standardized," prestigious alternative to Hungarian (Gal 1978); in a Detroit high school, female "burnouts" led the way in a new, stigmatized vowel shift (Eckert 1996); in Martha's Vineyard, men spearheaded the deviation from the standard in the development of a distinctive (and unprestigious) local register (Labov 1972). In some cultural contexts women are seen as the standard-bearers, the guardians of language; in other contexts they are seen as a destructive force.

Due to this tremendous cross-cultural difference in definitions of "feminine" and "masculine" language, sociolinguists and linguistic anthropologists have long debated whether gender is truly the axis along which men's and women's speaking styles are differentiated, or whether the connection to gender is mediated by some other attribute. Lakoff (1975), for example, theorized that the different speaking styles she observed were, first and foremost, distinguished by power: that women used more hedges, politeness markers, hypercorrect language, etc., because this was a *powerless* way of speaking. Penelope Eckert (1996) similarly suggests that "femininity" and "masculinity" are simply calques for "mitigation of power" and "affirmation of power"—in other words, what gets classed as "feminine" is that which disclaims power, and what gets classed as "masculine" is that which claims power. Elinor Ochs (1992) introduced the concept of *indirect indexicality*, arguing that particular speech forms index (point to) particular interactional strategies or qualities, which in turn index gender. Hedging, for example, indexes non-aggression, which indexes femininity.

One of the strengths of this "mediated indexicality" approach is that it accommodates the polysemy of ways of speaking; for example, verbal hedges might signify femininity in one context, but in other contexts they might index deference, or a formal situation, or any number of other factors that could call for indirectness. Another strength is that it highlights the arbitrariness of the associations between linguistic features and gender. There is nothing inherently "female" or "male" about particular ways of speaking (with the exception, perhaps, of pitch, though even that varies almost as much *within* gender categories as it does across them)—the links between gender and linguistic features are culturally and historically contingent, and rely on shared beliefs and conventions.

But in denaturalizing the links between linguistic features and gender, this approach sometimes instead naturalizes the links between linguistic features and power, assertiveness, directness, or whatever other mediating quality is suggested. Why, for example, is "asking questions" an example of conversational passivity? It could just as easily be framed as exerting control over the interaction, forcing one's interlocutor to provide information according to one's demands. Why are backchannels (saying things like "mhm" while someone else is speaking) supportive as opposed to egocentric? Particular personality traits and interactional effects do not *necessarily* follow from particular linguistic forms; rather, these connections are based on unconscious assumptions that speakers bring to the table and are culturally specific.

As a result, gaining power is not simply a matter of switching to "powerful" ways of speaking, despite what self-help books would have us believe. Women who attempt to speak more "assertively" by using language typically associated with men find themselves being labeled "bossy" rather than "forceful," "bitchy" rather than "authoritative." This is one of the reasons why other feminist sociolinguists have suggested that the causal link between powerful speech and gendered speech may run in the opposite direction: that instead of women speaking devalued styles because they lack power, particular linguistic styles are devalued *because they are spoken by women*. Daniel Maltz and Ruth Borker (1982) contend that gender differences in language use are the result of different childhood subcultures among boys and girls. Tannen (1990) similarly treats men's and women's conversational styles as an element of gender socialization, and argues that they are both equally efficacious in theory, but that women's speech is devalued and stripped of its power due to the sexism of mainstream culture. This once again leaves us with a chicken-and-egg dilemma that we can see echoed in broader feminist debates about the origins of gender inequality: which came first, the devaluing of women or the devaluing of femininity? And even more broadly, returning to gender performativity, which came first: women or femininity?

We can use historical and comparative ethnography to answer these questions diachronically, as scholars such as Sherry Ortner (1974) and Miyako Inoue (2002) have done. But we can also address the question synchronically, through a linguistic anthropological framework that can accommodate and articulate polysemy. Michael Silverstein's (2003) concept of "orders of indexicality" builds on Ochs's "indirect indexicality" to describe a cultural framework in which one signifier can simultaneously signify many different things—femininity, politeness, weakness, attractiveness, etc.—without one connotation having primacy over another. Indeed, what makes gendered signifiers so powerful is that their many connotations bolster one another, each seeming to be a natural corollary of the others. Consider the current public hand wringing about young American women using "vocal fry" (a gravelly quality that results from speaking at the lower end of one's pitch range, also known as "creaky voice"): it is variously described as ugly, unfeminine, rude, and a sign of mindless trend following (Fruehwald 2011). To defend any one of these descriptors requires leaning on the others. Why is vocal fry rude? Because it's ugly. Why is it ugly? Because it's unfeminine. Why is it a sign of mindless trend following? Because no woman would use it otherwise, because it's unfeminine. Why is it unfeminine? Because it's ugly and rude.

The constellation of descriptors ultimately relies on a co-constitutive relationship between femininity, pitch, and politeness, such that politeness and pitch are unconsciously assumed to directly correlate, both from person to person and from situation to situation (note that many women have a "polite voice" that is considerably higher in pitch than their regular speaking voice). As Judith Irvine and Susan Gal (2000) explain, cultural and linguistic ideologies tend to laminate collections of attributes together into "iconized," essentialized, seemingly seamless stereotypes. Disentangling these ideological recursions is an important step, academically and politically, for feminist anthropology.

A linguistic anthropological approach, with its focus on language ideologies, shifts the question from "do men and women actually speak differently?" to "what can we learn from the fact that we believe men and women speak differently?" And this question gets to the heart of gender inequality in American culture, because it uncovers the extraordinarily complex ideological framework that aligns gender in a seemingly self-evident way with power, race, class, nationalism, and the many other categories that make up social life.

LANGUAGE ABOUT GENDER

Language and Cognition

As this discussion of gendered language use demonstrates, feminist anthropologists and linguistic anthropologists alike have emphasized that language is not merely a tool for reference—it is a social tool as well, reflecting outward from the speaker, shaped by his or her particular location in the sociolinguistic landscape. But language doesn't just draw on experience; it also actively shapes experience. It is not merely a tool for reference, nor is it merely a tool for expressiveness: language exists outside of the control of any one individual, and as such it has the power to impose particular structures, both cognitive and social, upon each speaker. Thus it is also vitally important to study language *about* gender, because of what it reveals about the ways we think about gender and because it shapes gendered experience.

The question of the relationship between language and thought has attracted widespread debate amongst linguists and linguistic anthropologists. We know that languages can differ from one another tremendously; do these (syntactic, semantic, phonological, etc.) differences have cognitive impacts? Does the way we speak shape the way we think about the world? How could we possibly know if it does, given that we only have access to others' thoughts *through* language?

The debate over these questions has coalesced around the Sapir-Whorf Hypothesis, also called the theory of linguistic relativity. Linguistic relativity is perhaps one of the most widely misunderstood academic theories, thanks to its straw-manning by pop linguists such as Steven Pinker (2007). While volumes can be (and have been—see Lucy 1992b; Silverstein 2000) written about misconstruals of linguistic relativism, I will limit myself to a very brief summary of the issue.

The version of linguistic relativity that has made it into the public imagination is what has been called *strong* linguistic relativism (or linguistic determinism): the idea that language *limits* the sorts of things one can think about, that a speaker is *constrained* by the categories offered by his or her particular language. This is the version of linguistic relativism that motivates, for example, George Orwell's work—both the concept of "Newspeak" in *1984* (1949) and the concerns he expresses in his famous essay "Politics and the English Language" (1970 [1946])—but it is not the version of linguistic relativism advanced by (most) linguistic anthropologists, nor by the eponymous Edward Sapir and Benjamin Whorf.

The version of linguistic relativity that I put forth here differs from the popularized version in two significant ways. First, it deals with *habitual* thought, not the outer limits of what it is *possible* to think. For example, English speakers tend to envision time spatially, with the future to the right or forward, the past to the left or backward, and the here-and-now centered on the self. This does not mean that an English speaker *cannot* envision time in other ways—merely that it is not intuitive for an English speaker to do so. And this spatio-temporal metaphor, left unacknowledged and unchallenged, may shape a range of cultural practices, from aesthetic standards to the bodily use of space to the ways that events are scheduled.

Second, rather than looking at superficial lexical differences (the "Eskimos have *n* words for snow" trope), linguistic anthropologists who study relativism are focusing on deeper structures such as grammatical categories: do languages that encode different elements of the world, or encode the same elements in different ways, correlate with broader cognitive and behavioral differences? Is the phenomenological experience of speakers of languages without grammatical tense (for example, Mandarin) different from that of speakers of a language with an elaborate tense system (such as Spanish)? If a concept is represented as a noun in one language and a verb in another, does it influence how people talk and think about it? Fascinating work comparing, for example, languages with and without mass/count noun distinctions (such as English and Yucatec Maya, respectively) (Lucy 1992a; Lucy and Gaskins 2001), as well as languages with absolute (e.g., North/South/East/West) versus relative (e.g., left/right) spatial systems (Brown and Levinson 1993), suggests that different languages do indeed encode different habitual ways of thinking about and perceiving the world.

The relationship between language and cognition has wide-reaching implications for feminist anthropology, both theoretically and methodologically. It means that the ways we talk about gender (not just the ways that genders talk) can reveal and shape the ways we think (and act) about gender. The deep analysis of language is a vital component of the study of a culture, and specifically the study of gendered experience within a culture. Studying language—both language as an abstract system, and language in actual use—is important not only because a language is a window into cultural specificities but also because it is a central part of a culturally specific existence. In other words, language can tell us about a culture, but language also *is* culture.

The following sections provide an overview of two general areas where feminist and linguistic anthropology have intersected productively in the study of language about gender. The first is the eternally thorny issue of gender-neutral language, which in the United States has taken the form of two interconnected debates: can English be gender-neutral, and should it be in practice? The second is the matter of representation: how are men and women depicted in popular discourses, and what are the ramifications (and causes) of these representations?

Gender-Neutral Language

The push for gender-neutral language was, as mentioned in the introduction, both one of the strongest fronts of second-wave feminism and one of the strongest sources of backlash. In the United States, the debate over gender-neutral language has focused on two main dimensions of English usage: the use of masculine terms as generics (that is, to denote entities of indeterminate or mixed gender), and the use of gender-specific titles in situations where gender is not (or should not be) particularly relevant (e.g., *waiter/waitress, steward/stewardess*). Second-wave feminists made their mark on the linguistic landscape; these days, using "man" to mean "human" is widely understood as problematic. Many publishers' style guides include recommendations for avoiding masculine generics, and gendered job titles have been replaced with new, gender-neutral ones, such that we are now waited upon in restaurants by "servers" and on airplanes by "flight attendants."

But these changes have been neither painless nor complete. The counter arguments have been many: that this "political correctness" comes at the expense of clarity (if "they" as singular generic becomes common usage, how do we know whether someone is referring to one or many people?); of precision (don't we want our language to encode as much information as possible?); of beauty ("chairperson" is ugly, clunky, etc.). And, above all, that it is unnecessary—critics argue that "he" and "man" are perfectly serviceable as gender-neutral terms, and that everyone already understands them as such.

Indeed, it may not be inherently problematic to have a generic pronoun-feminine pronoun dichotomy (McConnell-Ginet 1979). If the same term can be used to successfully reference "men" and "people" in different contexts (we could even consider these two usages separate homonymic words), and a separate term successfully references "women," then our language is adequate for the referential needs of a society with binary gender categories.

But that is a big "if." Sociolinguists have shown, time and time again, that ostensibly gender-neutral terms are in fact implicitly gendered in use—that the generic "he," *even if it is recognized as a gender-neutral usage,* still conjures a male image (Eckert and McConnell-Ginet 2013). If "he" were truly gender-neutral, then the sentence "a nurse should always be compassionate toward his patients" would not be so jarring, nor would we immediately envision a male nurse, given that nurses are stereotypically female. Generic "he" and its assorted cousins do not successfully call to mind either a mixed-gender group or a person of indeterminate gender. (Indeed, at least among Western cultures, people tend to find it difficult if not impossible to imagine a genderless person; human beings, even hypothetical ones, must be either male or female.) Yet at the same time that the generic "he" erases women, its ostensible inclusiveness erases that very erasure; the illusion of gender neutrality neatly obscures the actual exclusion of women.

What we have here is the important distinction between language in theory and language in practice—what Ferdinand de Saussure (1983) called *langue* and *parole*, respectively. The systematic rules about how a language should "work"—grammatical formulae, dictionary definitions—do not always correspond with actual usage. Language in use is messy: ambiguous, open-ended, inherently imperfect, but generally sufficient for our needs. And it is this gap between theory and practice that linguistic anthropologists and sociolinguists have helped bridge, by focusing on the emic rather than (or in addition to) the etic. For a linguistic anthropologist, the question of what a word means cannot be answered by looking in a dictionary; it is in people's mouths, in the texts that circulate within a community, in the sedimented history of each instance of its use (McConnell-Ginet 2006). This emphasis on actors' own understandings of their actions is one of linguistic anthropology's primary strengths, just as a concern with actual lived experience is one of feminist anthropology's.

Abstract structure is still important, of course, but the questions that we (as feminist anthropologists and/or as linguistic anthropologists) ask about it are different. On the issue of gender-neutral language, moving beyond the question of individual instances of reference and what they mean, we can draw on linguistic relativity to ask: how might having a language with a generic-feminine dichotomy affect the way that speakers think about the world? What sorts of "habitual thoughts" might it foster, and what sorts of information does it make salient?

One way to frame the generic/feminine split is in terms of markedness: "she" is marked for gender while "he" is (at least in theory) not. The marked/unmarked distinction originates in structuralist linguistics, where it is used to refer to morphology—"lion" as unmarked versus "lioness" as marked, for example—or to semantic categories—particular forms being marked for animacy, modality, and so on. From the structuralist perspective, markedness is merely an etic system of coding; marked and unmarked exist in binary opposition, and the labels could easily be reversed. ("He" could be marked for gender non-specificity. The "missing" suffix of "lion" is what linguists call a "zero morpheme.") And indeed the mutual constitution of binary categories is an essential principle of both feminist and linguistic anthropology, which have emphasized that masculinity (and other unmarked social categories) are just as performative as their marked counterparts (Bucholtz 2011; Kiesling 2002; Kitzinger 2005).

But at the same time, the two categories are neither perceived nor experienced as equally performative. In practice, femininity is perceived and felt as a "divergence" from a neutral or unbiased baseline. In 1949, Simone de Beauvoir wrote: "The terms masculine and feminine are used symmetrically only as a matter of form. . . . In actuality the relation of the two sexes is not quite like that of two electrical poles, for man represents both the positive and the neutral, as is indicated by the common use of man to designate human beings in general; whereas woman represents only the negative, defined by limiting criteria, without reciprocity" (Beauvoir 1989, xxi). More than half a century later, much has changed, but the basic asymmetry remains. We can refer to this emic quality as "social markedness." A state of markedness simultaneously singles women out as particular—subject to special scrutiny and incapable of anonymity—and tokenizes them, rendering any given woman representative of womanhood in general. We can see it in the never-ending carousel of news stories about how "women" feel about one issue or another without accompanying articles about how "men" feel about it; we can see it in the way that stick figures representing "people" suddenly sprout skirts as soon as they are ushering children around (Wade 2013). Heteronormativity is another example of social markedness: note that Vaughn Walker, the district court judge who overruled California's same-sex marriage ban in 2010, was accused of being biased because of his homosexuality, while it was taken for granted that heterosexual judges were unbiased (despite the simultaneous argument that same-sex marriage was an issue that affected straight couples). Social markedness carries with it a psychological burden—from street harassment to stereotype threat—as well as the material burdens of navigating a set of public institutions designed with the "default" human being in mind. And in the realms where men are the marked category, for example, child care, men who participate face difficulties ranging from the superficially hegemonic (being referred to as "babysitters") to the restrictive (a lack of changing facilities in men's restrooms) to the dangerous (being accused of abducting a child who is throwing an inconvenient tantrum).

Linguistic markedness is neither necessary nor sufficient for the generation of social markedness, and of course we cannot know which "came first," but the two exist in a mutual feedback relationship, bolstering each other and resisting change. Thus, even if the generic-feminine grammatical division *were* referentially sufficient, we would still be left with a linguistic structure that encourages—note, not *forces*—speakers to attend to gender only and always with female subjects, viewing them as exceptions to a "genderless" (read: male) norm. Regardless of whether the social markedness or the linguistic markedness of women "came first," the two are in a dialogic, mutually reinforcing relationship. Linguistic anthropology's semiotic grounding gives us a theoretical framework that can account for the unmarked: both its *seeming* neutrality or semiotic "emptiness" and its *actual* role as one half of a dialectical pairing. A century ago, Edward Sapir (1963) set out to study language as a system of emic contrasts; today, feminist linguistic anthropologists are applying the same basic principles as they argue that "neutral" is an ideological construction, and indeed an especially pernicious one that obscures its own partiality.

Narrative Representations

Ultimately, the concern about gender-neutral language is about representation and inclusion: does our language use lead us to ignore people in ways that promulgate inequality? If, for example, a university is looking for a new president, and the job description uses masculine pronouns, will the search committee unconsciously think disproportionately of male candidates? If all of the materials circulated in a STEM (science, technology, engineering, and mathematics) workplace presume a male addressee, are women more likely to feel alienated from and uninterested in the job? When half the population's viewpoints and needs are unthinkingly viewed as "special interests," how does this shape a society and the experiences of its individual members?

The feminist concern with representation goes beyond the sorts of democratic anxieties that have preoccupied Americans for centuries (Gustafson 2008). The modern notion of representation is not merely about representation in the political sense of having one's voice heard, but in the cultural sense of seeing one reflected back to oneself in popular discourses. It is a visual metaphor ("representation" as depiction) as much as a verbal one ("representation" as proxy), and the questions it provokes are self-reflexive ("what do we see/hear/consume?") as much as they are critical ("what do those in power see/hear about us?"). As feminists and other civil rights activists have argued, if you do not see representations of people "like you"—or you only see negative representations—you will suffer as a result. And so will a society generally, because its discourses will be impoverished, only capturing a small sliver of the broad spectrum of human experience.

The under- and mis-representation of women in media is thus a perennial feminist concern. The cartoonist Alison Bechdel (1985) introduced a tongue-in-cheek tripartite test for movies: in order to pass the "Bechdel Test," as it has come to be called, a movie must include: 1) at least two named female characters; 2) who have a conversation with each other; 3) about something other than a man. The Bechdel Test is not, of course, a way of determining whether a movie is sexist or not; its value lies not at the level of the individual test case, but in the aggregate. When we see just how few movies pass the Bechdel Test, it hammers home the dearth of complex, realistic female characters who serve a purpose beyond "one-dimensional love interest."

It is not just popular media that have this gaping hole. Early feminist anthropological work sought to remedy precisely this sort of invisibility within the discipline: in the introduction to *Toward an Anthropology of Women*, Rayna Reiter (now Rapp) (1975) accused the field of ignoring women, arguing that social systems were inevitably described from the point of view of a male ego, that fieldworkers obtained information about women by asking men instead of directly talking to women, and that women's points of view were treated as less representative and central—in short, that typical ethnographies of societies were in fact ethnographies of the *men* in those societies.

In the case of anthropology, it is easy to see why this would be problematic: in the search for knowledge (and, nowadays, often social justice [Jean-Klein and Riles 2005]), we want to be as perceptive and thorough as possible. When talking about popular culture, the case is often more difficult to make, countered as it is with well-worn objections like "the media industry is just giving people what they want" and "it's just a movie/advertisement/book, what's the big deal?" But when we bring in linguistic anthropology's emphasis on narrative—as a central experiential dimension of human life, as a socially performative tool, and as a culturally specific structure—we wind up with an extremely compelling argument for the importance of representation.

Linguistic anthropologists have long stressed the importance of narrative as a tool people use to structure and interpret the world around them (Ochs and Capp 2001; Wortham 2001). Narratives enable people to make sense of their lives—to render orderly and coherent a complex and chaotic sociopolitical landscape. Autobiographical narrative has been an important ethnographic tool both for feminist anthropology—consider Faye Ginsburg's (1989) research on abortion activists—and for linguistic anthropology—for example, Jane Hill's (1995) classic article "The Voices of Don Gabriel." We self-reflexively narrate our lives as we live them, and then narrate them back to ourselves having lived them. In doing so, we interpret past actions and predict future actions, and inflect ourselves as heroes or villains. And often we do not merely *predict* future events but cause them: more than merely passive reflections of what has happened, narratives have performative power. The act of narrating transforms the narrative itself.

Narratives make life meaningful but they also constrain: they designate "beginnings" and "ends," suggest causal relationships, and draw on a set of characterological stereotypes that come with prepackaged qualities and potentials for action. (This is, of course, one of the fundamental tensions of human life: simplification is both necessary and limiting.) When we tell stories to ourselves, we are likely to draw from the existing pool of conventional, culturally specific narratives with which we are familiar. The sorts of people we can be, the paths our lives take, the actions we undertake to follow those paths—the possibilities of our lives, both short-term and long-term, are shaped by the existing stories we are already familiar with. And when the process fails us, when we find ourselves unmoored from a recognizable narrative path, we can feel vulnerable, frustrated, lonely, even paralyzed. Lack of representation and *mis*representation are both problematic.

The study of narrative and cultural representation is thus a crucial focal point for feminist anthropology. Thinking of culture as a set of scripts or "discourses" (Hall 1996) is a useful conceptual tool for analyzing, explaining, and critiquing hegemonic ideologies. For example, we can conceptualize "rape culture" as a set of cultural discourses that naturalize and encourage rape. These circulating narratives include: movies that portray a man's relentless pursuit of a woman as not just harmless but romantic, and define male "success" as obtaining sex; public speech that sorts rape victims into "genuine" and "non-genuine" or that uses intransitivity to frame rapists as not responsible (Clark 1998); literature that denies women sexual agency by portraying their desires as separate and alien (Haag 1992); police and court systems that evaluate rape victims against a script of how victims "typically" behave (Matoesian 2001); language that frames heterosexual intercourse as something men do to women, as a penis actively (even aggressively) penetrating a passive vagina (Helliwell 2000); and perhaps even, as Sharon Marcus (1992) suggests, certain second-wave feminist works (e.g., Dworkin 1987) that claim that rape is an inevitable byproduct of sexual interactions between men and women. This set of conventionalized narratives reinforces (and is in turn reinforced by) a particular set of habitual thoughts and behaviors among all societies, in which rape is likely to occur and unlikely to be prosecuted.

This is just one example of how dominant cultural narratives reinforce themselves, sculpting social life to meet their descriptive ends. The feminist concern with cultural representation is precisely an attempt to break this cycle of narrative self-reinforcement by diversifying the available narrative repertoire. We cannot change the centrality of narratives to our lives, but we can try to ensure that the narratives we can choose from are inclusive, flexible, and positive. Linguistic anthropology provides a set of ethnographic and analytical methods for uncovering, describing, and critiquing the implicit narratives that structure our lives, which is an essential step toward the creation of a set of cultural narratives that can accommodate social diversity.

CONCLUSION

In looking at gendered language (including ideologies *about* gendered language) and language about gender, both feminist anthropologists and linguistic anthropologists have demonstrated that language is incredibly powerful.

Language is powerful cognitively: language shapes the way we perceive the world, and thus the ways we behave toward ourselves and others. Language provides us with the schemas that make life manageable but at the same time constraining. Language is the mechanism by which implicit ideologies about gender (and its relationship to other categories) are inculcated in us from the moment we are born. Language is a window into collective beliefs about gender as well as individual experiences.

And language is powerful socially: it can be used to exclude, abuse, and threaten, as well as to include, encourage, and forge new intimacies. It helps us inhabit social roles, including gender, even without our being aware of it—and sometimes even against our will. Language is the primary vehicle for sexism, as well as the primary tool for combating it.

Alessandro Duranti (2011) recently suggested that the diverse field of linguistic anthropology was united by a shared ontological perspective of language as a "non-neutral medium." This chapter has highlighted just a few of the many meanings of this phrase. Language is "non-neutral" in the sense that (*pace* John Locke) there is no "objective" language; each language (like each culture) divides up the world in its own unique way, and thus each language encapsulates its own partial perspective of the world. Language is non-neutral in that it shapes the social world, rather than passively reflecting it. And language is non-neutral in the sense that even an unmarked signifier still signifies: "being ordinary" (Sacks 1985) is as much a social achievement as is belonging to a salient category.

We might similarly classify the purview of feminist anthropology as the study of gender as a non-neutral phenomenon. Over the past half-century, feminist anthropologists have shown that gender cannot be taken for granted as a preexisting, universal category; gender is experienced differently in different cultures, and no one system is more objective than another. Gender, like language, shapes the social world, though its influence is often hidden by ideologies that naturalize it. And gender is neither passive nor inhabited by default; it must be actively performed, regardless of whether actors or audiences realize that a performance is taking place.

Revealing this non-neutrality in the face of entrenched ideologies that obscure it has been a critical element of both feminist anthropology and linguistic anthropology. The two disciplines together have crafted incredibly powerful analytic tools in the fight for gender equality. Linguistic anthropology provides a robust theoretical framework for studying the ways that social difference is created, maintained, and altered; and feminist anthropology applies this framework to issues of the utmost importance, both at home and abroad. And as we face an era when, at least in the United States, the majority of sexism takes the form of implicit circumscription of social possibilities rather than explicit discrimination, a feminist linguistic anthropology will prove more important than ever.

ACKNOWLEDGMENTS

I would like to thank Ellen Lewin and Leni M. Silverstein for their invaluable help with this chapter as well as their tireless efforts, first in organizing the "Mapping Feminist Anthropology in the Twenty-First Century" panel at the 2013 American Anthropological Association Annual Meeting and then in putting together this volume. I am also indebted to the many colleagues whose feedback greatly improved the chapter, especially Rayna Rapp, Susan Gal, Jim Shliferstein, and my fellow participants in the AAA panel. Last but not least, I am eternally grateful to Sally McConnell-Ginet for introducing me to the field of language and gender.

REFERENCES

Austin, John L. 1975. *How to Do Things with Words*. 2nd ed. Cambridge, MA: Harvard University Press.

Beauvoir, Simone de. 1989. *The Second Sex*. Trans. H. M. Parshley. New York: Vintage Books.

Bechdel, Alison. 1985. *Dykes to Watch Out For*. New York: Houghton Mifflin.

Brown, Penelope, and Stephen Levinson. 1993. "'Uphill' and 'Downhill' in Tzeltal." *Journal of Linguistic Anthropology* 3 (1): 46–74.

Bucholtz, Mary. 2011. *White Kids*. New York: Cambridge University Press.

Butler, Judith P. 1990. *Gender Trouble: Feminism and the Subversion of Identity*. New York: Routledge.

Cameron, Deborah. 1995. *Verbal Hygiene*. New York: Routledge.

———, ed. 1998. *The Feminist Critique of Language: A Reader*. 2nd ed. New York: Routledge.

———. 2009. *The Myth of Mars and Venus: Do Men and Women Really Speak Different Languages?* Oxford: Oxford University Press.

Clark, Kate. 1998. "The Linguistics of Blame: Representations of Women in *The Sun*'s Reporting of Crimes of Sexual Violence." In *The Feminist Critique of Language: A Reader*, ed. Deborah Cameron, 183–197. New York: Routledge.

Duranti, Alessandro. 2011. "Linguistic Anthropology: Language as a Non-Neutral Medium." In *The Cambridge Handbook of Sociolinguistics*, ed. Raj Mesthrie, 28–46. Cambridge: Cambridge University Press.

Dworkin, Andrea. 1987. *Intercourse*. New York: Free Press.

Eckert, Penelope. 1996. "The Whole Woman: Sex and Gender Differences in Variation." In *The Matrix of Language: Contemporary Linguistic Anthropology*, ed. Donald Brenneis and Ronald Macaulay, 116–137. Boulder, CO: Westview Press.

Eckert, Penelope, and Sally McConnell-Ginet. 2013. *Language and Gender*. 2nd ed. New York: Cambridge University Press.

Faludi, Susan. 1991. *Backlash: The Undeclared War against American Women*. New York: Crown.

Fruehwald, Josef. 2011. "On Vocal Fry." *Val Systems*, December 16. http://val-systems.blogspot.com/2011/12/on-vocal-fry.html, accessed November 1, 2015.

Gal, Susan. 1978. "Peasant Men Can't Get Wives: Language Change and Sex Roles in a Bilingual Community." *Language in Society* 7 (1): 1–16.

Gavey, Nicola. 2005. *Just Sex? The Cultural Scaffolding of Rape*. New York: Routledge.

Ginsburg, Faye D. 1989. *Contested Lives: The Abortion Debate in an American Community*. Berkeley: University of California Press.

Goffman, Erving. 1979. *Gender Advertisements*. New York: Harper & Row.

Gustafson, Thomas. 2008. *Representative Words: Politics, Literature, and the American Language, 1776–1865*. 1st ed. Cambridge: Cambridge University Press.

Haag, Pamela. 1992. "In Search of 'The Real Thing': Ideologies of Love, Modern Romance, and Women's Sexual Subjectivity in the United States, 1920–40." *Journal of the History of Sexuality* 2 (4): 547–577.

Hall, Kira, and Mary Bucholtz, eds. 1995. *Gender Articulated*. New York: Routledge.

Hall, Stuart. 1996. "The West and the Rest: Discourse and Power." In *Modernity: An Introduction to Modern Societies*, ed. Stuart Hall, David Held, Don Hubert, and Kenneth Thompson, 185–227, Malden, MA: Wiley-Blackwell.

Haviland, John B. 1996. "'We Want to Borrow Your Mouth': Tzotzil Marital Squabbles." In *Disorderly Discourse: Narrative, Conflict, and Inequality*, ed. Charles L. Briggs, 158–203. New York: Oxford University Press.

Helliwell, Christine. 2000. "'It's Only a Penis': Rape, Feminism, and Difference." *Signs* 25 (3): 789–816.

Hill, Jane. 1995. "The Voices of Don Gabriel: Responsibility and Self in a Modern Mexicano Narrative." In *The Dialogic Emergence of Culture*, ed. Dennis Tedlock and Bruce Mannheim, 97–147. Urbana: University of Illinois Press.

Inoue, Miyako. 2002. "Gender, Language, and Modernity: Toward an Effective History of Japanese Women's Language." *American Ethnologist* 29 (2): 392–422.

Irvine, Judith T., and Susan Gal. 2000. "Language Ideology and Linguistic Differentiation." In *Regimes of Language: Ideologies, Polities, and Identities*, 1st ed., ed. Paul V. Kroskrity, 35–83. Santa Fe, NM: School of American Research Press.

Jean-Klein, Iris, and Annelise Riles. 2005. "Introducing Discipline: Anthropology and Human Rights Administrations." *PoLAR: Political and Legal Anthropology Review* 28 (2): 173–202.

Keenan, Elinor. 1989. "Norm-makers, Norm-breakers: Uses of Speech by Men and Women in a Malagasy Community." In *Explorations in the Ethnography of Speaking*, ed. Richard Bauman and Joel Sherzer, 125–143. New York: Cambridge University Press.

Kiesling, Scott. 2002. "Playing the Straight Man: Displaying and Maintaining Male Heterosexuality in Discourse." In *Language and Sexuality: Contesting Meaning in Theory and Practice*, ed. Kathryn Campbell-Kibler, Robert Podesva, Sarah Roberts, and Andrew Wong, 249–266. Stanford, CA: CSLI Publications.

Kitzinger, Celia. 2005. "'Speaking as a Heterosexual': (How) Does Sexuality Matter for Talk-in-Interaction?" *Research on Language and Social Interaction* 38 (3): 221–265.

Kramer, Elise. 2001. "The Playful Is Political: The Metapragmatics of Internet Rape Joke Arguments." *Language in Society* 40 (2): 137–168.

Labov, William. 1972. "The Social Motivation of a Sound Change." In *Sociolinguistic Patterns*, 1–42. Philadelphia: University of Pennsylvania Press.

Lakoff, Robin. 1975. *Language and Woman's Place*. New York: Oxford University Press.

———. 2000. *The Language War*. Berkeley: University of California Press.

Lee, Benjamin. 2001. "Circulating the People." In *Languages and Publics: The Making of Authority*, ed. Susan Gal and Kathryn Woolard, 164–181. Northampton, MA: St. Jerome Publishing.

Lucy, John. 1992a. *Grammatical Categories and Cognition: A Case Study of the Linguistic Relativity Hypothesis*. Cambridge: Cambridge University Press.

———. 1992b. *Language Diversity and Thought: A Reformulation of the Linguistic Relativity Hypothesis*. Cambridge: Cambridge University Press.

Lucy, John, and Suzanne Gaskins. 2001. "Grammatical Categories and the Development of Classification Preferences: A Comparative Approach." In *Language Acquisition and Conceptual Development*, ed. Stephen Levinson and Melissa Bowerman, 257–283. Cambridge: Cambridge University Press.

Maltz, Daniel, and Ruth Borker. 1982. "A Cultural Approach to Male–Female Miscommunication." In *Language and Social Identity*, ed. John J. Gumperz, 196–216. Cambridge: Cambridge University Press.

Marcus, Sharon. 1992. "Fighting Bodies, Fighting Words: A Theory and Politics of Rape Prevention." In *Feminists Theorize the Political*, ed. Judith Butler and Joan W. Scott, 385–403. New York: Routledge.

Matoesian, Gregory M. 2001. *Law and the Language of Identity: Discourse in the William Kennedy Smith Rape Trial*. New York: Oxford University Press.

McConnell-Ginet, Sally. 1979. "Prototypes, Pronouns, and Persons." In *Ethnolinguistics: Boas, Sapir, and Whorf Revisited*, ed. Madeleine Mathiot, 63–83. The Hague: Mouton.

———. 2006. "Why Defining Is Seldom 'Just Semantics': Marriage, 'Marriage,' and Other Minefields." In *Drawing the Boundaries of Meaning*, ed. Betty J. Birner and Gregory Ward, 223–246. Amsterdam: John Benjamins.

Ochs, Elinor. 1992. "Indexing Gender." In *Rethinking Context*, ed. Alessandro Duranti and Charles Goodwin, 335–358. Cambridge: Cambridge University Press.

Ochs, Elinor, and Lisa Capps. 2001. *Living Narrative: Creating Lives in Everyday Storytelling*. Cambridge, MA: Harvard University Press.

Ortner, Sherry B. 1974. "Is Female to Male as Nature Is to Culture?" In *Woman, Culture, and Society*, ed. Michelle Zimbalist Rosaldo and Louise Lamphere, 67–87. Stanford, CA: Stanford University Press.

Orwell, George. 1949. *1984*. London: Penguin.

———. 1970 (1946). "Politics and the English Language." In *A Collection of Essays*, 156–170. New York: Houghton Mifflin.

Pinker, Steven. 2007. *The Language Instinct: How the Mind Creates Language*. New York: Harper Perennial Modern Classics.

Reiter (Rapp), Rayna. 1975. "Introduction." In *Toward an Anthropology of Women*, ed. Rayna Reiter (Rapp), 11–19. New York: Monthly Review Press.

Sacks, Harvey. 1985. "On Doing 'Being Ordinary.'" In *Structures of Social Action*, ed. J. Maxwell Atkinson, 413–429. New York: Cambridge University Press.

Sapir, Edward. 1963. *Selected Writings of Edward Sapir*. Ed. David G. Mandelbaum. Berkeley: University of California Press.

Saussure, Ferdinand de. 1983. *Course in General Linguistics*. Ed. Charles Bally and Albert Sechehaye. Trans. Roy Harris. La Salle, IL: Open Court.

Silverstein, Michael. 2000. "Whorfianism and the Linguistic Imagination of Nationality." In *Regimes of Language: Ideologies, Polities, and Identities*, ed. Paul Kroskrity, 85–138. Santa Fe, NM: School of American Research Press.

———. 2003. "Indexical Order and the Dialectics of Sociolinguistic Life." *Language & Communication* 23 (3–4): 193–229.

Spender, Dale. 1980. *Man Made Language*. New York: Routledge.

Tannen, Deborah. 1990. *You Just Don't Understand: Women and Men in Conversation*. New York: HarperCollins.

Wade, Lisa. 2013. "Stick Figures and Stick Figures Who Parent." *Sociological Images*, March 2. http://thesocietypages.org/socimages/2013/03/02/stick-figures-and-stick-figures-who-parent.

Wortham, Stanton Emerson Fisher. 2001. *Narratives in Action: A Strategy for Research and Analysis*. New York: Teachers College Press.

THE CURIOUS RELATIONSHIP OF FEMINIST ANTHROPOLOGY AND WOMEN'S STUDIES

A. LYNN BOLLES

US feminist anthropology and women's studies claim the same origins in the anti-war and civil rights movements of the 1960s and 1970s. That era's activism generated a range of politics on behalf of and for women, from grassroots actions involving health, economic, and educational needs, to implementation of policy on state and federal levels, to increasing the number of women in the professoriate and to curricular reform in higher education. US women's studies afforded women an institutional base for activist work and for women-centered scholarship with an interdisciplinary scope. US feminist anthropology, emanating from that same activist source, questioned the parameters of the discipline itself. It questioned the devaluation of women anthropologists as scholars and colleagues and focused attention on how women were described and analyzed—or often ignored—as members of societies under study. Feminist anthropologists, particularly social and cultural scholars, joined forces with other social scientists, literary scholars, and historians (to name only some of the fields that contributed) to institutionalize interdisciplinary women's studies units on college campuses.

Over the years, both US women's studies and feminist anthropology have faced issues of identification and representation, and dealt with problems of inclusion, exclusion, institutional boundary setting, and activist engagement. While feminist anthropologists contributed to and worked in women's studies programs in many academic settings, they generally carried out their work within anthropology departments and focused their professional commitments within the larger discipline of anthropology. My main question is: why did these two areas of study about women and gender become disconnected in the kinds of scholarship produced and in higher education curricula? Basically how did feminist anthropology become divorced from the wider disciplinary project of women's studies?

To answer my main question, this chapter examines three areas that relate to the increasingly divergent emphases that have characterized feminist anthropology and women studies.

(1) What is the intellectual relationship between the field of feminist anthropology and interdisciplinary women's studies? (2) What are the theoretical concerns, methodologies, and actions shared by feminist anthropology and women's studies? (3) How do we account for the apparent distance between the two fields in recent years? I address these points in a genealogical fashion, highlighting the origins, the theoretical and methodological contributions, and the social concerns faced by both women's studies and feminist anthropology in order to understand the constrictions this separation imposed on both fields.

THE 1970S–1980S—WOMEN'S STUDIES

From the early days, women's studies (now often renamed gender or feminist studies or some other configuration of women, feminist, gender, and/or sexuality), was the domain of literary scholars and sociologists. This early start was very US-focused, sparked by women's liberation writing such as Betty Friedan's *The Feminist Mystique* (1963), Robin Morgan's *Sisterhood Is Powerful* (1970), and grounded in US "second-wave feminism." In 1977, the National Women's Studies Association (NWSA) was founded to professionalize academic efforts. Entering the 1980s, the discourse of women's studies focused on American women but began to consider issues and concerns across class, race, ethnicity, religion, sexuality, and other social differences. This change of direction was generated by the scholarship of black, Latina, and Asian American sociologists and literary critics. But importantly for this discussion, the interdisciplinary nature of women's studies, adapted to address important problems by using differing perspectives and methods than those found in traditional disciplines, waned. The emphasis centered not only on sociology and literary scholarship, but eventually on a cultural studies perspective (distinctive from the breadth, objective, and methodology of anthropology), as postmodernism took root in the US academy. With this shift, feminist anthropology, among other empirically based perspectives, lost significant presence in women's studies.

EVOLUTION OF FEMINIST ANTHROPOLOGY—THE PERSONAL AND PROFESSIONAL

By the late 1960s feminist anthropology was evolving as a subfield of anthropology and women's studies was developing as an interdisciplinary field of study. Feminist anthropology dealt with the pressing problems of deconstructing and dismantling the Eurocentric bias in the study of women and enhancing the valuation of women both as worthy subjects of investigation and as respected colleagues and scholars. Not until the mid-1970s did women in anthropology publically recognize their often-inequitable status in the discipline and in departments of anthropology. For example, even though she was the world's most famous twentieth-century anthropologist, Margaret Mead never obtained a regular faculty appointment at Columbia University. And although the contents of Peggy Golde's edited volume (1970) *Women in the Field* were not inspired by the women's movement, it became an influential text for women in the discipline who began to document the gender inequities in their graduate training, in their fieldwork settings, and in their being hired and retaining faculty positions in departments of anthropology. The professional stories told by two other anthropologists who later became distinguished professors offer a sense of the period. Leith Mullings (1997) recalled that she never considered herself a feminist until she personally recognized the telltale signs of gender bias in addition to the racial discrimination she faced in the early years of her career at Columbia. In 1975, as an assistant professor, Louise Lamphere filed charges of sex discrimination "on behalf of herself and all other persons similarly situated," charging Brown University's Department of Anthropology as being in violation of Title VII of the 1964 Civil Rights Act. The case, settled by Consent Decree before the scheduled trial, mandated Brown to follow court-ordered affirmative action policies that were monitored by a university committee over twenty years. This precedent greatly strengthened the positions of all women faculty members across the United States (Brown University 2013; *Lamphere v. Brown University* 1975).

EVOLUTION OF FEMINIST ANTHROPOLOGY—THE THEORETICAL

In the 1970s, feminist scholars in anthropology directed their attention to thorny scholarly issues, for example: where and how did female subordination appear and what should be made of the collisions of colonialism and neocolonialism in the locales of most anthropological study? In 1974 and 1975, the now classic volumes of feminist anthropology, the Michelle Rosaldo and Louise Lamphere (eds.) and the Rayna Reiter (now Rapp) (ed.) anthologies, were published. The contents of these texts are indicative of the engagement of anthropology with feminist thought at that time. In their introduction, Rosaldo and Lamphere (1974, 1) stated that the intent of the volume was not derived from some "sort of abstract intellectual curiosity" but rather that they sought approaches to understand their own situation. The chapters looked at ways that sexism produced female inequality and oppression. Rayna Rapp's foundational volume (1975) included essays on gendered interpretations of fossil records (Slocum) in addition to the ground-breaking chapter on sex and gender, Gayle Rubin's "The Traffic in Women: Notes on the 'Political Economy' of Sex." Over the decades, Rubin's chapter continues to influence discussions on compulsory heterosexuality as a human activity, gender in anthropology, women and gender studies, and LGBTQ studies.

By the beginning of the next decade, the production of feminist scholarship in anthropology was prodigious all over the world in all four subfields of the discipline. Social and cultural, medical, biological, linguistics, and archeological fieldwork was situated across the Western Hemisphere, Europe, and the wide expanse of the Global South.[1] Feminist anthropology also embraced theories and concepts generated in agronomy, economics, labor studies, political science, literary studies, psychology, primatology, paleontology, geography, and interdisciplinary area studies. More than ever before, feminist anthropology exercised its scholarly heterogeneity. Furthermore, as Ellen Lewin (2006, 13–19) critically recounts, the anthropology of women moved from an analysis of the status of women to one that engaged in gendering material and cultural conditions, nuanced in grounded meanings of difference. In 1988, as the number of women and men conducting feminist research grew, a new unit of the American Anthropological Association (AAA) was formed, the Association for Feminist Anthropology (AFA), providing professional recognition for this scholarly work.

BREAKING DOWN BARRIERS IN ANTHROPOLOGY

Besides coordinating feminist and gendered scholarship, the AFA aimed to broadly promote equity, inclusiveness, human rights, and social justice. As noble as this sounds, the AFA itself, as well as feminist anthropologists, still faced major obstacles to obtaining recognition and respect in the discipline. Sandra Morgen directed the federally funded Gender and Anthropology Project, with the aim to increase the recognition and value of gendered research in the academy. The end result of the project was a text, *Gender and Anthropology: Critical Review for Research and Teaching* (1989), and an assessment of introductory textbook publications. As editor of *Gender and Anthropology*, Morgen's goal was to provide anthropologists, across all areas of the discipline, with the knowledge to incorporate gendered subjects into their teaching. The chapter authors were all women, save for one; many were established experts in their fields, and a number were African American and Asian American. The project's textbook review team examined the leading introductory anthropology textbooks, recommending substantive revisions. All major publishers revised their materials, making title and subtitle changes; for example, no longer was "man the hunter" a descriptor of all early human activity and content that would meet the gender inclusive goals of the project was developed in response. The AAA provided every department of anthropology gratis copies of *Gender and Anthropology*.

Besides fulfilling the goals of the project, there was another outcome. For perhaps the first time, an edited volume by feminist anthropologists featured the scholarship of more than one non-white woman scholar. Although the number of feminist black, Latina, and Asian American anthropologists increased, it remained difficult at that time to recognize their work as feminist scholarship. As racialized anthropologists who were also women, they were viewed primarily on the basis of race/ethnic identity, or the location of their research site, such as Africa, Caribbean, urban America.[2] Such positionality limited the recognition that non-white feminist anthropologists received for their contributions to the field of anthropology as well as to women's studies.

All Women Are Not White

In this early period, two black feminist anthropologists voiced concerns about the limitations of a women's studies still rooted in the white women's liberation movement. Diane Lewis's (1977) "A Response to Inequality" noted that while there were a number of theories about female inequality, these analyses were limited by the single focus on sex (gender).[3] This view devalued the cause of black women's dual subordinate position via sex and race, and fueled grounds for mistrust of the theoretical contributions that might emerge from their scholarship. Johnnetta B. Cole's edited volume *All American Women* (1986) was critical in breaking through the silence on race, religion, age, and politics in women's studies. Cole (1986, xiii) asks, "How to explain the narrowness of women's studies in the 1980s?"

Race, Class, Gender, and Sexuality

By the early 1980s, women's studies programs and departments were burdened by misinformed popular culture definitions of feminism, as well as by their own biases and the exclusionary practices of racism and sexism. Significant fissions surfaced within the NWSA membership, caused by the exclusion experienced by feminists of color and lesbians—not a new issue for the US women's movement. During the early years of the women's movement, the Furies, a radical lesbian separatist group, spoke out about patriarchy and the homophobia of heterosexual feminists. Likewise, members of the Cohambee River Collective put forward "A Black Feminist Statement" (1982 [1977]) that chronicled crushing acts of homophobia, racism, and classism. After all, as the title of the 1982 pioneering volume attests, *All the Women Are White, All Blacks Are Men but Some of Us Are Brave* (Hull, Scott, and Smith 1982). NWSA had to introspectively grapple with and address the consequences of its own racist, homophobic, and classist biases.

The watershed moment occurred in 1981 at the annual NWSA conference held at Storrs, Connecticut, that turned into a nightmare as calls of homophobia and racism were echoed by many in attendance. Twenty years later, following the lead of black literary scholar and poet June Jordan, feminist theorist Carole McCann and feminist anthropologist Seung-Kyung Kim (2010, 152) recount this divisiveness when they state, "Who are 'we' outside the boundaries of the Northern white women's movement and feminist theory?" Part of the problem centered on the naming practices of identity of women's studies at that time. The identity label "women of color" was approved, but it, too, was a product of the US-based black and white racial dichotomy, and obfuscated differences of ethnicity, religion, language, class, and sexuality. These debates surrounding naming practices continued for the next few years as feminist scholars (anthropologists as well) sought ways to understand and acknowledge the multiple social and cultural locations of diversity.

One of the responses to addressing issues of social positioning and inequality came from the research of black, brown, Asian American, and European American progressive women scholars. *Standpoint theory,* a matrix of domination and intersectional approaches, offered a new epistemological toolkit. In particular, these approaches established historical, contextual, and philosophical reasoning for unpacking women's oppression, deciphering inequitable situations and suggesting ways to interpret women's past experiences by underscoring the variability of gender oppressions. Feminist philosopher Nancy Hartsock's (1983) "The Feminist Standpoint" argued that people's knowledge and perspectives were shaped by their own experiences in specific social locations and social groups. Knowledge is situated, depending on one's circumstances, and influenced or shaped in terms of place, experience, and relative power, as opposed to knowledge supposedly free of context and value.

Patricia Hill Collins took standpoint theory to the next level of analysis and interpretation. Incorporating black intellectual thought from the works of Frances Beale (1970), Toni Cade Bambara (1970), and Bonnie Thornton Dill (1979), among others, Collins's first published article on the subject, "Learning from the Outsider Within" (1986), acknowledged that black feminists were beginning to embrace the creative potential of their outsider status and using that position "wisely." As such, these scholars were placing themselves and their discipline "closer to the humanist vision implicit in their work—namely the freedom both to be different and part of the solidarity of humanity" (Collins 1986, 31). In defense of her analysis, Collins (1990) remarked,

> Thus Black feminist thought represents a partial perspective. The overarching matrix of domination houses multiple groups, each with varying experiences of penalty and privilege that produce corresponding partial perspectives, situated knowledges and, for clearly identifiable subordinate groups, subjugated knowledges. No one group has a clear angle of vision. No one group possesses the theory or methodology that allows it to discover the absolute "truth" or, worse yet, proclaim its theories and methodologies as the universal norm evaluating other groups' experiences. (Collins 1990, 221–238)

Not long after Collins's article appeared, legal scholar Kimberlé Crenshaw published "Demarginalizing the Intersection of Race and Sex" (1989). Crenshaw applied the framework of black feminist theory to an examination of court cases involving black women and coined the term "intersectionality." She explained that intersectional thinking provides the means for dealing with the simultaneous systems of domination experienced by women of color, and further explored how race and gender interact to shape the multiple dimensions of structural, political, and representational aspects of black women's lives. Intersectionality opened up a broad lens from which to examine multiple grounds of identity when considering how the social world is constructed (1989, 1422). Expanding her viewpoint, Crenshaw suggested that intersectionality could provide the means for dealing with other marginalizations as well as those of women of color, such as LGBTQ identity or disability. "Awareness of intersectionality can better acknowledge and ground the differences among us and negotiate the means by which these differences will find expression in constructing group policies" (Crenshaw 1989, 1422). In short order, intersectionality became a core concept for feminist theorizing across the disciplines, as it conveyed the sense that individual identity and social life are produced by multiple, overlapping, and contradictory systems of power that operate simultaneously (McCann and Kim 2010, 148). Intersectional feminist theory is powerful since it supplies the means to look at how gender, race, class, sexuality, nation, ethnicity, and age (to mention a few) are shaped by ideological systems and historical patterns of power, economics, and politics. Moreover, intersectionality became the mechanism by which to navigate and critique postmodern and poststructuralist theoretical positions in feminist discourse. It forged a fluid perspective for third-wave feminism to understand gender, sexuality, politics, and transnational feminism.

FEMINIST POSITIONS AND GLOBAL PROJECTS

While still very US-centered, women's studies scholarship began to consider issues and concerns outside of the United States, especially as more women from across the globe constructed their own programs of study, women-centered activism, and political agendas. Advanced by the UN Decade for Women (1975–1985), Copenhagen, Nairobi, Beijing, and Beijing + 5, US women's studies came face to face with women's movements and academic programs from across the globe. As global academic women's studies voices became increasingly more pronounced, questions were raised about terminology, the right to represent other women, and Western theories of women's oppression.

Feminist anthropologist Aihwa Ong argued (1988) that Western feminists tend to objectify non-Western women by relegating their status to that of the "Other." Ironically, a major achievement of Western feminism had been to demonstrate that, as the result of male and patriarchal philosophical constructs, Western women lacked a concept of self apart from the experience of Otherness: that is, they lacked a voice in assigning, categorizing, and evaluating who and what someone is or is not. Along these lines, Ong stated, "Feminist voices in the social sciences unconsciously echo the masculinist will to power in its relation to non-Western societies" (1988, 80). Further, she added, "When feminists look overseas, they frequently seek to establish their authority on the backs of non-Western women . . . the claim to common kinship with non-Western women is at best, tenuous, at worst, non-existent" (Ong 1988, 80). Given such criticism of "internationalizing" Western feminist thought, women's studies, with its foundation squarely rooted in the humanities, became imbedded in cultural studies and postmodernism, distancing itself from its anthropological counterpart.

Essential to postmodernism, a reaction to the assumed certainty of the scientific model, is the relationship of meaning, power, and social behavior within social orders. The inherent ability to problematize the conditions in which one's life depends on one's situation and knowledge of the place, experience, and relative power is extremely difficult. Knowledge from nowhere is never value free. As postmodern women's studies further developed, it tended to focus more on philosophical theory and less on its activist roots (see Lamphere, this volume, for an analysis of the continued activist roots of feminist anthropology). Issues of power and agency became ideological constructs divorced from their structural or material base, definitely not generated from face-to-face, on-the-ground encounters or human interactions. At one point, Ong referred to cultural studies and postcolonial scholars as well as some anthropologists as "universalizing arm chair theorists" (1999, 240).

Nonetheless, for those feminist social scientists and other empirical scholars, standpoint and intersectionality theorizing, in which everyone has a partial view and nobody commands a vantage point to stand and see everything, clearly reinforced the value of this approach. A partial view can still produce valuable, if not complete or perfect, knowledge. Some locations make it possible to ascertain positions and interlocking social systems, while others generate problematic interpretations when relying on partial views. Feminist social scientists, new to qualitative methods and, in particular, ethnography, found this approach appealing. It answered many dilemmas emerging from the fieldwork experience and allowed them the opportunity to stand back from their data sets and surveys, to engage in personal encounters as a valid methodology.

Still, during this period of questioning the authoritative position located in ethnography and the validation of a partial view of truth, feminist anthropology as an empirically based approach began to lose traction in the interdisciplinary project of women's studies. Between those who embraced the postmodern, unsullied but distanced approach that questioned the validity of ethnography and the entrenched sociological influence in women's studies, it seemed as if there was no room for feminist anthropologists to be truly invested in this intellectual project. A number of points underscore this statement.

First, since positionality was key to feminist research, what credence did any feminist anthropologist armed with the legacy of being "the child of imperialism" hold as an interpreter of someone else's culture, modes of behavior, belief systems, kinship, livelihoods, and more? Anthropologist Lynn Walter remarked, "No anthropologist has enough experience, nor any single representational work, enough voices (no matter how dialogical) to represent others" (1995, 274). Secondly, the laden expression "cross-cultural," often used as a descriptor of an anthropological perspective, spoke volumes of derision. Who had the right to speak for whom? Chandra Mohanty (2003, 19) chastised Western feminist discourse, and rightfully criticized the 1970s *Sisterhood Is Powerful* universalizing perspective. However, in her classic chapter, "Under Western Eyes," she wrote, "a cross-culturally singular, monolithic notion of patriarchy or male dominance leads to the construction of a reductive and homogenous notion of what I call the 'Third World difference'—the stable, ahistorical something that apparently oppresses most if not all women in these countries" (2003, 19 [1986, 333]). Mohanty's critique is well taken as she proposes a real call to decolonize feminist anthropology, sociology, and economics. In the notes to the original chapter Mohanty says, "A number of the texts written by feminist sociologists, anthropologists, and journalists are symptomatic of the kind of Western feminist work on women in the Third World that concerns me" (2003, 256). In fact, she rarely cites US feminist anthropologists, save for the Rapp, Rosaldo, and Lamphere texts and a 1980 *Signs* essay by Michelle Rosaldo. These limited references say much about how circumscribed feminist anthropology appeared to be at that time. That is, it appeared that Mohanty was simply not aware of the kind of work feminist anthropologists were doing and didn't know the extent to which similar questioning of colonialism was already under discussion in the discipline.

By 2003 Mohanty significantly revised "Western Eyes"; terms were recast and the arguments framed to emphasize an anti-globalization and anti-capitalist feminist praxis across the board. Still, women's studies graduate students, steeped in postmodernism and cultural studies/postcolonial studies texts, needed to be trained to see Mohanty's "Western Eyes" 1984 and 2003 versions as the evolution of an intellectual journey of transnational feminism in a particular historical context. Mohanty targets feminist pedagogy as a way to understand anti-globalization by telling alternative stories of difference, culture, power, and agency (2003, 459), thus introducing possible feminist solidarities across the divisions of place, identity, class, work, belief, etc., that can forge bridges and build alliances with activists. Moreover, these new political subjects can now refer to and reflect upon their own context of how race, class, and ethnicity matter and how these local differences define and affect women's forms of action. That is, members of non-Western and postcolonial societies demand to speak for themselves, requiring deeper reflection in Western feminist anthropology.

OUR JOINT STRUGGLES

Here is the puzzle. How does practical knowledge, rooted in the authority of anthropological representations and grounded in empirical and ethnographic evidence through the impartiality (partial and mediated view) of the anthropologist come to bear on the recounting and interpretation of other peoples' lives? Herein lies the precise moment when feminist anthropological contributions were lost in Mohanty's very influential text, and subsequently, in the women's studies enterprise. Even without naming feminist anthropology as tainted, the narrowness of who can be legitimately involved in the critique of and resistance to global capitalism, and who has the rights of representation, profoundly discredited the feminist anthropological project and the substantial body of literature it had already produced.

A clear example of this dilemma that appears in feminist texts is the use of the term "transnational." The term surfaced as a way to address women from Third World nations/ethnicities who reside within the "First World" (Western Europe, United States, Australia, and Canada) in addition to those living in the Global South. This nomenclature required reexamination because it made explicit the unequal positions that appeared in the larger scheme of globalization. Furthermore, "transnational" was not in the lexicon of many feminist anthropologists, as the specificity of location remained a constant in ethnographic work. However, the term globalization was gaining traction in many of the societies we studied, no matter where they were geographically located.

Globalization, according to a basic definition, is the process of international integration arising from the interchange of worldviews, products, and ideas, accelerated by advances in transportation, telecommunication, and generating the interdependence of economic and cultural activities. Through social media, the sharing of information and connections among individuals and groups is extraordinarily rapid. For women's studies, transnational feminism was fully embraced as an area of study, in part due to the process of globalization generated by the decades of UN-sponsored women's international conferences. Applying a transnational feminist perspective relies on the establishment of clear understanding and shared viewpoints in order to best communicate with one another. It is at this juncture that feminist anthropology and women's studies can or should have been partners in transnational discourses, enabled by the processes of globalization.

In a co-authored text, feminist scholars M. Jacqui Alexander and Chandra Mohanty drew attention to three important elements in their definition of the transnational: (1) a way of thinking about women in similar contexts across the world—women in different geographical spaces rather than as all women across the world; (2) an understanding of a set of unequal relationships among and between peoples, rather than as a set of traits embodied in all non-US citizens (particularly because US citizenship continues to be premised on a white, Eurocentric, masculinist, heterosexist regime); and (3) a consideration of the term *international* in relation to an analysis of economic, political, and ideological processes that require taking critical anti-racist, anti-capitalist positions that would make feminist solidarity work possible (1996, xix). These comments were directed to women's studies scholars who were forging ahead in their transnational projects, unmindful of colonial histories, let alone postcolonial situations, exercising a postmodern moment that asserted a person's agency and simultaneously denied a political stance.

These difficulties in method and theory prompted women's studies scholar Sally Kitch to say, "Women's Studies is still struggling to determine what the production of women's studies research means or what if anything distinguishes women's studies scholarship from scholarship on women and gender in other disciplines" (2003, 435). Furthermore, according to Kitch, the value of interdisciplinary work is the set of interconnections, continuity, and interrelations that are reciprocal and integrative. Generally, this set of processes became a mark of achievement in the field.

For feminist anthropologists, the goals outlined by Alexander and Mohanty were already in place. Their ongoing work proved it was possible to have authentic and ethical communication across the power borders of anthropology (Walter 1995, 280). The responses to the question of why we anthropologists do feminist anthropological work were being answered in practice. Lynn Walter (1995,

283) pinpointed some of those reasons when she asked the following: "What is the source or motive for the willingness of the anthropologist to be exchanged by the other, given that it is an anguish-provoking and time-consuming process? Perhaps the explanation is to be found in the critique of one's own culture, or maybe admiration of and identification with those under study, or as a search for conflict resolution?" (Walter 1995, 283).

At times, feminist anthropological work was in concert with US-centered black and Latina women scholars as they reflected on their own position as insiders, outsiders, or native anthropologists. There are two arguments presented here that shape the debate. The first entertained a postmodern perspective that focused on the anthropologist as minimally and situationally bicultural, engaged in both scholarship as well as everyday life. The second focused on the politics of the insider/outsider stance coupled with an overlapping debate about rights of representation.

Major criticisms emerged to question the "native" or insider identification that focused on the social and cultural differences between an inquiring anthropologist who may have affinities or connections (of varying sorts) with those who were under study. Two examples of this criticism come to mind. First is Ranu Samantrai's (2004) caustic review of *Black Feminist Anthropology* edited by Irma McClaurin (2001). Samantrai chides a number of the chapter authors over their "inability to grapple with their membership in the global aristocracy" with their claims of commonality and shared victimhood. Another view, by Kirin Narayan (1993), suggested that differences that come from being an anthropologist might outweigh the cultural identity of an insider. According to Narayan, the ideal was the quality of the relationships garnered with those one encounters in fieldwork. "Knowledge is situated, negotiated, and becomes part of the ongoing process that spans personal, professional, and cultural domains" (Narayan 1993, 682). Further, she remarked, "Writing texts that mix lively narrative and rigorous analysis involves enacting hybridity regardless of our origins" (Narayan 1993, 682). Her position aligns with some of the interesting politics of the postmodern moment where the interpretation of a social order centers around the individual—subject and researcher—rather than on a sense of a shared understanding of either party. This stance elides the hard road we face because of anthropology's identification as the "child of imperialism" and the often cited, "I think this anthropology is just another way to call me a nigger" (Gwaltney 1981, xvix).

The struggle to produce a self-reflexive perspective had important implications for the politics of representation. Is it possible to authenticate someone else's position? Without being able to answer this question, we faced a major obstacle in explaining what the meaning, relevance, and reward could be for doing ethnography. Do members of the society under study acquire nothing more than to benefit the researcher's career (Valentine 1983)? But, of course, not all feminist or progressive anthropology ends with policy outcomes. More than likely, the framing of the insider/outsider position reflects a point of personal politics. Feminist anthropologist Deborah A. Thomas, whose work focuses on Jamaica, remarked, "I have a personal and professional stake as a half-Jamaican, half-German-American, browning/redgirl/light-skinned, dreadlocked, middle class artist and intellectual" (2004, 16). Faye V. Harrison even titled her 2008 collection of essays *Outsider Within,* emphasizing her self-reflexive position in her scholarship and professional career as a black feminist anthropologist whose primary area of interest is in the African Diaspora. Often, the physical location of one's research is primarily inspired by personal politics. In an interview about the women's health movement and substance abuse, Sandra Morgen discussed how in the late 1970s, she chose the US northeastern community-based clinic where she spent over a year conducting fieldwork. "My choices were limited because of my interest in race and class along with gender and sexuality so [I looked] for a clinic that served a broad client base including women of color, poor and working class women" (in Travis 2012). As these cursory examples illustrate, no matter where feminist anthropological research occurs, the anthropologist remains the inquiring visitor.

Over twenty years ago, Aihwa Ong (1988, 80) argued that Western feminists tended to objectify non-Western women by relegating their status to that of the "other." Contemporary feminist anthropology is trying to redress this history through its process of recovery, historical analysis, and corrective personal politics. It might be easier for many feminists to follow democratic practices in the "safety" of the field where female anthropologists may pass as honorary males (in some societies), or as persons of higher status based on their membership in a Western culture (Visweswaran 1994, 29), than on the "home front" of their department or in the academy at large. This is part of the ongoing project of decolonizing feminist anthropology and the discipline as a whole (Bolles 2013, 58).

FEMINIST ANTHROPOLOGICAL SCHOLARSHIP

Early on, feminist anthropological work did make its way into women's studies curriculum, including ethnographies such as Carol Stack's *All Our Kin* (1974) and Marjorie Shostak's *Nisa: The Life and Words of a !Kung Woman* (1981). However, as women's studies increasingly became institutionalized, the uniformity of introductory texts contained few contributions from feminist anthropology or ethnography or even minimal interest in the role that culture plays in the study of identity, sexuality, cultural expression, and ethnography. Consequently, as women's studies remains US-centered, it continues to slight even the work of US-focused feminist anthropologists. In the rare instance where feminist anthropological work makes an appearance, it tends to be misused. Such is the case of Lila Abu-Lughod's contribution in the *Feminist Frontiers* 7th edition (2006), edited by Verta Taylor, Nancy Whittier, and Leila Rupp. The chapter "Do Muslim Women Really Need Saving?" looked at how then US First Lady Laura Bush's "saving Afghan women" project constructed Afghan women as people to be saved. Abu-Lughod examined the daily human costs these women paid due to the violence in their homeland, and convincingly argued that the patronizing quality of the rhetoric of saving women diminished the overall price paid. Without any intended irony, the chapter is located in the section called "Global Change" while in fact, the article is about US politics and US foreign policy.

But works by feminist anthropologists have in fact directly addressed Alexander and Mohanty's concerns about representation and Kitch's call for integrative research. Let me offer three noteworthy examples. First, let us consider *Zapotec Women: Gender, Class, and Ethnicity in Globalized Oaxaca* (2005) by Lynn Stephens. In a version significantly revised from her award-winning 1992 volume, Stephens's ethnography focuses on the interaction between local and global market forces, and the role of women and family textile production and marketing. Stephens engages in storytelling about the lives of her informants, interspersed by the successes and failures they experience in the competitive world of the international textile market. In this ethnography, Stephens demonstrates how the international market sets the pace of production and distribution of Oaxaca women whose livelihoods are tied to forces outside of their villages. Stephens captures their concerns and way of life in their own words. This allows for an integrative and reciprocal relationship between the ethnographer and the women with whom she works to share those experiences, thereby enabling readers to understand that connection (see Lamphere, this volume).

Another particularly noteworthy example of feminist anthropology's contribution to transnational feminism is *The Gender of Globalization* (2008) edited by Nandini Gunewardena and Ann Kingsolver. Their text relies mainly on ethnographic and feminist methods of analysis, and examines how local and global constructions of gender play out in the workings of transnational capital. In their introduction, Gunewardena and Kingsolver remark on how women "participate in, become drawn and incorporated into, are affected by, and negotiate their encounters with contemporary forms of global economic restructuring commonly referred to as globalization" (2008, 3). Ethnography plays an important role in their analysis, providing descriptive "thickness" to give a more nuanced understanding of globalization and the myriad ways in which its processes affect women's everyday lives. *The Gender of Globalization,* a product of the Association of Feminist Anthropology sponsored panels held during the 2003 annual meetings of the American Anthropological Association, received the 2011

Society for the Anthropology of Work Book Prize. Alicia DeNicola's review conveys how such feminist anthropological research yields an important contribution to feminist knowledge, saying, "One of the book's greatest strengths is that, as a collection, it addresses side by side the similarities between marginalized women in very different areas of the globe while never losing track of the particular differences that geography, class, caste, ethnicity, race, and even age can have on the ways in which women experience the problems and possibilities of globalization" (2008, 78). Taken as a whole, this text addresses both Mohanty and Kitch's concerns. From the individual book chapters, it is clear that across the globe, women's experiences in everyday life are dramatically influenced by the globalization recounted in ethnography.

The final example of how feminist anthropologists have addressed these issues is *Feminist Activist Ethnography* (2013), edited by Christa Craven and Dána-Ain Davis. The editors suggest that feminist ethnographers are in a key position to reassert central feminist connections among theory, methods, and activism. Chapters incorporate methodological innovations such as collaborative analysis and collective activism. This collection continues the crucial dialogue about feminist activist ethnography in the twenty-first century—situated at the intersection of engaged feminist research and activism in the service of furthering organizations, peoples, communities, and issues of social justice. The titles of the sections of the volume illustrate how feminist anthropologists use ethnography to test, query, and address current issues, framed by neoliberalism and the privatization, deregulation, and reduction of government spending that affords free reign to the open market. In the section titled "The Intimacies of Feminist Ethnography," for example, medical anthropologist Mary Anglin discusses how she applied a social justice framework when writing about women with breast cancer. Discussed elsewhere in this volume are issues of domestic violence, advocacy, food justice, reproductive rights, and the academy itself as a site of neoliberal policy. Elizabeth Chin's chapter examines how Institutional Review Board (IRB) rules often inhibit or limit activist feminist ethnographic projects due to the very nature of the structure of a process that is based on a positivist scientific model. In this very US-centered volume, ethnography, the cornerstone of feminist, sociocultural anthropology, is shown to be a powerful explanatory and critical tool that provides a political and economic understanding of issues facing women, children, and men in the twenty-first century. All the chapters detail the importance of race, gender, class, and other specific differences in a cultural context, thus giving meaning to the specificity of the social and economic environment context.

These three examples clearly demonstrate the power that ethnography can have as a methodological tool in conveying and interpreting the lives and experiences of women and their families. Are these anthropological texts? Yes, they are. Can they be considered women's studies texts? Of course! Women's studies scholars should use them since they provide the depth that a partial truth perspective can allow. The inordinate amount of detail generated in anthropological inquiry is something that makes it unique but often troublesome to those who rely on statistical reliability or who seek totally value-free authenticity. These examples of feminist anthropological work provide evidence of actual dialogue across methodological, geographical, social, and cultural borders.

CURIOUS RELATIONS: FEMINIST ANTHROPOLOGY AND WOMEN'S STUDIES

This inquiry into the relationship between feminist anthropology and women's studies asked three questions. As a way of examining the intellectual relationship, the shared theories, methods, and activism of these often overlapping fields of inquiry, we approach a point of resolution in the puzzling distancing of these two partners in their mutual feminist project. We see a narrative arc at play here: a history, points of tension, the unfolding of differing paths, and a resolution.

From the very beginning of the 1970s, as students, faculty, and activists, feminists worked together in partnership to develop an academic field called women's studies. In doing so, feminist scholars found themselves dividing their energies into fostering feminist thought in their disciplines as well as institution building. Based on any one institution's willingness and need to facilitate institutionalizing women's studies, the feminist scholars who championed the cause became part-time, or in some instances, solely members of departments in those academic units. However, the direction of these institutional and career choices was often based on numbers. To fill the growing demands of establishing women's studies units, larger numbers of literary scholars, sociologists, and historians were available in the academy than were anthropologists. Over the years the intellectual relationship between interdisciplinary women's studies and feminist anthropology became tenuous due to the dominance of a disciplinary emphasis from the humanities with an overlay of sociology. Further, as black, Latina, Native American, and Asian American feminist sociologists demonstrated, the narrowness of women's studies and the challenge of embracing intersectionality as an approach allowed for better understanding of US-centered research and scholarship. Postmodern thought placed empirically based feminist anthropology and women's studies not in partnership, but in a seemingly adversarial position. Further, given the historical role that anthropology played during the colonial era, feminists from the Global South rightfully questioned the authority that anthropologists and other social scientists wielded as experts. Members of the feminist anthropological community became self-critical regarding the rights of representation, their position as interpreters of cultures not their own, and the consequences of exerting inequitable power dynamics in "the field." At this point of great tension, women's studies, particularly as it developed a transnational perspective, moved away from feminist anthropology.

On the other hand, at the moment of disconnect, women's studies scholars also came to embrace qualitative research methods, especially ethnography. Currently, women's studies researchers value the face-to-face encounter dictated by ethnographic practice. Coming from qualitative sociology, grounded theory includes the time-honored anthropological practice of participant observation, one-on-one interviewing, and the use of public records and private documents such as photographs and other visual materials. These methods are now part of the women's studies research toolbox but often are not attributed to anthropology let alone feminist anthropology.

How to close the distance between these two partners in feminist scholarship? We must follow the words of Audre Lorde (1984, 122) who told us to "enrich our visions" in our "joint struggles." The best practice is investment in the future. As interdisciplinary scholars, women's studies researchers must mine all sources for the most pertinent, valuable materials and scholarship available for advancing their projects. Interest in earning advanced degrees in women's studies is evidenced by the growing number of doctoral programs in the field. In a similar fashion, students of anthropology turn to feminist anthropological research for direction in ethics and methods. The innovative approaches taken by feminist anthropologists illustrated in this chapter indicate the significance of the body of anthropological knowledge across the disciplines. Good scholarship requires a heavy dose of curiosity, particularly as our vision spans the globe, demands collaborative efforts, and inaugurates new technologies for research. The partners in feminism—women's studies and feminist anthropology—should rely on each other's strengths.

NOTES

1. Global South includes countries found in Africa, Latin America, developing Asia, and the Middle East. It refers to the comparative disadvantages in technology, education, infrastructure, and foreign exchange dependency on primary products.

2. Listed by generation are: Johnnetta B. Cole, Niara Sudarkasa, Diane Lewis, Yolanda Moses, Carolyn Martin Shaw, Sheila Walker, Patricia Guthrie, Angela Gilliam, Leith Mullings, Gwendolyn Mikell, Victoria Durant Gonzalez, Faith Mitchell, A. Lynn Bolles, Faye Harrison, Cheryl Mwaria, Signithia Fordham, Brackette Williams, Alaka Wali, Aihwa Ong, Patricia Zavella, Ruth Behar, Lila Abu-Lughod, Suad Joseph, and others.

3. Lewis's 1977 comments in *Signs* gave as the example *Women, Culture, and Society* edited by Rosaldo and Lamphere because although there were several models of female subordination, none of the chapters considers fully the structural position and theoretical implications of women subject to both racism and sexism.

REFERENCES

Abu-Lughod, Lila. 2006. "Do Muslim Women Really Need Saving?" In *Feminist Frontiers*, 7th ed., ed. Verta Taylor, Nancy Whittier, and Leila Rupp, 486–495. New York: McGraw-Hill.

Alexander, M. Jacqui, and Chandra T. Mohanty, eds. 1996. *Feminist Genealogies, Colonial Legacies, Democratic Futures.* New York: Routledge.

Beale, Frances. 1970. "Double Jeopardy: To Be Black and Female." In *The Black Woman: An Anthology*, ed. Toni Cade, 90–100. New York: Signet.

Bolles, A. Lynn. 2013. "Telling the Story Straight: Black Feminist Intellectual Thought in Anthropology." *Transforming Anthropology* 21 (1): 57–71.

Brown University. 2013. "Exploring the Legacy of Louise Lamphere v. Brown." http://www.brown.edu/research/pembroke-center/archives/christine-dunlap-farnham-archives/louise-lamphere-v-brown-university, accessed November 25, 2015.

Cade, Toni Bambara. ed. 1970. *The Black Woman: An Anthology.* New York: Signet.

Cohambee River Collective. 1982 (1977). "A Black Feminist Statement." In *All the Women Are White, All Blacks Are Men but Some of Us Are Brave*, ed. Gloria Hull, Patricia Bell Scott, and Barbara Smith, 13–22. New York: Feminist Press.

Cole, Johnnetta B., ed. 1986. *All American Women: Lines That Divide, Ties That Bind.* New York: Free Press.

Collins, Patricia Hill. 1986. "Learning from Outsider Within." *Social Problems* 33 (6): 14–32.

———. 1990. *Black Feminist Thought Knowledge, Consciousness and the Politics of Empowerment.* Boston: Unwin Hyman. 1986.

Craven, Christa, and Dána-Ain Davis, eds. 2013. *Feminist Activist Ethnography.* Lanham, MD: Lexington Books.

Crenshaw, Kimberlé. 1989. "Demarginalizing the Intersection of Race and Sex: A Black Feminist Critique of Antidiscrimination Doctrine, Feminist Theory, and Antiracist Politics." *University of Chicago Legal Forum*, 139–167.

———. 1991. "Mapping the Margins: Intersectionality, Identity Politics, and Violence against Women of Color." *Stanford Law Review* 43: 1241–1299.

Dill, Bonnie T. 1979. "Dialectics of Black Womanhood." *Signs* 4 (3): 543–555.

DeNicola, Alicia. 2008. "Review, *The Gender of Globalization.*" *Anthropology of Work Review* 29 (3): 78–79.

Friedan, Betty. 1963. *The Feminist Mystique.* New York: W. W. Norton.

Golde, Peggy, ed. 1970. *Women in the Field.* Berkeley: University of California Press.

Gunewardena, Nandini, and Ann Kingsolver, eds. 2008. *The Gender of Globalization.* Santa Fe, NM: SAR Press.

Gwaltney, John L. 1981. *Drylongso: A Self-Portrait of Black America.* New York: Random House.

Harrison, Faye V. 2008. *Outsider Within.* Urbana–Champaign: University of Illinois Press.

Hartsock, Nancy. 1983. "The Feminist Standpoint." In *Discovering Reality*, ed. Sandra. Harding and Merrill B. Hintikka, 283–310. Dordrecht: Reidel Publishing.

Hull, Gloria, Patricia Bell Scott, and Barbara Smith, eds. 1982. *All the Women Are White, All Blacks Are Men but Some of Us Are Brave.* New York: Feminist Press.

Kitch, Sally. 2003. "PhD Programs and the Research Mission of Women's Studies: The Case for Interdisciplinarity." *Feminist Studies* 29 (2): 435–447.

Lamphere v. Brown University. 1975. Rhode Island District Court Case No. Civ. A. No. 75-0140P.

Lewin, Ellen, ed. 2006. *Feminist Anthropology: A Reader.* Boston: Wiley-Blackwell.

Lewis, Diane. 1977. "A Response to Inequality: Black Women, Racism, and Sexism." *Signs* 3 (2): 339–361.

Lorde, Audre. 1984. *Sister Outsider*. Trumansburg, NY: Crossing Press.

McCann, Carole R., and Seung-kyung Kim, eds. 2010. *Feminist Theory Reader.* New York: Routledge.

McClaurin, Irma, ed. 2001. *Black Feminist Anthropology: Theory, Politics, Praxis, and Poetics.* New Brunswick, NJ: Rutgers University Press.

Mohanty, Chandra. 1984. "Under Western Eyes: Feminist Scholarship and Colonial Discourses." *Boundary* 2 (3): 333–358.

——— 1991. "Under Western Eyes" In *Third* World *Women and the Politics of Feminism*, ed. Chandra T. Mohanty, Ann Russo, and Lourdes Torres, 51–80. Bloomington: Indiana University Press.

———. 2003. *Feminism without Borders*. Durham, NC: Duke University Press.

Morgan, Robin, ed. 1970. *Sisterhood Is Powerful*. New York: Random House.

Morgen, Sandra, ed. 1989. *Gender and Anthropology: Critical Reviews and Research.* Washington, DC: American Anthropological Association.

Mullings, Leith. 1997. *On Our Own Terms*. New York: Routledge.

Narayan, Kirin. 1993. "How Native Is a Native Anthropologist?" *American Anthropologist* 95 (3): 671–686.

Ong, Aihwa. 1988. "Colonialism and Modernity: Feminist Representations of Women in Non-Western Societies." *Inscriptions* (3/4): 79–93.

———. 1999. *Flexible Citizenship: The Cultural Logics of Transnationality.* Durham, NC: Duke University Press.

Reiter (Rapp), Rayna, ed. 1975. *Toward an Anthropology of Women.* New York: Monthly Review Press.

Rosaldo, Michelle Z., and Louise Lamphere, eds. 1974. *Women, Culture, and Society*. Stanford, CA: Stanford University Press.

Samantrai, Ranu. 2004. "Review of *Black Feminist Anthropology: Theory, Politics, Praxis, and Poetics*, Irma McClaurin, ed." *American Anthropologist* 106 (1): 201–202.

Shostak, Marjorie. 1981. *Nisa: The Life of a !Kung Woman.* Cambridge, MA: Harvard University Press.

Stack, Carol B. 1974. *All Our Kin.* New York: Basic Books.

Stephens, Lynn. 2005. *Zapotec Women: Gender, Class, and Ethnicity in Globalized Oaxaca.* Durham, NC: Duke University Press.

Taylor, Verta, Nancy Whittier, and Leila Rupp, eds. 2007. *Feminist Frontiers*. 7th ed. New York: McGraw-Hill.

Thomas, Deborah A. 2004. *Modern Blackness.* Durham, NC: Duke University Press.

Travis, Trysh. 2012. "Points: The Blog of the Alcohol and Drugs History Society," September 13. https://ashsblog.wordpress.com/category/trysh-travis, accessed June 28, 2014.

Valentine, Betty Lou. 1983. *Hustling and Other Hard Work in the Ghetto*. New York: Random House.

Visweswaran, Kamala. 1994. *Fictions of Feminist Ethnography*. Minneapolis: University of Minnesota Press.

Walter, Lynn. 1995. "Feminist Anthropology?" *Gender and Society* 9 (3): 272–288.

PART II EXPANSIONS

Confronting Universals

WHEN NATURE/ CULTURE IMPLODES

Feminist Anthropology and Biotechnology

ELIZABETH F. S. ROBERTS

Feminist accounts of biotechnology, especially since the development of in vitro fertilization (IVF), have been thoroughly saturated with a "technological ambivalence" often dividing feminists in regard to effective action in the face of the "increased choice" structured by patriarchal, industrial capitalism (Franklin 2013a, 185–186). Guided by Donna Haraway, the influential feminist historian and philosopher of science, Sarah Franklin, a feminist anthropologist of biotechnology, has pointed out that technological ambivalence can serve as a resource for "forms of political organization and social change" where a new kind of unity might be founded in the ambivalence, partiality, and disrupted holism at play in the use of biotechnologies (Franklin 2013a, 186; Haraway 1991). What I trace in this chapter is how the technological ambivalence permeating feminist debate about biotechnology has also served as a resource for feminist anthropologists of science, medicine and technology to disrupt twentieth-century Euro-American certainties about the holism of nature and artificiality of technology.

Early feminist critics of assisted reproductive technologies (ARTs), who contributed significant and productive analyses of how reproductive technologies were constituted through patriarchal, capitalist systems, frequently made their arguments through evocations of nature. For those earlier authors, "mother machines" and "test tube women" were artificial technological interventions into natural reproductive processes (Arditti, Minden, and Klein 1984; Corea 1988). They, along with conservative critics of ARTs, were deeply concerned about human technological interference with nature and the commodification of natural reproductive material, women's bodies, and kin relations (Rae 1994; Rothman 1988). Likewise, Euro-American popular press stories continue to deploy nature in often breathless descriptions of how the use of IVF, egg donation and more recently, cloning, stem cells, and egg freezing, artificially manipulate nature.

While technological ambivalence is still central to feminist accounts of biotechnologies, including feminist anthropological accounts, that ambivalence tends no longer to focus on nature. We can see this is a recent online debate between three respected feminist medical anthropologists, Marcia Inhorn, Lynn Morgan and Janelle Taylor, who disagreed online about the politics of egg freezing for young academic women. Inhorn offered egg freezing as one solution, albeit imperfect, to the often necessarily delayed childbearing of academic women, while Morgan and Taylor decried this approach as ignoring larger structures that produce the quandary of delayed childbearing in the first place (Inhorn 2013; Morgan and Taylor 2013). Soon after, Sarah Franklin weighed in, contextualizing this particular debate as continuous with earlier feminist arguments that drew "fault lines in the sisterhood" over the use of reproductive technologies as "complicit with patriarchy." Franklin argued that this is not an either-or question, but that "solutions to the intractable problem of how women reconcile their reproductive status to other crucial aspects of their viable social identities need to accommodate a generous dose of ambivalence in order to be successful in the long run" (Franklin 2013b).[1] As Franklin demonstrated, the egg freezing controversy resonated with earlier feminist contestations about the use of reproductive technologies. Ambivalence continues, as clearly there is no one feminist anthropological position on biotechnologies, which makes for sharp and painful debates among often deeply collaborative scholar-activists. One key difference between the egg freezing and earlier debates, however, concerned the status of nature and technology themselves. Inhorn, Morgan, Taylor and Franklin have all conducted empirical fieldwork on how women live with and use biotechnologies, and they share the premise that biotechnologies are fully part of the human world, in all their ambivalent reality. Instead of debating the *nature* of these biotechnologies writ large or a presumed conflict between nature and biotechnology, the debate reflects differences in evaluating the *effects* of a specific biotechnological practice on gendered beings situated in a specific world where the question of what women's work ought to be is still up for grabs.

The clear absence of nature, then, tells us about the shifting place of nature in feminist anthropological analysis throughout the twentieth and early twenty-first century. As the debate suggests, the last few decades of feminist analysis of biotechnology have realigned nature, culture, and technology differently from earlier feminist and feminist anthropological accounts. Feminist anthropologists, in particular, have played a large part in dissolving nature's rhetorical hold on the social science analysis of medicine, science, and technology, by demonstrating how these systems have played such a large part in the naturalization of the racial and sexual stratifications of industrial capitalism. Claims to nature, then, can't be separated from the colonial and industrial processes that separated and essentialized nature in the first place, making appeals to nature ultimately a losing strategy for feminists concerned with legacies of sexual and racial essentialism. Insights about the problematic nature of nature, often stemming from the technological ambivalence of earlier contestations, have shifted feminist debates and helped build the fields of medical anthropology and science and technology studies (STS). Deploying insights from their own fieldwork and the now rich ethnographic record focused on women's encounters with biomedicine and biotechnologies, feminist anthropologists studying medicine and science currently insist on parsing the specific material–semiotic relations between people and the worlds they inhabit without an a priori assumption about what counts as nature or technology.

HARDENING NATURE

The distinction between nature and culture, which has been pivotal to the feminist anthropological analysis of biotechnology and to feminist anthropology more generally, was shaped within Enlightenment reason, itself a product of the European colonial project and its fortunes. Science, based on reason, was formulated as the active, male discovery of the disenchanted universal laws of *nature*—a passive, inert, feminized, and racialized domain (Daston and Galison 1992; Toulmin 1996). While science was the study of the natural material world, separate from human consciousness, and medicine the application of that study to bodily processes, technology came to describe the actively agentive process of controlling the passive natural world. Over the last few centuries, the technological innovations of *man* have been portrayed as both heroic (transcontinental railways! space exploration! the discovery of DNA!) and full of hubris (think *Frankenstein* through *The Terminator,* both anxiety-ridden narratives about artificial male creations). Within either portrayal, technology is an active doing upon to the fixed, natural world, an account which has shaped how biotechnologies, from gene splicing to IVF, have been experienced in much of the Euro-American world.

The logic behind the Enlightenment metaphysics that separated nature from both God and man, and divided subject from object, and mind from body, provided a basis for new kinds of human hierarchies based on the possession of reason, the ability to see the material world through unclouded senses. For the gentlemen of Western European science, women, the mad, the superstitious, children, and savages from colonized lands were less reasonable, making them less technological and closer to nature, an affinity that made it possible to study and manage these less reasoned groups with impunity (Ortner 1974).

While this transformation of nature into an entity separate from God and human reason was essential to the later emergence of the nature/nurture debates of the late nineteenth century, for the first few centuries after this separation, humans continued to be understood as shaped in continuous relation to the material world around them. At this point, nature was not an internal or determinist force (i.e., genes) that shaped humans separate from their conditions of life, as it came to be later. Within anthropology, we often point to the philosopher Johann Gottfried Herder (1744–1803) as providing us with the culture concept, coming from *Volkgeist*, the *spirit* of a people, which in American anthropology came to emphasize the ephemerality and non-materiality of culture as opposed to the hard reality of nature. However, Herder never opposed culture to nature or the material world, but instead linked culture to cultivation (as in agriculture), signifying specific groups of people embedded within a particular climate, geography, and language over time. Early evolutionary thinkers like Jean Baptiste Lamarck, who proposed the theory of acquired characteristics, also shared this prevalent sense of the continuing material process of organismal development through time. Standing in stark contrast to later nineteenth-century deterministic, biological theories of inheritance, Herder's and Lamarck's accounts of human development were steeped in temporal processes that surrounded an organism's gestation and life course. In other words, they envisioned relational processes, rather than a distinction between separate entities, that is, nature and culture.

Nancy Leys Stepan, a historian of eugenics and race, describes how, in nineteenth-century Western European thought as well as that of the United States, nature became "hard," less relational and more internal to individual organisms, a transformation that served to codify "natural" hierarchies of race and sex through the emergent fields of biology and scientific medicine (Stepan 1991). The last half of the century saw the beginnings of the politically powerful practice of debating whether human characteristics or behavior belonged to the discrete categories of inheritance or "institutional arrangements." These debates also contributed to creation and boundary maintenance between the hard sciences of nature and the soft sciences of society. Charles Darwin's evolution helped drive these debates, but his theory remained Lamarckian within his lifetime, insofar as he held that organismal change often came through the pressures of the external conditions of life.

It was Darwin's cousin, Sir Francis Galton, who promulgated the phrase "nature or nurture" in his 1874 argument for the innate inheritance of English male genius. Galton's assertion that social circumstances usually have very little to do with achievement was of a piece with the intertwined movement toward naturalized individualism in biological and economic theory, both of which imagined naturally bounded "hard" entities unshaped by context, able to move unencumbered through the world without drag. Similarly, turn-of-the-century biological scientist August Weismann theorized a "particulate" internal germ line, a mechanism that allowed organisms to exist and perpetuate themselves unaffected by external conditions (Keller 2010). This version of development limited the number of "actors" involved in reproduction to the essential germ or genes of individual men and women, not their surroundings. Weismann's model fit well with the late nineteenth-century liberal political economic theory that featured rational individual Euro-American male actors, whose reasoned natures allowed them to rise above passion and impulse.

Scientific and economic proponents of this new "hard" version of nature (e.g., Galton, Weismann, and Herbert Spencer) posited that since external social or historical influences did little to change an individual organism, there was no need to educate or support certain groups now defined as belonging to rigid biological categories, such as imbeciles, inferior races, females, and criminals. Thus, this version of nature removed the politics, history, and economics of institutions like American slavery from the understanding of differences in human development. Thus, new kinds of biological subjects were generated, whose roles were naturalized in the political economic order. This essentialized version of nature came to be shared even by Euro-American progressives. Increasingly, their arguments against conservatives focused on debates about which characteristics were innate, debates which accepted the existence of innate nature itself (Degler 1991; Keller 2010).

We can see how prevalent this version of nature became, even among social reformers, through the thought of two feminist thinkers and activists who had dramatically opposing views about the origins of sexual difference. In 1864, Frances Power Cobbe, a suffragist and anti-vivisection activist from a prominent Irish family, affirmed her agreement with John Stuart Mill in his argument against the legal subordination of women, but stood with Darwin against Mill in asserting that differences between men and women came from inherited qualities rather than education or life circumstances (Paul and Day 2008). A little while later, the American feminist anarchist Emma Goldman, coming from much more modest means, argued that education shaped capacities and sex differences. At the same time, in her 1912 tract advocating a new model of education, she wrote, "It is essential that we realize once and for all that man is much more of a sex creature than a moral creature. The former is inherent, the other is grafted on" (Goldman 2009). Cobbe's and Goldman's differences about the innateness of particular forms of human difference illustrate how, at their base, their arguments for nurture profoundly accepted the terms of a now hardened and essential nature.

CULTURE'S CONSTRUCTION

Early twentieth-century American anthropology was established on the basis of the now prevalent distinction between nature and nurture, as the novice discipline became central to national and international debates about what shapes human beings, especially in regard to race and sex. At first, culture was deployed to describe groups of people in their specific environments (e.g., Franz Boas's historical particularism), but in combatting scientific racism, cultural anthropologists came to explain human difference through an insistence on a malleable cultural variability, that like nurture, overlay a shared universal biology, forming a template that also informed theories of sex difference (Degler 1991).

Two of the first anthropologists to focus on women, Ruth Benedict and Margaret Mead, were tireless defenders of cultural variation and cultural malleability, specifically in their focus on how culture shapes personality. For Benedict, cultural anthropology was the study of what was not carried in the germ cell, or that which could not be altered (Benedict 1934). Mead's early and lasting fame came from her performance of a cultural anthropological veto, debunking the notion that adolescence was innately and universally stormy. In her Samoan monograph, among the first to foreground female experience at all, Mead found that female adolescence in Samoa offered a smooth transition into adulthood, unmarked by the psychological distress, anxiety, and confusion so common in the United States (Mead 1953). In Mead's later book, *Sex and Temperament in Three Primitive Societies*, she offered an early version of the sex/gender distinction by proposing that the personality qualities of men and women varied so widely in New Guinea that they could not be biological; thus the behaviors and roles of women and men everywhere were not innate (Mead 1963). For both Mead and Benedict the distinction was clear: nature determined universal traits and behaviors, while non-universal behavior (the non-germ) was the product of culture.

Mead and Benedict provided mid-twentieth-century cultural anthropology with the means of cultural critique, delivering examples of how the mechanism of human variability—culture—makes human life vary, thus launching a politics of comparison. With her *Redbook* columns, her close relationship to Dr. Benjamin Spock, and nationally televised interviews and recordings, it was Mead, especially, who became the public voice of anthropology, using cultural comparison to denaturalize entrenched ideas about child rearing and sex difference in the United States. She is one of several mid-century social scientists credited with convincing much of the American public about the weight of nurture within the nature/nurture debate (Degler 1991). The next generation of anthropologists critiqued the lack of attention to political economic histories in these cultural accounts, which assumed that cultures were formulated as discrete, ahistorical, integral wholes (Mintz 1985). And now, with double hindsight, we can examine how the mid-century cultural anthropologists who examined practices like puberty rites cross-culturally, without investigating the bodily processes themselves involved in puberty, ceded the very grounds of race and sex to nature and thus to biological determinists (Visweswaran 1998).

From the 1970s on, feminist anthropology, involved in interdisciplinary conversations with feminist historians, philosophers, political scientists, and literary theorists, extended the analysis of cultural and social forces as distinct from "nature," now explicitly addressing power relations and history. This work took place amid the rehardening of biological determinism, after a mid-century lull, through the rise of conservative sociobiology championed, across a range of fields, by biologists such as Richard Dawkins and political scientists such as Charles Murray. In combatting sociobiology and enduring social Darwinism, feminist anthropologists joined the broad humanities/social science project of social construction, an argument that our sense of reality is constructed through social forms, especially emphasizing the force of ideologies based in historical and political economic forms of dominance and inequality. One of the key contributions of feminist theory in this period was the social constructionist distinction between sex and gender, which provided a means to talk about social variations in gender across time and space (Rubin 1975). The sex/gender distinction prevented the conflation of biology with social, psychological, and cultural attributes, countering the biological determinism that equated women with their reproductive and domestic capacities. The specific contribution of feminist anthropologists to the analysis of the social construction of sex/gender continued to focus on ethnographically demonstrating that gender categories, institutions, and practices are shaped through relations of power. While not universal (although female subordination was understood to be), these categories are constituted differently in different places and hence not reducible to biology (Reiter [now Rapp] 1975).

As I'll describe next, "social construction" has recently come under critique from feminist anthropologists of science and medicine, and other STS scholars, for furthering enlightenment logics that separate the material from the ideational world; however, social construction contained important streams of thought that allowed for its very undoing. Sherry Ortner's classic and still rhetorically powerful 1974 article "Is Female to Male as Nature Is to Culture?" exemplifies both the further codification of nature/culture in this period and the possibility of its own dissolution. Through a comparative and structuralist tour of the ethnographic record, mixed with the feminist analyses of Simone de Beauvoir and Nancy Chodorow, Ortner argued that across the ethnographic record, "Women are seen as closer to nature, and nature is devalued because of the universally valued ability to manipulate and transcend nature." Read today, Ortner's proposal that women should become more aligned with "culture," which she defines as the control and transcendence of nature through "systems of thought and technology," is unsatisfying, because culture here partakes of the same Enlightenment logic that brought us the nature/culture divide and positioned women as closer to nature in the first place. At the same time, Ortner's analysis contains tantalizing possibilities that resonate with contemporary feminist thought. Anticipating thinkers like Margaret Lock and Donna Haraway, Ortner describes "a (sadly) efficient feedback system: various aspects of women's situation (physical, social, psychological) contribute to her being seen as closer to nature, while the view of her as closer to nature is in turn embodied in institutional forms that reproduce her situation" (Ortner 1974, 87). Here status and life circumstances bleed into each other, creating a feedback loop, superseding nature and culture, in making lived, sexed experience in the world.

NATURE IN QUESTION

Feminist anthropologists of the 1970s and 1980s focused on exploring the variability of gendered behavior and gender systems, a crucial background for understanding the emergence of a feminist anthropology of science, medicine, and biotechnology. Feminist anthropological revitalization of kinship studies provided much of the impetus, challenging the very nature of kinship and reproduction, and turning several feminist anthropologists' attention to the expert discourses of medicine and science that socially constructed relatedness and sex (Franklin 1995). This move also reflected a broader change within anthropology in which urban centers and institutions in the United States and Western Europe were now seen as important sites of anthropological analysis.

Much of the examination of medicine and science was inspired by poststructural accounts of how scientific medicine became a powerful form of governance by claiming itself to be about nature, thus outside of politics. Feminist scholars across several disciplines extended Michel Foucault's analysis of how expert discourse about supposedly apolitical, universal, and innate biological processes generated individuated, gendered, and raced bodies. As the philosopher Judith Butler contends, "the materialization of bodies as matter-prior-to-power is in fact power's greatest effect" (Butler 1993). Deploying poststructuralist approaches, feminist scholars delineated how expert categories such as "maternal and infant mortality," "reproductive health," "biological clocks," and "global health statistics" are naturalized in ways that have powerful material effects in shaping the life conditions of women and men as gendered/sexed beings (Adams and Pigg 2005; Casper 1998; Erikson 2001, 2012; Ginsburg 1998; Rapp 1999). Until recently, however, the bulk of these interrogations of body politics tended to focus on discourse, leaving aside bodily processes themselves.

Alongside feminist historians and philosophers, feminist anthropologists examined how the roles, characteristics, and trajectories of women and men, which can seem so private, personal, intimate, medical, natural, and biological, are thoroughly political and economic, and serve as a key site of global processes that are saturated with stratifications of race, labor, and class (Ginsburg and Rapp 1995). In particular, feminist anthropologists identified medicine, science, and biotechnology as key sites for the production of inequalities of sex and gender, not only in the Global North or in cosmopolitan centers of the Global South, but nearly everywhere.

Much of the feminist anthropological work that investigated the production of body politics emerged through the developing fields of medical anthropology and STS in the late twentieth century. Medical anthropology began as an applied endeavor, where anthropologists assisted biomedical, public health, and development experts, both internationally and domestically, in understanding how cultural context contributes to underlying biological etiologies of ill health (Foster and Anderson 1978). More critical strains of medical anthropology, developed in the 1970s and 1980s, criticized anthropology for serving as a handmaiden to biomedicine, which invariably individualizes and naturalizes health and disease as well as race and sex (Gordon 1988; Singer and Baer 1995). Through the critical analysis of medicalization, feminist medical anthropologists have documented how bodily processes come to be understood and managed through a primarily individualizing medical lens, therefore bracketing out the political and social world. Examples included the examination of the medicalization of baby feeding in shanty-town Brazil, where malnourished women pay for infant formula because their breast milk is "tainted" (Scheper-Hughes 1992) and plastic surgery performed on Asian women in the San Francisco Bay Area in the 1980s "enliven" their "passive" and "dull" eyes and noses (Kaw 1993). As several feminist medical anthropologists have argued, it's imperative to analyze these processes empirically, since women and their supporters respond to medicalization in often surprising and pragmatic ways that defy simple, one-dimensional, overly confident political prescriptions (Lock and Kaufert 1998). In other words, empirical ethnographic studies of science, medicine, and technology are often inherently ambivalent, as they map how patients come to make "choices" that make sense within the unequal distribution of resources and the ongoing stratifications of race, sex, and class.

The growth of medical anthropology, combined with the revitalization of kinship studies by feminist anthropologists, produced dynamic insights about the deployment of nature in the cultural construction of reproduction and kinship, especially in Euro-American sites (Weiner 1995). Along with the investigation of queer kinship and same-sex parenting, new assisted reproductive technologies provided an obvious site for anthropological investigations of "the natural order," especially sex and gender (Lewin 1993; Weston 1997). As has been pointed out in most feminist cultural anthropological accounts, by producing new Euro-American kinship configurations, queer kinship and assisted reproduction reordered both culture and nature, in ways that have contributed to their analytical undoing (Thompson 2005).

Feminist anthropologists have specifically analyzed practices such as abortion, infertility, birth, assisted reproduction, and same-sex parenting to great comparative effect. Critical analyses of pregnancy and childbirth demonstrate how processes deemed natural and universal in Euro-American contexts are thoroughly shaped within the material, semiotic, and relational contexts where they are situated (Ivry 2010; Jordan 1997; Pinto 2008; Van Hollen 2003). The anthropological literature on conception and abortion, for example, has illuminated starkly different conceptions of personhood, showing how personhood in various non-Western sites sometimes commences postpartum, and that frequently the concept of individual life holds little relevance to how new people are made. Such relativizing has served to provincialize the fixation in North American abortion debates on when life begins (Browner 1976; Conklin and Morgan 1996; Picone 1998; Taylor 2008).

As noted earlier, assisted reproductive technologies are an especially useful site for comparative work on biology, human life, and nature. Starting in the early 1990s, Marilyn Strathern drew on her longstanding delineation of relational personhood in New Guinea to analyze the Euro-American use of ARTs. Strathern outlined how in these contexts, ARTs created anxiety because of the Euro-American separation of nature from artifice (Strathern 2005). Strathern's work opened up a vast array of comparative questions for current ethnographers of reproduction, especially feminist anthropologists interested in examining the effects of the ARTs on women (Mamo 2007; Modell 1991). In line with Strathern's work, ethnographers who study the use of ARTs outside Europe and the United States and those who have made comparisons within Europe make it clear that anxieties about ARTs in these locales are based on a particular version of nature that is in fact regional and historical (Bamford 2007; Bharadwaj 2006; Handwerker 1995; Kahn 2000). Marcia Inhorn's ongoing work on the use of reproductive technologies across Lebanon, Egypt, and the United Arab Emirates demonstrates that concerns about the life of embryos are not universal and IVF practice within Islamic countries varies widely (Inhorn 1996; Inhorn, Chavkin, and Navarro 2014). In my own scholarship on ARTs in Ecuador, the work of Strathern and other feminist anthropological and STS scholars enabled me to notice how assisted reproduction in Ecuador was not experienced as an artificial imposition on natural biological processes because nature was not assumed to be stable or separate from human action (Roberts 2013).

While much of the feminist anthropological scholarship of medicine, science, and biotechnology since the 1980s made an implicit distinction between biological and cultural processes, this work, steeped in the ambivalence of examining processes that have profoundly complicated effects, eventually made it possible to trouble the categories of nature and culture that shaped how human life was framed in Europe and North America throughout the twentieth century (Franklin 1995). These insights resonate with recent critical work in feminist medical anthropology and STS that diffuse and redistribute the self-evident nature of nature and technology by examining how biological processes themselves are shaped through historic, economic, and political realities.

NATURE CONSTRUCTED

The feminist anthropology of science, medicine, and biotechnology is aligned with the work of other social scientists, feminist theorists, philosophers, historians, and sociologists who have increasingly found the nature/culture divide inadequate for describing the reality of human life. These scholars have argued that the continued assertion of social or cultural constructionism strengthens a sense of nature as a "space outside of human agency" (Helmreich 2009, 159) and contributes little to the analysis of women's experience, even in Euro-American sites. Some of these scholars have moved away from *social* constructionism toward constructionism, where the material world or what has been framed as nature is also understood as contingent (Haraway 1991; Latour 2005). Whereas social constructionism distinguishes the malleable, ideational social world from the fixed object world, constructionism challenges the distinction between social modes or narratives that organize "reality" in multiple ways on top of a singular set of underlying fixed universal biological processes. Within constructionism, objects and facts are both real and constructed, and ontologies are as multiple as epistemologies (Mol 2002).

Constructionist scholars argue for material interconnectedness, proposing terms like "nature/cultures" (Haraway 1991), or dispensing with the terms altogether, employing approaches that analyze the world without privileging natural phenomena as grounding universal or ultimate determinants of the "hard" truth. Following this logic, entities as different as women, men, scallops, water pumps, computers, legislatures, tomatoes, microorganisms, and divinities are all constructed and the task at hand is to investigate how they are made without engaging in domain classification and boundary policing. For instance, biologist Anne Fausto-Sterling provides a model for how sex and sexual inequality are made simultaneously through social, genetic, epigenetic, hormonal, and gonadal pathways that are impossible to separate into nature or culture (Fausto-Sterling 2012).

Constructionism changes the relationship of human activity to the material world, and redefines technology; it decenters human activity by examining it like anything else that shapes the world, for example, erosion, gravity, the movements of insects, all of which disperse heroic (male) accounts of technology based on knowing subjects that affect passive nature. Constructionism points to happenstance, unintended effects, and the distribution of agency among actors. Instead of characterizing technology as a fully agentive product of human intervention in the material world, constructionists describe technology as "an organ of the human species" (Canguilhem 1992, 55), or several species, for that matter, given that all kinds of creatures construct their world with external objects (Feeley-Harnick 2014). Thus, within a constructionist analysis, technology is not inherently alienating, although it certainly can be (Mol, Moser, and Pols 2010). Within constructionism, humans are part of the world, not outside of nature, an analytical stance that prevents certain groups (women, for example) from being "closer to nature." Constructionism allows us to examine the relative contribution of various forces at work in creating phenomena, for example, how humans are driving climate change and antibiotic resistance without engaging in a story of "nature lost" (Landecker 2015).

This recent transformation of nature within the social sciences is mirrored in the "hard" sciences themselves through bio-scientific efforts that posit complex conditioning entanglements between organisms and environment. The expanding fields of evolutionary developmental biology, epigenetics, and research into the microbiome and the exposome can be read as responses to the inability of deterministic genetics to provide full explanations for phenotype and behavior (Barker 1990; Jablonka and Lamb 2005; Jirtle and Skinner 2007). These approaches offer a framework for the study of the ways external environmental exposures such as pollutants and foods can alter the expression of genes and exert long-term effects on phenotype, even in adult bodies, brains, and behavior, through mechanisms such as epigenetic DNA methylation and exchanges between human and bacterial cells within the human body (Hewagama and Richardson 2009).

Overlapping interests, like these between the social and biological sciences suggest that the "science wars" of the 1980s and 1990s, during the heyday of sociobiology and social constructionism, are waning. I would argue that most feminist social scientists of science and medicine and biological scientists now share an intensive interest in how the world is made. Thus, feminist medical anthropology and STS have much to offer biological researchers, who still narrowly define what they call "social determinants" and continue to situate key disease-transmission mechanisms exclusively inside individual bodies rather than within larger histories (Lock 2013). For instance, epigenetics researchers in the United States tend to direct the implications of their findings on the effects of the uterine environment to the fetus or individuals rather than larger political economic infrastructural problems that shape disease. This approach makes women (yet again) as mothers, into reproductive "containers" whose bodies come to be appropriate sites for individual intervention and control especially among poor women of color (Mansfield 2012). And it seems that the recodification of thoroughly American stories of race and sex are at play in the work of microbiome researchers who claim that the vaginal microbial communities of Asian and Caucasian women are more alike than those of Hispanic and African American women. Instead of using their findings to complicate how race is constructed (i.e., possibly through shared histories, microbial communities, and/or consumption patterns), these researchers reessentialize racial categories through an old colonial template that "discovered" essential race and sex difference through female genitalia (Helmreich 2014).

Given the greater resources and status the biological sciences continue to enjoy, caution is warranted for the feminist anthropologists participating in the at-times exhilarating collapse of nature/culture. We need to ask: what work do these transformations do for our accounts of the world? Why are they possible now among both biological and social scientists? Whose interests do they serve (corporations, politicians, women, activists, academics)? And importantly, what does the implosion of nature/ culture do to all of the careful and important antiracist and progressive feminist work that deployed social constructionism as a way to combat the biological determinisms of race and sex? These questions are key, given that biological determinism is by no means dead, within and outside the academy, as we can see in the continued popularity of evolutionary psychology to explain the "innate" behavior of "choosy" women as they pick male mates, and "promiscuous" men who "need spread their seed," or the ongoing conflation of race with genes (Wade 2014). When nature is still cast as universal and immutable, constructionism—with its engagement with biology—could easily be read as taking the side of biological determinism.

To make an argument for the real but constructed character of race and sex is to court trouble; yet, several feminist scholars, including anthropologists, have indeed begun the work of deessentializing biology, giving it a political history that demonstrates how bodies themselves are constructed in particular times and places. For example, Margaret Lock's foundational book *Encounters with Aging* (1993) provided an early example of this comparative constructionist approach. At the time of her study, women in North America experienced hot flashes, while women in Japan did not (Lock 1993). Lock argued that these differences did not derive from dissimilar cultural perceptions but, more provocatively, that these different places produced different "local biologies," constructed "within fields of thick historical and economic relations resulting in human biological difference" (Lock and Nguyen 2010, 90). A "local biologies" approach accepts these processes as biologically real while simultaneously understanding them as historically contingent. In Lock's account, North American women's hot flashes were not "in their heads," but are part of their lived bodily experience of twentieth-century North American industrial life. Local biologies is now a central concept in contemporary medical anthropological and STS-informed anthropology. By analyzing phenomena without dividing them into cultural and natural domains, the concept of local biologies helps reformulate the analysis of gender, since it demonstrates that women's and men's biological processes are not universal, thereby dismantling a key argument of biological determinists about the essential nature of sex.

The decline of nature/culture distinctions in feminist analysis has also brought about the collapse of the certainty that the most relevant biological unit is the individual as *he* emerged in nineteenth-century European biological and economic narratives. As Donna Haraway argues, reproductive technologies are not only expensive techno-medical procedures that treat individual women's bodies, but are complex economic and biological processes, and along with IVF, diaper pins, home births, accounting techniques, population politics, breast milk, and baby formula, are all reproductive technologies (Haraway and Goodeve 2000).

Taking her cue from Haraway, feminist historian of science Michelle Murphy argues that if we ask, "Where does biological reproduction reside?" the answer "the body" is simply not up to the task (Murphy 2011). Murphy advances a framework of "distributed reproduction" that allows us to examine "what counts as biological reproduction by tracking the dispersion of sexed living beings into their infrastructural and political economic milieu" (Murphy 2011, 22). The notion of the individual body is not up to the task, for instance, of understanding how in Eastern Canada, only 35 boys are born for every 100 girls among the First Nations Aamjiwnaang peoples, while in the local waterways, the gonads and sex ratios of fish, fowl, and reptiles have also been dramatically altered (Murphy 2013). To grasp the biological level of sexed reproduction here, Murphy argues, we need to move beyond individual bodies and trace the specific tangles of science, nation states, capital, the malleable and vulnerable endocrine processes of fish and people, the fluid dynamics of rivers, and the techno-assemblages of chemical manufacture, population politics, and corporate tax policies.

Murphy's project also critiques heteronormative views of reproductive time that works through vertical generations. Her focus on time links her to scholars working under the rubric of queer biologies, another constructivist approach that explores and celebrates the vast array of the earth's biotic possibilities (e.g., that sex change is common among some species), while remaining critical of political-economic processes like the rampant chemical dumping that contributes to the current upswing in ambiguously sexed amphibians (Hayward 2011; Seymour 2013). Through a constructionist framework then, biology becomes a constructed domain requiring a broad analytic and ambivalent lens to fully account for the wide array of actors and processes involved in its production.

A constructionist framework can also expand our sense of what a biotechnology is. For example, in twentieth-century Euro-American contexts, regular monthly menstruation has been understood as a natural, timeless, female biological process. Throughout the twentieth century doctors have attempted to scientifically regulate the bodies of women who did not menstruate regularly; indeed, the technology of the birth control pill was developed around the assumed natural order of monthly periods. Later on, the assumption of a regular menstruation became a crucial platform for most ARTs that sought conception. Some strands of the feminist health movement from the 1970s also participated in the "nature" of monthly menstruation by celebrating women's powerful monthly "moon time," which contributed to later popular narratives about the female sociality produced in a monthly visit to the menstrual hut in small-scale societies (Baker 1978; Diamant 1997). More recently, though, biological anthropologists have found monthly menstruation to be a product of capitalist industrial processes that radically reduced family size, produced extremely effective, cheap, mass-produced, contraceptive methods and increased body size and lifespan, so that women in industrialized nations spend much less of their lives pregnant or nursing than among smaller scale non-industrial groups (Strassman 1999). Thus "moon time" is also cyclical, regularized, technological, capitalist time, and a menstruating woman might have been lonely in the menstrual hut.

Through a constructionist lens, we can analyze monthly menstruation as among the conditions of life in industrial capitalism, a non-agentive biotechnology in itself that regulates capitalist bodies, just as irregular menstruation is part of the conditions of life among non-industrial groups. Like menopause, neither menstrual pattern nor local biology is more or less natural or cultural, and both modes of existence have important and ambiguous material effects on women's lives. The increased rate of breast cancers in industrial societies might relate to increased cell division involved in monthly menstruation, while multiple pregnancies did and can shorten women's lives depending on life circumstances. Recent proposals by doctors, women's health advocates, and pharmaceutical corporations to hormonally end monthly menstruation do not have to be analyzed as departing from or bringing us back to nature, but do require a thorough examination of the unknown effects of introducing these hormones into women's bodies, as well as the interests of pharmaceutical companies, that are, of course, central to the workings of industrial capitalism. We can do a similar constructionist analysis of the consumption of hormones by transpeople, athletes, men with erectile dysfunction, and menopausal women, all groups who have been celebrated or excoriated through appeals to nature. This is complicated and ambivalent political work, when technology becomes biological process and nature no longer serves as a unified and holistic guide.

CONCLUSION

The insights of contemporary feminist anthropological approaches to medicine, science, and technology, in all their ambivalence, have played a large part in the dramatic change in the status of "nature" and "technology," both inside and outside of feminist theory and anthropology. In strands of social science and some areas of the life sciences, biological processes are no longer modeled as innate universals but rather located in time and space, an approach that makes it more difficult to maintain a qualitative difference between nature and culture, or nature and technology.

Thus, contemporary feminist anthropologists, enmeshed in ongoing technological ambivalence, base their arguments not on essentialist nature as their guide, but within an expanding approach that posits nature as constructed, and medicine, science, and biotechnologies as a set of practices and realities specifically embedded in particular material circumstances saturated with power relations that shape how differently situated people will use them. Contemporary debates about the use of biotechnologies illuminate an enduring feminist engagement with how sex/gender continually shapes the way people navigate complex life circumstances, especially those—deemed natural—focused on controlling female reproductive processes.

Feminist anthropological accounts about the entanglements of variable biologies, brought to the fore by the collapse of the nature/culture lens, resonate with larger feminist projects that contest determinisms of sexual and racial difference circulating under the depoliticized order of nature. These feminist contributions have the potential to transform conversations in anthropology more generally, influencing how we constitute our objects of study, what questions we ask, how we might collaborate across fields, and how to create new politics when nature/culture divides no longer configure the boundaries of our discipline.

ACKNOWLEDGMENTS

Profuse thanks to Ellen Lewin and Leni Silverstein for inviting me to participate in this volume and their wonderful encouragement and editorial acumen throughout the process. I'm indebted to Ara Wilson for her critical eye in the early stages of writing this chapter as well as for our ongoing conversations and debates about feminism and anthropology. Rayna Rapp's wise guidance and astute suggestions allowed me to frame the final version.

NOTE

1. Franklin's framing of this issue, as well as Inhorn's initial op-ed, allow us to address a vexing issue for any collectivist, progressive agenda: how to bring about broad social change, while also grappling with the reality of pressing problems at (what is experienced as) the "individual" level. This problem is especially relevant to the highly individualist context of the United States, where it is difficult to maintain a collective response in the face of the material experience of autonomy in complex life circumstances. For instance, how does a young, politically progressive, female academic in the United States, facing family-unfriendly policies, deal with the reality that she might have a hard time conceiving later on, when she is more financially and professionally secure? What is she to do even if she has been organizing for better working conditions, including family leave, inside and out of universities her entire adult life? That struggle is not nearly won, and probably won't be for years. This young woman might thoroughly historicize her desire to have children, as contingent on histories of race, sex, and industrial capitalism, and egg freezing might or might not be on the table, but under these non-ideal, individualizing conditions, her response might very well include more than a social activist way forward.

REFERENCES

Adams, Vincanne, and Stacy Leigh Pigg. 2005. *Sex in Development: Science, Sexuality, and Morality in Global Perspective*. Durham, NC: Duke University Press.

Arditti, Rita, Shelley Minden, and Renate Klein. 1984. *Test-Tube Women: What Future for Motherhood?* London: Pandora Press.

Baker, Jeannine Parvati. 1978. *Hygieia: A Woman's Herbal*. Albion, CA: Freestone Publishing.

Bamford, Sandra C. 2007. *Biology Unmoored: Melanesian Reflections on Life and Biotechnology*. Berkeley: University of California Press.

Barker, Charles. 1990. "The Fetal and Infant Origins of Adult Disease." *British Medical Journal* 301 (6761): 1111.

Benedict, Ruth. 1934. *Patterns of Culture*. Boston and New York: Houghton Mifflin.

Bharadwaj, Aditya, ed. 2006. "Sacred Conceptions: Religion and the Global Practice of IVF—Special Issue." *Culture Medicine and Psychiatry* 30: 423–425.

Browner, Carole. 1976. "Poor Women's Fertility Decisions: Illegal Abortion in Cali, Colombia." PhD dissertation, University of California, Berkeley.

Butler, Judith P. 1993. *Bodies That Matter: On the Discursive Limits of "Sex."* New York: Routledge.

Canguilhem, Georges. 1992. "Machine and Organisim" In *Incorporations*, ed. Jonathan Crary and Sanford Winter, 44–67. New York: Zone Books.

Casper, Monica J. 1998. *The Making of the Unborn Patient: A Social Anatomy of Fetal Surgery*. New Brunswick, NJ: Rutgers University Press.

Conklin, Beth A., and Lynn M. Morgan. 1996. "Babies, Bodies, and the Production of Personhood in North America and the Native Amazonian Society." *Ethos* 24 (4): 657–694.

Corea, Gena. 1988. *The Mother Machine: Reproductive Technologies from Artificial Insemination to Artificial Wombs*. London: Women's Press.

Daston, Lorraine, and Peter Galison. 1992. "The Image of Objectivity." *Representations* 40: 81–128.

Degler, Carl N. 1991. *In Search of Human Nature: The Decline and Revival of Darwinism in American Social Thought*. New York: Oxford University Press.

Diamant, Anita. 1997. *The Red Tent*. New York: St. Martin's Press.

Erikson, Susan. 2001. "Maternity Care Policies and Maternity Care Practices: A Tale of Two Germanys." In *Birth by Design: Pregnancy, Maternity Care, and Midwifery in North America and Europe*, ed. Raymond DeVries, Cecilia Benoit, Edwin Van, and Sirpa Wrede Teijlingen, 203–217. London, New York: Routledge.

———. 2012. "Global Health Business: The Production and Performativity of Statistics in Sierra Leone and Germany." *Medical Anthopology* 31 (4): 367–384.

Fausto-Sterling, Anne. 2012. *Sex/Gender: Biology in a Social World*. New York: Routledge.

Feeley-Harnick, Gillian. 2014. "Bodies Words and Work: Charles Darwin and Lewis Henry Morgan on Human–Animal Relations." In *America's Darwin: Darwinian Theory and US Literary Culture*, ed. Tina Ginaquitto and Lydia Fisher, 265–301. Athens: University of Georgia Press.

Foster, George McClelland, and Barbara Gallatin Anderson. 1978. *Medical Anthropology*. New York: Wiley.

Franklin, Sarah. 1995. "Science as Culture, Cultures of Science." *Annual Review of Anthropology* 24: 163–184.

———. 2013a. *Biological Relatives: IVF, Stem Cells, and the Future of Kinship, Experimental Futures, Technological Lives, Scientific Arts, Anthropological Voices*. Durham, NC: Duke University Press.

———. 2013b. "Egg Freezing Commentary." *Repronet*. https://www.facebook.com/AnthroRepro/posts/10151343049506470, accessed July 19, 2014.

Ginsburg, Faye D. 1998 (1989). *Contested Lives: The Abortion Debate in an American Community*. Berkeley: University of California Press.

Ginsburg, Faye D., and Rayna Rapp, eds. 1995. *Conceiving the New World Order: The Global Politics of Reproduction*. Berkeley: University of California Press.

Goldman, Emma. 2009. "The Social Importance of the Modern School." http://dwardmac.pitzer.edu/Anarchist_Archives/goldman/socimportms.html, accessed August 5, 2014.

Gordon, Deborah. 1988. "Tenacious Assumptions in Western Medicine." In *Biomedicine Examined: Culture, Illness, and Healing*, ed. Margaret M. Lock and Deborah R. Gordon, 19–56. Dordrecht: Kluwer Academic Publishers.

Handwerker, Lisa. 1995. "The Hen That Can't Lay an Egg: Conceptions of Female Infertility in Modern China." In *Deviant Bodies*, ed. Jennifer Terry and Jacquline Urla, 358–386. Bloomington: Indiana University Press.

Haraway, Donna Jeanne. 1991. *Simians, Cyborgs, and Women: The Reinvention of Nature*. London: Free Association.

Haraway, Donna Jeanne, and Thyrza Nichols Goodeve. 2000. *How Like a Leaf: An Interview with Donna Haraway*. New York: Routledge.

Hayward, Eva. 2011. "When Fish and Frogs Change Gender." *Indy Week*. http://www.indyweek.com/indyweek/when-fish-and-frogs-change-gender/Content?oid=2626271, accessed August 6, 2014.

Helmreich, Stefan. 2009. *Alien Ocean: Anthropological Voyages in Microbial Seas*. Berkeley: University of California Press.

———. 2014. "Homo Microbis: The Human Microbiome, Figural, Literal, Political." *Thresholds* 42: 52–59.

Hewagama, Anura, and Bruce Richardson. 2009. "The Genetics and Epigenetics of Autoimmune Diseases." *Journal of Autoimmunity* 33: 3–11.

Inhorn, Marcia. 1996. *Infertility and Patriarchy*. Philadelphia: University of Pennsylvania Press.

———. 2013. "Women, Consider Freezing Your Eggs." *CNN Opinion*. http://www.cnn.com/2013/04/09/opinion/inhorn-egg-freezing/, accessed July 19, 2014.

Inhorn, Marcia C., Wendy Chavkin, and José-Alberto Navarro, eds. 2014. *Globalized Fatherhood*. New York: Berghahn.

Ivry, Tsipy. 2010. *Embodying Culture: Pregnancy in Japan and Israel*. New Brunswick, NJ: Rutgers University Press.

Jablonka, Eva, and Marion J. Lamb. 2005. *Evolution in Four Dimensions: Genetic, Epigenetic, Behavioral, and Symbolic Variation in the History of Life*. Cambridge, MA: MIT Press.

Jirtle, Randy L., and Michael K. Skinner. 2007. "Environmental Epigenomics and Disease Susceptibilty." *Nature Reviews* 8: 253–262.

Jordan, Brigitte. 1997. "Authoritative Knowledge and Its Construction." In *Childbirth and Authoritative Knowledge: Cross-Cultural Perspectives*, ed. Carolyn Fishel Sargent and Robbie Davis-Floyd, 55–79. Berkeley: University of California Press.

Kahn, Susan. 2000. *Reproducing Jews: A Cultural Account of Assisted Conception in Israel*. Durham, NC: Duke University Press.

Kaw, Eugenia. 1993. "Medicalization of Racial Features: Asian American Women and Cosmetic Surgery." *Medical Anthopology Quarterly* 17 (1): 74–89.

Keller, Evelyn Fox. 2010. *The Mirage of a Space between Nature and Nurture*. Durham, NC: Duke University Press.

Landecker, Hannah. 2015. "Antibiotic Resistance and the Biology of History." Body & Society. Published online before print http://bod.sagepub.com/content/early/2015/03/25/1357034X14561341.abstract, accessed April 15, 2014.

Latour, Bruno. 2005. *Reassembling the Social: An Introduction to Actor-Network Theory*. Oxford: Oxford University Press.

Lewin, Ellen. 1993. *Lesbian Mothers: Accounts of Gender in American Culture*. Ithaca, NY: Cornell University Press.

Lock, Margaret M. 1993. *Encounters with Aging: Mythologies of Menopause in Japan and North America*. Berkeley: University of California Press.

———. 2013. "The Epigenome and Nature/Nurture Reunification: A Challenge for Anthropology." *Medical Anthropology* 32: 291–308.

Lock, Margaret M., and Patricia A. Kaufert, eds. 1998. *Pragmatic Women and Body Politics*. New York: Cambridge University Press.

Lock, Margaret M., and Vinh-Kim Nguyen. 2010. *An Anthropology of Biomedicine*. Oxford: Wiley-Blackwell.

Mamo, Laura. 2007. *Queering Reproduction: Achieving Pregnancy in the Age of Technoscience*. Durham, NC: Duke University Press.

Mansfield, Becky. 2012. "Race and the New Epigenetic Biopolitics of Environmental Health." *BioSocieties* 7 (4): 352–372.

Mead, Margaret. 1953. *Coming of Age in Samoa: A Psychological Study of Primitive Youth for Western Civilisation*. New York: Modern Library.

———. 1963. *Sex and Temperment in Three Primitive Societies*. New York: Morrow Quill Paperbacks.

Mintz, Sidney Wilfred. 1985. *Sweetness and Power: The Place of Sugar in Modern History*. New York: Viking.

Modell, Judith. 1991. "Last Chance Babies: Interpretations of Parenthood in an *In Vitro* Fertilization Program." *Medical Anthropology Quarterly* 5: 124–138.

Mol, Annemarie. 2002. *The Body Multiple: Ontology in Medical Practice*. Durham, NC: Duke University Press.

Mol, Annemarie, Ingunn Moser, and Jeannette Pols. 2010. *Care in Practice: On Tinkering in Clinics Homes and Farms*. Netherlands: Transcript-Verlag.

Morgan, Lynn, and Janelle Taylor. 2013. "Op-Ed: Egg Freezing: WTF?*." *The Feminist Wire*. http://www.thefeministwire.com/2013/04/op-ed-egg-freezing-wtf/, accessed July 19, 2014.

Murphy, Michelle. 2011. "Distributed Reproduction." In *Corpus: An Interdisciplinary Reader on Bodies and Knowledge*, ed. Monica J. Casper and Paisley Currah, 21–39. New York: Palgrave Macmillan.

———. 2013. "Distributed Reproduction, Chemical Violence, and Latency." *The Scholar and The Feminist Online*. http://sfonline.barnard.edu/life-un-ltd-feminism-bioscience-race/distributed-reproduction-chemical-violence-and-latency/, accessed August 7, 2014.

Ortner, Sherry B. 1974. "Is Female Male as Nature Is to Culture?" In *Woman Culture, and Society*, ed. Michelle Zimbalist Rosaldo and Louise Lamphere, 67–87. Stanford, CA: Stanford University Press.

Paul, Diane B., and Benjamin Day. 2008. "John Stuart Mill, Innate Differences, and the Regulation of Reproduction." *Studies in History, Philosophy, and Biomedical Science* 39: 222–231.

Picone, Mary. 1998. "Infanticide, the Spirits of Aborted Fetuses, and the Making of Motherhood in Japan." In *Small Wars: The Cultural Politics of Childhood*, ed. Nancy Scheper-Hughes and Carolyn Fishel Sargent, 37–57. Berkeley: University of California Press.

Pinto, Sarah. 2008. *Where There Is No Midwife: Birth and Loss in Rural India*. New York: Berghahn Books.

Rae, Scott B. 1994. *The Ethics of Commercial Surrogate Motherhood: Brave New Families?* Westport, CT: Praeger.

Rapp, Rayna. 1999. *Testing Women, Testing the Fetus: The Social Impact of Amniocentesis in America*. New York: Routledge.

Reiter (Rapp), Rayna, ed. 1975. *Toward an Anthropology of Women*. New York: Monthly Review Press.

Roberts, Elizabeth F. S. 2013. "Assisted Existence: An Ethnography of Being in Ecuador." *Journal of the Royal Anthropolgical Institute* 19 (3): 562–580.

Rothman, Barbara Katz. 1988. "Reproductive Technology and the Commodification of Life." In *Embryos, Ethics, and Women's Rights*, ed. Elaine Baruch, Amadeo D'Adamo, and Joni Seager, 95–100. New York: Routledge.

Rubin, Gayle. 1975. "The Traffic in Women: Notes on the 'Political Economy' of Sex." In *Toward an Anthropology of Women*, ed. Rayna Reiter (Rapp), 157–210. New York: Monthly Review Press.

Scheper-Hughes, Nancy. 1992. *Death without Weeping: The Violence of Everyday Life in Brazil*. Berkeley: University of California Press.

Seymour, Nicole. 2013. *Strange Natures: Futurity, Empathy, and the Queer Ecological Imagination*. Urbana: University of Illinois Press.

Singer, Merrill, and Hans Baer. 1995. *Critical Medical Anthropology*. Amityville, NY: Baywood.

Stepan, Nancy. 1991. *The Hour of Eugenics: Race, Gender, and Nation in Latin America*. Ithaca, NY: Cornell University Press.

Strassman, Beverly. 1999. "Menstrual Cycling and Breast Cancer: An Evolutionary Perspective." *Journal of Women's Health* 8 (2): 193–202.

Strathern, Marilyn. 2005. *Kinship, Law, and the Unexpected: Relatives Are Always a Surprise.* New York: Cambridge University Press.

Taylor, Janelle S. 2008. *The Public Life of the Fetal Ultrasound: Technology, Consumption, and the Politics of Reproduction.* New Brunswick, NJ: Rutgers University Press.

Thompson, Charis. 2005. *Making Parents: The Ontological Choreography of Reproductive Technologies.* Cambridge, MA: MIT Press.

Toulmin, Stephen. 1996. "Descartes in His Time." In *Discourse on the Method and Meditations on First Philosophy,* ed. David Weissman, 121–146. New Haven, CT: Yale University Press.

Van Hollen, Cecilia. 2003. *Birth on the Threshold: Childbirth and Modernity in South India.* Berkeley: University of California Press.

Visweswaran, Kamala. 1998. "Race and the Culture of Anthropology." *American Anthropologist* 100 (1): 70–83.

Wade, Nicholas J. 2014. *A Troublesome Inheritance: Genes, Race, and Human History.* New York: Penguin Press.

Weiner, Annette. 1995. "Reassessing Reproduction In Social Theory." In *Conceiving the New World Order: The Global Politics of Reproduction,* ed. Faye Ginsburg and Rayna Rapp, 407–424. Berkeley: University of California Press.

Weston, Kath. 1997 (1991). *Families We Choose: Lesbians, Gays, Kinship.* New York: Columbia University Press.

CONCEPTIONS OF CONTRACEPTIONS

Feminist Anthropological Perspectives on Men, Women, and Reproductive Health in Two K'iche' Maya Communities

MATTHEW R. DUDGEON

Both through rich ethnography as well as nuanced theory, feminist anthropologists have drawn attention to women's lives and voices and revealed structures of power that largely privilege men. In doing so, the field has responded to Rayna Rapp's pioneering critique of anthropology: "[m]en's information is too often perceived as a group's reality, rather than as only part of a cultural whole" (1975, 12). But while feminist anthropology has brought a focused lens to the understanding of women's lives, the anthropological study of men and masculinity has only slowly begun to appear in the field. Indeed, Matthew C. Gutmann (1997) has described an "awkward avoidance" of feminist theory in anthropological studies of men, calling for more theoretically engaged investigations of what men do and what they do to be men.

Yet by decentering men in anthropological studies, feminist anthropology nonetheless has contributed new theoretical tools for the study of masculinity. A crucial feminist insight has been the cultural construction of gender, with particular emphasis on representation, performance (see Butler 1990), and power. By emphasizing constructionism, many feminist anthropologists have moved away from more polarizing theoretical stances (see MacKinnon 1989) to argue that "some ways of being a man are valued more than others" (Cornwall 1997, 12). Judith Gardiner succinctly describes a formula for broadening feminist studies of gender which she advocates as well for the studies of men: investigation of "hierarchies of dominance, relatively defined gender, and multiple and interactive axes of social oppression" (Gardiner 2005, 47). Patricia Hill Collins (2004) and others have elaborated on this concept of intersectionality, showing how overlapping, interlocking patterns of inequality interact and produce one another in historical context. But suffusing these feminist categories is the concept of power (Butler 1993; Yanagisako and Delaney 1995): *agentic* power wielded by men over women, children, and other men, as well as *discursive* power that produces, among others, masculine subjectivities and subject positions.

In particular, I use as starting points two feminist anthropological concepts that engage gender hierarchies as well as gendered embodiment. I will explore the concepts of stratified reproduction and local biologies to examine how men and women in two K'iche' communities in Guatemala make decisions about and experience the consequences of contraceptive use. Faye Ginsburg and Rayna Rapp (1995) discuss *stratified reproduction* (Colen 1995), by which the reproduction of members of some groups is encouraged and facilitated, while that of others is limited and hindered. Thomas Csordas (1988, 1994a, 1994b), Susan Bordo (1990a, 1990b, 1993), and others have made persuasive arguments for the centrality of physical bodies for grounding cultural meanings. Margaret Lock (1993) explores the contingent, *local biologies* of human bodies, that is, the plasticity of those bodies in varying environmental contexts.

These specific theoretical tools from feminist anthropology—stratified reproduction and local biologies—inform my use and interrogation of R. W. Connell's (1987) concept of *hegemonic masculinity*, the structures and practices which support and enact male dominance of women generally and also of some men. These structures exist relative to less idealized, or subordinate masculinities. Here, using contraception as a focus, I look at the intersection of hegemonic masculinity with the stratification of reproduction and the vernacular interpretations of biomedical interactions in two K'iche' Maya communities in western highland Guatemala.

MASCULINITY IN MAYA COMMUNITIES: PATRIARCHY, RESPONSIBLE AND OTHERWISE

Drawing on feminist anthropological perspectives and applying them to men and masculinity, I try to understand some of the stark differences as well as diffuse commonalities I encountered between two indigenous K'iche' communities. Between December 2001 and December 2004, I conducted dissertation fieldwork for sixteen months in the K'iche' communities of Jun in Cantel municipality and ten months in the community of Keb' in Chajul municipality. There

I explored how men and women thought about, experienced, and engaged in biological and cultural reproduction after suffering genocidal violence targeting ethnic Maya in the western highlands (Dudgeon 2013). I chose to work in these two communities because they represent two very different historical trajectories and experiences during the Guatemalan civil war. Jun, in proximity to a large *ladino (mestizo*/Iberian-identified) departmental capital, saw relatively little overt violence during the civil war, while Keb' (one of several *Comunidades de Población en Resistencia,* or Communities of Populations in Resistance, as discussed later), continues to be comprised of war refugees and endured direct military incursions and deaths.

Jun is connected economically to the department capital, Cantel, and other predominantly indigenous communities through trade in *corte* (women's woven dresses). Families in Jun (population approximately 3,500) participate in many other cash-earning activities, the most prevalent being the weaving of cloth on foot-pedal looms. Cantel municipality was the first Maya community to reject military occupation and imposed *rondas,* or surveillance rounds that men were required to make during the civil war.

Keb', located in Chajul, by contrast, is a much smaller community of approximately 500 individuals located in the northern Chuchumatanes mountains. Home to a multilingual group of predominantly K'iche' and Ixil Maya, the community was originally created by a group of K'iche' settlers from nearby departments. The group increased greatly in size at the beginning of the civil war, when refugees from other areas in the Ixil triangle entered the area. During the following months and years, Keb' became a Community of Populations in Resistance, one of many internally displaced communities in the Ixcán jungle during the civil war. These communities remained perpetually mobile to evade military intrusions, caught between the Guatemalan military and the guerrilla armies of the western highlands. The community "came back to light" in 1993, at the time of relative return to normalcy in the area, but before the formal signing of the Peace Accords in December 1996.

Gender relationships have broadly been cast in Maya communities as patriarchal in nature, but their patriarchy differs markedly from that found among non-Maya groups in Guatemala. When contrasting *ladino* and Maya groups in a community near Guatemala City in the mid-twentieth century, Eileen Maynard (1974) suggests that Maya culture is characterized by "responsible patriarchy" while *ladino* culture is characterized by "irresponsible patriarchy" (see Bastos 2000). In irresponsible patriarchy, *ladino* women cannot rely on *ladino* men for economic or emotional support "because of the *machismo* concept which glorifies the exploitation of women" (Maynard 1974, 96). She goes on to say that:

> The patriarchy places the Indian as well as the *Ladino* woman in a lower societal position, limits her freedom, and subjects her to the frustrations of male infidelity. Since, however, the concept of Indian masculinity includes responsibility to the family of procreation, the Indian woman is much more secure both emotionally and economically. Marriage for the Indian woman means more of a partnership—a partnership marked not so much by a battle of the sexes as by mutual help. (Maynard 1974, 96)

Thus, *ladino* women have power precisely because men abdicate their familial responsibilities; yet, for Maya women "the source of a woman's power in the family lies in the cultural definition of her role, a definition that recognizes her importance as wife, mother, and economic partner. All these roles are complementary to the man's role" (Maynard 1974, 98). Ethnographies of gender relations in various Maya communities throughout Meso-America document aspects of gender complementarity between men and women as they affect economic support, alcohol use, and domestic violence (Eber 1995; McClusky 2001; Rossenbaum 1993).

Although K'iche' men's accounts of pregnancy, childbirth, and contraceptive use in Jun and Keb' lend support to Maynard's observation that a very different gendered power dynamic exists in Maya groups, the concept of responsible patriarchy falls short of explaining why Maya men are accountable to their families. Her idea of responsible patriarchy is evocative, and presages Connell's concepts of hegemonic masculinity. However, it is static insofar as it does not explain (nor seek to explain) the dynamics that produce and reproduce gender complementarity over time. Moreover, it is difficult to reduce gender complementarity to economic roles in a community like Jun, where few men work as subsistence farmers and many men work as weavers, drivers, and teachers, while women undertake work opportunities outside the home. Even in Keb', the traditional roles of men and women were challenged by and evolved during the hardships of the civil war. While gendered relations of power continue to influence reproductive decisions, at the same time, the negotiation and consequences of those decisions play key roles in the persistence and transformation of gendered relations in Jun and Keb'.

CONCEPTIONS OF CONTRACEPTIONS

The dynamics of contraceptive use in Jun and Keb' provide a lens for examining the contradictions and ambivalences many men feel surrounding gender roles and familial responsibilities that lie at the intersection of responsible patriarchy and hegemonic masculinity. I detail patterns of contraceptive use in these two K'iche' communities to suggest ways contraceptives are used and negotiated between men and women. I then examine the transformative capacity of contraceptives more generally, looking at fears that contraceptives interfere with both familial as well as fetal development, in terms of biomedicines seen as inappropriate for Maya bodies, and small families as incompatible with Maya households. I explore a particular case that brings into focus the embodied conflicts some K'iche' Maya experience in using contraception, one of a young girl born with malformation of the upper and lower extremities in Keb'. I conclude with reflections on contraceptive decision making and the consequences of those decisions in K'iche' communities in light of the dynamics of masculinity.

The prevalence of overall contraceptive use in Guatemala has risen steadily among both *ladino* and indigenous Maya groups, although at different rates. From 1978 to 1998, contraceptive prevalence increased from 28 percent to 50 percent among *ladinos* and rose from 4 percent to 13 percent among Maya (Bertrand et al. 1999; Bertrand, Seiber, and Escudero 2001); national data (Guatemala 2003) show Depo Provera injections dominated service provision for new users. These numbers demonstrate, but do not explain, contraception stratification in Guatemala. From a purely demographic perspective, Guatemala's low overall contraceptive prevalence is largely "explained" by ethnicity: the Maya, a large proportion of Guatemala's population, use biomedical contraceptives infrequently. But actual patterns of Maya contraceptive use demand a more nuanced explanation. First, Maya reproductive health has been differently valued by the state. For most of Guatemala's history, Maya populations have been characterized as a flexible rural workforce limited by relatively low population levels after the postcolonial population collapse. Only in the twentieth century did the Maya population recover to the point that it posed an increasing demographic challenge to the Guatemalan state, with growing demands for improved worker's rights, education, and health care. I have argued elsewhere that this perceived demographic threat by the Guatemalan state influenced its shift in tactics in the civil war from counter-insurgency targeting mainly guerrilla fronts to wholesale genocide. In other words, genocidal violence was directed at the reproductive capacity of Maya as an ethnic group (Dudgeon 2013). Maya access to and use of contraception, impacted by the state's stratification of reproduction programs through forces as disparate as genocidal violence and contraceptive provision, must be understood from the perspective of Maya experiences of and responses to that stratification. At the same time, contraception is a field upon which Maya men encounter and perform aspects of hegemonic masculinity, a field to which I now turn by looking at contraceptive negotiations between couples.

MASCULINITY, MACHISMO, AND CONTRACEPTION—HEGEMONIC MAYA MASCULINITIES

Focusing on the negotiation of contraceptive use within couples brings into relief the ambiguities that surround contraceptive decision making for K'iche' men and women. Understanding K'iche' men's behaviors and experiences concerning family planning means trying to view Mayan men *as men* and *as Maya*. I will highlight aspects of normative K'iche' masculinity—in Connell's terms, hegemonic masculinity—that play a role in contraceptive use as well as in other masculine activities, and that anchor the dyadic power dynamics Maynard describes as responsible patriarchy. While conscious of avoiding gender stereotypes (Brannon 2011), I argue that Maya masculinity has some identifiable elements and is characterized by a kind of *machismo* that, not unsurprisingly, differs from *machismo* in other parts of Latin America. Both men and women in Jun and Keb' say that men are *macho*, but see their behavior as different from *ladino* machismo. *Ladino* machismo embodies a brasher, more flamboyant masculinity, while Maya *machismo* incorporates or coexists with elements such as humility, dedication, and hard work, dimensions outlined below. I refer to this Maya form of *machismo* as *Mayachismo.*[1] In my ethnographic research, I tried to distill several important dimensions of K'iche' hegemonic masculinity in the communities in which I worked, which included productivity, control, respect, and growth.[2] While by no means universal or exhaustive, these aspects capture many of the ideals of masculinity that men mentioned in interviews about being men, corroborated by my participant observation efforts. Moreover, two of these dimensions, control and respect, lie on a continuum that extends to *machismo* as hyper-masculine; these two dimensions play strong roles in men's contraceptive decision making. Men's exertion of control and requirements for respect, I argue, are not necessarily experienced as *machista* by K'iche' Maya men or women; these are, in fact, ideal characteristics to be used *in moderation* and valued by men and women alike, albeit often to different degrees. K'iche' men are *machista* in so far as they exert excessive or unnecessary control within their households and demand excessive or undeserved respect from its members. Contraceptive decision making provides men in Jun and Keb' with opportunities for and challenges to exerting control and receiving respect in their households and communities.

PATTERNS OF CONTRACEPTIVE USE: CONTRACEPTIVE AMBIGUITY

Contraceptive availability, state-run or otherwise, affects but does not determine contraceptive use in rural areas like Jun and Keb'; nevertheless, contraceptive use provides a window on reproduction *within* a subordinated strata. To understand community contraceptive use in Jun, particularly Depo Provera, the dominant method, I used retrospective data on contraceptive users collected from both the *puesto de salud* (health post) of Jun as well as a local contraceptive provider for the formerly United States Association for International Development (USAID)-funded Association for the Well-Being of the Family, Guatemala, or APROFAM (n = 167); added together, these data represent a minimum number of ever-users in the community over approximately the previous five years. At the time of my fieldwork, several contraceptive methods were available free of charge from the health post as well as the health center in Jun, including oral contraceptive pills, Depo Provera shots, and condoms. In Keb', Depo Provera shots were the only contraception option available, provided by a Canadian non-governmental health organization.

Reproductive health adoption among Guatemala's Maya communities is highly stratified, and the dynamics of that stratification are poorly understood from a purely epidemiologic perspective. Maya reproductive health is differently valued from *ladino/a* reproductive health by the Guatemalan state, a fact made clear both by the targets of the genocidal violence throughout Guatemala's civil war as well as the limited, but growing resources devoted by the state to indigenous reproductive health, including contraception. Combining this broad concept of stratified reproduction—how reproduction is valued differently by different groups as well as *within* a group—with an analysis of Maya masculinity, I can see how, on the one hand, K'iche' Maya communities are thinking about and adopting artificial contraceptive methods, as well as how men and women approach and experience the consequences of contraception.

One hundred sixty-seven women, eighty-four of whom were residents of Jun, had requested a modern contraceptive method at the *puesto* or from the Asociación Pro-bienestar de la Familia de Guatemala, or the Association for the Well-being of the Family, Guatemala (APROFAM), between 1996 and 2002. Approximately 92 percent of these were Depo Provera users—the rest used either oral contraceptive pills (OCPs) at 7.5 percent or condoms at 2.5 percent. The 2.5 percent of condoms users were men, a finding corroborated by my own data gathered from men in Jun; the majority had never used condoms, and those few who did (or had a friend who had) suggested condoms would only be used with paid sex workers.

Using these data, it is reasonable to estimate that, of all the women of fertile age who lived in Jun (741, a number taken from a larger demographic survey), a minimum of 14 percent had used some form of modern contraception in the past five years. This figure is consistent with regional and national contraceptive prevalence rates among Maya women. For Depo Provera injections and OCP use between 1996 and 2002, the average age of user initiation was 25.7 years, but there was a bi-modal distribution of number of users—one peak at age twenty-three and another around age thirty-three.

In Jun, comments about contraception from male and female informants as well as *comadronas* (traditional birth attendants or midwives) helped me to make sense of this pattern, as well as to comprehend the ambiguities many men and women felt about using contraception. Depo Provera use, even among couples in which there was cooperation, is not unproblematic. While discussing Depo Provera use with a female informant, she mentioned that some cautioned against Depo Provera, saying that it causes a woman to become *muy hombre* or very masculine, for two reasons. First, she had heard that it changes women's bodies to be more masculine. Second, it potentially allows women to have sex without becoming pregnant, in other words, to behave like a man, a theme I will explore later. One male informant wondered if his friend's first wife's early use of Depo Provera might have contributed to their later problems having children. Another father had thought about contraception after his third child, but wanted his wife to wait just a little longer in case they decided on a fourth, because you could not be sure what the chemicals in contraceptives did to your body. Rosalia, a twenty-two-year-old unmarried woman who worked as one of my field assistants, was taking OCPs because she had been diagnosed with irregular periods (likely due to polycystic ovarian syndrome), but worried that she would not be able to have children later because of her OCP use. Angela, a twenty-seven-year-old mother of two, had started using Depo Provera after the birth of her second child. She had her first child when she was nineteen, soon after marriage, and was very happy to have had two children early. "Now I can use the shot and not worry: we know we can have children." Doña Elena, a *comadrona* who also worked as a contraceptive provider, was even more direct.

> Few women who just married come to me for contraception. I think they should, so that they can wait and enjoy each other, save some money, build a house. But the father-in-law [of the young woman] will say, "Why would you build a house if you don't have children?" So the couple will stay with the father-in-law, with his father. She would never use contraception first [before having children], because then if they have problems [conceiving] it is to blame.

Many women are waiting to initiate contraception until they have had one or two children already and their fertility has been proven. Those women then use contraceptives to delay second or third births. The data showing an increase in contraceptive initiation by women in their thirties likely represent women's desire to avoid further pregnancies once they have completed their desired family size and want to more tightly control their reproductive careers. My research directly addresses the roles men play in these patterns.

K'iche' men express a range of opinions about contraceptive use, including support, skepticism, and open opposition. Importantly, however, many male informants, single as well as married, corroborated that they did not or would prefer not to use contraceptives before having at least one child—desires reflected in my earlier data on timing of contraceptive initiation.

Men I interviewed cooperate with their wives' contraceptive use, meaning that they know about their wives' use of Depo Provera or OCPs, and decide with them when to start. Some men accompany their wives on visits to a contraceptive provider to demonstrate their support. When I interviewed Horacio, a thirty-four-year-old weaver, during a visit with his wife to get her Depo Provera shot at the health post, he said that he came because he felt it was important that he "take an interest" in her health and "provide her support." The couple had decided together only to have two children because they wanted to be able to "better their [children's] lives." He knew other people saw him come, he said, which might deter other men because it would open them up to gossip. Some members of the community saw contraception as a sin, and others would question why a man would let his wife use contraception—but he felt that his family was his business.

Jorge, a twenty-two-year-old single male, said, "When you get married, you are very ready to have children, to have your little family—that's the reason [to marry]!" Enrique, a twenty-four-year-old who is also single, expressed concerns about having children early in marriage: "you want to have things prepared, some money, maybe a little house. It is hard." Nevertheless, he did not think he would choose contraception before having a first child. "If you love [your wife] then you take what is given. Don't get in the way." He did add, though, "It depends on the woman." Some young male informants like Lionel, a nineteen-year-old new father of a two-month-old, wanted to take a wait-and-see approach. He was not against contraceptives, but maybe not right away or very soon, and "maybe we will talk with the *comadrona*. She might know something natural."

Some women in the community do not inform their husbands when they are using contraceptives, in particular Depo Provera. Given the central location and public nature of the health post, it is difficult but not impossible for women to obtain contraceptives there without arousing notice in the community. However, it is precisely because some women hide their contraceptive use from their husbands that they choose to pay private providers: Doña Elena estimated that fifteen of her thirty-five clients, or around 43 percent, hide their Depo Provera use from their husbands. Indeed, the popularity of Depo Provera injections over pills may lie precisely in the possibility of its hidden use, a view Doña Elena endorsed. One female participant, a thirty-nine-year-old mother of five, said that she hid her Depo Provera use from her husband because "he would hit me if he knew" but that "having another child now would be too much."

CONTRACEPTION USE AND STRATIFIED REPRODUCTION

Men's contraceptive use in Jun and Keb' seems to be related to their overall family and household health priorities. Both men and women in Jun report that it is necessary for a couple to decide together if they want to use contraceptives—a decision made "under the covers." However, women were more likely to report that either the man or the woman would make the decision, while almost all men agreed that the couple together makes the decision. Men's attitudes toward children and their priorities for their children's health often revolve around the provision of the material conditions for the production of household health while leaving some details of maternal and child health to their wives and to *comadronas.* A family case study reveals some of the important differences in what contraceptives mean for men who are using them. Interviews with four men in a single family—two brothers and two of their brothers-in-law—illustrate how men experience contraceptive use very differently even as they actively cooperate in its usage.

Daniel, Alfonzo, Pedro, and Marcos are all members of the extended Kek family into which Pedro Saq' married. Their families are relatively wealthy—Daniel and Alfonzo are partners in a successful business in town with their father; Marcos works in that business, as did Pedro until several years ago. All their wives use Depo Provera. Daniel is forty-one years old and has two children, aged eleven and seven. He works as a teacher and runs several small businesses. His wife has used contraception since their last child. She also acts as a *comadrona* and contraceptive provider in Jun and has worked with health projects outside the community. Daniel actively supports his wife's decision to use contraceptives and to have a job, which sometimes requires overnight stays outside of the community.

Reflecting on his own attitudes toward deciding with his wife to use contraceptives, Daniel claimed that he wanted to give his children the best possible—*lo mejor posible.* Daniel has opened various businesses and describes himself as an entrepreneur; he plans to send his two children to private high school and prizes their academic achievements. As Daniel pointed out, part of providing for his two children meant that he and his wife spaced their births so that they can concentrate resources on a small number of children.

Alfonzo, thirty-eight, has recently returned from the United States, where he spent two years working in a car wash. His wife and the younger of his two sons, who is now four, accompanied him, while his older son, nine, remained in Jun with his wife's parents. Now working again in the family business, he has a two-story house, a truck, and a car. Alfonzo is known for doting on his wife and children. His wife does not work outside the home. Of the three brothers in the family, Alfonzo is the "lucky one" according to Daniel.

Marcos, thirty-seven years old, is married to Veronica, a nurse. He has a history of drinking, womanizing, and physical violence toward both his wife and his oldest daughter, who is fifteen. His youngest daughter is eight. His son died several years ago at age eleven. He lives with his parents-in-law outside of his natal community. Sober for three years and participating in Alcoholics Anonymous, he attributes his diagnosis of diabetes as the impetus to change his lifestyle.

Pedro, twenty-eight, and his wife Andrea (a nursing assistant and nursing student), have a six-year-old son. Moving from his natal community, he worked in the family business for five years. He had found a similar but better-paying job in Quetzaltenango, but was recently laid off, and had since returned to working intermittently for his wife's family.

The contrast among the four couples is striking. Both Daniel and Alfonzo completed high school and are successful businessmen. They cooperate closely with their wives, who at times work outside the home, and whose salaries, though not substantial, supplement the household income. In short, Daniel and Alfonzo represent versions of K'iche' Maya hegemonic masculinity: they are highly productive; they exert paternalistic control over their families but encourage their wives to participate actively in household decisions; they hold positions of community and familial respect; and they have pursued paths of personal, financial, and spiritual growth over time. Although Maya reproductive health and masculinity have and continue to be valued differently from those of their *ladino* counterparts by the state, Daniel's and Alfonzo's choices to use contraceptives are anchored in their local positions as men among men.

Marcos and Pedro, on the other hand, have problematic relationships with their wives that include histories of heavy drinking and physical abuse. Their wives are both nurses and work outside the community, while neither Marcos nor Pedro finished primary school. They represent aspects of non-hegemonic or subordinate, Maya masculinity, with personal shortcomings in economic productivity and personal growth (impacted both by poverty and alcohol use) that have negatively affected the control and respect they command in their households and community. For all of these couples, contraception is part of a conscious plan for improving their families, offering their children *lo mejor*. However, for Daniel and Alfonzo, contraceptive use has helped them to realize economic goals and reinforced their sense of (hegemonic) masculine self-worth, while at the same time carefully navigating their reproductive trajectories with their partners. This was evidenced for Alfonzo by a lavish prenatal shower he threw for his expectant wife, a custom he brought with him from the United States, complete with elaborate decorations that included "thought" balloons reflecting the unborn fetus' hopes, dreams, and conversations held between Alfonzo and the fetus prior to birth.

For Marcos and Pedro, the benefits of contraception are just as direct but personally less tangible. Their wives have achieved higher levels of education than the vast majority of women in their community and work as professionals outside the home. They have fewer children than most families, and their offspring are in private schools. However, in the intersectional context of Maya stratified reproduction and subordinated masculinity, the nearly identical choices and demographic outcomes of these men as compared with their brothers-in-law have resulted in very different consequences for their masculine sense of self.

Pedro and Marcos both link using contraception with other problems in their lives. Other men have chided Pedro for having only one child, questioning if he is really a man—especially since his wife works outside the home. He privately fears that her work gives her the opportunity to take advantage of not having to risk getting pregnant, and expresses doubts about having married so early. Marcos expresses guilt about the death of his son, which he attributes indirectly to his poor fathering because of his alcohol use. Contraception is part of the cooperative compact he has with his wife in light of his former indiscretions, but he nonetheless expresses sadness at the loss of his only son, with the opportunity for more sons effectively foreclosed.

It is important to note that Pedro and Marcos are not viewed by most of the community or by their wives as particularly "bad" or *machista* men. They cooperate with their wives in many ways and also want smaller families. However, the negative aspects of contraceptive usage have been minimized for Daniel and Alfonzo, but not for Marcos and Pedro. Marcos and Pedro, I believe, fear that they have lost control and balance in their households and their lives. Though they have been economically productive, by their community's standards, I believe that some of their anxiety is rooted in their relative dependence on their wives and on their wives' families in spite of the fact that they are more financially secure than many other men in their community. Contraception usage has complicated their sense of loss of control, and crystallized some of the issues these men feel about their positions. They have sought to reassert control over themselves and their families that, at times, has taken the form of drinking alcohol, pursuing relationships with other women, and resorting to physical violence. Marcos himself has made some of these links explicit in his narrative about his attempts to confront and overcome his alcoholism. At the same time, however, I sensed an ambivalence for Marcos toward contraception (one which I note he never directly articulated) because contraception meant he would not have another son.

Daniel and Alfonzo, however, have maintained their productivity, respect, and control; they have good jobs and have made other investments that have allowed them to take advantage of having fewer children. They can afford to allow their wives to work or not outside the home if they wish, and they weather criticisms from non-family members in part because they are progressing, moving their families forward. Alfonzo explicitly notes that spacing births has allowed him to be the kind of father that he wants to be, providing opportunities for his children, from lavish baby showers to private education. Moreover, Alfonzo notes he does not see contraception as troubling while he is away from the community for extended periods, as it may be for some men who may fear contraception encourages promiscuity. Rather, he sees having fewer children as having made his travel more flexible, because he has been able to take his wife and a child with him for some stays outside the community.

Thus, while I argue that no single Maya hegemonic masculinity exists, nevertheless, ways of being a Maya man differ from other regional masculine types (see Gutmann 1996; Lancaster 1992). At the same time, contraceptive use is not simply dictated by ideals or even practical, everyday realizations of masculinity. Decisions about contraceptive use play a direct role in men's feelings about themselves as men as well as what they think of as a man—*contraceptive decisions are masculinity in practice and have practical implications for masculinity.* For some of the men with whom I worked, contraceptive use has become part of a coherent, even idealized, picture of what it means to be a Maya man. In contrast, for other male informants, contraceptive use is a source of anxiety about their masculinity. While I cannot offer a full explanation for the low rates of contraceptive use among Maya groups in Guatemala, my research does provide some insight into: (1) how the mere statistic of increasing rates of contraceptive use among Maya does not capture the range of experiences, including decisions and feelings about the consequences of those decisions, Maya men have with contraception, and (2) cultural concerns which, if directly addressed, might improve men's willingness to use contraception.

CONTRACEPTIVE TRANSFORMATION AND LOCAL BIOLOGIES

In Keb', while all births are attended by *comadronas,* mostly male traditional healers (*curanderos*) also play important roles in providing reproductive health care to the community. Biomedical health care is limited to a small health post stocked with basic medicines and run by resident health promoters under the guidance of a local health coordinator as part of the Extension of Coverage program. Cuban doctors also visited the community once every few weeks. A census conducted with sixty-three women of reproductive age (18–45) showed that contraceptive prevalence was similar to that of Jun, at around 20 percent; all contraceptive use in Keb' was Depo Provera injection. Compared with Jun, the comparable prevalence of contraceptive use is striking; it occurs in spite of much lower average maternal and paternal education and income, and in the context of the communities' direct and long-term experiences with genocidal violence during the Guatemalan civil war, a point to which I return later. However, as in Jun, the use of Depo Provera injections in Keb' was not unproblematic.

One prominent healer in Keb', Don Sebastian, provided health care to many women in the community, addressing their individual illnesses as well as overseeing their care during pregnancy and childbirth. Some couples came to him both for pregnancies and for their children's illnesses, with pregnant women sometimes asking him to perform ceremonies so that their pregnancy would go well and they would have an uncomplicated delivery. Couples, he said, should participate together in these ceremonies of protection, because the baby developing in the uterus of the woman was part of both the father and the mother. As a couple, they were susceptible to attack and so the presence of both parents was required for the best defense of the fetus. This kind of prophylactic ceremony was important to avoid future complications during childbirth.

The source of these fears is complex. Don Sebastian, like other healers with whom I spoke, adhered to a syncretic Maya religion that incorporated some elements of Catholicism, including a belief in a pervasive evil force in the world, personified by the devil, who might be responsible for miscarriages. Bad luck, "bad destiny," a weak constitution, or past transgressions might also be in play. But Don Sebastian and other healers also were concerned about the important threat posed by the dead. Deceased members of the community could cause bad fortune or ill health, and would do so if surviving friends or family had offended or injured them prior to or after death. In Keb', however, the dead posed an additional threat because so many community members had been killed during the civil war and were either improperly or never buried. The community, situated close to the site of many of these deaths as well as to the clandestine cemeteries used at the time, was under continual spiritual threat—but not from any malice that the dead held for the living. Rather, because of the way their lives had been taken, the dead continued to long for life and connection with the living, especially with a vulnerable being like a developing fetus.[3]

Don Sebastian described the particular case of a couple from a nearby community that had experienced multiple infant deaths. The couple, Ixil-speaking relatives of Don Sebastian's wife, had had seven infant deaths, after each infant had lived between two weeks and two months. Don Sebastian, using divination, "asked questions of his table"—beans and stones—to determine the cause of their repeated reproductive loss. "It came out of the question that the two of them had the same date of birth on the Mayan calendar, and that there was a *choque* or a collision, because the two were equal. To solve the problem, I had to look for their day for the two of them and then perform a ceremony on that day to talk with the *nahual* and to ask the *nahual* to allow them to have children, and they now have several."[4]

Don Sebastian was adamant about not treating women who were using Depo Provera for any illness. The problem, he said, was the possibility that Depo Provera would "cross" with the natural medicine he used. On the one hand, he explained, he felt that the people in this community are *naturales,* literally "naturals," a word sometimes used as a synonym for indigenous or Maya. He meant that their bodies are more accustomed to natural medicine, as opposed to *ladino* bodies or foreign bodies like my own that were both built for and used to artificial medicines like pills and injections. He did not mean to imply that pills and injections didn't work on Maya bodies, but rather that the latter had less affinity for artificial medicines and more affinity for natural medicines—a kind of ethnotheory of Lock's local biologies (1993). Moreover, he said, natural medicines and artificial medicines worked along different lines; they had different powers, and so could "cross" in someone who was trying to use both, with unhealthy consequences—a deleterious drug interaction between indigenous and biomedicines related to local differences in indigenous bodies. Although he knew of other, more natural means of avoiding and terminating pregnancy, he personally preferred not to use them. He said he felt that the woman was the one who had to make the decision to employ a medicine like Depo Provera, because she is an adult and it is her body. But, he cautioned that she would then have to live with the consequences of her decision, one of which was that he would not treat her for other illnesses while she was using the injection.

These reasons, particularly the last, need to be contextualized in terms of Don Sebastian's position in the community vis-à-vis hegemonic masculinity and the broader gendered relations of power among the community's health providers. Don Sebastian and several of his brothers (who are also healers) formed a politically important, if not central, power bloc in the community. The brothers often banded together on issues in community debates. Moreover, Don Sebastian and his brothers were seen as powerful healers who, if angered, might use their powers in retaliation. Thus, Don Sebastian was respected (and feared) and exerted some control over his family and community. Because of the nature of his powers as a healer, he was often viewed with wary caution.

Don Sebastian discussed one case where problems of the crossing of Maya and Western medicine arose. The daughter of a community member, now four years old, had been born with congenital deformations: all four limbs were poorly developed, and her feet and hands had some webbing. Since her birth, she had undergone multiple surgeries to correct some of these deformities, and was scheduled for additional procedures as she grew older. Of note, I did by chance encounter one of her surgeons outside the community; he confirmed that more surgeries were planned as well as that the cause of these malformations was unknown to her doctors, but was unlikely to be caused by Depo Provera.

In this case, Don Sebastian felt that the deformities had been caused by the Depo Provera injections that the mother had received prior to her pregnancy. He was unsure if the couple had previously been using Depo Provera, had accidentally become pregnant, and then had received an additional injection after the start of the pregnancy, or if they had used the injection, knowing that the wife was pregnant in order to provoke an abortion. He thought that part of the problem was that they had also come to him to try a natural remedy while also using Depo Provera, and that the medicines had "crossed," causing the deformities in the baby. From that time on, he was determined to only treat women who had used Depo Provera in the past for nothing more serious than a headache or diarrhea. He mentioned, however, that pregnant women in general, were in a delicate, vulnerable state and he preferred to treat them only externally, administering a massage or blowing on them rather than providing a tea that would affect them internally.

By contrast, Domingo was a charismatic community leader who trained local people to work in the small health outpost in Keb' and in several other surrounding communities in coordination with a Canadian NGO and a few Cuban doctors. His wife, Ana, a respected *comadrona*, also helped to spearhead the effort to provide Depo Provera. As early adopters themselves, their advocacy in large part explains the community's relatively high prevalence of Depo Provera usage. They have five children that Ana declared were enough. Their oldest son was in high school outside the community, and they also hoped to send their second eldest son to school. Currently, they were helping this son, his wife, and their newborn who live with them. Domingo and Ana both linked their decision to adopt contraceptives to their experiences during the civil war. Ana had delivered many infants under duress during the conflict, and although conditions in the community had improved, those experiences of privation influenced how she felt about women having too many children. For his part, Domingo felt that one of the hardest lessons he learned from the civil war was the need to provide an education for his children, so that they would acquire an awareness of and connection to the larger world, something he did not have during the conflict. Contraception was one part of that effort.

Don Sebastian's example of this "crossing" case is more complex when considered within the local context of reproductive health care provision in Keb', specifically, in the gendered intersection of Maya healing and biomedicine involving Don Sebastian and Ana. As a male healer who sometimes works in reproductive health issues, Don Sebastian has avoided prescribing the use of most biomedical interventions including Depo Provera. Ana, herself a *comadrona*, someone familiar with other traditional remedies, does provide Depo Provera. Don Sebastian quite explicitly embodies the contrast between the male-dominated domain of Maya healing with both biomedicine and the work of the *comadrona.* He works with his wife in what he sees as the correct, complementary relationship: she attends births for which he provides spiritual protection. Ana's advocacy of Depo Provera, and biomedicine more generally, complicates this relationship. The interaction between biomedical Depo Provera and Maya healing practices demonstrated the incompatibility of the two forms of medicine for Don Sebastian; he believes biomedicine is inappropriate for Maya bodies in the context of the complementary, gendered relationship between Maya healing and the practices of the *comadrona*. Still, there appears to be some fluidity and flexibility in local understandings of Maya biologies in the use and incorporation of biomedicines like Depo Provera, since many Maya avail themselves of Guatemala's plural medical system. Nevertheless, the implications of Maya hegemonic masculinity reverberate through the community's reproductive health care system.

Ultimately, however, for the residents of Keb' and other communities with active indigenous healers, strong ties exist between the individual and her biological and environmental place, as mediated by the *nahual.* While an aspect of the divine, the *nahual* is also animalistic in nature, connected with the natural world in which the individual is born, having its own passions and appetites. The *nahual,* which comes into being as the fetus develops and is born, may produce illness at any point in the life of the individual since its nature may conflict with the path an individual chooses. As such, an individual could live a life out of balance, out of harmony with the *nahual* or other more traditional practices.

MAYA MASCULINITY AND ITS INTERSECTIONS WITH CONTRACEPTION

My research revealed that men's roles and experiences related to reproduction and reproductive health are filled with conflict, requiring them to negotiate actively among competing beliefs, demands, and expectations. I used data from interviews and participant observation to illustrate some of the areas in which men express equivocal beliefs about how they should participate in different aspects of the reproductive health of their wives, including contraceptive use, prenatal care, childbirth, and parenting. Reproduction and family loom large in men's expressed ideals of masculinity and masculine experience, yet just as importantly, K'iche' men feel at once removed from *and* involved in their wives' and children's lives. Many of the K'iche' Maya men with whom I worked expressed thoughts about changing their roles as husbands and fathers from what they themselves experienced as children and young men. Women as well expressed some ambivalence about men's roles, moving between what they characterize as more traditional male roles and newer models of masculinity. Importantly, men and women also are able to articulate differences between Maya masculinity and other models of *machismo* perceived to prevail in *ladino* groups.

In this investigation of Maya masculinity, I have tried to show how the hierarchical intersections of stratified reproduction and local biologies contribute to define hegemonic masculinity. In the communities in which I worked, and I suspect in other parts of Guatemala where Maya reproduction has long been stratified, that stratification has implications for men in terms of the ways being a man are valued. Likewise, in Jun and Keb', local interpretations of the workings of reproductive bodies have implications for men's understandings of themselves and their families. Ultimately, however, rigid structural and hierarchical formulations fall short in practice. Instead, what is required is close ethnographic analysis to understand men's lived anxieties, conflicts, and successes and how these feelings affect reproductive decisions. At this point in time, K'iche' Maya men tack back and forth between different dimensions of masculinity as part of their strategies for encountering and overcoming struggles, including their decisions about marriage, children, family, and community. Statistical patterns of contraceptive use alone are unable to capture the ways in which Maya masculinity is deployed and experienced in contraceptive decision making. More to the point, Maya men's ambivalence about contraceptives affects how couples use family planning even as these couples' experiences with contraception play a role in how men think of themselves as modern *and* Maya. Contraception in Maya communities occurs against the dynamic backdrop of men's and women's understandings of themselves and their bodies as Maya, and their local biologies change the consequences of contraception for those Maya men and women. Ultimately, these insights into Maya men and Maya masculinity draw from, and indeed require, a nuanced feminist anthropology of stratified reproduction.

NOTES

1. *Mayachismo* is a neologism not used by any of the members of the communities of Jun or Keb'. I shared it with men and women with whom I worked and it received some validation (and appreciative chuckles).
2. For an extensive discussion of these dimensions, see Dudgeon 2013.
3. This threat to pregnancy in Keb' is part of a larger cultural syndrome of illness referred to locally as *mala hora*, literally "bad hour"; see Dudgeon 2013 for an extended discussion.
4. The *nahual* is a spirit-animal-guide that comes into being on the day that an individual is born and is related to the Maya calendar day name of one's birthday.

REFERENCES

Bastos, Santiago. 2000. *Poderes y Quereres: Historias de Género y Familia en los Sectores Populares de Ciudad de Guatemala.* Guatemala: Facultad Latinoamericana de Ciencias Sociales (FLACSO).

Bertrand, Jane, Sandra Guerra de Salazar, Lidia Mazariegos, Ventura Salanic, Janet Rice, and Christine Kolars Sow. 1999. "Promoting Birthspacing among the Maya-Quiche of Guatemala." *International Family Planning Perspectives* 25 (4): 160–167.

Bertrand, Jane, Eric Seiber, and Gabriela Escudero. 2001. "Contraceptive Dynamics in Guatemala: 1978–1998." *International Family Planning Perspectives* 27 (3): 112–118, 136.

Bordo, Susan. 1990a. "Feminism, Postmodernism, and Gender-Skepticism." In *Feminism/Postmodernism*, ed. Linda J. Nicholson, 133–156. New York: Routledge.

———. 1990b. "'Material Girl': The Effacements of Postmodern Culture." *Michigan Quarterly Review* 29 (4): 653–677.

———. 1993. *Unbearable Weight: Feminism, Western Culture, and the Body.* Berkeley: University of California Press.

Brannon, Linda. 2011. *Gender: Psychological Perspectives.* 6th ed. Boston: Allyn & Bacon.

Butler, Judith. 1990. *Gender Trouble.* Berkeley: University of California Press.

———. 1993. *Bodies That Matter: On the Discursive Limits of "Sex."* New York: Routledge.

Colen, Shellee. 1995. "'Like a Mother to Them': Stratified Reproduction and West Indian Childcare Workers and Employers in New York." In *Conceiving the New World Order: the Global Politics of Reproduction*, ed. Faye D. Ginsburg and Rayna Rapp, 78–102. Berkeley: University of California Press.

Collins, Patricia Hill. 2004. *Black Sexual Politics: African Americans, Gender, and the New Racism.* New York: Routledge.

Connell, Raewyn W. 1987. *Gender and Power: Society, the Person, and Sexual Politics.* Stanford, CA: Stanford University Press.

Cornwall, Andrea. 1997. "Men, Masculinity and 'Gender in Development.'" *Gender & Development* 5 (2): 8–13.

Csordas, Thomas J. 1988. "Embodiment as a Paradigm for Anthropology." *Ethos*: 5–47.

———, ed. 1994a. *Embodiment and Experience: The Existential Ground of Culture and Self.* Cambridge, New York: Cambridge University Press.

———. 1994b. "Introduction: The Body as Representation and Being-in-the-World." In *Embodiment and Experience: The Existential Ground of Culture and Self*, ed. Thomas J. Csordas, 1–24. Cambridge: Cambridge University Press.

Dudgeon, Matthew R. 2013. "Birth after Death: Men and Reproduction in Two K'iche' Maya Communities." PhD dissertation, Emory University.

Eber, Christine. 1995. *Women and Alcohol in a Highland Maya Town: Water of Hope, Water of Sorrow.* Austin: University of Texas Press.

Gardiner, Judith Kegan. 2005. "Men, Masculinities, and Feminist Theory." In *Handbook of Studies on Men and Masculinities*, ed. Michael S. Kimmel, Jeff R. Hearn, and Robert W. Connell, 35–50. Thousand Oaks, CA: Sage Publications.

Ginsburg, Faye D., and Rayna Rapp, eds. 1995. *Conceiving the New World Order: The Global Politics of Reproduction.* Berkeley: University of California Press.

Guatemala, Ministerio de Salud y Asistencia Social, Instituto Nacional de Estadística. 2003. Encuesta Nacional de Salud Materno Infantil 2002: Mujeres. Ciudad de Guatemala.

Gutmann, Matthew C. 1996. *The Meanings of Macho: Being a Man in Mexico City.* Berkeley: University of California Press.

———. 1997. "Trafficking in Men: The Anthropology of Masculinity." *Annual Review of Anthropology* 26: 385–409.

Lancaster, Roger N. 1992. *Life Is Hard: Machismo, Danger, and the Intimacy of Power in Nicaragua*. Berkeley: University of California Press.

Lock, Margaret M. 1993. *Encounters with Aging: Mythologies of Menopause in Japan and North America*. Berkeley: University of California Press.

MacKinnon, Catharine A. 1989. *Toward a Feminist Theory of the State*. Cambridge, MA: Harvard University Press.

Maynard, Eileen. 1974. "Guatemalan Women: Life Under Two Types of Patriarchy." In *Many Sisters: Women in Cross-Cultural Perspective*, ed. Carolyn J. Matthiasson, 77–98. New York: Free Press.

McClusky, Laura J. 2001. *Here, Our Culture Is Hard: Stories of Domestic Violence from a Mayan Community in Belize*. Austin: University of Texas Press.

Reiter (Rapp), Rayna. 1975. *Toward an Anthropology of Women*. New York: Monthly Review Press.

Rossenbaum, Brenda. 1993. *With Our Heads Bowed:The Dynamics of Gender in a Maya Community*. Albany, NY: Institute for Mesoamerican Studies.

Yanagisako, Sylvia Junko, and Carol Lowery Delaney, eds. 1995. *Naturalizing Power: Essays in Feminist Cultural Analysis*. New York: Routledge.

THE BODY AND EMBODIMENT IN THE HISTORY OF FEMINIST ANTHROPOLOGY

An Idiosyncratic Excursion through Binaries

FRANCES E. MASCIA-LEES

Once the purview of medical science and philosophy, "the body" emerged in the mid- to late 1970s as a central site from which feminist scholars questioned the ontological and epistemological basis of almost all forms of inquiry. Over the decades, the body remained central to feminist analyses and activism within and outside the academy. For feminists of this period, it was clear that questions of power and oppression could not be addressed without first challenging ideologies that naturalized gender and other differences through discourses, representations, and practices of the body. Thus, the body became a fertile site from which feminists mounted refutations of abstract, naturalizing models and ideologies and interrogated operations of power and possibilities for agency and political change, signaled by such titles as *Our Bodies/Ourselves* (Boston Women's Health Book Collective 1973), *Of Woman Born* (Rich 1976), and *The Female Eunuch* (Greer 1970). At the same time, we amassed a voluminous archive highlighting physical and symbolic assaults on women's bodies, whether through poverty, rape, lack of reproductive choice, domestic violence, pornography or "compulsory heterosexuality" (Rich 1980).

THE BODY IN EARLY FEMINIST ANTHROPOLOGY

One of the most influential early discussions of the body in feminist anthropology was Sherry Ortner's now classic article "Is Female to Male as Nature Is to Culture?" (1974) in the ground-breaking volume *Woman, Culture, and Society* (Rosaldo and Lamphere 1974). Drawing on Simone de Beauvoir, Ortner asserted that women's universal subordination "all begins . . . with the body and the natural procreative functions specific to women" (Rosaldo 1974, 73). Although one is not born, but, rather, becomes a woman, according to Beauvoir, the female body "enslaves her to the species" (Beauvoir 1953, 239) while the male transcends biological existence by means of goal-oriented, meaningful action (Beauvoir 1953, 58–59). "Woman" for both Beauvoir and Ortner has been defined by man/men, she is denigrated because she is "nature" to man's "culture," "other" to man's "self," "object" to man's "subject." Beauvoir's prescription was for women to become subjects or agents, an issue that became increasing central to feminist anthropology over succeeding decades (and whose roots were already apparent in some chapters in *Woman, Culture, and Society* 1974, such as Collier 1974; Lamphere 1974; and Stack 1974). Yet many feminists continued to focus on women's secondary status, building their arguments on some version of this basic conception: despite being a cultural construction, a woman's body and its functions suited her to certain roles (especially motherhood), and not others, which in turn excluded her from the public sphere, resulting in universal female subordination.

Of course, not all feminist anthropologists shared this early diagnosis, notably authors in the collection *Toward an Anthropology of Woman* (Reiter [now Rapp] 1975), which followed on the heels of *Woman, Culture, and Society*. In seeking explanations for sexual inequality worldwide, they turned more to questions of variation in women's status across cultures than to universal subordination, more to Marx (and thus class, modes of production, reproduction, and labor) than to Beauvoir (and thus subjective consciousness/objective body).

Perhaps the most serious and direct refutation came from the chapters in the edited volume *Nature, Culture, Gender* (MacCormack and Strathern 1980) which not only questioned claims of women's universal subordination, but also exposed the binary opposition between nature and culture—and its association with female/male—as a product of Western thinking, not ethnographic reality. Many of the issues in early feminist anthropology were directly related to the concerns of the women writing about them, who engaged in the larger US women's liberation movement and were demanding concrete changes, including the entry of more women into the (public) workplace and increased male participation in the (private) domestic realm. The public/private distinction, buttressing notions of universal subordination, was thus questioned for its ethnocentrism. Rosaldo (1980) herself critiqued the public/private distinction that she and Louise Lamphere laid out in *Woman, Culture, and Society* (1974) early on.

It was not long before feminist anthropology, and the larger feminist movement of which it was a part, was also critiqued for its construction of *the* body as insufficiently attuned to what it means to be a woman whose body and experiences are marked not just by gender but also by racial, ethnic, or other forms of difference. The fiction and non-fiction writing of women of color (from various disciplines) such as bell hooks (1981), Cherríe Moraga and Gloria Anzaldúa (1981), Audre Lorde (1984), Maxine Hong Kingston (1975), and others opened a space within feminism for consideration of the racialized female body, ushering in decades of scholarship on the body and identity, intersecting axes of identification, and situated knowledges. In anthropology specifically, the volume *Black Feminist Anthropology* (McClaurin 2001) challenged white feminists to consider the contributions of black women's research and writing on such issues to the subdiscipline. Despite this prodding, Lynn Bolles has recently argued that feminist anthropologists have not come far in this effort. She points to "glaring omissions in citations" of black feminist anthropologists in feminist anthropological literature and states that black women continue to be excluded "from discussions that establish recognition in the field" (Bolles 2013, 57).

I do not wish to rehash these arguments, which have generated decades of productive feminist analyses. Despite its limitations, adopting "gender" as a universal conceptual category in early feminist work did emphasize the social and cultural construction of some differences and challenged androcentrism and some forms of biological determinism, thereby laying a foundation on which today's feminist anthropology has been able to build. Similarly, early attempts to contend with categorical thinking led to the exposure of the active semiotic chain in Western thinking that underscores multiple forms of oppression, linking not only the mind/body to male/female, culture/nature, subject/object, self/other, and public/private, but also to rational/irrational (emotional), white/black, traditional/modern, civilized/primitive and West/non-West. Scholars demonstrated how these associations endlessly reinforce one another—buttressing their status as "truth"—privileging some interests over others and producing hierarchies of meaning and value with concrete material effects (e.g., inclusion/exclusion). These analyses revealed the long history in Western thinking of the valorization of the male as a white Western, rational, agentive self—the Cartesian subject—over the irrational, emotional, female Other, objectified as body. Patricia Hill Collins wrote of the implications of the dichotomous categories of race in the United States: "One must either be Black or white in such thought systems—persons of ambiguous racial and ethnic identity constantly battle with questions such as 'What are you anyway?' This emphasis on quantification and categorization occurs in conjunction with the belief that either/or categories must be ranked. The search for certainty of this sort requires that one side of a dichotomy be privileged while its other is denigrated" (Collins 1990, 225).

Feminist scholars from across the disciplines took on each of these dyads in turn. Attacks on the (Western) self/(non-Western) Other and the primitive/civilized constructions, for example, were launched by a growing number of postcolonial scholars, including feminist anthropologists, exposing the role they played in maintaining colonial oppression. The nature/culture, human/animal, human/machine divides were powerfully challenged by such notions as "the cyborg" (Haraway 1985), while the rational/irrational binary that structured male-based sciences came under close scrutiny, blossoming into Science and Technology Studies (see, e.g., Harding 1986).[1]

Some feminists dealt with these hierarchical bifurcations by reappraising the terms in the equation, reversing their valuation. For example, since the body had been seen as a site of women's devaluation, Anglo-American radical feminists reclaimed it as a source of empowerment while French feminists envisioned a challenge to phallogocentrism—with its notion of the monolithic self as male—in the "sexual organ that is not one" (Irigaray 1985) and "*l'écriture féminine*" (feminine writing from the body, Cixous 1980). Although the impact of such French feminist thinking was significant for some Anglo-American feminist analyses, it was largely—although not totally—ignored in feminist anthropology. It was seen as reasserting a biological essentialism into the discussion of sexual difference, an assumption that has, however, been debated rigorously in the larger feminist literature.[2]

Given the significance of the active semiosis of binary categories in maintaining power relations, my interest here is in tracing the theoretical and methodological effects of the gradual unraveling of these and other oppositional categories by feminist scholars, particularly anthropologists. In the 1980s, poststructuralism reformulated our thinking about the binary opposition—and the notion of the dialectic closely tied to it (as I discuss later)—powerfully disrupting feminist understandings of the body and subjectivity. To track these influences, I take an admittedly idiosyncratic excursion through some of these challenges. My interest is in assessing their implications for a feminist politics of the body, especially within feminist anthropology today. I do not, however, attempt to provide a comprehensive review of the larger feminist or feminist anthropological literature on the body, or the larger corpus of anthropological research on the body and embodiment, which does not necessarily claim feminist roots, but which is often animated by some similar and overlapping concerns.

ANTHROPOLOGY OF "THE BODY"

The body as an object of analysis was rare in the discipline in the first half of the twentieth century, although Marcel Mauss's "Techniques of the Body" (2000) and Mary Douglas's *Natural Symbols* (1970) were early, now classic, exceptions. Mauss anticipated the emergence of the "embodiment turn" within anthropology in the later decades of the twentieth century with his concept of habitus: "all the acquired habits and somatic tactics that represent the 'cultural arts' of using and being in the body and in the world" (see Scheper-Hughes 1994, 185). Despite this early foundation, little work in anthropology focused directly on the body until the last decades of the twentieth century. For example, in anthropology there were almost no dissertations focused on the body in the 1970s and earlier. But the impact of feminism significantly directed scholarly attention to the body and by the 1980s there were, on average, forty dissertations focused on the body each year, and in the 1990s, seventy-five every year of that decade (see Halliburton 2002). Thus, since the 1980s, the body has increasingly served as the basis for a large number of inquiries in anthropology, both feminist and otherwise. To a great extent, this is also because, as Steven Van Wolputte (2004, 252) has put it, "the history of the body in anthropology (both as an object of study and as an analytical metaphor) is a history of notions of self, person, and subject history," making it central to many ethnographic studies.

Another important strand in theorizing the body in the 1980s took place at the confluence of feminist and medical anthropology. Feminist medical anthropology—with its focus on such experiences as pain, illness, suffering, and disability—threw into relief ontological questions concerning the nature of the body (Bendelow and Williams 1998), while the political-economic and ideological dimensions of healing and care, as well as suffering, violence, and trauma, became increasingly central (see, e.g., Kleinman, Das, and Lock 1997; Scheper-Hughes 1993). In 1987, Emily Martin published *The Woman in the Body*, revealing how medical knowledge imposes control over women's minds and bodies, making a significant contribution to a feminist medical anthropology that by the early 1990s provided growing numbers of critical examinations of the imbrication of inequalities in science, biomedicine, and reproductive technologies.

In the same year as Martin's groundbreaking book, feminist medical anthropologists Nancy Scheper-Hughes and Margaret Lock's "The Mindful Body" (1987) provided a blueprint for understanding the body as multiple, as consisting of three bodies: the body-self, the social body, and the body politic. These categories represented not only separate and overlapping units of analysis, but also different theoretical approaches and epistemologies: phenomenology, structuralism and symbolic anthropology, and poststructuralism respectively (Scheper-Hughes and Lock 1987, 8). Their notion of a non-bifurcated body-self was part of a larger move in anthropology to adopt phenomenological frameworks to disrupt the opposition of mind to body and subject to object such that by the mid-1990s, much anthropological work rarely spoke of *the* body. The literature not only became pluralized during this period, talking about "bodies" and allowing for multiple differences, but also turned to understanding the body as "lived," as an experiential "being in the world," a topic to which I will return later.

CONTENDING WITH BINARIES

If such efforts to question binary conceptual categories in the 1980s made inroads into the US academy through feminist analyses, the translation into English of Jacques Derrida and Michel Foucault during this period shook the infrastructure of many disciplines. Their attacks on totalizing Western metanarratives—including the belief in universal reason associated with the Cartesian rational, white male subject—fueled an intensive critique of the bifurcated categories which ordered knowledge and experience and sustained such "truths." In its Derridean form poststructuralism was, among other things, the very attempt to undo the binaries underlying Western thought and to critique the dialectic that sought to transcend them through synthesis. Deconstruction was conceived as the moment when a binary opposition contradicts itself, undermining its own authority. Deconstructionists, thus, sought to problematize the very possibility of the reconciliation of the terms in a binary, emphasizing instead their difference, perpetual interplay, and indeed, what Derrida calls, their very "undecidability." Rather than the synthesis or transcendence of terms in the dialectic sought by G.W.F. Hegel (where the negation inherent to it inevitably serves the positive), deconstructionists highlighted an endless deferral or slippage of meaning. Indeed, to be an effective counter to the continental philosophy that had inscribed these terms as truths, Derrida contended that deconstruction needed to create new concepts, not to synthesize the terms in opposition, but to mark their difference, eternal interplay, and tension.

Just as Derrida, so did Foucault reject the Hegelian orthodoxy of abstract dialectical thinking (Dreyfus and Rabinow 1983). Foucault's (1975) focus on power and the disciplined body, in which he linked subjectivity to subjection (the docile body), profoundly resonated with many feminist scholars. He argued that *subjectivity*, produced through discourses and practices, situated individuals in relation to power, *subjecting* them to the forces of economics, law, social traditions, and the circumstances of history. Subjectivity was, for Foucault, part of the process that "naturalizes" relations of power, situating people within them. However, although a potent framework for understanding the relationship of power to subjectivity, some feminists argued that Foucault failed to denaturalize the body even as he presented the body as a socially constructed artifact of power.

His analysis of the body as a mere surface upon which history is written, presumed, some feminists argued, an inanimate and politically benign and passive body waiting to be inscribed by a multiplicity of external forces of power, indeed, a preexisting, precultural body that reinstituted mind/body, subject/object, culture/nature distinctions, but as I have argued elsewhere, only "reclaimed" the body once it was divested of its association with the biological and, thus, the female (Mascia-Lees and Sharpe 1992).

Judith Butler, both influenced by Foucault and writing in opposition to him, deconstructed the nature/culture divide in another way, focusing on the sex (biology)/gender (social) binary that had become an integral part of much Anglo-American feminism. She argued that feminists had made a mistake by asserting that "women" are a group with common characteristics and interests due to their sex, an argument, as noted earlier, that was already fully advanced by women of color, lesbians, and the differently abled, for example. Butler concluded that the sex/gender divide performed "an unwitting regulation and reification of gender relations," reinforcing a binary view of gender in which human beings are divided into two clear-cut groups, women and men (Butler 1998, 278).

Although feminism rejected the idea that biology is destiny, Butler argued that feminism's claim that masculine and feminine genders are constructed upon "male" and "female" bodies, reinforced that very notion (Butler 1990). Her account of gender as the product of repetitive and stylized body performances, which produce the mistaken belief that gender is real, and therefore that something inevitable (i.e., "natural")—the sex of the body—must be undergirding it had a widespread impact on feminist thinking across disciplines. Queer theory took up this conceptualization rigorously and explored its implications while Butler's ideas were also applied to an understanding of other forms of identity in fields such as cultural studies. Stuart Hall, for example, drew on Butler to assert that racial and cultural identity is created and recreated through the repetition of embodied practices, conceptualizing it as "a temporary attachment to the subject positions which discursive practices construct for us" (Hall 2002, 6).

DEALING WITH THE AFTERMATH: THE DEATH OF THE SUBJECT

These various assaults on oppositional categories and dialectical thinking—feminist, deconstructive, and Foucauldian—took a toll on feminist politics, and by the 1990s, a major discussion ensued about their impact on political action. Many feminists had been attracted to poststructuralism because of its focus on "difference," but when subjectivity became a product of representation and discourse (or some other signifying system), and gender a (mere) result of performativity, a dilemma was created: "through its very anti-essentialism [feminism] risk[ed] undercutting the basis of a politics of action based upon gender difference" (Myers 2010). Some worried that a feminism based on the sameness/difference split was running out of theoretical and political steam.

Subjectivity understood as subjection was widely critiqued for precluding the possibility of resistance, although many feminists continued to grapple with overcoming Foucault's totalizing view of power and to put his ideas in the service of feminist goals. Others, such as Gayatri Spivak (1996), called for the replacement of the notion of an essential female identity with the concept of "strategic essentialism," a temporary solidarity for the purpose of social action, a notion echoed in Julia Kristeva's (1986) call for using "women" as a political tool without attributing ontological integrity to the word. Corporeal feminists (e.g., Braidotti 1994; Grosz 1994) argued that the binaries—mind/body, subject/object—could be collapsed and a politics retained after poststructuralism because in the conceptualization they advocated, sexuality still had priority: "being a women is always already there as the ontological precondition for my existential becoming a subject" (Braidotti 1994, 187). This poststructuralist assault on subjectivity also raised other suspicions, prompting some feminists to question the timing of the "death of the subject": why, they wondered, was the subject decentered at the very moment that the West's "others" were gaining a voice and claiming subjective status (see Mascia-Lees, Sharpe, and Cohen 1989)?

DEALING WITH THE AFTERMATH: WRITING THE MATERIAL BODY OUT OF THEORY

Critically, for many feminists as well as other scholars, poststructural theories' linguistic turn also occluded the materiality of the body, only appearing to problematize the division of mind/body, subject/object, and self/other, as numerous critiques of Foucault revealed. As Terry Turner put it, "Foucault's body has no flesh" (1994, 36). Micaela di Leonardo and Roger Lancaster also took to task the purely discursive analyses of gender and sexuality underlying poststructuralist thinking, arguing against the disembodied nature of discourse that obscured the actual lives of humans and the material conditions affecting them (1996). This assessment was shared by Susan Bordo (2003) who argued that by ignoring the materiality of the body, poststructuralist theorists failed to see that cultural discourse has real embodied consequences. Butler's work was questioned in this regard as well: some critics argued that her performative account failed to address how the materiality of the body enters into a sense of self.

THE EMBODIMENT TURN IN ANTHROPOLOGY

In response to the disappearance of the body in the face of assaults on Western oppositional thinking, many anthropologists—feminist and otherwise—increasingly turned to phenomenology, and found in it a way to confront mind/body, subject/object dualisms. Just as Scheper-Hughes and Lock had offered the mindful body, other anthropologists drew on Maurice Merleau-Ponty's (1962) notion of "embodiment" to offer a non-dualistic understanding of the body in which the body is not an object to be studied in relation to culture, but is the subject of culture. As Thomas Csordas offers, embodiment is not only a way of living or inhabiting the world, but the "existential ground of culture and self" (1994, 4). In Merleau-Ponty's (1962) phenomenological framework, the body and mind are indistinguishable; we experience them together as an existential process operating in every human activity. In other words, subjectivity and meaning are no longer sited in the internal, individual subject but produced through the adjustment of bodies to one another and the world: bodies continually become us and we continually become our bodies. Body-selves come into being through intersubjective co-production of the world. Using the term "body-subject" to capture this, he rejects any absolute opposition between self and world. Instead Merleau-Ponty argues that such body-subjects are extended and immersed in multiple worlds, continuously shuttling between representation and the immediacy, indeterminacy and sensibility of the world, all in the context of making sense of lived experience in an intersubjective world of shared meaning (Olkowski 2002). As Russell Keat points out (2013), the concept of embodiment also collapses the division between thought and sensation since both are understood to occur against a background of perceptual activity that we always already understand to be within a state of embodiment. Our bodies are not "object-like instruments of a guiding, knowing, intending consciousness"; it is the body itself, which understands what to do and how to do it; it is the body's intentionality which directs us toward the world (Keat 2013, 7).

Embodiment as an analytical category thus collapses distinctions between mind and body, subject and object, self and world, interiority and exteriority, thought and sensation. Desjarlais and Troop suggest that within a phenomenological framework the distinction between textuality and materiality is also erased as theorists examine "the intersection of concrete bodily experiences, forms of knowledge, and practice with political, social, economic, and discursive formations with the operations and felt immediacies of bodies" (2011, 90).

Although Merleau-Ponty's work helps overcome dichotomous thinking, he is not without his critics. Frantz Fanon, for example, presents a criticism of Merleau-Ponty in *Black Skin, White Masks* (1986), and both Beauvoir and Irigaray argue that Merleau-Ponty's idea of the body-subject is a generalized, universalized concept that ignores gender. Recently, a spate of new writings has sought to reexamine Merleau-Ponty's ideas in terms of these criticisms. Johanna Oksala, for example, argues that "there can be no one universal or inherent normativity of the [situated] living body" (Oksala 2006, 221).[3] Feminist philosopher Gayle Salamon agrees in her recent review of Olkowski and Weiss's edited volume, *Feminist Interpretations of Maurice Merleau-Ponty* (2006), finding a shared agenda between feminism and phenomenology: "like feminism," she writes, "phenomenology understands its project to be an unsettling of the fantasy of a universal perspective, and the means by which it accomplishes this unsettling is careful and close attention to the perspectival nature of experience and of the world" (2008), helping to explain the significance and embrace of his ideas by anthropologists.

THE AFFECTIVE TURN

It is not Merleau-Ponty, but Giles Deleuze, however, to whom influential recent theorists, particularly of queer theory and cultural studies, have looked to blur lines not only between mind and body, but also perceiver and perceived, objective reality and subjective experience. Although both philosophers posit a human body continuous with the world, they differ in identifying the locus of sensation and affect (del Rio 2005). Merleau-Ponty locates them in subjective experience, while Deleuze treats sensation and affect "as material flows whose individuation and exchange does not rest upon subjectified intentions, but rather upon the workings of a non-organic, anonymous force or life" (del Rio 2005, 62). Because of their similarities as well as their differences, del Rio suggests that the ideas of both philosophers are equally necessary (2005, 62).

Affect, understood as a function of embodiment, Tom Csordas argues, is a condition of intentionality and existence, a feature of intersubjectivity, not subjectivity (2009). Affect, in other words, is what allows the body-self to be an open system, "always in concert with its virtuality, the potential of becoming" (Pelligrini and Puar 2009, 37). Affect's use by many theorists is an attempt to represent the unrepresentable: to capture the potentiality of the "intensities" that are transmitted between and among bodies and objects. It is this characteristic, I suggest, that gives the concept of affect such promise for a feminist anthropology. For, as Csordas points out, affect is part of the intersubjectivity of the world; once we understand this, questions of politics, persuasion, and power quickly open up (1993).

Affect, however, is a notoriously slippery term. For Melissa Gregg and Gregory Siegworth, the editors of *The Affect Reader*, conceptually affect "is a means to account for the relational capacities that belong to the doings of the body or are conjured by the world-belongingness that gives rise to the body's doing"

(2010, 9). In this description, Gregg and Siegworth follow the Deleuzian tradition of contemporary founding theorists of affect, Eve Sedgwick and Brian Massumi, to understand affect as a non-conscious experience of intensity, the body's ability to *affect* and *be affected*. In this formulation, affect is understood to proceed directly from the body, circulating both within and between bodies, "it is non-cognitive and separate from meaning, interpretation, and representation" (Leo 2011, 2).

This brand of affect theory, focused on intensities and their transmission, offers new ways to reconfigure the relationship of body, experience, subject, and world. However, it is not without its critics. Ruth Leys (2011), for example, worries that, since within this framework, meaning, belief, and cognition are separate from affect, automatic preconscious bodily reactions, and responses, it creates a materialist theory of the body and emotion, thus ignoring ways to study the body that do not reproduce the dichotomy of mind and matter, and reinforces the same dualism of the subject and object it seeks to undo.

For other scholars, affect is often more inflected with notions of emotion, feeling, and sensation (Pelligrini and Puar 2009, 36–37). Feminist queer theorists Lauren Berlant (2011) and Ann Cvetkovitch (2012), for example, work with the notion of affect to explore public feelings in the United States. Although there is debate over the relationship of affect to emotion, Michael Hardt remarks that a focus on affect draws attention to the body and emotions. It does so, however, by introducing an important shift:

> The challenge of the perspective of the affects resides primarily in the synthesis it requires . . . because affects refer equally to the body and the mind . . . because they involve both reason and passions. Affect requires us . . . to enter the realm of causality, but they offer a complex view of causality because the affects belong simultaneously to both sides of the causal relationship. They illuminate . . . both our power to affect the world around us and our power to be affected by it, along with the relationship between these two powers. (Hardt 2007, iv)

The work of Berlant (2011) and Cvetkovitch (2012) are exemplary illustrations of this shift. Their political engagement is meant to expose how and why feelings and emotions (assumed to be private, personal experiences) influence politics and maintain oppression, focusing on "how capitalism feels." Claiming that the present is perceived affectively before it is understood in other ways, Berlant exposes the emotional resonances of contemporary neoliberal capitalism in the United States where people cling to hopes and desires that subvert their ability to thrive, calling this "cruel optimism" (2011). As Leo describes her work, she is interested in analyzing "where affect mediates between identity and desire, enabling a more pointed understanding of the labor of subjectivity, the tiring work of 'life-building'" (2011, 112).

Cvetkovitch examines "depression" in the United States, similarly, not as the private disease of an individual body, but as a public feeling, arguing that the lived experience of neoliberal capitalism is "feeling bad" (2012). She provocatively asks us to understand the depression that as feminist scholars we may feel as affective acknowledgment of our own political failures and disappointments. Just as an earlier feminism collapsed the public/private divide by exposing the "personal as political," so studies of public feelings expose the political construction of such affective experiences as intimacy,[4] belonging, and exclusion. Cvetkovitch, however, reveals her discomfort with the affective turn because "it implies there is something new about the study of affect when, in fact . . . this work has been going on for quite some time"; now, however, it has often come to signal the turn to the Deleuzian tradition (Cvetkovitch 2012, 4). She prefers invoking the notion of feeling precisely because it is intentionally imprecise; for her it signifies both embodied sensations and psychic/cognitive experiences, implying mind and body integration (Cvetkovitch 2012, 4).

The Deleuzian conception of affect as pure intensity has not made as deep an incursion into feminist anthropology as it has in text-based disciplines, where the project is often to perform sensation through the writing itself. Feminist anthropologist Kathleen Stewart's exquisite book of ethnographic vignettes, *Ordinary Affect* (2007), is one exception. As Ben Highmore (2010) describes it, "her work is aphoristic, descriptive, and evocative." It reveals the arbitrary experience of everyday life. As Stewart herself describes it: "The writing here has been a continuous, often maddening, effort to approach the intensities of the ordinary through a close ethnographic attention to pressure points and forms of attention and attachment . . . each scene is a tangent that performs the sensation that something is happening—something that needs attending" (Stewart 2007, 5).

AFFECT AND EMBODIMENT IN FEMINIST ANTHROPOLOGY

Although it may go without saying, work on affect in anthropology is fundamentally work in the anthropology of embodiment, since affect is intrinsically embodied. In the rest of this chapter, I explore a few examples of recent writing by feminist anthropologists who have also turned to affect in their analyses. I am interested in how they put affect to work for them as a concept, and emphasize those feminist anthropologists who have clearly turned to this concept as a way of continuing to address dichotomous and dialectical thinking in their analyses. These works, of course, do not jettison other ideas—Foucault, Bourdieu, and Butler, for example, remain relevant—but affect offers an important lens through which these theorists' works are filtered.

Several recent authors have turned to affect to show how public and private spheres are melded in particular ethnographic contexts as affect is mobilized to produce neoliberal subjects. Carla Freeman (2011) extends Arlie Hochschild's (1983) notion of "affective labor"—the commercialization of emotional labor under post-Fordism that requires the suppression of certain emotions and affects to suit a growing service economy—into the current neoliberal context of Barbados. There, women seeking new paths to upward mobility do not suppress feeling as in Hochschild's (1983) analysis as much as cultivate a particular neoliberal subjectivity: the "entrepreneur of the self," who must not only retrain and procure the new skills and networks that entrepreneurship requires, but also embrace a flexible self-making, involving caring for one's health, one's mind, and one's body (Freeman 2011, 356). A woman's emotional need for support, comfort, love, nurturance, and intimacy, once structured by kinship, marriage, parenting, religion, and class status, now gives way to a culture of "self-examination" in the service of creating a happier and better self in which "the importance of affective labor in their businesses resonates closely with the emotional labors they perform in their private, domestic life" (Freeman 2011, 364).[5]

Ana Yolanda Ramos-Zayas (2011) investigates how the inducement or suppression of emotion constructs neoliberal subjectivities in the interracial US urban schools she studies and how affects—the organization of feelings and sentiments—and emotions are produced and experienced within the context of racialization. She shows that Latinos, both US and immigrant, are racialized through the adoption of affective behaviors and expressions, the emotional styles associated with their black classmates. Specifically, they learn to "be hard," an attribute they see as "an almost unalterable quality attributed to the African American psyche" and thereby come to embody race. Learning negative affect—"being able to be dark and having a different public mood"—enables Latino kids to gain "urban competency" (Ramos-Zayas 2011, 28). At the same time, they must let go of the affective qualities associated with the neoliberal workplace: compulsory happiness, requiring them to calibrate the kinds and limits of the embodied racialized affect (Ramos-Zayas 2011). In her larger work, *Street Therapists*, Ramos-Zayas argues that affect is not only embodied and learned in the racialization of Latinos in Newark, but that it is also central to the nation-state's constitution of racial subjects, both blacks and Latinos. She turns to affect—as well as feelings, emotional styles, and sentiments—to reveal "the complexity of an interiority that always-already occupies a social and political space" (2012, 285) without reverting to explanations historically grounded in human psychology.

Yael Navaro-Yashin (2012) works through another set of boundaries. In her ethnography, *Make-Believe Space: Affective Geography in a Postwar Polity*, she draws on affect's transmissibility to explore the "affective geography" created in the aftermath of Turkish Cypriots' 1974 occupation of Greek Cypriots' former space after the latter's forced departure. Here, she claims, affect circulates among people, space, and objects, as Turkish Cypriots begin to occupy Greek Cypriots' abandoned homes and use their objects, producing troubling sentiments. Turkish Cypriots are bothered by their own looting of the objects left behind by Greek Cypriots and become melancholic about the ruins of war and their "ghostly presence" that spreads across the landscape. Turning to affect allows Navaro-Yashin to explore the role of materiality in the creation of subjectivity as she confronts the complication of yet another conceptual bifurcation: the ephemeral and the tangible. She argues that affect is not just mediated and qualified by the people experiencing it, but is concrete and palpable (Navaro-Yashin 2012). However, in making this claim, she questions those affect theorists who wish to study subjectivity outside registers of the linguistic or symbolic, taking aim specifically at Actor Network Theory (ANT), which, to understand the nature of the "social," treats humans and non-humans as equal "actants" in a network of relationships, thus assuming the indeterminacy of the actor (see, for example, Latour 2005). Critics have argued that ANT does not adequately account for the ability of humans to reflect (through language), and thus possess intentionality (see, e.g., Winner 1993). Navaro-Yashin lodges this critique thus: "an observation of the affect transmitted through the rusty environment of northern Cyprus does not lead me simply to discard language and subjectivity. For I also observed that my informants' subjectivities were shaped by and embroiled in the ruins which surrounded them" (Navaro-Yashin 2012, 5). Navaro-Yashin's concern here raises a central question for future analyses: "how must affect theorists understand 'language' in order to oppose it to 'felt bodily intensity'" (McGrail, Davie-Kessler, and Guffin n.d.)?

Saba Mahmood employs the notion of "affective embodied experience" to understand how difference is lived, produced, and experienced among a group of women in Egypt involved in the women's mosque movement, part of the larger Islamic Revival there (2005, 2). In this movement, women cultivate piety through an embodied practice of ethics that Western feminists have tended to view as undermining women's autonomy and freedom. Asking why women would participate in their own subordination, Mahmood argues that liberal feminists have sought to highlight points of resistance in their analyses, understanding women's choices within the construct of structure/agency. Mahmood questions this binary, and the focus on resistance attendant to it. She shows how these Egyptian women's activities, which they see as necessary to the cultivation of a pious Islamic self, have enabled them for the first time to participate in what has historically been the sole domain of men in Islamic practice: holding public meetings in mosques to instruct each other in the proper reading of Islamic texts, forms of bodily comportment, and performance of Islamic social practices (Mahmood 2005; also see Jamal 2008). Women's participation in this movement thus transforms the public sphere as women assert their presence, even as they do so by committing to certain patriarchal narratives about "woman's virtue"—their shyness, modesty, and humility (Mahmood 2005, 6). Mahmood also urges scholars to reconsider the secular and religious divide underpinning much of liberal feminist thinking, to enable new understandings of the complexity of lived, embodied experience in different ethnographic contexts.

As this brief review suggests, many feminist anthropologists do not clearly distinguish among "affect," "emotion," "feeling," and "sentiment." Although Cvetkovich, as described earlier, prefers this messiness, anthropologists Analiese Richard and Daromir Rudnyckyj (2009) disagree. They call for more analytical clarity on this point, arguing that affect should not be conflated with these other terms because "it is [the] dynamic and reflexive quality of affect and its ability to act upon (or affect) action that makes it analytically valuable" (Richards and Rudnyckyj 2009, 59). In comparison to these other terms, they contend that "affect is useful because it is inherently reflexive and intersubjective, referring to relations practiced between individuals"; this is in contrast to emotion, which, they suggest, still "bears the spectre of a psychological individualism" (Richards and Rudnyckyj 2009, 57). Indeed, in their work on affect and neoliberalism, they invoke the idea of "economies of affect"[6] because, they argue, it gives analytical purchase "to the connection between economic transformations and affective transactions" (Richards and Rudnyckyj 2009, 58). Their contention deserves attention. The recent profusion of studies in which feminist anthropologists invoke sentiment, emotion, feeling, and affect in different ways requires a close and critical exegesis beyond the scope of this chapter, to assess the potency attributed to affect theory by many scholars and to illuminate and refine our analytical distinctions and precision. This seems particularly salient in work that focuses on emotion, which has long been of importance to feminist anthropology, and which has not only contested the emotional/thinking binary, revealing it as a product of Western conceptualizations (Lutz 1988), but has treated emotions as a product of social interaction (Abu-Lughod 1986; Rosaldo 1980).

In my own research (Mascia-Lees 2011), I have developed the term "aesthetic embodiment" as a means to circumvent some of the assumptions and confusions that often underlie the use of affect in feminist studies. In his review of *The Affect Theory Reader* (2010),[7] Russ Leo (2011) claims that this otherwise groundbreaking text is presentist: "Except for the frequent citation of Spinoza, there is scarcely a reference to any writer or event prior to the twentieth century. This risks losing sight of the development of alternative theories and approaches to affect that have marked much of Western and Eastern—indeed, World—philosophy, aesthetics (in the broadest sense), religion, and therapeutic discourses." Because "affect belongs to aesthetics" and aesthetics "serves as a point of contact between the inextricable fields of politics and everyday life" (Leo 2011), my development of the concept of "aesthetic embodiment" enables me (see Mascia-Lees 2011) to explore questions of intersubjectivity, interobjectivy, and political/subject formation by subjecting them to the lens of Marx, Morris, Williams, Benjamin, Buck-Morss, and Jameson rather than Spinoza, Deleuze, Massumi, and Sedgwick (see Mascia-Lees 2011).

My recent ethnographic work, for example, focuses on how commodity capitalism is experienced, sensed, embodied, and made meaningful by a contemporary group of craftspeople and their customers who produce and consume a particular style of architectural and domestic goods associated with the hugely influential nineteenth-century British Socialist Arts and Crafts Movement. I show how this aesthetic is one that involves multiple sensory experiences and is simultaneously prereflective and self-reflexive, perceptual and conceptual, affective and cognitive, intersubjective and interobjective. It may grow out of a romanticism that offers consumers a respite from a commodity culture they can never really escape, but it clearly offers them an ethics that enables them to navigate its anonymity and excesses in a humanistic way (Mascia-Lees 2011).

Specifically, submersion in this embodied aesthetic creates a means for subverting commodity fetishism as well as a mode of attention (see Csordas 1993) to everyday detail that hones sensory receptivity to the specificity of things, an immersion that involves turning a critical eye on the way they think of everyday practices, linking affect to aesthetics and embodiment to politics. Although this may not necessarily provide producers and consumers with a transformative politics (although I would argue it does for many), this conclusion differs distinctly from those that understand neoliberal late capitalism as primarily depressive or cruel.

As an exercise, I suggest that exploring or developing alternative concepts can reveal the limitations of affect theory as well as its potency, and enable feminist anthropologists to develop their analyses in different directions, directions that might be more useful to their particular feminist politics.

CONCLUSION

So where does this leave today's feminist anthropology now that its central categories have been seriously problematized? As Ellen Lewin describes this circumstance, "Feminist anthropology's fate seems to be to deconstruct itself: its object is no longer as firmly female as it was thirty years ago, nor are its practitioners any longer willing to make facile assumptions about how to understand sex and gender. Its frame of reference is no longer clearly culture, its understanding of the body where it all starts no longer confident" (2006, 28).

In contemporary feminist anthropology, "the body" is conceptualized as simultaneously subject and object, symbol and material, individual and social, and deeply embedded in an intersubjective world of people and objects constituting lived experience, and thus can no longer be the object of analysis. Just as the anthropology of the body has transmuted into an anthropology of embodiment, so too has the feminist anthropology of the body. I suggest that what links much of the current work I have described to an earlier feminist anthropology is the continued search for concepts that allow us to analyze power, politics, and inequality in ways that address the limitations of binary dualisms that while confronted in theory, continue to operate within larger social contexts to buttress unequal power relations.

In saying this, I am suggesting that the feminist anthropological project is still alive in newer work, although it may be harder to recognize now that feminism's initial central organizing concepts have been challenged and lost some of their potency: gender, subjectivity, interiority, and agency, for example. The power differentials that spawned an earlier feminist anthropology persist and grow, taking on new forms, and feminist anthropologists today invoke a revised vocabulary to confront their current manifestations. All of the newer works on affect in anthropology reviewed here are concerned with questions of inequality or social justice. "Body-self," "intersubjectivity," "interobjectivity," and "affect," for example, are just some of the terms being used more frequently today to try to capture, evoke, and explain different ways of "being in the world," a world that continues to teem with material inequalities, injustices, and oppression.

ACKNOWLEDGMENTS

This chapter is based on two earlier versions I presented in 2013, both events organized by Florence Babb: an invited session of the 112th Annual Meeting of American Anthropological Association, "Feminist Publics, Current Engagements: Gender, Culture, and Society Forty Years Later" to recognize and honor the publication of *Woman, Culture, and Society*; the other was a conference on "Feminist Publics, Current Engagements: Gender, Culture, and Society Forty Years Later," University of Florida, Gainesville, Florida. I am deeply indebted to Florence for her insight, energy, and dedication to organizing these events. I am profoundly grateful to Alisse Waterston who read an early version of this chapter. While the ideas are my responsibility, her critical insights and probing questions pushed me to think harder about some of the central ideas with which I was grappling and, in doing so, helped me offer a stronger argument. I appreciate that Ellen Lewin and Leni Silverstein have pulled together this much-needed volume and included my chapter in it, and appreciate their helpful feedback.

NOTES

1. However, see Martin's recent work which shows that the rational/irrational boundary has yet to be fully challenged (2009).
2. See Csordas (2011) for his recent incorporation of the ideas of these theorists into his notion of embodiment as a methodological field.
3. See Olkowski and Weiss (2006) for recent reassessments of Merleau-Ponty's importance for feminist thinking, although not without criticism.
4. An exploration of the politics of intimacy has suffused feminist anthropology in the last decade: see, for example, Freidman (2006), Illouz (2007), Povinelli (2006), Stoler (2002), and Wilson (2004).
5. See Muehlebach (2011) and Nouvet (2014) for other recent works illuminating the relationship of affective labor to neoliberalism in different ethnographic contexts.
6. This is distinct from Sara Ahmed (2004) who uses the phrase "affective economies." The authors suggest that while Ahmed is describing how emotions bind subjects together into collectivities, they are more concerned with how the transaction of affect enables forms of connection at a distance.
7. Also see *The Affective Turn: Theorizing the Social* (Clough and Halley 2007).

REFERENCES

Abu-Lughod, Lila. 1986. *Veiled Sentiments: Honor and Poetry in a Bedouin Society*. Chicago: Chicago University Press.

Ahmed, Sara. 2004. "Affective Economies." *Social Text* 79, 22 (2): 117–139.

Beauvoir, Simone de. 1953. *The Second Sex*. Trans. Howard M. Parshley. Harmondsworth: Penguin.

Bendelow, Gillian, and Simon J. Williams. 1998. *The Lived Body: Sociological Themes, Embodied Issues*. London: Routledge.

Berlant, Lauren. 2011. *Cruel Optimism*. Durham, NC: Duke University Press.

Bolles, A. Lynne. 2013. "Telling the Story Straight." *Transforming Anthropology* 21 (1): 57–71.

Bordo, Susan. 2003. *Unbearable Weight: Feminism, Western Culture, and the Body*. Berkeley: University of California Press.

Boston Women's Health Book Collective. 1973. *Our Bodies/Ourselves*. New York: Simon and Schuster.

Braidotti, Rosi. 1994. *Nomadic Subjects: Embodiment and Sexual Difference in Contemporary Feminist Theory*. New York: Columbia University Press.

Butler, Judith. 1990. *Gender Trouble: Feminism and the Subversion of Identity*. New York: Routledge.

———. 1998. "Subjects of Sex/Gender/Desire." In *Feminism and Politics*, ed. Anne Phillips, 273–294. Oxford: Oxford University Press.

Cixous, Helene. 1980. "The Laugh of the Medusa." In *New French Feminisms: An Anthology*, ed. Elaine Marks and Isabelle De Courtivron, 245–264. Amherst: University of Massachusetts Press.

Clough, Patricia Ticineto, with Jean Halley, ed. 2007. *The Affective Turn*. Durham, NC: Duke University Press.

Collier, Jane Fishburne. 1974. "Women in Politics." In *Woman, Culture and Society*, ed. Michelle Z. Rosaldo and Louise Lamphere, 89–96. Stanford, CA: Stanford University Press.

Collins, Patricia Hill. 1990. *Black Feminist Thought: Knowledge, Consciousness, and the Politics of Empowerment.* New York and London: Routledge.

Csordas, Thomas. 1993. "Somatic Modes of Attention." *Cultural Anthropology* 8 (2): 135–156.

———. 1994. "Introduction." In *Embodiment and Experience*, ed. Thomas Csordas, 1–24. Cambridge: Cambridge University Press.

———. 2009. *Cultural Anthropology*, supplemental material. http://www.culanth.org/articles/301-somatic-modes-of-attention/, accessed May 24, 2015.

———. 2011. "Embodiment: Agency, Sexual Difference, and Illness." In *A Companion to the Anthropology of the Body and Embodiment*, ed. Frances E. Mascia-Lees, 137–156. Malden, MA: Wiley-Blackwell.

Cvetkovich, Ann. 2012. *Depression: A Public Feeling.* Durham, NC: Duke University Press.

del Rio, Elena. 2005. "Alchemies of Thought in Godard's Cinema: Deleuze and Merleau-Ponty." *SubStance* 108, 34 (3): 62–78.

Desjarlais, Robert, and C. Jason Throop. 2011. "Phenomenological Approaches in Anthropology." *Annual Review of Anthropology* 40: 87–102.

di Leonardo, Micaela, and Roger Lancaster. 1996. "Gender, Sexuality, Political Economy." *New Politics* 6 (1): new series. http://nova.wpunj.edu/newpolitics/issue21/leonar21.htm, accessed May 24, 2015.

Douglas, Mary. 1970. *Natural Symbols: Explorations in Cosmology.* London: Barrie & Rockliff, Cresset Press.

Dreyfus, Hubert, and Paul Rabinow. 1983. *Michel Foucault: Beyond Structuralism and Hermeneutics.* Chicago: University of Chicago Press.

Fanon, Frantz. 1986. *Black Skin, White Masks.* Trans. Charles Lam Markmann. London: Pluto Press.

Foucault, Michel. 1975. *Discipline and Punish: The Birth of the Prison.* New York: Vintage Books.

Freeman, Carla. 2011. "Embodying and Affecting Neoliberalism." In *A Companion to the Anthropology of the Body and Embodiment*, ed. Frances E. Mascia-Lees, 353–369. Malden, MA: Wiley-Blackwell.

Friedman, Sara. 2006. *Intimate Politics: Marriage, the Market, and State Power in Southeastern China.* Cambridge, MA: Harvard University Press.

Greer, Germaine. 1970. *The Female Eunuch.* New York: McGraw-Hill.

Gregg, Melissa, and Gregory J. Seigworth, eds. 2010. *The Affect Theory Reader.* Durham, NC: Duke University Press.

Grosz, Elizabeth. 1994. *Volatile Bodies.* Bloomington: Indiana University Press.

Hall, Stuart. 2002. "Who Needs Identity?" In *Questions of Cultural Identity*, ed. Paul duGay and Stuart Hall, 1–17. Thousand Oaks, CA: Sage.

Halliburton, Murphy. 2002. "Rethinking Anthropological Studies of the Body: Manas and Bodham in Kerala." *American Anthropologist* 104 (4): 1123–1134.

Haraway, Donna. 1985. "A Manifesto for Cyborgs: Science, Technology, and Socialist Feminism in the 1980s." In *Feminism/Postmodernism*, ed. Linda Nicholson, 190–233. New York: Routledge.

Harding, Sandra. 1986. *The Science Question in Feminism.* Ithaca, NY: Cornell University Press.

Hardt, Michael. 2007. "Foreword: What Affects Are Good For." In *Theorizing the Social*, ed. Patricia Ticineto Clough with Jean Halley, iv–xiii. Durham, NC: Duke University Press.

Highmore, Ben. 2010. "Something Ordinary." *Reviews in Cultural Theory* 1 (1). http://www.reviewsinculture.com/?r=15, accessed May 24, 2015.

Hochschild, Arlie. 1983. *The Managed Heart*. Berkeley: University of California Press.
hooks, bell. 1981. *Ain't I a Woman?: Black Women and Feminism*. Boston: South End Press.
Illouz, Eva. 2007. *Cold Intimacies: The Making of Emotional Capitalism*. Cambridge: Polity.
Irigaray, Luce. 1985. *This Sex Which Is Not One*. Trans. Catherine Porter with Carolyn Burke. Ithaca, NY: Cornell University Press.
Jamal, Amina. 2008. "Review of *Politics of Piety: The Islamic Revival and the Feminist Subject, An Enchanted Modern: Gender and Public Piety in Shi'i Lebanon, and Performing Islam: Gender and Ritual in Iran*." *Journal of Middle East Women's Studies* 4 (3): 121–128.
Keat, Russell. 2013. *Merleau-Ponty and the Phenomenology of the Body*. http://www.russellkeat.net/admin/ers/51.pdf, accessed May 24, 2015.
Kingston, Maxine Hong. 1975. *The Woman Warrior: Memoirs of a Girlhood among Ghosts*. New York: Vintage Press.
Kleinman, Arthur, Veena Das, and Margaret Lock, eds. 1997. *Social Suffering*. Berkeley: University of California Press.
Kristeva, Julia. 1986. *The Kristeva Reader*. Ed. Toril Moi. New York: Columbia University Press.
Lamphere, Louise. 1974. "Strategies, Cooperation, and Conflict among Women in Domestic Groups." In *Woman, Culture and Society*, ed. Michelle Z. Rosaldo and Louise Lamphere, 97–117. Stanford, CA: Stanford University Press.
Latour, Bruno. 2005. *Reassembling the Social: An Introduction to Actor-Network-Theory*. Oxford and New York: Oxford University Press.
Leo, Russ. 2011. "An Archive for Affect Theory." *Reviews in Cultural Theory* 2 (2). http://www.reviewsinculture.com/?r=61, accessed May 24, 2015.
Lewin, Ellen. 2006. "Introduction." In *Feminist Anthropology: A Reader*, ed. Ellen Lewin, 1–38. Malden, MA: Wiley-Blackwell.
Leys, Ruth. 2011. "The Return to Affect: A Critique." *Critical Inquiry* 37 (3): 434–472.
Lorde, Audre. 1984. *Sister/Outsider*. Berkeley, CA: The Crossing Press.
Lutz, Catherine. 1988. *Unnatural Emotions: Everyday Sentiments in a Micronesian Atoll and Their Challenge to Western Theory*. Chicago: University of Chicago Press.
MacCormack, Carol, and Marilyn Strathern, eds. 1980. *Nature, Culture, and Gender*. Cambridge: Cambridge University Press.
Mahmood, Saba. 2005. *Politics of Piety: The Islamic Revival and the Feminist Subject*. Princeton, NJ: Princeton University Press.
Martin, Emily. 1987. *The Woman in the Body: A Cultural Analysis of Reproduction*. Boston: Beacon Press.
———. 2009. *Bipolar Expeditions: Mania and Depression in American Culture*. Princeton, NJ: Princeton University Press.
Mascia-Lees, Frances E. 2011. "Aesthetic Embodiment and Commodity Capitalism." In *A Companion to the Anthropology of the Body and Embodiment*, ed. Frances E. Mascia-Lees, 3–23. Malden, MA: Wiley-Blackwell.
Mascia-Lees, Frances E., and Patricia Sharpe. 1992. "The Marked and the Un(re)marked: Tattoo and Gender in Theory and Narrative." In *Tattoo, Torture, Mutilation, and Adornment: The Denaturalization of the Body in Culture and Text*, ed. Frances E. Mascia-Lees and Patricia Sharpe, 145–169. Albany: State University of New York Press.
Mascia-Lees Frances E., Patricia Sharpe, and Colleen Cohen. 1989. "The Postmodernist Turn in Anthropology: Cautions from a Feminist Perspective." *Signs*, 7–33.
Mauss, Marcel. 2000. "Techniques of the Body." In *Beyond the Body Proper: Reading the Anthropology of Material Life*, ed. Margaret M. Lock and Judith Farquhar, 50–68. Durham, NC: Duke University Press.

McClaurin, Irma, ed. 2001. *Black Feminist Anthropology*. New Brunswick, NJ: Rutgers University Press.

McGrail, Richard, Jesse Davie-Kessler, and Bascom Guffin, eds. n.d. "Affect, Embodiment, and Sense Perception." *Cultural Anthropology*. http://www.culanth.org/curated_collections/16-affect-embodiment-and-sense-perception, accessed May 24, 2015.

Merleau-Ponty, Maurice. 1962. *Phenomenology of Perception*. Trans. James Edie. Evanston, IL: Northwestern University Press.

Moraga, Cherríe, and Gloria Anzaldúa, eds. 1981. *This Bridge Called My Back: Writings by Radical Women of Color*. New York: Kitchen Table, Woman of Color Press.

Muehlebach, Andrea. 2011. "On Affective Labor in Post-Fordist Italy." *Cultural Anthropology* 26 (1): 59–82.

Myers, Diana. 2010. "Feminist Perspectives on the Self." *Stanford Encyclopedia of Philosophy*. http://plato.stanford.edu/entries/feminism-self/, accessed May 24, 2015.

Navaro-Yashin, Yael. 2012. *The Make-Believe Space: Affective Geography in a Postwar Polity*. Durham, NC: Duke University Press.

Nouvet, Elysée. 2014. "Some Carry On, Some Stay in Bed: (In)convenient Affects and Agency in Neoliberal Nicaragua." *Cultural Anthropology* 29 (1): 80–102. http://dx.doi.org/10.14506/ca29.1.06, accessed May 24, 2015.

Oksala, Joanna. 2006. "A Phenomenology of Gender." *Continental Philosophy Review*. http://philpapers.org/rec/OKSAPO, accessed May 24, 2015.

Olkowski, Dorothea. 2002. "Flesh to Desire: Merleau-Ponty, Bergson, Deleuze." *Strategies: Journal of Theory, Culture & Politics* 15 (1): 11–24.

Olkowski, Dorothea, and Gail Weiss, eds. 2006. *Feminist Interpretations of Maurice Merleau-Ponty*. State College: Pennsylvania State University Press.

Ortner, Sherry. 1974. "Is Female to Male as Nature Is to Culture?" In *Woman, Culture and Society*, ed. Michelle Z. Rosaldo and Louise Lamphere, 68–87. Stanford, CA: Stanford University Press.

Pelligrini, Ann, and Jasbir Puar. 2009. "Affect." *Social Text* 100, 27 (3): 35–38.

Povinelli, Elizabeth. 2006. *The Empire of Love: Toward a Theory of Intimacy, Genealogy, and Carnality*. Durham, NC: Duke University Press.

Ramos-Zayas, Ana Yolanda. 2011. "Learning Affect/Embodying Race." In *A Companion to the Anthropology of the Body and Embodiment*, ed. Frances E. Mascia-Lees, 24–45. Malden, MA: Wiley-Blackwell.

———. 2012. *Street Therapists: Race, Affect, and Neoliberal Personhood in Latino Newark*. Chicago: University of Chicago Press.

Reiter (Rapp), Rayna, ed. 1975. *Toward an Anthropology of Women*. New York: Monthly Review Press.

Rich, Adrienne. 1976. *Of Woman Born: Motherhood as Experience and Institution*. New York: W. W. Norton.

———. 1980. "Compulsory Heterosexuality and Lesbian Experience." *Signs* 5 (4): 631–660.

Richard, Analiese, and Daromir Rudnyckj. 2009. "Economies of Affect." *Journal of the Royal Anthropological Institute* 15: 57–77.

Rosaldo, Michelle. 1974. "Woman, Culture, and Society: A Theoretical Overview." In *Woman, Culture, and Society*, ed. Michelle Z. Rosaldo and Louise Lamphere, 17–51. Stanford, CA: Stanford University Press.

———. 1980. "The Use and Abuse of Anthropology: Reflections on Feminist and Cross-Cultural Understanding." *Signs* 5: 389–417.

Rosaldo, Michelle Z., and Louise Lamphere, eds. 1974. *Woman, Culture, and Society*. Stanford, CA: Stanford University Press.

Salamon, Gayle. 2008. "Review of Feminist Interpretations of Maurice Merleau-Ponty." *Notre Dame Philosophical Reviews: An Online Journal*. https://ndpr.nd.edu/news/23754-feminist-interpretations-of-maurice-merleau-ponty/, accessed May 24, 2015.

Scheper-Hughes, Nancy. 1993. *Death without Weeping*. Berkeley: University of California Press.

———. 1994. "Embodied Knowledge: Thinking with the Body in Critical Medical Anthropology." In *Assessing Cultural Anthropology*, ed. Robert Borofsky, 229–239. New York: McGraw-Hill College.

Scheper-Hughes, Nancy, and Margaret Lock. 1987. "The Mindful Body: A Prolegomenon to Future Work in Medical Anthropology." *Medical Anthropology Quarterly*, n.s. 1 (1): 6–41.

Spivak, Gayatri. 1996. *The Spivak Reader*. Ed. Donna Landry and Gerald MacLean. New York and London: Routledge.

Stack, Carol. 1974. "Sex Roles and Survival Strategies in an Urban Black Community." In *Woman, Culture, and Society*, ed. Michelle Z. Rosaldo and Louise Lamphere, 118–128. Stanford, CA: Stanford University Press.

Stewart, Kathleen. 2007. *Ordinary Affects*. Durham, NC: Duke University Press.

Stoler, Ann. 2002. *Carnal Knowledge and Imperial Power: Race and the Intimate in Colonial Rule*. Berkeley: University of California Press.

Turner, Terrence. 1994. "Bodies and Anti-Bodies: Flesh and Fetish in Contemporary Social Theory." In *Embodiment and Experience*, ed. Thomas Csordas, 27–47. Cambridge: Cambridge University Press.

Van Wolputte, Steven. 2004. "Hang on to Your Self: Of Bodies, Embodiment, and Selves." *Annual Review of Anthropology* 33: 251–269.

Wilson, Ara. 2004. *The Intimate Economies of Bangkok: Tomboys, Tycoons, and Avon Ladies in the Global City*. Berkeley: University of California Press.

Winner, L. 1993. "Upon Opening the Black Box and Finding It Empty: Social Constructivism and the Philosophy of Technology." *Science, Technology, & Human Values* 18: 362–378.

DISCIPLINE AND DESIRE

Feminist Politics, Queer Studies, and New Queer Anthropology

MARGOT WEISS

Gender and sexuality, feminist and queer—these four terms and their sometimes-contested interrelationships are the subject of this chapter. Like others in this volume, I aim to highlight the legacies of feminist anthropology; my particular task is to explore these legacies in terms of contemporary queer anthropology. But I intend to go about my task queerly. I do not proceed linearly or forge a progressive narrative, where queer might take the place of feminist, or where proper objects, once demarcated, might stay put. Instead, I stage a series of analogical readings of feminist and queer studies and their proper objects and political investments, alongside the questions of political desire and institutionalization, before turning to the possibilities of a critical queer studies and its relationship to anthropology. My hope is that these readings might yield helpful ways to think about queer anthropology today.

I begin with well-trodden ground: the delineation of gender as the domain of feminist studies, and sexuality as the domain of queer studies. We can locate this split in two distinct moments: efforts in the 1980s to disconnect studies of gendered oppression from studies of sexuality, and efforts in the 1990s (and later) to move away from seemingly exclusive identity terms (*women* or *gay/lesbian*) and toward purportedly inclusive ones (*gender, sexuality, queer*). These are moments others in this volume explore, so I won't linger on these details. Instead, I focus on two questions of continued relevance: the problematic of institutionalization (and the closure or fixity institutionalization represents) and the problematic of good enough objects—objects that might satisfy the political desires we have invested in them.

Examining the political aspirations we invest in our disciplines, I explore how the desire to exceed the limits of institutionalization has sparked a critical queer studies, one that is attentive to both particularity and to a larger global context. Detouring through some of the new work in queer studies that, in my analysis, is compatible with cultural anthropology, I focus on the places where queer analytics aim to surpass proper objects and pat political interpretations. I conclude with a survey of what I term the "new queer anthropology," which seeks to remake its objects and analytics by pushing its key terms—*queer* and *anthropology*—into uncharted territories. Throughout, I remain attuned to what I see as the key tension driving queer studies in and outside anthropology: the ways disciplinary desires produce new political and intellectual possibilities, even as we remain attached to the conditions of their emergence.

PROPER OBJECTS: GENDER AND SEXUALITY

Let's start with proper objects. No matter how many times she tells us it just wasn't so, most of the stories about the founding of queer studies start with Gayle Rubin's 1984 essay "Thinking Sex," and in particular that one part, toward the end of the essay, that goes: "I want to challenge the assumption that feminism is or should be the privileged site of a theory of sexuality. Feminism is the theory of gender oppression. To assume automatically that this makes it the theory of sexual oppression is to fail to distinguish between gender, on the one hand, and erotic desire, on the other" (1993 [1984], 32). The essay was intended, as she explains, to enable us to "think about oppression" and "the structures of sexual stratification" (Rubin 1994, 90) beyond binary gender, "presumptions of heterosexuality, or a simple hetero-homo opposition" (Rubin 1994, 70). She protests in a 1994 interview with Judith Butler, "I think those last few pages [of "Thinking Sex"] have been overinterpreted as some huge rejection or turn-about on my part. I saw them more as a corrective, and as a way to get a handle on another group of issues . . . issues of sexual difference and sexual variety" (67).[1]

But although Rubin did not intend "to found a field" or argue that feminism "should not work on sexuality" (1994, 88), it is a testament to the power of her words that the essay was taken as such. Indeed, the *Lesbian and Gay Studies Reader*—the first of its kind to anthologize the field—begins with Rubin's essay, drawing on it to argue for lesbian and gay studies as an (at least semi-) autonomous field for the study of sexuality. As the editors write, "lesbian/gay studies does for sex and sexuality approximately what women's studies does for gender" (Abelove, Barale, and Halperin 1993, xv).

Yet how, analytically, might we cordon off "sex and sexuality" from "gender"? As Judith Butler writes in "Against Proper Objects," such a division between sexuality and gender denies both "the normative operation of gender in the regulation of sexuality" (perhaps Butler's main contribution to the field of queer theory) and, as she puts it, the "constitutive ambiguity of 'sex,'" where sex points to both gender/embodiment and sexuality/desire (1994, 6). Immediately, then, we have proper disciplinary objects that refuse to stay put—a dilemma perhaps obvious to anthropologists trained to see gender more as an "entry point into complex systems of meaning and power" and "less as a structure of fixed relations," as Kamala Visweswaran describes disidentificatory feminist ethnography (1997, 593). If gender and sexuality cannot be neatly separated—as indeed they cannot in studies of travesti sex workers (Kulick 1998) or *mati* work (Wekker 2006) or men who have sex with men (Boellstorff 2011; Padilla 2007) or transnational gayness (Manalansan 2003; Rofel 1999), to draw on the range of topics central to recent queer ethnography—neither are they identical, which we can see when we scale down to any particular cultural milieu.

Take, as a brief case in point, the different mappings of gender and social power in Evelyn Blackwood's *Falling into the Lesbi World* (2010) and Tom Boellstorff's *The Gay Archipelago* (2005). Comparing these two stellar ethnographies of same-sex desire and sexuality in Indonesia illuminates the crucial difference sex and gender, in combination with desire, make in terms of access to public spaces, familial autonomy, mobility, and other markers of social power and sexual possibilities. Blackwood's ethnography of lesbi tombois and their girlfriends in West Sumatra emphasizes the (re)mappings of gendered binaries and power, whereas Boellstorff's emphasizes the emergence of *gay* and *lesbi* sexual subject positions in a national context. Taken together, these two ethnographies highlight *both* divergence between gendered experiences and identities in local communities *and* strengthened connections between lesbi, tombois, girlfriends, *gay* men, and *warias* across Indonesia, and in global or transnational LGBT/queer circuits.[2]

But if the analytical separation of gender and sexuality is conceptually untenable, it remains the case that this purported separation fosters, in Butler's terms, foundational "territorial claims," claims that continue to map disciplines and secure institutional authority (1994, 6). Butler calls for both feminist and queer studies to "move beyond and against those methodological demands which force separations in the interests of canonization and provisional institutional legitimation," to remain open to other differences such as race or class, and to think "against the institutional separatisms which work effectively to keep thought narrow, sectarian, and self-serving" (1994, 21). Indeed, it is the demands of legitimacy and legibility that call for the impossible separation of objects as a mechanism of institutional authority, and it is my contention that this is a key legacy that both feminist and queer anthropology confront today.

AWKWARD RELATIONS, POLITICAL DESIRES: FEMINIST STUDIES AND QUEER STUDIES

If the first legacy is a kind of closure-through-institutionalization that, simultaneously, produces women's studies and gay and lesbian studies as figuratively autonomous fields, the second is its dialectical other: the desire to think "against the institutional separatisms" and limitations institutionalization portends. I refer, of course, to the shift from *women* to *gender* and from *gay and lesbian* to *queer.* This shift is far more than semantics—as any linguist could tell you—but what I want to focus on is the way this shift was (is) guided by a political desire for better, more expansive concepts, methods, and disciplines. As Robyn Wiegman has argued, for scholars working in women's studies, the move to *gender* was a response to the failure of *women* to account for *all* women. *Gender*, then, could include men and masculinity, as well as queer and transgender. Perhaps it would be more inclusive, complex, sophisticated, and intersectional than the former object, *women* (Wiegman 2012, 39–40).

I will spend some time on Wiegman's argument because it helps us think about the political investments we make in and through our objects of study. For the hope that this new object could dislodge the false universalizations that seemed to plague women's studies relies, as Wiegman argues, on a "transferential idealism": that *gender* might save us, conceptually *and* politically, moving us forward, in a progressive march toward "representational inclusion, historical precision, subjective complexity, social reparation, and theoretical sophistication" (40). This move—which entailed renaming women's studies programs (to feminist studies, gender studies, or a combination), rethinking curricula, and remapping the field—rested on the belief that "gender will be capable of giving us everything that women does not . . . will be adequate to all the wishes that are invested in it" (Wiegman 2012, 42). In short, that our object will satisfy our feminist political desires.

The search for a perfect or fully inclusive object is akin to the desire to find the perfect terminology that will yield a one-to-one correspondence between language and our social world, a desire Boellstorff critiques as the "logic of enumeration"[3] (2007b, 18; see also Weiss 2011a). Yet still, this wish or desire, invested in an object, is a central legacy for us today in both feminist and queer studies. Both, as politically motivated fields, aim to do "justice with, to, and through our objects of studies," even as our objects are always "incommensurate with the political desire invested in them" (Wiegman 2012, 42). If this is true of gender, which continues to strain under the sometimes-inclusion of the rapidly expanding field of trans studies,[4] perhaps the same might be true in queer studies (née gay and lesbian studies). Yet while the dynamics of the good-enough object in feminist and queer studies suggests certain parallels, the object relations in each are not precisely analogous.

Just as women's studies began to question its foundational object, *women*, so too did lesbian and gay studies—moving away from *gay* and *lesbian* to *queer*. The shift in terminology entailed interrogating the conceptual content of homosexuality and, indeed, sexuality itself (Weston 1993, 346). But unlike *gender*, these queries, in queer studies, took the form of an "internal critique" of lesbian and gay studies, rather than the substitutive search for a new perfect object (like *gender*). In other words, *queer*, at least in its early 1990s formulation, was less an object and more a provocation, a critique of the "fixed sexual identity" or "'thing' called homosexuality" offered by gay and lesbian studies (Weston 1993, 348).

This is where feminist and queer studies' object relations diverge. Feminist studies, in moving toward *gender*, sought an object capacious enough to withstand the political desires invested in it, desires formulated according to identification with one's object. The convergence (and mutual identification) between subject and object in feminist studies seemed necessary for political solidarity; it is this purported convergence that generates the "awkward relationship" between feminism and ethnography that Marilyn Strathern (1987) and Judith Stacey (1988) have so cogently outlined. In queer studies, on the other hand, one does "justice to or with one's object of study by steadfastly refusing identification" (Wiegman 2012, 97)—by *not* assuming self-identical or indexical relations between author and object—but instead focusing on category confusion or *transgression*.

Queer, then, is not a more inclusive or robust category of identity—indeed, in feminist foremothers Eve Sedgwick's (1993) and Judith Butler's (1993) work, *queer* is profoundly anti-identitarian. Queer is a political location, that which is, in Michael Warner's oft-cited phrase, resistant "to regimes of the normal" (1993, xxvi; see also Berlant and Warner 1998), a category for the "transgressive aspects of gender and sexuality" (Weston 1993, 348). In the decades since 1993, Wiegman argues, the centrality of anti-normativity or transgression to the concept of queer has dovetailed with its quasi-institutionalization in the academy; as she writes, anti-normativity serves today as queer studies' "guiding frame and political guarantee" (2012, 341).[5]

Yet for all this divergence between identification (in feminist studies) and anti-identitarian fracturing (in queer studies), the political desires that subtend each field are not so neatly opposed. Indeed, in many ways, queer studies echoes and inverts feminist studies' awkward relationship between self, object, and political desire. *Queer* is simultaneously a disciplinary object, an analysis (or, in stronger terms, an epistemology), and a political stance. As a political stance, queer studies tends to describe the critic *through* the object, cloaking our own "professional investments in the noble rhetoric of the political desire that incites it" (Wiegman 2012, 314)—even as it is precisely the "inherently radical political position" of queerness that underwrites its institutional authority (308–309, 341–342). The (partial) institutionalization of Queer Theory in the academy demands a continual reinvestment in that dynamic, which sustains the critical authority of the interdiscipline *and* the radicality of our own queer political desires.

In both feminist and queer studies, then, the field imaginary, as Wiegman puts it, is one that promises to support the critic's political desires through the object. And yet, the failure of the hoped-for equivalence between politics and professionalization often leads to frustration or disappointment: "what happens," Wiegman asks, "when what you once loved no longer satisfies your belief that it can give you what you want?" (2012,10). This happened in queer theory, of course. Indeed Teresa de Lauretis, the first person to use the phrase "queer theory" in print in her 1991 introduction to a special issue of *differences,* turned away from the term a mere three years later, claiming that it had become "a conceptually vacuous creature of the publishing industry" (de Lauretis 1994, 297). De Lauretis's complaint is one of institutionalization—institutionalization as unwanted normalization.

With *queer,* de Lauretis hoped for a way to "transgress and transcend" discursive categories; *queer,* she imagined, might investigate the formations of identities across time and space and in the intersections of race, gender, and class, rather than assume them (1991, iii). Above all, *queer* promised a "conceptual and speculative" opening for de Lauretis. "Can our queerness act as an agent of social change," she asked, "and our theory construct another discursive horizon, another way of living the racial and the sexual?" (1991, xi). This was the possibility of *queer,* in the early 1990s at least: a "site of collective contestation, the point of departure for a set of historical reflections and future imaginings," as Butler rather hopefully wrote. Even so, for Butler, *queer* can only have this political value insofar as the term remains undomesticated—"never fully owned, but always and only redeployed, twisted, queered from a prior usage and in the direction of urgent and expanding political purposes" (1993, 19). Similarly, Lauren Berlant and Michael Warner worried over the potential calcification of "queer theory" as it was being absorbed into the academy and suggest "queer commentary" instead as an inclusive academic and activist project that could be "radically anticipatory," "trying to bring a world into being" (1995, 344, 347).

This short history of *queer* is painfully ironic: what was, at its start, an opening to new possibilities has, as it has become institutionalized in the academy, taken on its own normative anti-normativity. We can see why this frustrated de Lauretis—as soon as queer is marked off, it is absorbed by precisely those institutions it seeks to critique—and also why Butler urges us to avoid marking territory in a bid for institutional recognition: "There is more to learn from upsetting such grounds . . . and resisting the institutional domestication of queer thinking. . . . For normalizing the queer would be, after all, its sad finish" (1994, 21).

But, as I will detail in the next section, institutionalization has not been the end of queer. Instead, we might take a lesson from feminist studies and see that it is precisely the frustration of the (political-analytical) desires that motivated the field to begin with that moves queer studies in new directions. The transference of our political desire onto a disciplinary object (like *queer*) generates "predictable disappointment, if not at times political despair" (Wiegman 2012, 322). Still, this is the logic of field formation—an "affective failure" that simultaneously "restores the horizon of possibility" by promising new objects or analytics that might achieve our political desires (322). In the same way that women's studies sought new political horizons through gender (however we wish to evaluate its relative success), the "ongoing revision and differentiation" that we can see in queer regenerates the field through our own political frustrations. Thinking about queer studies' temporality in this way, we might see institutionalization—and its attendant complicity with precisely the "exclusions by which [queer] is mobilized" (Butler 1993, 20)—as perhaps less a mark of failure, and more a sign of the productive social conditions that guide both our scholarly and sexual pursuits. If this is the case, then we might say that the cordoning off of gender and sexuality, feminist studies and queer—along with the constitutive exclusions and impossible incommensurabilities that those divergences put into place—has also recharged the political desires we've brought to our objects and our disciplinary work.

As I hope I've shown, it is not that feminist studies and queer studies are neatly analogous; in the case of feminist studies, we've sought a more perfect object (gender), whereas in queer studies, we've sought an object equivalent to our politics (the resistant queer). I have spent some time unpacking queer studies' political-disciplinary attachment to anti-normativity because, and crucially for anthropologists, the valorization of anti-normativity as a merged object-cum-political-analysis within queer studies can produce work that turns away from, rather than engages, the social world. This happens when queer studies becomes a prescriptive project—one that a priori assumes that all queer objects are anti-normative. It is this that, I think, might motivate some anthropologists' suspicion of queer studies (as anti-empirical or overly abstracted). Yet still, in queer studies (and feminist studies), I would argue that the limitations of these objects vis-à-vis our desires also serve as prompts that push us toward new objects, new analyses, new horizons.

REMAPPING BOUNDARIES: ANTHROPOLOGY AND CRITICAL QUEER STUDIES

In her cogent analysis of the ethnocentrism of queer studies, Elisabeth Engebretsen argues that "despite a growing appreciation in queer studies of the complexities of contemporary global sexualities and genders . . . there seems to be little genuine effort to re-visit and revise" foundational analytical concepts (2008, 90). Queer studies, she argues, rests on a "particular definition of sexual meanings and research questions and objects" (91). As long as this is the case, the descriptions of non-US genders and sexualities offered by anthropologists simply operate as "data on the half shell" (as Kath Weston so brilliantly put it [1998]); they do not challenge the theoretical paradigms and exclusions that undergird queer studies itself.

Engebretsen's is one of a number of anthropological critiques of queer studies' US-focus (and presumptions), even in its transnationalizing or globalizing key.[6] I certainly don't dispute the claim that queer studies does not pay attention to anthropology—and not *only* because I am a disciplinary chauvinist; it is a source of continual frustration for queer anthropologists that we specialize in exactly the sort of theoretically sophisticated, locally grounded, transnational analysis that "transnationalizing" queer studies claims to want. Indeed, to peruse the American Anthropological Association annual conference program or the nominees for the Association for Queer Anthropology's annual Ruth Benedict Prize is to be awed by sophisticated, cutting-edge theoretical-empirical work on nationalism and sexuality, on queer and trans transnational politics, on queer modes of belonging and futurity, on language and its sexual politics, on queer activisms in locations across the world. But still, I think there is another possible relationship between cultural anthropology and queer studies—a more synergistic one with what might be called a critical queer studies.[7]

I'll take as my starting point the 2005 special issue of *Social Text*, "What's Queer About Queer Studies Now?" Editors David Eng, J. Jack Halberstam, and José Muñoz answer their own question (and sound rather anthropological), writing that their queer studies "insists on a broadened consideration of the late twentieth-century global crises that have configured historical relations among political economies, the geopolitics of war and terror, and national manifestations of sexual, racial, and gendered hierarchies" (2005, 1). Naming empire, globalization, neoliberalism, sovereignty, immigration, and citizenship, alongside race, class, and nation, as key terrains for queer studies in the early 2000s, the editors herald a queer studies that does not retain *queer's* strict relationship to sexuality (and certainly not identity) (2005, 2). What I call a critical queer studies also troubles a strict attachment to *anti-normativity.* As Eng, Halberstam, and Muñoz note, we are witnessing the growth of "queer liberalism," which attempts "to reconcile the radical political aspirations of queer studies . . . with the contemporary liberal demands of a nationalist gay and lesbian US citizen-subject petitioning for rights and recognition before the law" (2005, 10). This emergence, they write, "challenges us to reconsider some of the canonical ideas of the field," including "normal and antinormal" (2005, 13).

Critical queer studies troubles both sexuality as the proper object of queer studies and the assumption that *queer* is always oppositional (to the state, capitalism, and the like) by moving queer analysis in two directions: toward the more specific or particular, and toward broader global or transnational flows. (It might be the special province of anthropology to aim to do both of these at the same time.) So, for example, Roderick Ferguson argues that the centralization of sexuality as the "propertied object" of queer studies has elided the ways that sexuality is "constitutive of and constituted by racialized gender and class formations" (2005, 87, 88). He urges us to take inspiration from women of color feminism and insist on "the historical specificity and heterogeneity of 'sexuality,' a specificity and heterogeneity denoted as racial difference" in the United States (86). From the other direction, Chandan Reddy's work seeks to uncover the US state's operations as a form of "freedom with violence" that fuses state protection with legitimated state violence against racialized, non-normative others (2011; see also Puar 2007).

These are just two examples of US-focused queer studies work that tends, at least in my reading, to complement queer anthropology by foregrounding social specificity and embedding queer subjects and communities within broader national imaginaries and political economies. I make no claims as to the global reach of this work. Indeed, although it might be the case that US queer studies, perhaps unsurprisingly, tends to presume an American national context, it is also the case that this concentration has fostered much of queer studies' best work. Like ethnographic work, such critical queer scholarship can help us better understand the specificity of a US racialized sexuality or the nexus of the US nation and queerness.

It is beyond the task of this chapter to survey the entire field of queer studies, but these new directions suggest that the frustrations arising from an institutionalized and normative anti-normativity, alongside an expansion of the boundaries of "sexuality," have generated a critical queer studies that—to me—connects to the work that we are doing in queer anthropology. What, for example, might be learned by reading work in queer Marxism, queer affect, or queer of color critique alongside ethnographic examinations of queer globalization, neoliberalism, and imperialism? In my own work on the sexual politics of BDSM (bondage and discipline, domination/submission, sadomasochism), generative frictions between ethnography and queer and feminist studies shaped my analysis of race, gender, and late capitalist cultures of neoliberalism (Weiss 2011b).

Similarly, my current research on how queer left activists conjure new visions of queer social and economic justice has benefitted from exploring concepts like potentiality, endurance, and futurity across and between ethnographic and non-ethnographic registers (especially Berlant 2011; Dave 2012; Muñoz 2009; and Povinelli 2011). The analytical and political stakes of that project are, of necessity, in dialogue with interdisciplinary queer studies work that challenges progressive narratives of activism (Hanhardt 2013) and situates queer politics in the broadest sociopolitical frame (Haritaworn, Kuntsman, and Posocco 2014). I offer these rather mundane examples of my own interdisciplinarity to destabilize, rather than reentrench, an assumed oppositionality between queer studies and anthropology. That such synergies are possible is one of the hallmark strengths of anthropology's promiscuous theoretical purview. Indeed, we all might take a note from the debates around the proper objects of feminist and queer studies and resist the "methodological demands which force separations in the interests of canonization and provisional institutional legitimation" (Butler 1994, 21).

But taking that lesson a bit further, as I aim to do in this chapter, we can see that the normalization institutionalization carries offers not only (some) legitimation, but also serves as a productive limit that might spur new relationships between queer studies and anthropology. For example, Scott Morgensen's *Spaces between Us* (2011) is situated on the borders of anthropology, queer studies, and native studies; his work not only challenges disciplinary norms, but also the ground—white settler colonialism—upon which our disciplines function. Departing dramatically from ethnocartographic studies of Indian (Native American) gender and sexuality, including analyses of two-spirit people, Morgensen's book is as much a critique of queer studies as it is of anthropology's appropriation of Native peoples' sexualities, genders, and lands. Other collaborations aim to recalibrate disciplinary ways of knowing, as with the generative collaboration between Lauren Berlant and Katie Stewart on "Sensing Precarity"—the experience of living in a vulnerable, collapsing present.[8] In my analysis, such collaborations between queer studies and anthropology draw on both fields' frustrations and desires—for better objects, more powerful methods, more robust politics—and, in so doing, seek to produce new ways to comprehend the textures of social life.

QUEER HORIZONS: TOWARD A NEW QUEER ANTHROPOLOGY

And so finally we arrive at what I am calling a new queer anthropology. To be sure, the new queer anthropology appeared on the scene dragging some serious baggage in the form of the fraught problematics of institutionalization I've detailed earlier (between gender and sexuality, feminist and queer studies, and queer studies and anthropology). And queer anthropology, although still a tiny subset of the larger anthropological world, has achieved some institutional legitimacy: it has its own AAA section, book prize, courses, and review essays such as this one. And so, as we might expect, queer anthropology shares many of the same frustrations (about institutional closure and limitations) and desires (for more expansive, more political objects) that power its sister fields. With "new queer anthropology," then, I mean to refer not only to very recent trends in queer cultural anthropology, but to a queer anthropology that encounters *queer* and *anthropology* as generative limits, and seeks to reimagine both terms as proper objects and ways of knowing.

First, *queer.* In her recent *Queer Activism in India,* Naisargi Dave cites David Halperin's definition of *queer* as "whatever is at odds with the normal, the legitimate, the dominant . . . a horizon of possibility whose precise extent and heterogeneous scope cannot in principle be delimited in advance" (quoted in Dave 2012, 20). This double definition points first to the meaning long accepted: queer is anti-normative, perhaps transgressive. But it also, and this is where I begin to see a new *queer* in queer anthropology, points toward queer as an emergence, a potentiality, a utopic desire for something not yet, something yet to come (Muñoz 2009, 21, 25–26)—even as it also creates new limitations, normalizations, or boundaries.

We can see this dynamic in Dave's ethnography, which details the emergence of lesbian activism in India. Yet her analysis does not follow a straight narrative of LGBT progress. Instead, Dave pays particular attention to tensions between affect (as what is not-yet delimited [2012, 10]) and norm (as the consolidation of affect into a social and historical form). So, for example, a lesbian networking list or the debates between activist groups that favor different forms of politics *both* spark new hopes, desires, and possibilities *and* produce norms of what lesbians or sexual justice can or should be. For Dave, then, *queer* serves as a "horizon of possibility," an "ethical aspiration" to create a new "radical world" (Dave 2012, 20). Yet containment, "the fixing of potential into certain normative forms—is an inevitable part of activism," and, I would add, queer anthropology, too (2012, 203).

It is not that the anti-normative meaning of queer has been entirely effaced. Many anthropologists use *queer* to signal that which is non-normative (identities or practices that challenge normative gender roles) and transgressive (those that challenge heteronormative sexuality)—while also noting a less-than-oppositional relationship to normativity. For example, in Evelyn Blackwood and Mark Johnson's introduction to a special issue on "Queer Asian Subjects," they write that *queer* highlights "the possibilities and constraints of different systems of gender/sexuality" that produce "both normative and transgressive bodies and practices" (2012, 442). Similarly, Jafari Allen explains that his use of *queer* references the non-normative erotic subjectivity of the black homosexual and gender non-conforming Cubans with whom he works *and* the ways queer is "an insistence on potentiality or concrete possibility for another world" (2011, 195). These definitions, then, take up sexual and gender non-normativity, yet also move it somewhere else. In this way, *queer* in new queer anthropology is less a repetition of the queer = transgressive analysis Wiegman describes as normative anti-normativity, and more an invitation—at least as long as we are trying to do justice to our (ethnographic) object.

Engebretsen opens her ethnography *Queer Women in Urban China* with a discussion of her use of *queer*. Her book is an analysis of the emergence of *lala* social-sexual identity and community in Beijing, in the context of changing gender and sexual politics within a rapidly transforming China, with new modern discourses of individualism and choice. For Engebretsen, *queer* marks the "sexual and gender nonnormativity" of Chinese lesbians (2013, 8) even as she interrogates—through close ethnographic analysis of both social particularity and broader context—the "powerful ways that hegemonic norms continue to define girls' and women's scope for meaningful independence and agency" (2013, 8). But her work also questions *queer's* purported anti-normativity, especially in terms of the ways that the *lalas* with whom she worked sought normalcy. It is not only the political weight of anti-normativity that is at stake here, but more crucially the ethnographic analysis of social intelligibility itself, in the form of regulatory norms (like gender) upon which all subjects (queer or not) depend—a critique that dovetails with queer of color interventions such as Cathy Cohen's (1997). In this way, Engebretsen's ethnography is an analysis of the "meaningful and complex ways that normativity remains a central aspiration for, as well as limitation to, same-sex desires and life strategies"—an exposition of the desire for social normativity alongside "new queer imaginaries" (2013, 13, 28).

The dynamic of opening/potential and closure/norm in these ethnographies parallels that in queer (and feminist) studies: *queer's* expansion becomes the grounds of its institutional restriction. In this case, typical of anthropology and of a piece with *gender*, *queer* issues an invitation or entry point into complex mappings of a social field: linkages of racialization, sexuality, nation; divergent political imaginaries; the ways queerness can serve liberal, neoliberal, and radical projects alike. There are no political guarantees in this invitation, which means that *queer* can't secure a political stance for either the object or the ethnographer. Queer, then, does not only, perhaps not even primarily—in my maybe idiosyncratic reading—point to the range of divergent or transgressive sexual (and gendered) practices. Instead, and building on the existent incommensurability of gender and sexuality across cultures, *queer* might trouble the categories through which "normativity" itself—as a social and historical praxis—is mobilized.[9]

I might be prompted by my own enthusiasm about what Elizabeth Povinelli has termed an "anthropology of potential" or "of the otherwise" (2012, 2001), one that is still built on the unstable and unsatisfying grounds of what is. But I seem to share this enthusiasm with others in queer anthropology who are invested not so much in a proper object or analytic, but in queer political desire itself. For example, Shaka McGlotten's recent special issue on black queer studies asks us to imagine queerness as speculative, "a wondering curiosity" or practice "of experimentation" (2012, 3). Martin Manalansan, in his tribute to the work of Liz Kennedy, writes that he sees Kennedy in relation to queer studies, since both "take up the cudgels of a dissident life" to provide "some sense of hope and future for people who have felt unwanted, isolated, ostracized, and somewhat unsure about their own survival" (2011, 17,16). Queer studies feeds on a critical hope, what Lisa Duggan and José Muñoz call a "collective hope without delusion"—a desire for an otherwise grounded in our ongoing social world (2009, 276). In this way, *queer*, in both queer studies and anthropology, is tied to the conditions that necessitate its emergence, yet those conditions serve as limitations that produce the impetus to generate something new.

If the new queer anthropology seeks not only to question what we thought we knew about *queer* (gender, sex, sexuality, and normativity), it also asks what might count as *anthropology*. This part is, by necessity, a bit sketchier, since these theorizations are emergent. This new queer work aims to queer the *anthropos*, the species or subject of anthropology—it is, in other words, post- or extra-human. I'll gesture to two lines of inquiry in this new work: multispecies ethnography (anthropology beyond the human/species) and ontological anthropology (anthropology beyond the "living" world).

S. Eben Kirksey and Stefan Helmreich define multispecies ethnography as focused on "the host of organisms whose lives and deaths are linked to human social worlds" (2010, 545). Studying entanglements or "contact zones where lines separating nature from culture have broken down" (2010, 546), such ethnography builds on the work of Donna Haraway and other feminist theorists of "naturecultures" (2003). Multispecies ethnography branches into the ecological and environmental as well as the ethical and political, pressuring the proper object of anthropology as it interrogates lines between human, animal, other; biological and cultural. While one could assert that all of this work is queer in the sense of challenging normative epistemological boundaries, some of it is explicitly queer, and addresses particular relationships among gender, sexuality, embodiment, and social normativity. Interdisciplinary work in queer animal studies and queer ecologies, for example, seeks to challenge the sexual biopolitics of nature (Giffney and Hird 2008; Mortimer-Sandilands and Erickson 2010). Eva Hayward's ethnography of cup coral (*Balanophyllia elegans*) at the Long Marine Laboratory in Santa Cruz, California, is a sophisticated ethnographic example of queer multispecies analysis. Hayward is interested in the laboratory as "an arena where species meet" (2010, 581). This focus enables Hayward to build a "sensorial ensemble" (2010, 593) based on the sensory connections between her body and the corals she prods and pokes. The linking between queer people and coral—perverts and inverts (invertebrates)—is a form of "tranimal" ("an enmeshment of 'trans' and 'animals'"). Hayward not only challenges assumptions about normative/natural sex (and reproduction) but more fundamentally, analyzes the "appearing and disappearing boundaries between the human, the postanimal (human and non-human), the in-un-human, and the animal" (2010, 595).

Multispecies ethnography might queer borders between human and animal; it might also take up human and non-human boundaries. While not ethnographic, Mel Chen's recent *Animacies* (2012) offers cultural and linguistic readings of animacy hierarchies (human > animal > vegetable > mineral) as they are linked to racial hierarchies (and crosscut by sex, gender, and disability). Allied with work in queer studies that confronts necropolitics or disposability, Chen seeks to broaden the way we understand the (political) relationships between the living and the dead, animate and inanimate. For this reason, *Animacies* can be read as an example of the "new materialism," work that attends to what Jane Bennett calls "vibrant matter," or the capacity of things to act (2009). In anthropology, especially in science and technology studies, this has taken the form of an "ontological turn" away from interpretation or hermeneutic analysis. As Martin Holbraad explains, "Rather than using our own analytical concepts" to answer "why the Nuer should think that twins are birds," for example, "we should be asking . . . What must twins be, what must birds be" in this conceptual universe? (Carrithers et al. 2010, 184). In this way, ontological anthropology seeks not only new objects (things, inanimate matter, diseases), but a new method to encounter ethnographic objects within their own reality (or plural realities).

As of now, there is a limited archive of queer ontological theorizations; theoretical physicist Karen Barad's queer, feminist notion of "agential realism" is perhaps the best known (2007). In anthropology, Annemarie Mol's work connects ontological methodologies to the study of disease, asking not how "medicine *knows* its objects," but how it "*enacts*" them through practices (2002, vii). S. Lochlann Jain's approach to breast cancer is particularly suggestive, exploring cancer not as an object of knowledge, but "as a creative force . . . that can powerfully organize relationships" between gender, sexuality, the body, temporality, risk, capitalism, health care, and more (2013, 233). Such work in extrahuman anthropology seeks to trouble the boundaries between human and world, nature and culture, yielding a queer analysis of ensembles/assemblages and non-humans as political actors. The ontological turn, then, might reanimate the question not only of the proper objects of anthropology (the human) but also the way we might know those objects—and therefore of the epistemology of anthropology. In this way, *queer* might generate a new way of knowing that pushes us past *anthropology*, too.

FEMINIST, QUEER, REDUX

These examples of the new queer ethnography are not intended to be complete nor even particularly laudatory. I offer them as provocations—not endorsements. For I don't imagine that either a *queer* queer or a non-anthropos anthropology will finally overcome queer anthropology's frustrating attachments to its objects or its methods. Instead, what I take from these excursions in the history of feminist and queer studies is precisely the inverse: our desire to overcome our own attachments is what motivates our search for an otherwise, for an object and a mode of analysis that could do justice to our hopes and dreams—political or analytic (or both). That this may never be achieved is, perhaps, to our and our fields' benefit.

Imagining queerness and anthropology as sites of hope, potential, or aspiration for something better, anthropologists seem, to me, not to confuse their objects with their own desires, nor to expect—frustratingly—a commensurability between self and other, at least not by investing in *queer*. In a way, Wiegman's analysis of the disappointment we might feel when our objects fail us, or fail to measure up to the political commitments we have invested in them, is inverted in queer anthropology. For the lesson here is not so much that our object will always fail us, but that we might always fail our objects. This is, I suspect, the condition of doing ethnographic research: all we know is that we never know enough.

And this, finally, is what I think brings these interdisciplinary dreams and desires together: neither an agreement over gender or sexuality as proper objects, nor even a territory battle over them, but instead a shared frustration in the limitations of our ways of knowing to do justice to our objects, or ourselves. This state of frustration, in queer anthropology as in feminist studies and queer studies, has led us toward new objects and new analytics that draw on the incommensurability of our political desires and our objects to bring a new future into view. It's the task before us, then, to keep struggling to do justice both to our objects and our political commitments—knowing that institutional closures also might open us to new ways of knowing, and achieving, that which we hold most dear.

NOTES

1. In 2011 Rubin reflects, "While the essay has sometimes been interpreted as a rejection of feminism, I saw it as completely within the best traditions of feminist discourse, particularly the constant self-critical striving toward more analytic clarity and descriptive precision about inequality and injustice" (2011, 37). This "self-critical striving" is central to both queer and feminist studies, as I aim to show.

2. Boellstorff defines *waria* as "male-to-female transvestites" (2005, 11). There is a parallel between the necessity of analyzing gender alongside sexuality and the longstanding complaint that much of queer anthropology is centered on the experiences of (cisgendered) men and "gay" desire, in contrast to more limited work on (cisgendered) women, transgender identities, "lesbian" or other non-gay desires or sexualities (see Blackwood and Wieringa 1999, 39). The anthropology of sexuality (or LGBT anthropology) only began to take up a broader range of topics—lesbian practices, transgender identities and communities, and even heterosexuality and sexual practices like BDSM—in the 1990s. Even so, queer anthropology—and queer studies in general—is not necessarily a *feminist* queer anthropology; queer analyses do not always center intersections of gender, sexuality, the body, and social power (see Lewin 2002). Further, as Elizabeth Kennedy argues, while gay anthropology in the 1980s paid little attention to women, gender, or lesbians, feminist anthropology was not a particularly friendly site for research on gays, lesbians, or sexuality either (2002, 99–100). In this way, the legacy of the proper object debates is a constitutive limitation in both queer and feminist studies.

3. Indeed, nearly every queer ethnography begins with a discussion of the impossibility of proper terminology. While these debates are in no way settled, I do think that queer anthropology has recognized that linguistic purity is impossible, especially given the multiplicities of transnational flows and frictions.

4. As Gayle Salamon argues, although women's studies has struggled to incorporate (unevenly, sometimes unsuccessfully) "the work of women of color, lesbians, sex radicals, and queers," trans studies presents a singular challenge to the field: a "breaking apart" of the category woman and a "new articulation of the relationships between sex and gender" especially for emergent genders (2010, 97–98). See also Susan Stryker on transgender studies as "queer theory's evil twin" (2004, 212).

5. Anti-normativity is not the only epistemological norm within queer studies. For reasons of space, I will merely gesture to three other consolidations of *queer*: around a normative (cisgendered) mode of embodiment, sex, and gender; around racialization in the form of universalized whiteness; and around sexuality-as-identity, an effacement of the more unruly psychodynamics of desire.

6. Overviews of transnational queer studies include Grewal and Kaplan 2001 and Cruz and Manalansan 2002. See also debates about "globalizing gayness"—not only Dennis Altman's infamous essay (1997), but also Bacchetta 2002, Boellstorff 2003, and Manalansan 1995. Critiques of queer studies' effacement of everyday social life include Lewin and Leap 2002, 10–11, and 2009, 6–8.

7. The most intricate and useful reading of the relationship between queer studies and anthropology remains Tom Boellstorff's *A Coincidence of Desires* (2007a).

8. Papers from the original 2011 AAA panel, "Sensing Precarity," are archived at Lauren Berlant's blog Supervalent Thought: http://supervalentthought.com/.

9. It is, of course, these incommensurabilities that have driven much of the anxiety over the applicability of "Western" concepts (like gay, lesbian, queer) outside their sites of origin.

REFERENCES

Abelove, Henry, Michèle Aina Barale, and David M. Halperin, eds. 1993. *The Lesbian and Gay Studies Reader.* New York: Routledge.

Allen, Jafari S. 2011. *¡Venceremos?: The Erotics of Black Self-Making in Cuba.* Durham, NC: Duke University Press.

Altman, Dennis. 1997. "Global Gaze/Global Gays." *GLQ: A Journal of Lesbian and Gay Studies* 3 (4): 417–436.

Bacchetta, Paola. 2002. "Rescaling Transnational Queerdom: Lesbian and Lesbian Identity—Positionalities in Delhi in the 1980s." *Antipode* 34 (5): 947–973.

Barad, Karen Michelle. 2007. *Meeting the Universe Halfway: Quantum Physics and the Entanglement of Matter and Meaning.* Durham, NC: Duke University Press.

Bennett, Jane. 2009. *Vibrant Matter: A Political Ecology of Things.* Durham, NC: Duke University Press.

Berlant, Lauren. 2011. *Cruel Optimism.* Durham, NC: Duke University Press.

Berlant, Lauren, and Michael Warner. 1995. "What Does Queer Theory Teach Us about X?" *PMLA* 110 (3): 343–349.

———. 1998. "Sex in Public." *Critical Inquiry* 24 (2): 547–566.

Blackwood, Evelyn. 2010. *Falling into the Lesbi World: Desire and Difference in Indonesia.* Honolulu: University of Hawai'i Press.

Blackwood, Evelyn, and Mark Johnson. 2012. "Queer Asian Subjects: Transgressive Sexualities and Heteronormative Meanings." *Asian Studies Review* 36 (4): 441–451.

Blackwood, Evelyn, and Saskia E. Wieringa. 1999. "Sapphic Shadows: Challenging the Silence in the Study of Sexuality." In *Female Desires: Same-Sex Relations and Transgender Practices across Cultures,* ed. Evelyn Blackwood and Saskia E. Wieringa, 39–63. New York: Columbia University Press.

Boellstorff, Tom. 2003. "Dubbing Culture: Indonesian Gay and Lesbi Subjectivities and Ethnography in an Already Globalized World." *American Ethnologist* 30 (2): 225–242.

———. 2005. *The Gay Archipelago: Sexuality and Nation in Indonesia.* Princeton, NJ: Princeton University Press.

———. 2007a. *A Coincidence of Desires: Anthropology, Queer Studies, Indonesia.* Durham, NC: Duke University Press.

———. 2007b. "Queer Studies in the House of Anthropology." *Annual Review of Anthropology* 36 (1): 17–35.

———. 2011. "But Do Not Identify as Gay: A Proleptic Genealogy of the MSM Category." *Cultural Anthropology* 26 (2): 287–312.

Butler, Judith. 1993. "Critically Queer." *GLQ: A Journal of Lesbian and Gay Studies* 1 (1): 17–32.

———. 1994. "Against Proper Objects." *differences: A Journal of Feminist Cultural Studies* 6 (2/3): 1–26.

Carrithers, Michael, Matei Candea, Karen Sykes, Martin Holbraad, and Soumhya Venkatesan. 2010. "Ontology Is Just Another Word for Culture." *Critique of Anthropology* 30 (2): 152–200.

Chen, Mel Y. 2012. *Animacies: Biopolitics, Racial Mattering, and Queer Affect.* Durham, NC: Duke University Press.

Cohen, Cathy. 1997. "Punks, Bulldaggers, and Welfare Queens." *GLQ: A Journal of Lesbian and Gay Studies* 3 (4): 437–465.

Cruz, Arnaldo, and Martin F. Manalansan, eds. 2002. *Queer Globalizations: Citizenship and the Afterlife of Colonialism.* New York: New York University Press.

Dave, Naisargi N. 2012. *Queer Activism in India: A Story in the Anthropology of Ethics*. Durham, NC: Duke University Press.

de Lauretis, Teresa. 1991. "Queer Theory: Lesbian and Gay Sexualities." *differences: A Journal of Feminist Cultural Studies* 3 (2): iii–xviii.

———. 1994. "Habit Changes." *differences: A Journal of Feminist Cultural Studies* 6: 296–313.

Duggan, Lisa, and José Esteban Muñoz. 2009. "Hope and Hopelessness: A Dialogue." *Women & Performance: A Journal of Feminist Theory* 19 (2): 275–283.

Eng, David L., Judith Halberstam, and José Esteban Muñoz. 2005. "Introduction: What's Queer About Queer Studies Now?" *Social Text* 84–85, 23 (3–4): 1–17.

Engebretsen, Elisabeth Lund. 2008. "Queer Ethnography in Theory and Practice: Reflections on Studying Sexual Globalization and Women's Queer Activism in Beijing." *Graduate Journal of Social Science* 5 (2): 88–116.

———. 2013. *Queer Women in Urban China: An Ethnography*. New York: Routledge.

Ferguson, Roderick A. 2005. "Of Our Normative Strivings: African American Studies and the Histories of Sexuality." *Social Text* 84–85, 23 (3–4): 85–100.

Giffney, Noreen, and Myra J. Hird, eds. 2008. *Queering the Non/human*. Hampshire, UK: Ashgate Publishing.

Grewal, Inderpal, and Caren Kaplan. 2001. "Global Identities: Theorizing Transnational Studies of Sexuality." *GLQ: A Journal of Lesbian and Gay Studies* 7 (4): 663–679.

Hanhardt, Christina B. 2013. *Safe Space: Gay Neighborhood History and the Politics of Violence*. Durham, NC: Duke University Press.

Haraway, Donna J. 2003. *The Companion Species Manifesto: Dogs, People, and Significant Otherness*. Chicago: Prickly Paradigm Press.

Haritaworn, Jin, Adi Kuntsman, and Silvia Posocco, eds. 2014. *Queer Necropolitics*. New York: Routledge.

Hayward, Eva. 2010. "Fingeryeyes: Impressions of Cup Corals." *Cultural Anthropology* 25 (4): 577–599.

Jain, S. Lochlann. 2013. *Malignant: How Cancer Becomes Us*. Berkeley: University of California Press.

Kennedy, Elizabeth Lapovsky. 2002. "These Natives Can Speak for Themselves: The Development of Gay And Lesbian Community Studies in Anthropology." In *Out in Theory: The Emergence of Lesbian and Gay Anthropology*, ed. Ellen Lewin and William L. Leap, 93–109. Urbana: University of Illinois Press.

Kirksey, S. Eben, and Stefan Helmreich. 2010. "The Emergence of Multispecies Ethnography." *Cultural Anthropology* 25 (4): 545–576.

Kulick, Don. 1998. *Travesti: Sex, Gender, and Culture among Brazilian Transgendered Prostitutes*. Chicago: University of Chicago Press.

Lewin, Ellen. 2002. "Another Unhappy Marriage? Feminist Anthropology and Lesbian/Gay Studies." In *Out in Theory: The Emergence of Lesbian and Gay Anthropology*, ed. Ellen Lewin and William L. Leap, 110–127. Urbana: University of Illinois Press.

Lewin, Ellen, and William Leap, eds. 2002. *Out in Theory: The Emergence of Lesbian and Gay Anthropology*. Urbana: University of Illinois Press.

———, eds. 2009. *Out in Public: Reinventing Lesbian/Gay Anthropology in a Globalizing World*. Malden, MA: John Wiley & Sons.

Manalansan, Martin F. 1995. "In the Shadows of Stonewall: Examining Gay Transnational Politics and the Diasporic Dilemma." *GLQ: A Journal of Lesbian and Gay Studies* 2 (4): 425–438.

———. 2003. *Global Divas: Filipino Gay Men in the Diaspora*. Durham, NC: Duke University Press.

———. 2011. "Horizons of Hope: Queer Futures and the Legacy of Elizabeth Lapovsky Kennedy." *Voices* 11 (1): 16–18.

McGlotten, Shaka. 2012. "Always Toward a Black Queer Anthropology." *Transforming Anthropology* 20 (1): 3–4.

Mol, Annemarie. 2002. *The Body Multiple: Ontology in Medical Practice.* Durham, NC: Duke University Press.

Morgensen, Scott Lauria. 2011. *Spaces between Us: Queer Settler Colonialism and Indigenous Decolonization.* Minneapolis: University of Minnesota Press.

Mortimer-Sandilands, Catriona, and Bruce Erickson, eds. 2010. *Queer Ecologies: Sex, Nature, Politics, Desire.* Bloomington: Indiana University Press.

Muñoz, José Esteban. 2009. *Cruising Utopia: The Then and There of Queer Futurity.* New York: New York University Press.

Padilla, Mark. 2007. *Caribbean Pleasure Industry: Tourism, Sexuality, and AIDS in the Dominican Republic.* Chicago: University of Chicago Press.

Povinelli, Elizabeth A. 2001. "Radical Worlds: The Anthropology of Incommensurability and Inconceivability." *Annual Review of Anthropology* 30: 319–334.

———. 2011. *Economies of Abandonment: Social Belonging and Endurance in Late Liberalism.* Durham, NC: Duke University Press.

———. 2012. "The Will to Be Otherwise/The Effort of Endurance." *South Atlantic Quarterly* 111 (3): 453–475.

Puar, Jasbir K. 2007. *Terrorist Assemblages: Homonationalism in Queer Times.* Durham, NC: Duke University Press.

Reddy, Chandan. 2011. *Freedom with Violence: Race, Sexuality, and the US State.* Durham, NC: Duke University Press.

Rofel, Lisa. 1999. "Qualities of Desire: Imagining Gay Identities in China." *GLQ: A Journal of Lesbian and Gay Studies* 5 (4): 451–474.

Rubin, Gayle. 1993 [1984]. "Thinking Sex: Notes for a Radical Theory of the Politics of Sexuality." In *The Lesbian and Gay Studies Reader*, ed. Henry Abelove, Michèle Aina Barale, and David M. Halperin, 3–44. New York: Routledge.

———. 1994. "Sexual Traffic (Interview)." *differences: A Journal of Feminist Cultural Studies* 6 (2–3): 62–99.

———. 2011. "Blood Under the Bridge: Reflections on Thinking Sex." *GLQ: A Journal of Lesbian and Gay Studies* 17 (1): 15–48.

Salamon, Gayle. 2010. *Assuming a Body: Transgender and Rhetorics of Materiality.* New York: Columbia University Press.

Sedgwick, Eve Kosofsky. 1993. "Queer and Now." In *Tendencies*, 1–20. Durham, NC: Duke University Press.

Stacey, Judith. 1988. "Can There Be a Feminist Ethnography?" *Women's Studies International Forum* 11 (1): 21–27.

Strathern, Marilyn. 1987. "An Awkward Relationship: The Case of Feminism and Anthropology." *Signs* 12 (2): 276–292.

Stryker, Susan. 2004. "Transgender Studies: Queer Theory's Evil Twin." *GLQ: A Journal of Lesbian and Gay Studies* 10 (2): 212–215.

Visweswaran, Kamala. 1997. "Histories of Feminist Ethnography." *Annual Review of Anthropology* 26: 591–621.

Warner, Michael. 1993. "Introduction." In *Fear of a Queer Planet: Queer Politics and Social Theory*, ed. Michael Warner, vii–xxxi. Minneapolis: University of Minnesota Press.

Weiss, Margot. 2011a. "The Epistemology of Ethnography: Method in Queer Anthropology." *GLQ: A Journal of Lesbian and Gay Studies* 17 (4): 649–664.

———. 2011b. *Techniques of Pleasure: BDSM and the Circuits of Sexuality*. Durham, NC: Duke University Press.

Wekker, Gloria. 2006. *The Politics of Passion: Women's Sexual Culture in the Afro-Surinamese Diaspora*. New York: Columbia University Press.

Weston, Kath. 1993. "Lesbian/Gay Studies in the House of Anthropology." *Annual Review of Anthropology* 22: 339–367.

———. 1998. "The Bubble, the Burn, and the Simmer: Locating Sexuality in Social Science." In *Long Slow Burn: Sexuality and Social Science*, 1–27. New York: Routledge.

Wiegman, Robyn. 2012. *Object Lessons*. Durham, NC: Duke University Press.

PART III REVERBERATIONS

Transnational Encounters

A GREATER MEASURE OF JUSTICE

Gender, Violence, and Reparations

KIMBERLY THEIDON

It was 1975 when Susan Brownmiller published *Against Our Will: Men, Women, and Rape,* a feminist classic that was widely credited with changing public attitudes and debates about rape in the United States. In her wide-ranging analysis, men rape because they can, and rape is framed not as an act of lust, but as an expression of domination and violence. Her conceptualization became a key framing device for feminists throughout the 1970s and 1980s, as they sought to "desexualize" rape by laying bare its dimensions of power and coercion, and to counter victim-blaming by arguing that rape was "the female fear," a "special fear," rather than a female provocation.[1] As she argued, "From prehistoric times to the present, rape has played a critical function. It is nothing more nor less than a conscious process of intimidation by which all men keep all women in subjugation . . . [and] . . . rape becomes an unfortunate but inevitable by-product of the necessary game called war" (Brownmiller 1975, iv).

It was feminist activism that led to a change not only in perceptions, but also in international jurisprudence. Security Council Resolution 1820 challenges the inevitability argument, calling for the prevention and sanction of conflict-related sexual violence deployed against women and girls. It notes that

> rape and other forms of sexual violence can constitute a war crime, a crime against humanity or a constitutive act with respect to genocide . . . [and] . . . affirms its intention, when establishing and renewing state-specific sanction regimes, to take into consideration the appropriateness of targeted and graduated measures

> against parties to situations of armed conflict who commit rape and other forms of sexual violence against women and girls in situations of armed conflict. (Security Council Resolution 1820 [2008])

The juxtaposition of Brownmiller and Resolution 1820 can be read as a story of (Western) feminist triumph; that is the story I wish to unsettle in this chapter. The centrality of conflict-related sexual violence on the international agenda is an achievement, but it comes at a cost. As we shall see, even the most expansive definition of sexual violence results in a limited grasp of the gendered dimensions of war.

Over the past twenty years, there has been increased international attention to conflict-related rape and sexual violence. In March 1994, the United Nations established a Special Rapporteur on Violence Against Women to examine the causes and consequences of gender-based violence, especially rape and sexual violence targeting women and girls.[2] Additionally, the UN's ad hoc International Criminal Tribunals for the former Yugoslavia and Rwanda—countries where conflict-related sexual violence in the early 1990s captured international attention on an unprecedented scale—greatly advanced efforts to codify sexual and reproductive violence. The jurisprudence resulting from these two tribunals classified systematic rape and other sex crimes as war crimes, crimes against humanity, and forms of genocide. The Rome Statute of the International Criminal Court, adopted in 1998, built on and extended those advances, providing a broader basis for prosecuting sexual crimes (including rape, sexual slavery, enforced prostitution, forced pregnancy, enforced sterilization, or any other form of sexual violence of comparable gravity) as violations of international laws on war, genocide, and crimes against humanity. No longer would sexual crimes be considered merely "moral offenses" or "injuries to honor or reputation" as they had been defined in the Geneva Conventions (1949).

On a complementary front, a series of UN Security Council Resolutions focused on the important role women play in conflict prevention, resolution, and peace-building efforts, while simultaneously denouncing the use of rape and sexual violence against women and girls in situations of armed conflict. Collectively known as the Women, Peace, and Security Agenda, these resolutions (1325, 1820, 1888, 1889, 1960, 2106, and 2122) demand the complete cessation of all acts of sexual violence by all parties to armed conflicts, with each successive resolution lamenting the slow progress made to date on this issue.

The Women, Peace, and Security Agenda—and various sexual violence summits and celebrity spokespeople—have overwhelmingly focused on women and girls as victims of sexual violence during armed conflict. Strikingly absent in this agenda are men and boys as *victims* of sexual violence, women as *perpetrators* of violence, and the broader goal of gender equality. The focus on "conflict-related sexual violence" also has temporal and geographical implications: the Women, Peace, and Security Agenda draws attention to the front lines of war and to extraordinary forms of sexual violence bracketed in time, which may result in obscuring the less dramatic yet everyday forms of gender-based violence that distort the lives of women and girls, men and boys. It also leaves men and boys as perpetrators hovering in the margins of the resolutions or, at best, as "those secondarily traumatized as forced witnesses of sexual violence against family members" (UN Security Council Resolution 2106 [2013]).

In what follows I complement ongoing research that I have conducted in Peru since 1997 with reports from the Peruvian Truth and Reconciliation Commission (PTRC) to explore four themes. I begin by discussing the Peruvian TRC and how it implemented a "gender focus" in its investigations and in its final report. Influenced by the feminist campaign to "break the silence" around rape as an intrinsically emancipatory project, the PTRC actively sought out first-person accounts of rape, with rape understood to be the emblematic womanly wound of war. I will analyze what a focus on rape and sexual violence brings into our field of vision, and what it may obscure. Between the trope of "unspeakable atrocities" and the call to "break the silence," a great deal was being said. A critical rereading of the PTRC's 2003 final report reveals that women frequently spoke about the systematic violation of their social, economic, and cultural rights—injuries that cannot be reduced to the violation of bodily integrity, as horrible as that violation may be. I will also discuss what women have talked about with my research team and me. When speaking outside the "victim-centered" space of the PTRC (or in the offices of the National Victims Registry), women narrated much more complicated stories about war and its effects, and about the multiple roles they assumed during the armed conflict and its aftermath. In these nuanced stories, women challenged some common sense notions of gender and war, and provided us with an opportunity to think beyond rights and remedies to a more robust sense of gender and harm, of gender and justice.

I will then discuss how rape between men and women—and between men—was a form of establishing relations of power and "blood brothers" at the nexus of gender, ethnicity, and social class. The literature on male-dominant environments, such as armed groups, indicates that these groups utilize elaborate socialization mechanisms that are especially relevant to understanding the roles some men assume during conflict.[3] From illegal armed groups to state-sponsored militaries, induction into male-dominant groups frequently involves brutal or demeaning rites of passage. I will discuss how men are both perpetrators *and* victims of sexual violence, and what the erasure of the latter means in terms of gender-based violence, essentialisms, and the politics of victimhood. After considering the massive sexual and gender-based violence that characterized Peru's internal armed conflict, I conclude with some reflections on the possibility of reparations, and on how feminist anthropology can contribute to achieving a greater measure of justice in the aftermath of profound harm.

COMMISSIONING GENDER

> "A fate worse than death": Any misfortune that would make life unliveable, especially rape or loss of virginity. The phrase was formally a euphemism for rape.[4]

On August 28, 2003, the Commissioners of the Peruvian Truth and Reconciliation Commission (PTRC) submitted their Final Report to president Alejandro Toledo and the nation. After two years and some 17,000 testimonies, the commissioners had completed their task of examining the causes and consequences of the internal armed conflict that convulsed the country during the 1980s and 1990s. The PTRC determined that almost 70,000 people had been killed or disappeared, and that 75 percent of the casualties were rural peasants who spoke some language other than Spanish as their native tongue. Thus, the distribution of deaths and disappearances reflected longstanding class and ethnic divides in Peru.

Although the PTRC was given a gender-neutral mandate, feminists were successful in insisting that the commission think about the importance of gender in its work. Drawing upon previous commissions in Guatemala and South Africa, they argued for proactive efforts to include women's voices in the truth-seeking process. This reflected the desire to write a more "inclusive truth," as well as developments in international jurisprudence with regard to sexual violence. In light of concerns that "perhaps the most commonly underreported abuses are those suffered by women, especially sexual abuse and rape" (Hayner 2010, 77), efforts were made to encourage women to come forward. "Gender sensitive" strategies were employed with the goal of soliciting women's testimonies about rape and other forms of sexual violence, with rape understood to be the emblematic womanly wound of war. The results? Of the 16,885 people who gave testimonies to the PTRC, 54 percent were women and 46 percent men (PTRC 2003, 3:64). Thus, many women did come forward to provide their testimonies: they spoke a great deal, but not necessarily about sexual violence—at least not in the first person. The total number of reported cases of rape was 538, of which 527 were committed against women and 11 were crimes against men (PTRC 2003, 8:89). The commission's effort to provide a "fuller truth" about the use of sexual violence by various armed groups was met with a resounding silence.[5]

Shame is frequently cited as the reason women and men do not speak about sexual violence, and this is certainly one explanatory variable. But to assume shame may inadvertently convey reactionary messages about purity, chastity, and cleanliness—and may imply that a rape survivor is "damaged goods." Although the phrase "rape is a fate worse than death" became somewhat of a mantra within international conflict feminism, we should consider the troubling message this sends to the thousands of people who have survived this brutal form of violence.[6] Additionally, survivors may have forged a different relationship with their past, however painful it might have been. Outside the victim-subject position assigned to them by the PTRC, women often spoke with defiance, courage, pride, or rage about their experiences of sexual violence, narrating heroism in a multitude of guises. These stories are at odds with the abject rape script too frequently foisted upon survivors.

Indeed, in constructing the "rape victim" as a transnational phenomenon for activist purposes, international conflict feminism may have unintentionally revived an essentialized notion of "woman," eliding feminist and postcolonial critiques of this monolithic category. Insights regarding intersectionality and the politics of positionality, in this context, seem to have ceded to a victim-centered politics that elides the heterogeneity of women's experiences.[7] As Ratna Kapur has argued, "The victim-subject relies on a universal subject: a subject that resembles the uncomplicated subject of liberal discourse. It is a subject that cannot accommodate a multi-layered experience" (2005, 99). The repeated emphasis on "conflict-related sexual violence against women and girls" risks erasing social context and the cultural meanings assigned to sexual violence and its legacies. Additionally—and ironically, given the tenacious effort to have sexual violence recognized as a war crime and a crime against humanity—sexual violence might not be what women categorize as the worst violation they have endured during times of war. For example, I found that survivors of sexual violence in Peru may consider the loss of entire families due to brutal massacres, or to the slow grinding death of starvation, to be the most searing aspect of the internal armed conflict. Sexual violence may not be at the top of some women's hierarchy of harms; thus, more emphasis should be placed on discovering local women's priorities, including their views of what constitutes redress and justice. The risk of overemphasizing the sexual and penetrative violation of women's bodies is that women are reduced to sexualized objects to which damage is done, eliding both their protagonism in the face of danger as well as the more complicated stories women tell about war and its effects. The literature on truth commissions has lamented that women "do not talk about themselves," but rather about the suffering of others.[8] However, in foregrounding the ways in which violence has affected their homes, personal spaces, communities, and their loved ones, women *are* talking about themselves. They are narrating the violation of what, in many societies, are their areas of expertise, and they often do so in the voice of the witness rather than that of the victim.[9] A feminist theory of harm might begin with understanding the importance of connectivity and interdependence in many women's lives given their roles as caregivers in most societies. I recall the many times women in Peru lamented "we were both mother and father during those years" or insisted, "When children are hungry, it is the mother who must respond." These women were clear that when children and families are in danger, it is women who must shoulder the struggle of daily life. Thus we might begin with a more fundamental question: what exactly *is* the injury?

LIBERAL LIMITS

Recall that women provided over half of the testimonies compiled by the PTRC. What *did* they talk about? Women offered tremendous insight into the gendered dimensions of war, and the ways in which violence permeated all spheres of life. They spoke about the challenges of keeping children fed, homes intact, livestock safe; the search for missing loved ones; the lacerating sting of ethnic insults in the very cities in which they sought refuge: women spoke about familial and communal suffering, and about the quotidian aspects of armed conflict. When people go to war, caregiving can become a dangerous occupation. While they did not provide the emblematic rape narrative, these wide-ranging and diffuse harms are precisely how many women experienced this war. While the international focus on conflict-related rape and sexual violence has been a hard-won achievement, it comes at a cost. Even a broad definition of sexual violence results in a narrow understanding of the gendered dimensions of war, and of the full range of harms that women (and men) experience and prioritize.

What do women name as violence? The focus on bodily integrity, while important, flows from a focus on the so-called first-generation human rights (civil and political rights protected by a variety of treaties following World War II). The "second-generation" rights—social, economic, and cultural—have taken longer to be enforceable and remain "soft law" standards in most instances. However, as illustrated by my research in Peru, the emphasis women place on the violation of social, economic, and cultural rights should inform accountability dialogues and transitional justice debates in the aftermath of armed conflict.

Transitional justice is a field of postwar inquiry and intervention focused on addressing the legacies of past human rights violations in the hope that doing so will build a more peaceful and just future, and may include tribunals, war crimes prosecutions, memorials, reparations, and truth commissions (Teitel 2002). Transitional justice imports many elements of the liberal human rights tradition, with its foundation in Enlightenment principles of individual freedom; the autonomous individual and the social contract; the public sphere of secular reason; the rule of law; and the centrality of retributive justice, particularly in the form of criminal justice and prosecutions. Some have referred to this as the "liberal peace-building consensus," and acknowledge the many contributions this approach has made to postconflict reconstruction (Philpott 2007).

Liberal legalism, however, has both strengths and weaknesses. Feminist legal theorists have provided compelling critiques of law and liberalism, underscoring the failure of both to adequately capture the experiences of women. Fionnuala Ní Aoláin has referred to this as the "problem of capture" (2009). As she argues, "The idea of harm to women has been central to women's placement in legal discourse. Such placement, however, is not synonymous with status and recognition" (2009, 2–3). Indeed, the conceptual and practical consequences of such efforts frequently affirm women's secondary and disjunctive social status, and give rise to regulatory or protectionist legal regimes that may be constraining and paternalist in their application.[10]

In *Caring for Justice* (1999), Robin West argues that more effort has been invested in the deployment of law as an instrument of redress than concern with a more fundamental set of questions: what does harm entail and how should we know it and recognize its manifestations? Limiting accountability to the categories prescribed by law may exclude many of the everyday experiences of women who live in conflict settings. The structure of law and its normativity may include the use of relatively rigid categories. If violations fit a certain category, they are included. If not, they are rendered invisible and the harm is not recognized as a legal matter. This has tremendous impact on potential forms of redress.

At present, reparations programs and other forms of redress operate on the principle that "where there is a right, there is a remedy." This is part of the problem: the classic violations enshrined in human rights treaties default to masculinist normativity and legal categories that fail to capture what many women prioritize as the most harmful consequences of war. Within the "thick descriptions" women provided to my research team and me is the material necessary to develop a feminist theory of harm that could allow us to craft transformative—not just palliative—reparations.

Reparations programs now figure as a staple ingredient of transitional justice endeavors. Priscilla Hayner, in her recently updated text on truth commissions, notes that it is only within the last decade that there has been a significant expansion in the literature on reparations (2010). This increase reflects the growing recognition that reparations are an integral component of justice. Research across postconflict contexts indicates that satisfying demands for justice requires more than *just* doing something *to* the perpetrators; it means doing something *for* the victim-survivors as well.[11] However, as noted, reparations programs and other forms of redress operate on the maxim "where there is a right, there is a remedy." Thus, the liberal legal realm is characterized by an "accountability approach" in which the daily violence women experience has yet to be legally defined, and this same reductive logic can result in reparations programs that are woefully insensitive to the many other ways in which girls and women experience war. There is forced labor, coerced marriage, forced sterilization, displacement, male-biased land tenure systems and inheritance patterns, chronic health problems stemming from sexual violence and malnutrition, and the sharp rise in female-headed households and the feminization of poverty. These gender-based harms are overwhelmingly borne by women and girls, and prosecuting sexual crimes alone will not achieve the transformative structural changes that are required at the international and domestic levels. "In an effort to respond to the massive damages left in the wake of the internal armed conflict, the Peruvian TRC designed the Program of Integral Reparations (PIR) as a form of 'reaffirming the dignity and status of the victims, and offering hope for the future despite the loss of loved ones or the interruption of life projects'" (PTRC 2003, 9: ch. 2, 2).

The PIR was explicitly linked to the goals of national recovery and sustainable peace, and was hailed as one of the most comprehensive reparations programs in the world to date. The commission's "gender sensitive" approach was considered a model for future transitional justice processes. However, a decade later, many victim-survivors insist that the PIR has failed them, particularly in regard to gender-based and sexual violence. For the thousands of women—and men—who were subjected to these brutal forms of violence, the reparations program is simply "*una burla más*" (just one mockery more). How did this come to pass?

The reasons are multiple, but in part reflect the fact that reparations programs by definition construct categories and hierarchies of victimhood, and these categories in turn oblige people to produce particular speech acts and to occupy defined subject positions. Reparations convert certain forms of speech into reparable categories of redress. In order to be accredited as a rape victim in Peru, for example, an individual must provide detailed information to the National Victims Registry (RUV), which will in turn evaluate the victim's statement to determine whether the individual has or has not told the truth about the violation she or he suffered. As noted earlier, women and men overwhelmingly refused to speak about rape in the first person during the PTRC, yet the reparations program forces them to do so in the hope of securing some form of justice. Silence is not "reparable." And yet, what if someone does not wish to inhabit the "rape victim" category? What does it mean to be asked to narrate your life in a discourse that does not do you justice?

Or to narrate one's life only to have it deemed "unthinkable." There are more silences at work in this story, and one tenacious silence concerns men as victims—not just perpetrators—of sexual violence.

ERASURES

> Some of the recruits were really young. They were just adolescents. They didn't want to participate [in the rapes]. If someone refused, the rest of the men would take him aside and rape him. All of them would rape him, with the poor guy screaming. They said they were "changing his voice"—with so much screaming, his voice would lower and he wouldn't be a woman anymore. (Former member of the Peruvian navy, cited in Theidon 2012, 135)

I turn now to the men, convinced that a gendered perspective on war should include an analysis of men and masculinities; "gender" is too frequently a code word for "women," leaving men as the unquestioned, unmarked category.[12] Gender-sensitive research should include studying the forms of masculinity forged both during armed conflict, and as one component in reconstructing individual identities and collective existence in the aftermath of war. Additionally, given that women survivors of sexual violence are unjustly made to bear the narrative burden for these crimes, involving men in our research on sexual violence has been crucial.

One aspect of shifting the narrative burden would include research with the rapists. In his thought-provoking article "Military Rape," anthropologist Roland Littlewood reviews the dominant models used to explain rape during war, and lays out a series of compelling questions for further research:

> What is the immediate motivation of the military rapist? What are his notions of sexual pleasure, of his usual sexual pleasure, his expectations of fatherhood? What does he think he is doing? . . . We need to know much more about the soldier's view at the time of his act. How does he consider and deal with the conventional objections to rape? Perhaps by dehumanization, which then justified violence as a collective practice? But then how does he justify sexual intercourse with a "non-human"? (Littlewood 1997, 13)

He acknowledges these questions will be difficult to answer given the "near impossibility of research in humans . . . and because of the post-conflict disgust, on the part of both the principal and his surviving victim, which prevents any sort of detailed contextual study" (Littlewood 1997, 13). Although these issues do pose methodological challenges, I strongly suggest we disturb the silence of the male perpetrators, and learn to listen differently to male victim-survivors.

There is not just one explanation or motivation for sexual violence during armed conflict. As with any sort of human action, the specificities matter. Indeed, the specificities are key to moving beyond the "boys will be boys" shrug of inevitability to understanding when and where sexual violence occurs; which individuals or groups are targeted and why; who the perpetrators are; and the types of sexual violence practiced, and how these may vary across time, space, and armed groups.

In her comparative research, Elisabeth Wood has employed the concept of a "repertoire of violence" to refer to the range of violent acts an armed group deploys. She then examines whether or not sexual violence figures in to that broader repertoire. Wood has found that different forms of violence do not co-vary; in other words, even in highly violent conflicts, the use of sexual violence may be either very low or virtually non-existent. This has led her to state that rape is not inevitable in war, a conclusion which leads to a series of important consequences (Wood 2006). Investigating this variation moves beyond essentializing arguments about men, guns, and testosterone: understanding variation allows us to identify those factors that encourage—or may serve to limit—the deployment of sexual violence. It becomes easier to hold perpetrators accountable if we can demonstrate that rape and other forms of sexual violence are *not* "an unfortunate but inevitable by-product of the necessary game called war" (Brownmiller 1975, iv).

My research and the Peruvian TRC's final report reveal that patterns of sexual violence varied across armed parties to the conflict. Shining Path guerrillas were more inclined toward sexual slavery and mutilation, forced nudity, and coerced abortions; the Peruvian armed forces were more likely to engage in sexual torture and gang rape. Indeed, as my research showed, when women described their experiences of rape, it was never one soldier but rather several. "They raped the women until they could not stand up." The soldiers were mutilating women with their penises, and the women were bloodied. These were blood rituals.[13]

When analyzing gang rape, we should think about why the men raped this way. An instrumentalist explanation would indicate that the soldiers raped in groups in order to overpower a woman, or so that one soldier could serve watch while the others raped. However, it would be a limited reading to attribute this practice to the necessity for pure force or standing watch. When a soldier pressed his machine gun into a woman's chest, he did not need more force. When the soldiers came down from the bases at night to rape, "privacy" was not their primary concern. They operated with impunity.

Clearly there is a ritualistic aspect to gang rape.[14] Many people related that after killing someone, the soldiers drank the blood of their victim, or bathed their faces and chests with the blood. Blood ties were established between soldiers, and bloodied wombs birthed a lethal fraternity. These blood ties united the soldiers, and the bodies of the raped women served as the medium for forging those ties.

In their analysis of rape during the 1992–1994 Bosnian war, Bulent Diken and Carsten Bagge Laustsen suggest that gang rape forges a "brotherhood of guilt" based in part upon the abjection of the victim (2005, 113). For the authors, men's guilt is the key emotion: guilt unifies the perpetrators, and rape is the rite of initiation. Additionally, they argue that shame resists verbalization while guilt incites it: "whereas guilt can be verbalized and can perform as an element in the brotherhood of guilt, shame cannot, which is why it often results in trauma. War thus both creates and destroys communities [of the perpetrators and the victims respectively]" (2005, 114).

Gang rape not only breaks the moral codes that generally order social life: the practice also serves to eradicate shame. Committing morally abhorrent acts in front of others not only forges bonds between the perpetrators but also forges *sinvergüenzas*—shameless people—capable of tremendous brutality. To lose the sense of shame—a regulatory emotion because shame implies an Other in front of whom one feels ashamed—creates men with a recalibrated capacity for atrocity. Guilt unifies; shame individuates. Acts that obliterate shame also obliterate a sense of self, contributing to processes aimed at subsuming individuality to create group cohesion and "selflessness" in the service of a collective. Additionally, there is a temporal aspect to understanding these acts and the men who engage in them—and to understanding why the solidarity of guilt may give way to a deep sense of shame over time. In my research, I am struck by the fact that "men don't talk," at least not in the first person, about their participation in rape.

But they certainly do talk during the act itself. Women (and men) emphasize what the soldiers said while raping them: "*Terruca de mierda*" (terrorist of shit; shitty terrorist), "*ahora aguanta, India*" (now take it, Indian), "*carajo, terruca de mierda*" (damn it, terrorist of shit), and "*India de mierda*" (shitty Indian). The soldiers were marking their victims with physical and verbal assaults. Importantly, in my conversations as well as in the testimonies provided to the PTRC, acts of sexual violence were almost always accompanied by ethnic and racial insults, prompting me to consider the ways in which gender, racial, and military hierarchies converged during the internal armed conflict.

Where did the soldiers learn this behavior, and acquire such virulent disdain for people ethnically similar to themselves? I suggest we look to the barracks. Drawing upon her research in Guatemala, Diane Nelson has written that, "Reports of brutal barracks training suggest that internalized racism is a tool used to break the boys down so they may be remade as soldiers, in part by promising them marks of ladino identity (modern bourgeois practices like wearing shoes and eating meat) and of masculinity. Mayan men are often feminized in relation to traditional practices and in their limited power vis-à-vis the ladino" (Nelson 1999, 91). Military service, for all of its abuses, is thus a way to become "less Indian" in a context in which "the Indian is often coded as female" (Nelson 1999, 182).

This holds true in Peru as well where young rural men swelled the lowest ranks of the army, and were subject to brutal military socialization. *"Los antiguos"* (senior officers and more seasoned soldiers) referred to these young men as *"los perros"* (the dogs); the former soldiers we interviewed summed up their basic training as *"la perrada"*—a dog's life.[15] They recount being forced to lick the floors of filthy latrines, to sleep with dirty flea-infested blankets, to kill dogs and subsequently drink their blood and eat their raw flesh. These men also described severe beatings and lacerating verbal harassment as punishments for even minor infractions.

Included in the verbal harassment were ethnic insults. The recruits were darker-skinned men from the sierra serving under lighter skinned officers from the coast. Class standing and military rank magnified ethnic difference, which was further enforced by the use of sexual violence, especially rape. In our interviews, former soldiers assured us that "sex was 80 percent of the conversations we had every day." Who could *"tirar"* (rape) another was a determining factor in deciding who was the *"más macho,"* and the first one to anally rape another man came out, literally, on top. Just as rank determined who would go first when raping civilians, that same hierarchy was repeated within the barracks. The gang rapes began with the highest-ranking officer and ended with the lowliest recruit. Rape was a means of establishing hierarchies, between armed groups and the population, and within the armed forces themselves. Several former soldiers described the use of sodomy on young recruits who were reluctant to demonstrate the "appropriate" level of aggression vis-à-vis the civilian population. In other instances, we were told that if a recruit refused to participate in the raping, he would be shot and his family told that he died in combat. Thus, I stress the importance of understanding men as both victims *and* victimizers during times of conflict, a recognition that need not devolve into a lack of accountability or endless moral elasticity.

Holding people accountable means having a clear understanding of the forms of violence practiced and suffered, by whom, and in what context. This may involve listening differently to male victims, as I have suggested, which could change what we think we know about sexual violence. Across the board in Peru, Quechua-speakers frequently used veiled speech when talking about rape and other forms of sexual violence. The verbs I heard most often were *fastidiar* (to bother), *molestar* (to harass), *abusar* (to abuse), and *burlar* (to make fun of or to take advantage of someone). Context is crucial to understanding the meaning of what an individual was actually communicating, and we now know that the gender of the speaker also influenced what was heard and how it was coded by the PTRC.

Political scientist Michelle Leiby reviewed a sample of 2,500 testimonies given to the Peruvian TRC, examining what people had said and how the acts they described were coded into the database. When she analyzed the original testimonies (and worked with native Quechua speakers to capture the nuances of language), Leiby found that 22 percent of the victims of sexual violence were men (2009, 82). In the PTRC's coding, "The rape of men is treated inconsistently—coded as either sexual violence or torture, and sometimes not recorded at all" (2009, 82).[16] Evidently, what determined whether a particular act was coded as sexual violence rather than torture often depended not on the act itself, but on the gender of the body upon which the act was performed. The erasure of sexualized violence against men yields stereotypical victim-perpetrator binaries, and reinforces the image of women as persons to whom sexual crimes *essentially* occur. Women get raped; men, apparently, do not.[17]

I think here of Michel-Rolph Trouillot's work on silences in the making of historical sources (1995). He was examining a slave revolt in Haiti, and its apparent absence in history. Of interest here is the category of the "unthinkable"; for French colonialists, it was unthinkable that black slaves could successfully organize and execute a revolution (that sort of thing took place in France, not some distant slave outpost!). By exceeding conceptual limitations of the possible, the slave revolt never made it into the archives.

For certain testimony takers and database designers in Peru, men as victims of sexual violence was "unthinkable," and the stories men told about being raped, sexually tortured, mutilated, or humiliated were largely erased. Thus, an important silence entered into and molded the archive. Statistics have powerful knowledge effects, and archives are more than a mere collection of documents that define a culture at a particular moment. As Michel Foucault argued, archives are more than institutions neutrally established to preserve texts. Rather, the archive is "the law of what can be said," and the law of how what is said is transformed, used, and preserved (1982, 127). In this instance, the archive leaves us with essentialized notions of victims and perpetrators, categories too frequently assumed to map seamlessly onto gendered dichotomies as well. Gender is reduced to women; gender-based violence reduced to rape; and the more complicated stories people tell about war are at risk of becoming *unthinkable* and therefore, erased.

CONCLUSIONS

> Anthropologists have been accused of making the social so complex as to make it useless for any policy purposes that demand some reduction of complexity. However, in my experience it is precisely when anthropologists are able to convey the meaning of an event

> in terms of its location in the everyday, assuming that social action is not simply a direct materialization of cultural scripts but bears the traces of how these shared symbols are worked through, that it can be most effective. (Das 2007, 217)

I wish to conclude by reflecting on the contributions feminist anthropology can make to the issues raised in this chapter. The feminist commitment to gender equality, combined with anthropological theories and methods, can contribute to achieving a greater measure of justice in the aftermath of war. Given the limitations of quantitative data collection on sensitive subjects such as gender-based and sexual violence, sustained ethnographic research can fill important gaps in our knowledge. I focus on five points: generating new forms of evidence that can assist in shifting the narrative burden for sexual violence from women without jeopardizing their right to reparations; qualitative research that can establish patterns and systematicity regarding the use of sexual violence in order to contribute to accountability efforts; including men in our research as both perpetrators and victims; capturing the cultural meanings of sexual violence and its legacies; and contributing to feminist theorizing on harm and redress.

When people talk about sexual violence, they talk a great deal about silences. What to do with these silences—how to listen to them, how to interpret them, how to determine when they are oppressive and when they may constitute a form of agency, how to understand silences and and the ways in which they contour the archives—is a subject of much concern and debate.[18] For an earlier wave of feminists, "breaking the silence" regarding rape and other forms of sexual violence was an important rallying cry. The contribution these feminists made to changing societal perceptions and advancing international jurisprudence was vitally important. However, I advocate moving from "breaking the silence" to learning to respect certain silences and the people who maintain them. Drawing upon her research on women's interactions with the South African TRC, Nthabiseng Motsemme has emphasized, "[the] ways in which silence can also be viewed as 'present' and 'speaking,' rather than 'absent' and 'voiceless'" and thus "becomes a site for creating meanings and forms of enablement for those at the margins" (2004, 926). Silences, in the plural, may preserve life and community, and perform important work in reconstituting self and the everyday. Rather than the incitement to speech about rape as the cornerstone of an emancipatory project, I caution against tying the right to redress to speech, and to speech of a particular kind.

How many times have victim-survivors repeated their stories of suffering with justice a distant horizon? What *are* the consequences of conflating persons with their injury, or narratively harnessing them to that experience? Of reducing a human being to his or her wound? In her critique of liberalism and justice,

Wendy Brown cautions against "wounded attachments" as a means of "doing politics." As she argues, an identity politics based upon a logic of pain—one in which politicized identity is founded upon a wounded character—has limited emancipatory potential because it tethers the individual to ontological claims of suffering, which breeds a politics of recrimination and rancor (Brown 1993). It can also give rise to a politics of victimhood in which narration serves to solidify injury as the core of a person's subjectivity, rather than a means of scripting a new self, a new future.

Anthropological methods can contribute to changing this dynamic. I have never asked anyone if they were raped. Long-term research and the relationships one forges over time change the nature of our interactions and allow us to eschew the interview format in lieu of informal conversations and participant observation. We are positioned to capture nuance, listen for silences, "thick descriptions"—and construct powerful arguments based upon qualitative data. After years of working with communities throughout the highlands in Peru, I have been able to discern patterns to the sexual violence—an ethnographic mapping, if you will. In each community in which a military base had been established during the internal armed conflict, there was a sustained level of sexual abuse against the civilian population. The preponderance of "third-person" conversations, triangulated with the PTRC's final report and our interviews with former soldiers, have established this fact. This pattern contributes to building a reasonable "assumption model" regarding the use of sexual violence; such anthropological data could relieve people from being forced to narrate their individual experiences in order to be considered potential beneficiaries of reparations.[19]

At its best anthropology disrupts both universalizing and essentializing discourses by insisting on complexity in our analyses. Drawing upon the vast literature from gender and particularly masculinity studies, feminist anthropology combines its methods and theories to explore the multiple femininities and masculinities forged during conflict and postconflict periods, and to examine how these converge and diverge from preexisting gender regimes. David Morgan has noted that, "Of all the sites where masculinities are constructed, reproduced, and deployed, those associated with war and the military are some of the most direct" (Morgan 1994, 165). Calling attention to the plurality of masculinities, for instance, could help researchers tease out why and when masculinity and the exercise of violence fuses, and how to disentangle the two more effectively in the aftermath of armed conflict. Additionally, capturing local understandings of sexuality could call into question the theories of heterosexual male sexuality that infuse the inevitability arguments, while also researching the pleasure of the rapist. If an earlier generation of feminists strategically disarticulated rape and sexuality to lay bare its violent and dominating aspects, more fully understanding how men achieve erections and orgasms in situations of bloody gang rape or coercion could help to inform efforts to reconstruct masculinities following periods of armed conflict.

Additionally, Paul Richards has argued that, "Ethnography is a tool to probe the social content of war" (1996, 8). Anthropologists are poised to capture the *cultural meaning* of rape and other forms of sexual violence, which has tremendous implications for theory and intervention. For example, in Peru we found that many women referred to the soldiers as "animals." While this may at first seem nothing more than a standard wartime form of discursive dehumanization, attentiveness to language use is important. Why "animals"? We have discovered that the soldiers sodomized women, frequently in public venues in front of family members and the broader community. Women have made clear that anal intercourse is not an acceptable form of sexual activity for them; indeed, they assured us that only "animals have sex that way," and that God considers it sinful for human beings to engage in such practices. Thus, some women's shame extended beyond their loved ones; in God's eyes, they are degraded sinners as well. The psychological legacies of such acts should inform reparations programs and orient psychological services.

Finally, research makes clear that women have been overwhelmingly excluded from peace agreements and national rebuilding efforts, and that the additional burdens women assume as a result of armed conflict are often left unaddressed. Of course, peace agreements are just one step in lengthy transitional processes. Former UN Secretary General Kofi Annan defined transitional justice as "[t]he full range of processes and mechanisms associated with a society's attempts to come to terms with a legacy of large-scale past abuses, in order to ensure accountability, serve justice, and achieve reconciliation. These may include both judicial and non-judicial mechanism, with differing levels of international involvement (or none at all) and individual reform, vetting, and dismissals, or a combination thereof."[20] Among that full range of mechanisms are reparations programs. As I have argued, perhaps one of the gravest problems with reparations programs is that the forms of harm experienced by women tend to be classified as less serious or secondary in relation to the human rights violations suffered by men—or to be rendered invisible. A leader in the field of gender and reparations is Ruth Rubio-Marín whose work focuses on how to harness the transformative potential of reparations to destabilize gender hierarchies.[21] In part she advocates moving from a rights-based to a harms-based approach when designing reparations programs, a move toward which ethnographic research has much to contribute. As she argues, due to the gender bias of many rights systems, reparations (when conceived as redress for the violations of such rights) are likely to reproduce gender biases (2006, 31). In contrast, focusing on "harms" can capture the wider range of consequences that women disproportionately bear:

> Indeed, the need to identify who, beyond the rights holder, has been individually or collectively affected by the violation and deserves redress allows movement beyond the rights paradigm in one concrete way that may be fundamental to women, namely by bringing to the fore the interrelatedness of the harms and the ways in which the diffuse nature of harms affects women specifically. For instance, although, strictly speaking, there is no human right not to be widowed; the harm done to women whose husbands are executed or disappeared can nevertheless find adequate recognition through this harms-based notion of victim. (2006, 31)

As I have demonstrated, feminist anthropology can contribute to theorizing gender-based harms via attention to historically, culturally, and economically situated women and men, and researching their priorities and concepts of redress. One criticism of international conflict feminism has been its Western bias, which in turns leads to interventions that smack of an earlier era of colonial impositions. However, by combining gender theory with postcolonial critique, twenty-first-century feminist anthropology can insist—again and loudly—on intersectionality and the importance of capturing local specificity without losing sight of the globalized world in which we all seek to make our way.

NOTES

1. See Helliwell 2000 for a useful critique of this approach based upon her research in a Dayak community in Indonesian Borneo.
2. For an excellent analysis of the Violence Against Women movement, international human rights, and their "vernacularization," see Merry 2006.
3. The classic work on male fraternities is Peggy Sanday's *Fraternity Gang Rape: Sex, Brotherhood, and Privilege on the College Campus* (1990). On military socialization, the literature is vast; a good place to start is with Joshua Goldstein's *War and Gender: How Gender Shapes the War System and Vice Versa* (2001); Lt. Col. Dave Grossman's *The Psychological Cost of Learning to Kill in War and Society* (1996); and Richard Holmes's *Acts of War: The Behavior of Men in Battle* (1989). For a fascinating analysis of how torture may be resignified as a source of pride and a route to male authority, see Julie Peteet, "Male Gender and Rituals of Resistance in the Palestinian 'Intifada': A Cultural Politics of Violence" (1994). In addition to academic and practitioner texts and documents, some of the finest work has been authored by former soldiers themselves. For an overview of key texts, see Keith Brown and Catherine Lutz, "Grunt Lit: The Participant Observers of Empire" (2007).
4. I searched for the origin of the phrase, and the answer varies. See Nigel Rees's entry in *The Cassell's Dictionary of Clichés* (1996) for an overview of sources.
5. For a detailed discussion of these issues, see Theidon 2007 and 2012.
6. The term "international conflict feminism" is one I borrow from Vasuki Nesiah (2009).
7. I invoke, of course, Kimberlé Crenshaw's concept of intersectionality (1989), as well as the abundant postcolonial critiques, including Anzaldúa (2012), Kapur (2005), and Mohanty (1988).
8. For example, see Hayner (2010) and Ross (2002).

9. See Fiona Ross for her insightful analysis of women's testimonies to the South African TRC (2002).
10. See Elizabeth Bernstein (2012) for an insightful analysis of how laws aimed at eradicating human trafficking have inadvertently limited the mobility of female migrants and sex workers who may find that such labor allows them to support their families and achieve economic independence.
11. In 2005, the United Nations approved the UN Basic Principles and Guidelines on the right to a Remedy and Reparation for Survivors of Violations of International Human Rights and Humanitarian Law. These Basic Principles establish minimum standards that require remedies, and state that reparations must "be adequate, effective, prompt, and appropriate."
12. On the need for an anthropology of men and masculinity, see Gutmann 1997.
13. In this section I draw upon my book *Intimate Enemies: Violence and Reconciliation in Peru* (2012).
14. For her discussion of war rape and male bonding, see Enloe 1988.
15. I conducted this phase of my research with the able assistance of Edith Del Pino, Lenor Rivera, and Mariano Aroñes. We were funded by the Weatherhead Center for International Affairs, Harvard University.
16. The most frequent forms of sexual abuse suffered by men was sexual humiliation (46 percent) followed by sexual mutilation (20 percent), then sexual torture (15 percent), and rape (15 percent) (Leiby 2009).
17. Space limitations do not allow me to adequately address certain domestic legal systems and the gendered pronouns used in the rape laws. In some countries men cannot "legally" be raped because the law only recognizes female victims. In other cases, "sodomy" may be illegal, and thus a man who comes forward to denounce having been raped is a criminal not a victim.
18. Veena Das has suggested that women's silence about rape may be a form of agency—perhaps the only form available to women—and thus silence does not necessarily signify the absence of linguistic competency but rather the active refusal to allow it (1987). See also Butalia (2000) and Ross (2003).
19. See Guillerot 2006 on the possibilities of designing accurate assumption models for the purpose of accountability and reparations.
20. Report of the Secretary General on the Rule of Law and Transitional Justice in Conflict and Post-Conflict Societies, S/2004/616.
21. See Ruth Rubio-Marín, ed., What Happened to the Women? Gender and Reparations for Human Rights Violations (2006); and The Gender of Reparations: Unsettling Sexual Hierarchies While Redressing *Human Rights Violations* (2009).

REFERENCES

Anzaldúa, Gloria. 2012. *Borderlands: La Frontera. The New Mestiza*. 4th ed. San Francisco: Aunt Lute Books.

Bernstein, Elizabeth. 2012. "Carceral Politics as Gender Justice? The 'Traffic in Women' and Neoliberal Circuits of Crime, Sex, and Rights." *Theory and Society* 41 (3): 33–59.

Brown, Keith, and Catherine Lutz. 2007. "Grunt Lit: The Participant Observers of Empire." *American Ethnologist* 34 (2): 322–328.

Brown, Wendy. 1993. *States of Injury: Power and Freedom in Late Modernity*. Princeton, NJ: Princeton University Press.

Brownmiller, Susan. 1975. *Against Our Will: Men, Women, and Rape*. New York: Simon and Schuster.

Butalia, Urvashi. 2000. *The Other Side of Silence: Voices from the Partition of India*. Durham, NC: Duke University Press.

Crenshaw, Kimberlé. 1989. "Mapping the Margins: Intersectionality, Identity Politics, and Violence against Women of Color." *Stanford Law Review* 42: 1240–1299.

Das, Veena. 1987. "The Anthropology of Violence and the Speech of Victims." *Anthropology Today* 3 (4): 11–13.

———. 2007. *Life and Words: A Descent into the Ordinary*. Berkeley: University of California Press.

Diken, Bulent, and Carsten Bagge Laustsen. 2005. "Becoming Abject: Rape as a Weapon of War." *Body and Society* 11 (1): 111–128.

Enloe, Cynthia. 1988. *Does Khaki Become You? The Militarisation of Women's Lives*. London: Pandora Press.

Foucault, Michel. 1982. *The Archaeology of Knowledge*. New York: Vintage Books.

Goldstein, Joshua S. 2001. *War and Gender: How Gender Shapes the War System and Vice Versa*. New York: Cambridge University Press.

Grossman, David. 1996. *On Killing: The Psychological Costs of Learning to Kill in War and Society*. New York: Back Bay Books.

Guillerot, Julie. 2006. "Linking Gender and Reparations in Peru: A Failed Opportunity." In *What Happened to the Women: Gender and Reparations for Human Rights Violations*, ed. Ruth Rubio-Marín, 136–182. New York: Social Science Research Council.

Gutmann, Matthew C. 1997. "Trafficking in Men: The Anthropology of Masculinity." *Annual Review of Anthropology* 26: 385–409.

Hayner, Priscilla. 2010. *Unspeakable Truths: Transitional Justice and the Challenge of Truth Commissions*. 2nd ed. London: Taylor and Francis.

Helliwell, Christine. 2000. "'It's Only a Penis': Rape, Feminism, and Difference." *Signs* 25 (3): 789–816.

Holmes, Richard. 1989. *Acts of War: Behavior of Men in Battle*. New York: Free Press.

Kapur, Ratna. 2005. *Erotic Justice: Law and the New Politics of Postcolonialism*. Delhi: Permanent Black.

Leiby, Michelle. 2009. "Digging in the Archives: The Promise and Perils of Primary Documents." *Politics and Society* 37: 75–99.

Littlewood, Roland. 1997. "Military Rape." *Anthropology Today* 13 (2): 7–16.

Merry, Sally. 2006. *Human Rights and Gender Violence: Translating International Law into Local Justice*. Chicago: University of Chicago Press.

Mohanty, Chandra. 1988. "Under Western Eyes: Feminist Scholarship and Colonial Discourses." *Feminist Review* 30: 61–88.

Morgan, David H. J. 1994. "Theater of War: Combat, the Military, and Masculinities." In *Theorizing Masculinities*, ed. Harry Brod and Michael Kaufman, 165–182. London: Sage Publications.

Motsemme, Nthabiseng. 2004. "'The Mute Always Speak Out': On Women's Silences at the Truth and Reconciliation Commission." *Current Sociology* 52 (2): 909–932.

Nesiah, Vasuki. 2009. "Feminist Interventions: Human Rights, Armed Conflict, and International Law." *Proceedings of the 103rd Annual Meetings of the American Society of International Law* 103: 67–69.

Ní Aoláin, Fionnuala. 2009. "Exploring a Feminist Theory of Harm in the Context of Conflicted and Post-Conflicted Societies." University of Minnesota Law School, Legal Studies Research Paper 09–45.

Peruvian Truth and Reconciliation Commission (PTRC). 2003. *Informe Final de la Comisión de Verdad y Reconciliación*. 9 vols. Lima, Peru: Peruvian Truth and Reconciliation Commission.

Peteet, Julie. 1994. "Male Gender and Rituals of Resistance in the Palestinian 'Intifada': A Cultural Politics of Violence." *American Ethnologist* 21: 31–49.

Philpott, Daniel. 2007. "Religion, Reconciliation, and Transitional Justice: The State of the Field." New York: Social Sciences Research Council Working Papers, October.

Rees, Nigel. 1996. *The Cassell's Dictionary of Clichés*. New York: Cassell.

Richards, Paul. 1996. *Fighting for the Rain Forest: War, Youth, and Resources in Sierra Leone*. London: Heineman.

Ross, Fiona. 2002. *Bearing Witness: Women and the Truth and Reconciliation Commission*. London: Pluto Press.

Rubio-Marín, Ruth, ed. 2006. *What Happened to the Women? Gender and Reparations for Human Rights Violations*. New York: Social Science Research Council.

———. 2009. *The Gender of Reparations: Unsettling Sexual Hierarchies While Redressing Human Rights Violations*. Cambridge: Cambridge University Press.

Sanday, Peggy. 1990. *Fraternity Gang Rape: Sex, Brotherhood, and Privilege on the College Campus*. New York: New York University Press.

Teitel, Ruti. 2002. *Transitional Justice*. Oxford: Oxford University Press.

Theidon, Kimberly. 2007. "Gender in Transition: Common Sense, Women and War." *Journal of Human Rights* 6 (4): 453–478.

———. 2012. *Intimate Enemies: Violence and Reconciliation in Peru*. Philadelphia: University of Pennsylvania Press.

Trouillot, Michel Rolph. 1995. *Silencing the Past: Power and the Production of History*. New York: Beacon Press.

United Nations Security Council. Resolution 1325. 2000. (S/RES/1325).

———. Resolution 1820. 2008. (S/RES/1820).

———. Resolution 1888. 2009. (S/RES/1888).

———. Resolution 1889. 2009. (S/RES/1889).

———. Resolution 1960. 2010. (S/RES/1960).

———. Resolution 2106. 2013. (S/RES/2106).

———. Resolution 2122. 2013. (S/RES/2122).

West, Robin. 1999. *Caring for Justice*. New York: New York University Press.

Wood, Elisabeth. 2006. "Variation in Sexual Violence during War." *Politics and Society* 34 (3): 307–341.

COOKING WITH FIREWOOD

Deep Meaning and Environmental Materialities in a Globalized World

MEENA KHANDELWAL

For feminist anthropologists, collaboration with engineers can be more than awkward; it can be hazardous to your mental health. Scholars in the social sciences, humanities, and area studies strive to cultivate a rich sense of context, language, locality, region, history, and social position. Engineers aim to universalize: biofuel is energy, which is they quantify and compare across contexts. Feminist anthropologists purge passive voice from our writing. Engineers prefer it. In my collaboration with a professor of mechanical engineering, H. S. Udaykumar ("Uday"), even the simplest task of agreeing on a title for a joint presentation becomes a comedy of errors. Yet the project challenges me to confront what I never learned in grade school: because trees sequester carbon, deforestation is a major cause of increased greenhouse gases. Similarly, he must learn some feminist basics. Having promised to deliver a guest lecture in my transnational feminism course, he innocently asked in a hurried e-mail: "What time do you want me to be at your transsexual feminism class?" Collaboration across such gaping divides has enabled me to "see" new things, but having to explain disciplinary truisms to an outsider who has competing views also revealed multiple contradictions, not only between social science and applied science as expected, but also between the generally "allied" fields within which I work. It is these tensions between anthropology, feminist studies, and area studies that I contemplate here.

This collaboration between myself and Uday provided experiential lessons for me to think through the sometimes incompatible approaches to food taboos and preferences in relation to environment, anthropology, feminism, and South Asian studies. This conversation across disciplines is not something I pursue simply to provoke. Rather, I argue, it is crucial if we are to address urgent problems in the world, for these tend to be simultaneously material, social, and imaginative—in both cause and effect. Is it possible to consider, if not fully synthesize, divergent theoretical and methodological tools in order to better understand both deep meaning and environmental realities, and the relationship between them, in the context of economic and cultural globalization?

THE ORIGIN STORY OF A PROJECT

The interdisciplinary dialogue I describe here began with a product: a solar cook stove. My aim here is to highlight the process of collaboration, which raised questions about this goal without dismissing the potential benefit of technological innovation in cook stoves. Why stoves? In January 2011, Uday took a group of engineering students from the University of Iowa to southern Rajasthan in India to learn about deforestation and sustainable technologies. They went to the Aravalli region, a hilly strip of forests that separates two ecological zones. On one side is the vast Thar desert, and on the other is semi-arid scrubland suitable for agriculture. The Aravallis prevent the desert from spreading over the croplands of northern India. Maxine Weisgrau (1997) observed that deforestation in this region sets off a chain of ecological events with dramatic impacts on residents' quality of life, particularly for those already marginalized. Destruction of forest in the Aravallis led to monsoon irregularities, droughts, loss of human life and livestock, crop failures, and out-migration of men (Weisgrau 1997, 136). The Government of India has since the time of independence recognized deforestation as a problem (Kumar 1993, 182). In Rajasthan as in much of rural India (and the world), firewood is gathered by women and girls who trek increasingly long distances to find it. Over three decades ago, Bina Agarwal (1983) identified the dire consequences of deforestation and firewood scarcity for women. Aside from the challenge of collecting wood in the face of deforestation, burning it to cook food emits household air pollution not only deadly to women and children (because of their physical proximity to cooking fires) but also harmful to wider populations and the earth's climate.

Uday has been working for a few years to design a solar cooker. For decades, however, efforts to diffuse improved stoves (to increase efficiency or reduce smoke) on the part of government agencies, development organizations, researchers, and inventors have been notoriously unsuccessful in India

(Subramanian 2014). Uday's solar prototype met the same fate. He was working with two NGOs, Climate Healers and Foundation for Ecological Security (FES), which distributed solar cookers in the village of Karech, only to find them gathering dust a year later. Uday's current goal is to improve the design so that women will want to use the cookers. When he learned that I was a feminist anthropologist, he approached me with a question, or rather, a plea: "how can we get these women who reside on the frontier of the Aravallis to adopt solar cookers and stop cutting firewood?"

My response was skeptical: "it cannot possibly be the case that these women living at a bare subsistence level are the cause of this deforestation? What kind of commercial logging is going on?"

"No logging," he was sure. "There are no roads."

As an anthropologist, I was also curious: "did you and your students go with the women on their treks to collect firewood?"

"No," he said. "We were too lazy."

These kinds of conversations occur everywhere. Typically, that would be the end of that. We critique; they ignore our insistence on grounded knowledge in their rush to fix problems. Uday's project began with the naïve assumption that freeing women from this task would result in a cascade of positive consequences, such as reforestation, better health, reduced drudgery, and girls' schooling. Anthropologists understand that cause and effect is not so simple when it comes to human behavior. As it turns out, the following winter, Uday and his students did accompany the women on their wood-cutting excursions and learned that women did not approach this work as drudgery. They were laughing, singing, trashing their husbands, and teasing the foreigners for their inability to lift seventy pounds of wood and navigate treacherous terrain in their fancy hiking boots as they themselves carried heavy loads across steep and rocky paths in long skirts and rubber flip flops. Harvesting wood is women's work; it is arduous, yes, but also creates community. Feminist anthropology has shown that gender segregation, stereotypically associated with premodern patriarchy, creates female social spaces of pleasure and solidarity from which women may act in their own interests (Arora-Jonsson 2009; Gururani 2002; Jassal 2012; Maggi 2001; Natarajan 2000). Uday further learned that even if wood is a form of energy, it is not simply biofuel; the women barter and sell wood to meet household needs. It is a form of currency that women control.[1] With these insights—wood is not solely a vault for carbon but is also a form of community and currency—the conversation became more interesting and began to feel like collaboration. Still, I had nagging doubts: were we focusing on women's informal economic activity and ignoring the bigger problem: legal or illegal commercial activity? At the very least, we must wonder: if wood is no longer necessary, will these women's lives improve? If they adopt solar cookers, will they stop cutting wood or simply harvest it to sell for profit? If they stop cutting wood, will the forests grow back? Will the girls go to school? These are not simple matters of cause and effect.

THE VALUE OF AWKWARD

The initial encounter described earlier was an awkward conversation between researchers with goals and assumptions that arise from different epistemologies. Despite this, or perhaps because of it, a mechanical engineer and a feminist anthropologist talking past each other can yield new insights. It makes us pose questions that would not otherwise arise in our own disciplines, and the knowledge we produce is an effect of the questions we ask. The insights Uday and I each brought to the table seem, frankly, quite obvious in our own fields, but I suggest that the sum is greater than the parts.

In her 1987 essay, now a classic in feminist anthropology, Marilyn Strathern suggested that anthropology's resistance to feminist thinking was the paradoxical product of intellectual proximity. For example, both fields promote difference, gender in one case and culture in the other. Then, asks Strathern, why such awkwardness? Her answer is that feminism attempts to undo its Other (patriarchy), while anthropology has a different relationship to its Other (defined as an alien culture); rather than attacking the culture being studied, anthropology deliberately sustains its foreignness. The anthropologist and informant have different interests, observes Strathern, but feminists claim shared interests with those they study. Feminism mocks the anthropological pretension of joint authorship with informants (a claim popular in the late 1980s) and insists that any dialogue that occurs in ethnographic encounters is by definition asymmetrical, while anthropology mocks the feminist pretension of achieving distance from its own patriarchal culture. Feminism and anthropology, concludes Strathern, are in a sense irrelevant to each other, and both fields, I once thought, are irrelevant to research in applied science.

Much has changed since Strathern's 1987 essay. Some anthropologists have employed postcolonial, indigenous, and feminist perspectives to critique the discipline's investments in maintaining difference. Feminists have seen the emergence of transnational theories in response to critiques that Global North feminism fails to interrogate its own geopolitical position. Transnational feminism responds to critiques that feminism is too deeply embedded in perspectives variously identified as liberal, Western, First World, and Global North and thus addresses what Strathern identified as anthropology's "mockery" of feminism. Because my analysis in this chapter is informed by transnational feminism, let me summarize its critiques of Global North feminism.

It presumes a shared goal of global sisterhood unencumbered by analysis of colonial legacies and ongoing capitalist transformation such as Structural Adjustment Programs (Alexander and Mohanty 1997; Lugones 2010). It explains the oppression of so-called Third World Women as caused by reified notions of tradition and culture stripped of history and economy (Narayan 1997; Nnaemeka 2005, 37). It tends to equate modernity with the West and with liberatory visions (Bernal 1994) and women's liberation with such privileges as consumption and freedom to travel the world (Kaplan 1995). Its focus on agency erroneously assumes all women long for autonomy and aim to challenge social norms and those who don't lack agency (Mahmood 2005). Global North feminism concentrates too much on how we liberated Westerners can help those in the Global South, but not enough on how our own foreign policy and funding structures, whether government aid or private philanthropy, constrain people from pursuing their own interests. Instead, recipients of aid are encouraged to focus on a single predetermined issue—eradication of female circumcision, LGBT rights, access to credit/debt systems—that donors deem important at a given moment in history (Alvarez 2008; Ford-Smith 1997).

Transnational feminism aims to decolonize Western feminist theory and its essentialist constructions of subaltern people in the Global South by: showing how people's lives are locally and historically grounded, while also delineating non-local processes; addressing difference among Third World women; attending to the material, concrete realities of their lives; and identifying linkages between subaltern groups in Global North and Global South contexts. As such, it would seem to bridge the gap Strathern first identified between anthropology and feminism. Anthropologists have made crucial contributions to the field of transnational feminism. Are we no longer then haunted by Chandra Talpade Mohanty's accusation that anthropology has been one of the most influential forms of knowledge produced by colonial rule and that it has historically authorized the objectification of women in the Global South in the form of "The Native Woman" (Mohanty 2003, 74–76)? For me, an unexpected collaboration with an engineer has lent new urgency to this question, as a debate about solar cookers in Rajasthan quickly became a debate about globalization and the politics of food, one that revealed contradictions between anthropology and feminism—further complicated by area studies.

DEFINING A PROBLEM IN THE ARAVALLIS

Deforestation is a truly "wicked problem" (Rittel and Webber 1973), but defining this problem in a given place—its causes and solutions—is no simple task. My disciplinary training primed me to be skeptical of the assumptions underlying

Uday's initial plea for advice on how to get rural women to adopt solar cookers. My initial response might seem predictable, given my schooling in postcolonial, feminist, and anthropological scholarship. This is what I know: (1) the trope of rescue is deeply colonial; (2) positionality is foundational to knowledge production; (3) postwar development agendas often solidify old-order geopolitical inequalities; and (4) the hubris of modernization narratives is based on unilineal accounts of progress unsupported by evidence. This is what I wanted to understand: who bears responsibility for causing environmental degradation in the Aravallis—and for fixing it? The policies of Global North countries have tended to focus on increasing population (i.e., high fertility of poor women in the Global South) instead of high consumption, for example. Such policies shift the blame for environmental degradation away from middle-class and elite consumption patterns and toward marginal populations, whose children have a tiny footprint, and further erase the reasons for high fertility that include elevated infant mortality rates (Hynes 1999). In their study of rural communities, anthropologists also examine the role of industrial development, extraction of commodities, and the consumption practices of those living elsewhere, for these tend to have greater environmental impact than indigenous subsistence patterns. Environmental historians of South Asia Madhav Gadgil and Ramachandra Guha (1995) have suggested that all of India's population can be divided within three general categories. There are omnivores, affluent people who consume things produced all over the world; ecosystem people, who depend on the natural environments of their own locality to meet their basic needs; and ecological refugees, whose local ecosystems are degraded. Solar cookers were intended for ecosystem people on the brink of becoming refugees, and it seemed backward to point to their livelihood activities as the cause of deforestation. What is the role of the Indian state, commercial logging, and urbanization? These are valid anthropological questions, but, to be fair, the engineering perspective was not as simple as it first appeared.

Uday defines the problem thus: women cut tree branches. Cows roam the hills, grazing on saplings. Behind them come herds of goats that dig up and consume even the roots. By the time the goats are finished, nothing will grow back. Deforestation leads to drought in southern Rajasthan, and intensifies global warming to boot. Persistent drought makes agriculture tenuous, so people turn to livestock to supply the increasing demand for meat and dairy products in urban India and other countries, hence a vicious cycle.[2] Conceptualizing the problem thus, Uday proposes two solutions.

SOLAR COOKERS AND VEGAN DIET

One solution is to develop a solar cooker targeted at poor people in rural Rajasthan who currently rely on biofuel for cooking; it should be simple in design, cheap to produce, made from local materials, easy to repair, and capable of meeting local cooking needs. Replacing primitive technology with solar cook stoves is a quintessential modernization project. Engineers want to fix things and are optimistic about their ability to do so through technological innovation. Cultural anthropologists and postcolonial scholars have amply demonstrated the harmful ecological and economic impacts of many post-World War II development projects, but Cheryl McEwen argues that postcolonial studies scholars focus too much on discourse instead of material realities, too much on the past instead of the present, and, ultimately, that their oppositional stance has had little impact on North–South power relations (McEwen 2001). Most anthropologists, however, do not tend to see it as our job to offer solutions. For some, this is because the pursuit of scientific objectivity and empirical investigation—the pursuit of truth—must precede any thoughtful decision about where, when, and how exactly to intervene. Others, influenced by postcolonial and postmodern theories, are reluctant to prescribe solutions because of the discipline's historical complicity with colonialism. In an acrimonious debate, Nancy Scheper-Hughes (1995) calls for a politically engaged, militant anthropology that enables researchers to intervene in the face of human suffering, while Roy D'Andrade (1995) insists that "speaking truth to power" requires finding out the truth through scientific generalizations and objectivity. In a thoughtful response to the "objectivity and militancy" debate, Laura Nader suggests that the best anthropology requires quantitative and qualitative models, humanism along with some kind of science, good writers and good thinkers, and a deep respect for both integrative thinking and empiricism (1995, 427). I suggest that this hybrid approach could also be collaborative. We must retain insights about discursive forms of mystification from critical theories, while also seeking solutions, lest we be too absorbed in a passionate argument about neoliberalism to notice when the conference hotel falls into the ocean. It is easy to be sanctimonious in one's critique of development, viewing it as naïve at best and neocolonial at worst, when one is sitting on the sidelines; the more urgent challenge is to continue to ask critical and reflexive questions about power even while getting one's hands dirty in social change projects. Whether we blame Rajasthan's deforestation on colonialism, postcolonial development, cooking with wood, or affluent people's taste for meat, it does not change our current problem. Climate change is pulling the villagers of Karech into a globalized world that is not of their making or choosing. A central question thus remains: what should be done about their plight and by whom?

Even if a solar cooker is unlikely to "fix" the deforestation problem, it could bring multiple benefits. According to feminist scholar Patricia Hynes, Somali women who used a pilot solar cooker were happy to avoid the hazards of the snakes, scorpions, and bandits they would encounter on excursions to find wood; no longer did they have to trade food for fuel when they fell short of wood. The solar cooker gave them rest and time for other tasks. Somali women also did not have to worry about smoke inhalation or their children being burned. The food, they said, even had a better taste. Moreover, the cooker can pasteurize water and milk, and women can use their meager income to purchase fresh food rather than fuel (Hynes 1999, 189–190). Similarly, it is clear that women in Karech village are not categorically opposed to new technologies as evidenced by their rapid embrace of solar lanterns (supplied by Climate Healers) and cell phones (purchased). These lanterns have helped women avoid snakebites when going out in the predawn darkness. But, research shows that new technologies may both undermine and reinforce established gender roles (Doron 2012, but also see Ghertner 2006). Given the dire threat of deforestation, innovations in stove technology could have positive impact, especially in Rajasthan where sun is the most abundant energy source.

Environmentalists tend to identify rural people's demand for wood as the cause of deforestation, but the wood fuel shortage in India is more accurately a symptom rather than a cause of deforestation (Swaminathan 1999, 171). Regardless of whether cooking with fire is a major cause of deforestation in the Aravallis or not, it is without a doubt a problem for women both in terms of wood scarcity and health. But, defining something as a "women's issue" also marginalizes it, as we have seen with domestic violence and rape in the United States and elsewhere. In India, state resources from the energy sector aimed at improved cook stove technologies have seen a sharp decline (Swaminathan 1999, 168). The launch of Global Alliance for Clean Cookstoves in 2010 by Hillary Clinton has directed more resources and attention toward improving cook stoves, though most models continue to be based on biofuel energy (Subramanian 2014). If three billion people in the world depend on locally available biomass for their daily energy needs, the impact of this reliance on people's health and ecosystems is massive, seemingly irreversible and tragic; cooking with wood is both essential and unsustainable (Yadama 2013, 40). The question of cooking technologies is part of this collaborative project but not my main focus here.[3]

Instead, what I wish to engage in this chapter is Uday's second proposed solution: convince the world's affluent to renounce meat and dairy. Though our discussion started with cook stoves, I quickly found myself facing urgent arguments for a vegan diet as the single most important thing each of us can do to stem climate change. Thus, I outline the different, sometimes incompatible, approaches to animal foods that permeate research in anthropology, feminism, and South

Asian studies. I do so in order to show that public engagement with authentic problems necessitates bringing into this dialogue an analysis of deeply held meanings about, for example, sacred cows on the one hand, and the materiality of environmental change on the other hand. Attention to this dialogic process brings clarity to some of the sacred cows of our respective disciplines and should also inform activism.

Uday's assessment is that we cannot place environmental catastrophes at the doorstep of Third World overpopulation, because First World consumption is at least as significant. On this point, scholars in the three fields in which I work all agree. Shifting from a narrow focus on firewood harvesting to other causes of deforestation in the region, the questions became more compelling to me. With the coming of the British to India, both forests and people who lived in or around them came to be "managed" as a resource within a broader system of production (Hardiman 1994, 105). By the early 1800s, vast amounts of high-quality teak was being extracted for the building of British warships, but eventually the demand for teak for railway construction exceeded that of ships (1994, 119). The Indian railway system enabled more efficient extraction and exportation of resources. In 1864, the colonial state established the Indian Forest Department, not to conserve forests but to maintain a cost effective timber supply; the colonial-era assault on South Asia's forests was both unprecedented and irreversible (Das 2011, 48). Deforestation for commercial use and development has continued at a rapid pace in the postcolonial era (Gadgil and Guha 1995).

Uday, along with one of our other collaborators, Sailesh Rao, founder of Climate Healers and a former engineer, argues that the fate of the Aravalli forests today reflects a deep intertwine of cooking practices and the production of animal-derived food commodities to meet the skyrocketing external demand for milk, beef, and mutton (Rao 2011). If this trend continues, on the horizon loom desertification and a landscape inhospitable to human life. On a per person basis, notes Uday, there are three main sources for the huge footprint of middle-class people in the West—driving cars, heating and cooling, and eating animal products—and going vegan is the single most effective measure that we as individuals can take to stem climate change. It is at this point that our collaboration became more challenging. The demand for animal products is pushing deforestation across the world, and the call for affluent people to become vegans makes sense from an energy and climate perspective. Why, then, did it make me bristle?

It is well-established that the environmental cost of elite and middle-class lifestyles is shifted to marginalized communities. It is not possible for anyone, including myself, someone with access to private cars and an incredible variety of foods, to opt out of intervening in their lives. The rhetoric of doing so, whether in the name of cultural relativism or refusing First World privilege, belies the urgent environmental realities that connect rich and poor, Global

North and Global South, in an asymmetrical relationship. Those who provide labor, fueling increased consumption, are often the people dispossessed of their natural resources; additionally, they live with the waste of others' consumption and face the most immediate impact of environmental decline (Gadgil and Guha 1995; Guha 2006; Shiva 2008). Calls for veganism in the name of stemming climate change challenge us to consider deep meanings about food as the material realities of energy, food, and waste. What then should we eat? Below I consider what my distinct fields—South Asian studies, anthropology, and feminist studies—have to say about this matter in order to attempt to answer this question.

WHAT'S THE BEEF ABOUT?: THE CULTURAL POLITICS OF BEEF IN SOUTH ASIAN STUDIES

Scholars and activists concerned about the relationship between food production and the environment in South Asia have no choice but to consider the volatile, but unique, politics of dairy and meat consumption in India. This necessitates engagement with scholarship in South Asian studies which explores the specificities of history, region, politics, religion, and culture (Adcock 2010; Khare 1976; Khare and Rao 1986; Lodrick 2005), even if its attention to deep meaning counters the universalizing tendencies of materialist approaches. Area studies scholars have documented upper-caste Hindu stigmatization of beef eating in India, where it is the most marginalized groups—Dalit, Muslim, and Christian—who eat beef (Chigateri 2010).[4] Parvis Ghassem-Fachandi (2010) argues that public (Hindu) discourse expressing disgust toward beef and those who eat it may be directly linked to the 2002 Gujarat violence that left some 1,500 people, mostly Muslims, dead. That same year, there was a murder of five Dalit men because of a rumor that they openly slaughtered a cow in Haryana (Jodkha and Dhar 2003). The facts of both incidents are contested. Were the men in Haryana simply transporting a dead cow or a load of skins, both of which are customary activities associated with their low status? Did the police spread the rumor? Did the mob that killed the men mistake them for Muslims? More recently, when Dalit students at Osmania University in Hyderabad organized a beef festival to protest what blogger Murali Shanmugavelan (2012) calls Hindu "food fascism," feminist supporter, writer, and poet Meena Kandaswamy, apparently deemed a traitor to her religion, was threatened with gang rape and acid attacks by Hindu militants. Hindu nationalists have idealized the vegetarian diet as essential to Hinduism, despite historical evidence that vegetarianism developed later than they claim. Further, recent polls suggest that only a minority of India's population is strictly vegetarian, even if overall meat consumption is very low compared to other countries.[5] But because the politics of meat in South Asia are deeply linked to caste hierarchies, religious hostilities, Hindu nationalism, and horrific violence (news reports of attacks on those who consume beef continue as this book goes to press), progressives are generally not willing to take a public stance against eating meat. Vegetarian rhetoric is too easily associated with Hindu militancy. Unlike Uday, I cannot isolate veganism as the answer to a set of complex realities and contradictions.

However, Uday and Sailesh connected the dots for me, linking dairy and meat production, bovine density, deforestation, loss of ground water, and persistent drought. Close to half (45 percent) of the world's land area is currently used for livestock production, and livestock has emerged as one of the top contributors to our most serious environmental problems: deforestation, desertification, overuse of fresh water, emission of greenhouse gases (GHGs), and diversion of food for use as feed (UNEP; Steinfeld and Gerber 2010). According to the UN's Food and Agricultural Organization (FAO) mapping, India is bovine density central. The 2012–2013 annual report of the government's Department of Animal Husbandry, Dairying, and Fisheries report that India is home to over half of the world's buffalo population and about 15 percent of its cattle. It is now the largest producer of milk in the world and has seen heavy growth in meat production. India has only 2.29 percent of the world's land but maintains over 10 percent of the world's livestock population, according to this report (FAO 2005). Dairy and beef production are discursively opposed but materially linked. As someone trained to analyze the relationship between social organization and symbolic worlds, it was an epiphany to "see" the material link between dairy and meat industries, and the contribution of both to environmental degradation.

The link between dairy and meat production has profound implications for understanding the politics of food in India. The country's bovine density appears to be the result of the high value placed on cows (state bans on their slaughter intensify their environmental impact) and their products. Contemporary Hinduism, particularly in north India with its ancient pastoral history, constructs milk as the perfect, pure food, and beef as polluting. Milk production and consumption has skyrocketed in India (and China) and is associated with national development and child growth (Wiley 2011, 2014). However, this issue cannot simply be explained in terms of Hindu cow veneration, for cows are just one kind of bovine. First, cows are female, so the increased focus on dairy production yields an excess of useless male calves and older female animals. Second, there has been no cultural elaboration, demarcation, marking, or protection of most of India's milk and beef supply, which comes from water buffaloes (Wiley 2014). While India's constitution calls for a scientific approach to animal husbandry and the protection of cows, it leaves regulation to the states. A report by the government's National Commission on Cattle (2002) observes that various states have enacted "cow" protection laws that only refer to the female animal, rendering a bull, bullock, and even a calf available for slaughter. Moreover, there is widespread transportation of cattle across state lines to evade protective laws. The commission calls for a uniform national plan to end this confusing and inconsistent patchwork of state laws. Indeed, in spring 2015, the state of Maharasthra extended a ban on cow slaughter to bulls and oxen and criminalized the sale of beef (Shibu 2015). The shifting legal terrain of the meat industry reflects the volatile politics of religion and caste rather than a significant political debate about environment and climate change.

Thus, the availability and affordability of beef is the byproduct of the high value placed on milk products. The poor drink relatively little milk, because of its high market value. Beef is cheap and available precisely because so many upper-caste Hindus want milk but not meat. It is a byproduct of dairy production, hence India's status as a major exporter of beef and leather. Bovines, both sacred cows and not-so-sacred buffaloes, are an environmental problem. Worldwide, the increasingly intensive production of ruminant sources of protein (beef, sheep, goat, milk) is a direct cause of environmental degradation, not only because cattle eat greenery and produce methane, but because forests are cleared to create pasture and grow food for animals. This is particularly acute in contexts of intensive, industrial beef production. For example, Brazil has one of the highest rates of tropical deforestation caused by intensive cattle ranching to supply markets in China, Russia, and the United States (Walker, Patel, and Kalif 2013). By contrast, Rajasthan's semi-arid ecosystem is different, and livestock here are raised by extensive rather than industrial means, but their increasing population is one cause of alarming environmental damage.

If Hindu public discourse values the purity and nutritional content of milk and evokes disgust toward beef and beef-eaters, considering the material and systemic link between dairy and meat production reveals a profound contradiction in these public discourses that is not at all evident when one looks only at the symbolic meaning of food. Focusing on meat as a cause of environmental decline is risky business in South Asia, given the politics of caste and Hindu nationalism. Shraddha Chigateri (2010) notes that Dalits point to the upper-caste hypocrisy embedded in the twin notions that milk is the perfect food and meat is associated with dirtiness and lack of self-control. Vegan activists make this move with a different purpose, employing a materialist framework that is neither South Asia-centric or even human-centric. Dalits and vegans put milk and beef in the same category. The former argue that both are good forms of nutrition, while the latter argue that humans must renounce both to address climate change.

Political issues cross geographic spaces with odd results. The right to abortion, a central plank of US liberal feminism, takes on a different meaning in contexts where a female fetus might be targeted for abortion (a problem in some parts of India), or where women are more concerned with the right to keep their children than to abort them, as is so often true in US minority communities that have lost children to adoption, foster care, or assimilationist boarding schools. So it is with meat. I have found myself in the disorienting situation where Indian scholars visit the Midwest and proudly declare their wish to eat a steak or hamburger as a badge of being a progressive (anti-caste) Indian. Such an act belies a stunning lack of awareness of the different politics of meat in the Midwest, where activists and scientists blame industrial meat production for the loss of groundwater, water contamination, brutal treatment of animals, and deliberate recruitment of undocumented and refugee workers who are too vulnerable to complain about their abysmal working conditions.[6] In the politics of meat, place and culture matter. And so does professional or academic discipline. And yet, the materiality of bovines' environmental impact—their food, their methane, their milk, their flesh—exists, regardless of what or how we think about it.

MEAT AS A SYMBOL OF EGALITARIAN SOCIETIES IN ANTHROPOLOGY

My resistance to promoting veganism as a solution was not only shaped by the field of South Asian Studies, but also by anthropology. Anthropologists understand the importance of food practices to identity and community, which leads us to highlight difference rather than to universalize. Depending on theoretical perspective, some anthropologists focus on food materialities and others on the cultural patterns of meaning across domains that are neither concrete nor measurable (Gold 2014).[7] Most of us don't generally set out to change the cultures we study, for interventions aimed at helping people can have unintended consequences. Moreover, our discipline has long detailed the harm done to people and communities by the arrogance of those (colonizers, missionaries, development experts) who intervene in the name of uplift, rescue, modernization, education, or conversion. Cultural relativism, despite various critiques, remains foundational to the field and teaches us to appreciate difference and avoid judgment of cultural practices that depart from our own, including diverse food preferences and taboos. Anthropologists have produced a rich body of scholarship critically analyzing food systems and the shift from subsistence to market production. We have mapped the latter's relationship to environmental decline, indebtedness of farmers, globalization, health, and exploitative labor practices and have offered policy recommendations (Striffler 2005). But, anthropologists have stopped short of proposing any particular diet as a solution.

I suggest that there is more than cultural relativism at stake when anthropologists confront food politics. Meat seems to have a special place in the hearts of anthropologists. Ramachandra Guha (2006) identifies three distinct environmental utopias: agrarianism, wilderness thinking, and scientific industrialism. Anthropology has a long history of research on agrarian, pastoral, and foraging societies, as well as scholarship documenting people's efforts to protect their ways of life from state-sponsored industrialism and its inherent structural violence. Agriculture and raising livestock tend to be deeply integrated activities among peasant communities, and anthropologists are keenly aware of the importance of domesticated animals in economic, social, and religious life, particularly when they are one among diverse subsistence strategies. Thus, anthropologists resist calls for universal solutions to environmental problems caused by mono-cropping and industrial food production. If some scientists call for a massive shift to more energy-efficient, plant-based foods for a "small planet" (Henning 2011), and others say that only place-based research can find solutions tailored to diverse ecosystems (Janzen 2011), anthropologists will generally agree with the latter.

Wilderness thinking, Guha shows, is deeply rooted in the US experience, and exemplified by our system of national parks; "primitivism" is one particular strand of wilderness thinking. Primitivists glorify a pre-agrarian state of harmony with nature that was rudely shattered by the white man; they posit that hunter-gatherers were the first, and perhaps the only, genuine environmentalists and tend to believe that it is only in hunting-gathering societies that we find relative gender equality (Guha 2006, 80). One standard feature of introductory contemporary textbooks in anthropology is a refutation of the notion that life for hunter-gatherers was generally difficult and short. Richard Borshay Lee's work documents the rapid process by which the !Kung of Botswana, who formerly lived long and leisurely lives as foragers, were pushed into settled communities to eke out a precarious living by herding, farming, and craft production. Their shift away from foraging is a story of loss: loss of sovereignty, dignity, and quality of life (Lee 2012). Yes, in anthropology, hunting for food is associated with small-scale societies who, in part because of their small population size, have generally survived without depleting resources until incorporated into larger markets and states.

Of course, if we imagine ourselves in solidarity with some of the most marginalized communities in the world, this begs the question of: "what should we do in response to rapid environmental change?" Hunting and animal husbandry are at the very center of the anthropological canon, but feminists have an entirely different relationship to meat, as I discuss later. If gender studies department events tend to offer vegetarian fare, my experience tells me that anthropologists prefer a pig roast. Does the departmental pig roast evoke a romance with the distribution of meat described in so many classic ethnographies, an acknowledgment of a precolonial era in which hunter-gatherers lived in dignity throughout the world? My most recent invitation to an anthropology department pig roast was accompanied by the following assurance: "no worries, veggie burgers will also be provided." Anthropology's food multiculturalism celebrates diversity in food customs as the appropriate cosmopolitan stance. However, anthropological work on food commodities shows that food is not simply a matter of taste, identity, and symbolic meaning, but is simultaneously also a matter of who produces what for whom and at what environmental cost. Food multiculturalism, like other forms of multiculturalism, is the anti-politics of our time, one that celebrates diversity while erasing material and structural inequalities.

ANIMAL PRODUCTS IN FEMINIST ENVIRONMENTALISM

On the frontier of the Aravalli hills it is women who trek ever longer distances to find increasingly scarce wood so that their families can enjoy food cooked according to their preferences. Feminist scholars and activists have outlined the ways women are the "social shock absorbers" (Harrison 1997, 452, citing Sparr) of deteriorating economic conditions under structural adjustment programs, since it is they who mediate the crises of declining public health, education, and wages. Their unpaid domestic labor and concentration in the growing informal sector mean that women carry the burden of making ends meet at the household level (Deere 1990; Harrison 1997).

The production of dairy and meat appears to be one major cause of deforestation in Rajasthan; rural people produce this food for external markets. As if concerns about cattle eating up plants and releasing methane were not enough, Uday and Sailesh began to send me links to feminist blogs. In one of these, animal rights activist Patricia Tallman writes about industrial dairy being a patriarchal system of subjugating females: "Their exploitation begins with forced impregnation in a device termed the 'rape-rack.' Calves are viewed only as instruments for lactation." I was only peripherally aware of eco-feminist research and activism on the treatment of animals. In a surprise turn of my collaboration, applied scientists sparked me to explore existing feminist research on animal-based food.

If training in both South Asian studies and anthropology primed me to resist vegan advocacy, feminist frameworks are far more amenable to such positions since feminist scholarship explicitly demands radical shifts in culture. In US public culture, we often see a dismissal of both vegans and feminists as zealots for their commitment to a vision and to social transformation. Feminist scholars have incorporated non-human animals into analyses of gender, social justice, and rights. (See Weiss, this volume.) Indeed, early feminist calls for vegetarianism by such thinkers as Carol Adams (1990) and Josephine Donovan (1990) provoked critiques by other feminist scholars who consider this stance ethnocentric and a prerogative of elites (George 1994, 2000). These continuing debates in feminist scholarship on both environment and animals, and the links between them, are some of the most provocative and intellectually challenging areas of research and activism (see Bailey 2007; Lucas 2005; Seager 2003).

Ecofeminists have been particularly vocal in promoting the feminist–vegetarian connection; they generally share two beliefs: one is that men and women act in fundamentally different ways; women are more compassionate, egalitarian, and community-minded, while men are more competitive and individualistic. Another is that male exploitation of women is comparable to human exploitation of animals, and it is for this reason that feminists should renounce meat. Ecofeminists draw an analogy between social reproduction ("women's work") and the exploitation of animal reproductive capacities to produce dairy and eggs with increasing efficiency. These insights also produce the moral logic of ethical veganism. Similarly, feminist animal rights activists have exposed the similarities in structures of oppression across gender, race, class, and species, and the gendered assumptions that underlie human relationships to non-animals (Seager 2003). Do animals have consciousness or social awareness? To what extent do they show cognitive skills, curiosity, and problem-solving capacity? Feminists have pointed out that these debates are reminiscent of colonial and racist discourses (Seager 2003).

Feminist environmentalism dismisses the essentialist aspects of ecofeminism in favor of solutions and ideas grounded in the political economy. This approach focuses less on promoting a particular kind of diet, or on the ethical treatment of animals, and more on the political economies of food access, security, and production. In the Indian context, this debate is exemplified in the different approaches of Vandana Shiva and Bina Agarwal (Gaard 2011). As Shubhra Gururani observes, in the 1980s ecofeminist Shiva popularized the view that women are closer to nature and more willing to conserve it, thus reproducing romanticized views of women, and Asian women in particular. Agarwal offered an alternative perspective grounded in ethnographic research that focuses on women's marginalization inside and outside the household, and that attends to the class, caste, and gender impacts of environmental degradation (Gururani 2002, 231–232). Cathryn Bailey (2007) notes that women are almost universally the worst fed, with animal protein often reserved for men. This is widely documented in India. Other critics of ecofeminism's stance that all feminists must eschew meat have pointed out, first, that it is a privilege to be able to turn away food and, second, that killing animals for food does not have the same meaning everywhere and in all contexts (Bailey 2007). Thus, beef might be a delicacy for elites in one context and a cheap, accessible source of protein for poor communities in another. In their critique of resource commodification, feminist political ecologists would want to know who produced a particular food, under what conditions, for whose consumption, and whose profit (Seager 2003, 172)? From this perspective, it does not much matter whether the food is beans or a burger.

If animal rights activists protest cruel treatment of animals, Uday frames the issue of meat first and foremost in terms of energy systems, and so does not accept organic, free-range livestock happily roaming bucolic farms as a solution, for it requires even more intensive use of resources to produce "humane" meat as compared to animal confinements. Animal rights activists, radical veganism, and feminist environmentalism do not always focus on the material, physical environment and its limits. Despite the challenges of collaboration across such gaping divides, entering into these awkward, "undisciplined" conversations has led to new, pressing questions and unforeseen solutions.

AN ARGUMENT FOR AWKWARD INTERDISCIPLINARITY

The politics of food is simultaneously local, national, and transnational. A campus beef festival in Hyderabad is a Dalit student protest against local and national Hindu values that stigmatize beef and its consumers. Yet, in another part of India, Lucia Michelutti (2008) describes a different politics of meat. A Yadav community in Mathura adopted the pure lacto-vegetarian diet (dairy but no meat) of trader castes in the early twentieth century but also claimed Rajput origins (castes of warriors and rulers). For Rajput men, consumption of meat and alcohol cultivates the aggressive masculinity required of rulers. Today, these Yadav men identify themselves as politicians from strict vegetarian homes and yet they consume chicken, goat, and whiskey at riverside picnics, away from wives and domestic space, to both enhance their masculinity and to create a sense of secular democratic unity with their Muslim allies. As situational meat-eaters from a vegetarian community, they legitimize their behavior as necessary for politicians (Michelutti 2008).

It is hard to imagine how veganism might enter these debates, the terms of which are defined by interlinked domains of meaning that have a deep history in India. One set of meanings is that meat, though impure according to Brahmanical values, gives physical strength but also heats the body and incites sexual desire and anger. Thus, it is considered appropriate both for those lacking in self-control and for the strong and powerful leaders who must fight military and political battles. Another set of meanings is that milk is a pure, wholesome, and nutritious food that strengthens the body, sharpens the intellect, and cools the emotions to enable self-control. Chicken is heating and milk is cooling. An argument for veganism that reshuffles viscerally felt categories of meaning by use of such universal measurements of energy and environmental cost is an awkward intervention into mainstream Indian discourses of food.

As with food politics, the materiality of food production and consumption is simultaneously local, national, and transnational. We all live, however differently positioned, in a globalized economy in which the poor are not only barred access to what the rich consume but also face the most direct environmental impact of others' consumption. Economic liberalization and export processing zones have intensified the extraction of resources. Cultural anthropology and postcolonial studies have tended in recent decades to focus on meaning and the discursive production of people, objects, and forests, in part as a rejection of reductive materialism. We produce knowledge as if physical ecological constraints are irrelevant. We only get away with this if we avoid awkward conversations with others who do not share our assumptions. However, it is then difficult to ask the question: what should we do about it? "This is the question," says Baviskar, "that recent studies have shied away from, preferring a more hands-off delineation of power as diffuse and immanent, a characterization that lends itself to political quietism" (2010, 217–218). She contrasts this tendency with the work of historian Ramachandra Guha, who treats the environment as a material and symbolic entity that sustains both livelihoods and a life of the imagination. The tendency Baviskar identifies blinded me to seeing what should have been self-evident: India's increasing beef exports are targeted for political attack by Hindu nationalist politicians as immoral and shameful, but the growing meat industry is a byproduct of increasing milk production that is a result of the state-led "white revolution" (the result of the world's largest dairy development program launched by India in 1970) and a source of national pride. Moreover, the latter contributes to a bovine density rate that spells trouble for the environment.

Engineers' training blinds them to many things, as well, but this is not my focus here. To consider food preferences only in terms of caste politics or religious beliefs is also, ironically, to depoliticize them, to ignore the material economy of production, consumption, and waste. Politics is not only about representation but is also about the materiality of its production, consumption, and waste. Feminist political ecology focuses on unequal access to and control over resources, economies of unequal development, and the environmental impacts of the forced integration of local environments and communities into global capital, military, and trade regimes (Seager 2003, 171–172). It is feminists' willingness to address the questions "What should we do?" and "How can we make a better world?" that enables us to enter awkward conversations about the urgent problems of our time.

As Strathern argued, anthropology and feminism are in a relationship of mutual mockery. I argue that this awkwardness persists today and is precisely what makes feminist anthropology such a vibrant area of new research. I do not share engineering's faith in silver bullets, whether First World veganism or Third World solar cookers. Anthropology has taught me that culture and social organization are complex and imbued with power, but it also tends to leave me feeling that our most urgent problems are too complex to solve. Anthropologists set out to observe humanity in all its diversity. While some of us become advocates along the way, this work is often separate from our academic work. Thinking through the politics of meat suggests that anthropology continues to be in an uncomfortable relationship with feminism's unapologetic goal to change the world. Perhaps there is no resolution to these disciplinary differences, but awkward is good. It keeps us from getting too comfortable in our disciplines. An awkward conversation is different from a debate, where two parties take opposing stances while agreeing on the terms of discourse (see Ginsburg 1989; Mani 1990). If we want to address the problems of our day, such as climate change, we must be willing to enter into awkward conversations with, for example, engineers and applied scientists.

I have shown how anthropological and feminist perspectives make different contributions to our understanding of the fuel crisis, deforestation, and drought in rural Rajasthan where communities are pulled into a globalized economy and environmental crises not of their own making. It is more urgent than ever to bring together analyses of deep meaning, globalization, and new environmental realities, but this necessitates stepping out of our comfort zones. One certainty is that there is no neutral space from which we can escape the messy politics of social change. Nor is there a moral high ground from which progressive academics can conclude that those involved in development, social change work, and activism are naïve (though that may be true) and can never succeed in creating real change, despite their good intentions. The conceit of cultural relativism aside, there is no opting out of this process, for middle-class folk are already involved in transforming other people's lives in distant places through what we consume every day. Our food, coffee, shoes, clothes, and gadgets already link us to the lives of people whose cultures we may not want to disturb. It may be difficult to connect the dots or we may choose not to do so. These commodities are produced elsewhere, or they are labeled "made in America" with raw material extracted from faraway places by people recruited from elsewhere. So the question is not whether to intervene in other people's lives—we are doing so already—but rather how and on what terms.

ACKNOWLEDGMENTS

I am indebted to H. S. Udaykumar and Sailesh Rao for initiating the conversation at the heart of this chapter, for providing feedback and, in general, for their good humor. I am grateful to Matt Hill, Jacki Rand, Rosemarie Scullion, Katina Lillios, and Deborah Whaley for their encouragement and suggestions and to Ellen Lewin and Leni Silverstein for inviting me to participate in a commemorative AFA session at the 2013 meetings of the American Anthropological Association. I presented versions of this chapter at the Annual Conference on South Asia at the University of Wisconsin, Madison (2013), the Department of American Studies at University of Iowa (2014), the Centre for the Study of Law and Governance at Jawaharlal Nehru University (2015), and the Center for South Asia at the University of Wisconsin, Madison (2015)—and benefited tremendously from lively discussions at these venues.

NOTES

1. Our preliminary field observations based on short visits to Karech suggest that women control the use and trade in fuelwood, but extended ethnographic research, still in the planning stages, is necessary to confirm this impression. A report produced from an Asian Institute of Technology workshop found that women's involvement in the wood fuel business across Asia tends to be small-scale, scattered, and informal, while men control large commercial enterprises (Babar 2001).
2. Weisgrau reports that the poorest households in this part of Rajasthan are the largest consumers of wood (1997, 138). Bullocks and cows are the most valuable animals, while goats are kept by the poorest people for both milk and meat (120).
3. We have brought several other colleagues into this project, including Matt Hill, Paul Greenough, Marc Linderman, Jerry Anthony, and Misha Quill. We are currently preparing co-authored manuscripts to share our findings on the diffusion (or lack thereof) of improved cook stoves in India.
4. As a child of an intercaste marriage (Punjabi Brahmin and Uttar Pradesh-Baniya), I grew up in assimilation era-US eating beef and other meat. In young adulthood, I became lacto-vegetarian. Later, I spent two years doing doctoral research on Hindu renunciation in Haridwar, where meat and eggs are prohibited. Despite twenty-five years of being a vegetarian, I never maintained a strict vegetarian household.
5. A 2006 survey conducted by Yogendra Yadav and Sanjay Kumar of the Centre for the Study of Developing Societies (CSDS) showed that the popular image of a vegetarian India is not accurate. The Hindu-CNN-IBN poll found that only 31 percent of Indians (but 55 percent of Brahmins) claim to be (lacto)-vegetarians ("The Food Habits of a Nation," *The Hindu*, August 14, 2006).
6. By the 1980s, the meat industry had become one of the most dangerous, difficult, and low-paid occupations in the United States (Fink 1998; Striffler 2005). Moreover, industrial meat and feed production has contaminated our waterways in the Midwest. In protest, animal rights activists have sought jobs on farms with the intent of exposing abuses using video, and, in response, Iowa became the first state in the US to adopt a law prohibiting people from using false pretenses to gain entry or employment in an agricultural production facility (Colb 2012).
7. The debate generated by the work of Marvin Harris (1966) explaining India's sacred cows is too lengthy and complex to address here, but Henderson (1998) provides a useful summary of cultural ecology and symbolic approaches to the sacred cow complex in India.

REFERENCES

Adams, Carol. 1990. *The Sexual Politics of Meat: A Feminist-Vegetarian Critical Theory*. New York: Continuum.

Adcock, Cassie. S. 2010. "Sacred Cows and Secular History: Cow Protection Debates in Colonial North India." *Comparative Studies of South Asia, Africa, and the Middle East* 30 (2): 297–311.

Agarwal, Bina. 1983. "Diffusion of Rural Innovations: Some Analytical Issues and the Case of Wood-Burning Stoves." *World Development* 11 (4): 359–376.

Alexander, M. Jacqui, and Chandra Talpade Mohanty. 1997. "Introduction: Genealogies, Legacies, Movements." In *Feminist Genealogies, Colonial Legacies, Democratic Futures*, ed. M. Jacqui Alexander and Chandra Talpade Mohanty, 13–42. New York: Routledge.

Alvarez, Sonia. 2009. "Beyond NGOization? Reflections from Latin America." *Development* 52 (2): 175–184.

Arora-Jonsson, Seema. 2009. "Discordant Connections: Discourses on Gender and Grassroots Activism in Two Forest Communities in India and Sweden." *Signs* 35 (1): 213–240.

Babar, Aneela Zeb. 2001. "Gender Issues in Wood Energy: Gender, Technology, and Development." 5 (2): 331–334.

Bailey, Cathryn. 2007. "We Are What We Eat: Feminist Vegetarianism and the Reproduction of Racial Identity." *Hypatia* 22 (2): 39–59.

Baviskar, Amita. 2010. "*The Unquiet Woods* and Indian Environmental History." In *The Unquiet Woods: Ecological Change and Peasant Resistance in the Himalaya*, 20th anniversary ed., ed. Ramachandra Guha, 213–232. Ranikhet: Permanent Black.

Bernal, Victoria. 1994. "Gender, Culture, and Capitalism." *Comparative Studies in Society and History*. 36 (1): 36–67.

Chigateri, Shraddha. 2010. "'Glory to the Cow': Cultural Difference and Social Justice in the Food Hierarchy in India." *Journal of South Asian Studies* 31 (1): 10–35.

Colb, Sherry F. 2012. "Iowa Passes an 'Ag-Gag' Law: The Power and Limits of Free Speech." *Verdict*, May 16. https://verdict.justia.com/2012/05/16/iowa-passes-an-ag-gag-law, accessed October 29, 2015.

D'Andrade, Roy. 1995. "Moral Models in Anthropology." *Current Anthropology* 36 (3): 399–408.

Das, Pallavi. 2011. "Colonialism and the Environment in India: Railways and Deforestation in 19th Century Punjab." *Journal of Asian and African Studies* 46 (1): 38–53.

Deere, Carmen Diana. 1990. *Household and Class Relations: Peasants and Landlords in Northern Peru*. Berkeley and Los Angeles: University of California Press.

Donovan, Josephine. 1990. "Animal Rights and Feminist Theory." *Signs* 15 (2): 350–375.

Doron, Assa. 2012. "Mobile Persons: Cell Phones, Gender, and the Self in North India." *Asia Pacific Journal of Anthropology* 13 (5): 414–433.

Fink, Deborah. 1998. *Cutting into the Meatpacking Line*. Chapel Hill: University of North Carolina Press.

Food and Agriculture Organization of the United Nations. 2005. Livestock Sector Brief: India. July.

Ford-Smith, Honor. 1997. "Ring Ding in a Tight Corner: Sistren, Collective Democracy, and the Organization of Cultural Production." In *Feminist Genealogies, Colonial Legacies, Democratic Futures*, ed. M. Jaqui Alexander and Chandra Talpade Mohanty, 213–258. New York: Routledge.

Gaard, Greta. 2011. "Ecofeminism Revisited: Rejecting Essentialism and Re-placing Species in the Material Feminist Environmentalism." *Feminist Formations* 23 (2): 26–53.

Gadgil, Madhav, and Ramachandra Guha. 1995. *Ecology and Equity: The Use and Abuse of Nature in Contemporary India*. New Delhi: Penguin Books.

George, Kathryn Paxton. 1994. "Should Feminists Be Vegetarians?" *Signs* 19 (2): 405–434.

———. 2000. *Animal, Vegetable, or Woman? A Feminist Critique of Ethical Vegetarianism*. Albany: State University of New York Press.

Ghassem-Fachandi, Parvis. 2010. "On the Political Use of Disgust in Gujarat." *South Asian History and Culture* 1 (4): 557–576.

Ghertner, D. Asher. 2006. "Technology and Tricks: Intra-Household Technology Implementation and Gender Struggles." *Gender, Technology, and Development* 10 (3): 281–311.

Ginsburg, Faye. 1989. *Contested Lives: The Abortion Debate in An American Community*. Berkeley and Los Angeles: University of California Press.

Gold, Ann Grodzins. 2014. "Food Values Beyond Nutrition." In *The Oxford Handbook of Food, Politics, and Society* (Oxford Handbooks Online), 1–14. Oxford: Oxford University Press.

Government of India. Annual Report 2012–2013. Department of Animal Husbandry, Dairying and Fisheries, Ministry of Agriculture. New Delhi: GOI.

Guha, Ramachandra. 2006. *How Much Should a Person Consume? Environmentalism in India and the United States*. Berkeley: University of California Press.

Gururani, Shubhra. 2002. "Forests of Pleasure and Pain: Gendered Practices of Labor and Livelihood in the Forests of the Kumaon Himalayas, India." *Gender, Place, and Culture* 9 (3): 229–243.

Hardiman, David. 1994. "Power in the Forest: The Dangs, 1820–1940." In *Subaltern Studies VIII: Essays in Honour of Ranajit Guha*, ed. David Arnold and David Hardiman, 89–147. New Delhi: Oxford University Press.

Harris, Marvin. 1966. "The Cultural Ecology of India's Sacred Cattle." *Current Anthropology* 7: 51–66.

Harrison, Faye V. 1997. "The Gendered Politics and Violence of Structural Adjustment: A View from Jamaica." In *Situated Lives*, ed. Louise Lamphere, Helena Ragone, and Patricia Cavella, 451–455. New York: Routledge.

Henderson, Carol. 1998. "The Great Cow Explosion in Rajasthan." In *Advances in Historical Ecology*, ed. William Balée, 349–375. New York: Columbia University Press.

Henning, Brian G. 2011. "Standing in Livestock's 'Long Shadow': The Ethics of Eating Meat on a Small Planet." *Ethics & the Environment* 16 (2): 63–93.

Hynes, H. Patricia. 1999. "Consumption: North American Perspectives." In *Dangerous Intersections: Feminist Perspectives on Population, Environment, and Development*, ed. Jael Silliman and Ynestra King, 189–201. Cambridge, MA: South End Press.

Janzen, H. H. 2011. "What Place for Livestock on a Re-Greening Earth." *Animal Feed Science and Technology* 166–167: 783–796.

Jassal, Smita Tewari. 2012. *Unearthing Gender: Folksongs in North India*. Durham, NC: Duke University Press.

Jodhka, Surinder S., and Murli Dhar. 2003. "Cow, Caste, and Communal Politics: Dalit Killings in Jhajjar." *Economic and Political Weekly*, January 18, 174–176.

Kaplan, Caren. 1995. "The Body Shop." *Social Text* 3: 45–66.

Khare, Ravindra S. 1976. *Culture and Reality: Essays on the Hindu System of Managing Foods*. Simla: Indian Institute of Advanced Study.

Khare, Ravindra S., and Madhugiri S. Rao, eds. 1986. *Food, Society, and Culture: Aspects of South Asian Food Systems*. Durham, NC: Carolina Academic Press.

Kumar, Radha. 1993. *The History of Doing*. London and New York: Verso Press.

Lee, Richard Borshay. 2012. "The Hunters: Scarce Resources in the Kalahari." In *Conformity and Conflict*, 14th ed., ed. James W. Spradley and David W. McCurdy, 73–86. New York: Pearson.

Lodrick, Deryck O. 2005. "Symbol and Sustenance: Cattle in South Asian Culture." *Dialectical Anthropology* 29: 61–84.

Lucas, Sheri. 2005. "A Defense of the Feminist–Vegetarian Connection." *Hypatia* 20 (1): 150–177.

Lugones, Maria. 2010. "The Coloniality of Gender." In *Globalization and the Decolonial Option*, ed. Walter D. Mignolo and Arturo Escobar, 369–390. London and New York: Routledge.

Maggi, Wynne. 2001. *Our Women Are Free*. Ann Arbor: University of Michigan Press.

Mahmood, Saba. 2005. *Politics of Piety*. Princeton, NJ: Princeton University Press.

Mani, Lata. 1990. "Contentious Traditions: The Debate on Sati in Colonial India." In *Recasting Women: Essays in Indian Colonial History*, ed. Kumkum Sangari and Urvashi Vaid, 88–126. New Brunswick, NJ: Rutgers University Press.

McEwan, Cheryl. 2001. "Postcolonialism, Feminism, and Development: Intersections and Dilemmas." *Progress in Development Studies* 1 (2): 93–111.

Michelutti, Lucia. 2008. "'We Are Kshatriyas but We Behave Like Vaishyas': Diet and Muscular Politics among a Community of Yadavs in North India." *South Asia: Journal of South Asian Studies*, n.s. 31 (1): 76–95.

Mohanty, Chandra Talpade. 2003. *Feminism without Borders*. New Delhi: Zubaan.

Nader, Laura. 1995. "Comments." *Current Anthropology* 36 (3): 426–427.

Narayan, Uma. 1997. *Dislocating Cultures*. New York and London: Routledge.

Natarajan, Kanchana. 2000. "Interfeminine Bonding." *Journal of Women's History* 12 (3): 13–22.

Nnaemeka, Obioma. 2005. "African Women, Colonial Discourses, and Imperialist Interventions." In *Female Circumcision and the Politics of Knowledge*, ed. Obioma Nnaemeka, 27–45. Westport, CT: Praeger.

Rao, Sailesh. 2011. *Carbon Dharma: The Occupation of Butterflies*. Udaipur District, India: Climate Healers Publishers.

Report of the National Commission on Cattle. 2002. Department of Animal Husbandry & Dairying, Ministry of Agriculture. Government of India.

Rittel, Horst W. J., and Melvin M. Webber. 1973. "Dilemmas in a General Theory of Planning." *Policy Sciences* 4: 155–169.

Scheper-Hughes, Nancy. 1995. "The Primacy of the Ethical: Propositions for a Militant Anthropology." *Current Anthropology* 36 (3): 409–420.

Seager, Joni. 2003. "Pepperoni or Broccoli? On the Cutting Wedge of Feminist Environmentalism." *Gender, Place, and Culture* 10 (2): 167–174.

Shanmugavelan, Murali. 2012. "Food Fascism: The Vegetarian Hypocrisy in India." *The Independent*, April 30. http://blogs.independent.co.uk/2012/04/30/food-fascism-the-vegetarian-hypocrisy-in-india/, accessed June 14, 2014.

Shiva, Vandana. 2008. *Soil Not Oil*. Boston: South End Press.

Steinfeld, Henning, and Pierre Gerber. 2010. "Livestock Production and the Global Environment: Consume Less or Produce Better?" *Proceedings of the National Academy of Sciences of America* 107 (43): 18237–18238.

Striffler, Steve. 2005. *Chicken: The Dangerous Transformation of America's Favorite Food*. New Haven, CT: Yale University Press.

Subramanian, Meera. 2014. "Deadly Dinners." *Nature* 509 (7502): 548–551.

Swaminathan, Padmini. 1999. "The Gendered Politics of Fuel in India." *Gender, Technology, and Development* 3 (2): 165–187.

Thomas, Shibu. 2015. "HC Declines Stay on Beef Ban Law, But Directs State Not to Take Coercive Steps for Possession." Times of India, April 29. http://timesofindia.indiatimes.com/india/HC-declines-stay-on-beef-ban-law-but-directs-state-not-to-take-coercive-steps-for-possession/articleshow/47093193.cms, accessed October 29, 2015.

Walker, Nathalie F., Sabina A. Patel, and Kemel A. B. Kalif. 2013. "From Amazon Pasture to the High Street: Deforestation and the Brazilian Cattle Product Supply Chain." *Tropical Conservation Science* 6 (3): 446–467.

Weisgrau, Maxine K. 1997. *Interpreting Development: Local Histories, Local Strategies*. Lanham, MD: University Press of America.

Wiley, Andrea S. 2011. "Milk for 'Growth': Global and Local Meanings of Milk Consumption in China, India, and the United States." *Food and Foodways* 19: 11–33.

———. 2014. *Cultures of Milk*. Cambridge: Harvard University Press.

Yadama, Gautam N. 2013. *Fires, Fuel, and the Fate of 3 Billion: The State of the Energy Impoverished*. New York: Oxford University Press.

FEMINIST ANTHROPOLOGY

Approaching Domestic Violence in Northern Việt Nam

LYNN KWIATKOWSKI

Throughout the twenty-six years of their marriage, her husband had beaten Xuân,[1] a fifty-three-year-old Vietnamese woman living in Hà Nội when I spoke with her in 2013.[2] Xuân said, "He beats me, and I go out to the road. When I return [to our house], he hits me and throws things at me." Xuân's experience of domestic violence is somewhat unusual in that, in addition to her husband's beatings, her daughters, who were then in their mid-twenties, had encouraged their father to hit their mother. The daughters would become upset with Xuân when she sold food in front of their house, interfering with Xuân's youngest daughter's hair-styling business that was located inside the house. Xuân continued, "I've been beaten on my arms and legs, and my face often has been swollen. I have gone to the police station many times. They called my husband and me to go to the police station. They called me to go first and then called him and interviewed him alone." She said she does not know if the police had punished her husband. For example, in addition to, or instead of, arresting men accused of domestic violence and charging them with a criminal violation, a police officer told me that the police have: warned or reprimanded the men; compelled them to make a commitment to ending their violence against their wives; fined them for a civil violation; or required the men to participate in a reconciliation process with their wives. Each of these penalties is identified in Việt Nam's domestic violence law (National Assembly, Socialist Republic of Viet Nam 2007, 15). Xuân guessed they may have punished her husband, but she said the police never arrested him. She asked for and received help from the Việt Nam Women's Union, a local shelter in her community, the leader of her neighborhood, and members of her community's reconciliation committee.[3] They all gave the same advice to Xuân, her husband, and children: make peace in the family. The Women's Union and the reconciliation committee also told Xuân to be less angry because she and her husband are older now. Her husband and older daughter initially treated her more kindly following these visits, but soon her husband hit her again. Xuân said his abuse toward her had lessened, though. Although a new domestic violence law had been approved in Việt Nam in 2007, Xuân's husband continued to beat her six years later, despite the many forms of assistance she had obtained from community officials and leaders in her attempt to end her husband's violence against her.

In recent years in Việt Nam, domestic violence has become a significant subject of discussion in the media and among Vietnamese government policymakers and officials, international development and donor organization personnel, local non-governmental organization (NGO) professionals, and members of the general population. By 2013, government officials felt a pressing need to address "some of the major issues behind rising domestic violence" (*ThanhNienNews .com* 2013).[4] The media and scholars have asserted that domestic violence has recently been increasing due to difficulties in meeting the demands of the market economy since the mid-1980s, and changes occurring with the "modernization and industrialization" of Việt Nam (*Thanh Nien News* 2013). Based on my discussions with people in Hà Nội, the perceived increase in domestic violence is likely due to the public's greater awareness of the problem.

These developments occurred six years after the approval of Việt Nam's first domestic violence law which "regulates the prevention and control of domestic violence, protecting and assisting the victims of domestic violence; [and] the responsibilities of individuals, families, organizations, institutions in domestic violence prevention and control" (National Assembly, Socialist Republic of Viet Nam 2007, 1). Also, for nearly two decades international organizations, local NGOs, and scholars have introduced new discourses about gender violence and women's rights, including women's right to freedom from violence and to freely choose among existing and new options on how to address domestic violence. These organizations have introduced fresh approaches to assisting abused women and preventing domestic violence through internationally funded programs, such as support clubs for abused women, counseling centers staffed by trained counselors for women facing gender violence and other problems, and a Western-style shelter. Some but not all of these approaches have been adopted by the Vietnamese government.

My study of domestic violence in northern Việt Nam highlights the ways that intersecting and sometimes contradictory local and transnational sociocultural forces have influenced the experiences of abused Vietnamese women. In this chapter, I show how individuals and communities can sometimes internalize, while they also simultaneously resist, gendered and other cultural discourses that allow for the persistence of gender violence within the current historical context. More specifically, many Vietnamese people, including some women abused by their husbands, regard women's positions as wives and mothers in their families as taking priority over their own needs, while they also support women's right to be free from violence. The contemporary Vietnamese state promotes both of these discourses. The tensions between Confucian ideologies of femininity and familial duty and present-day global discourses of women's rights have even made their way into the recently approved Vietnamese domestic violence law. I argue that even when legal redress is available and when women are able to undertake action on their own behalf, many abused women are still caught up in a Confucian-influenced understanding of women's subordination to men in marriage, and their obligation to sacrifice their own happiness, and even safety, to keep their families together. While no monolithic conception of a Confucian tradition exists in Việt Nam, maintaining family harmony is a paramount value, although, in reality, this understanding sustains marital conflict, unhappiness, and wife abuse. Thus, I highlight how multiple identities and beliefs shape the ability of legal measures against domestic violence to be effective.

FEMINIST ANTHROPOLOGICAL THEORY AND DOMESTIC VIOLENCE RESEARCH

Since the 1970s, feminist anthropologists have brought to the forefront the importance of analyzing gender violence cross-culturally. My research in Việt Nam has taken the approach, shared by other feminist anthropologists, of examining domestic violence as it transpires at intersecting interpersonal, community, state, and global levels (Adelman 2004; Hautzinger 2007; Merry 2006). In doing so, I move beyond the personal relationships of spouses, gender, and family power relations in play at the community level, by adding a cultural and political economic context present at the state and global levels. Madelaine Adelman (2004) proposes an anthropological political economy of domestic violence to analyze women's experiences of domestic violence. She shows how the interrelated domains of political organizations and economic structures at national and global levels influence them, as well as dominant family ideologies expressed through state policies. In a similar vein, Dana-Ain Davis analyzes domestic violence experienced by black women in the United States, in the context of welfare reform, race, and local economics. Davis also draws on black feminist theory to understand the effects of welfare reform in the United States on black women escaping domestic violence, as well as the resistances and resilience of the women with whom she conducted research (Davis 2006). Likewise, through ethnographic research, M. Cristina Alcalde (2010) closely examines the ways that structures of racism, sexism, and poverty intersect with other forms of violence that occur on the institutional and political levels. She shows how these factors contribute to the domestic violence experienced by mostly non-white, poor, rural-to-urban migrant women in Lima, Peru, as well as their resistance to oppression. Drawing on these approaches, I analyze domestic violence in Việt Nam as it transpires at intersecting interpersonal, community, state, and global levels.

In recent years, feminist anthropologists and other social scientists have emphasized the importance of understanding the complicated ways in which global forces such as the international human rights movement against violence to women, women's rights organizations, global feminism, international development processes, and global health practices all influence both our understanding of gender violence and our approaches to alleviating such violence in local communities cross-culturally (Johnson 2009; Merry 2006). For example, political scientist Janet Elise Johnson's (2009) informative study of gender violence in post-Soviet Russia focuses on whether or not different types of foreign interventions addressing gender violence are achieving objectives upon which global feminists have agreed, including fostering women's mobilization and activism, cultivating a new public awareness of violence against women, shifting policy and practice toward recognizing gender violence as a human rights violation, and undermining the sex/gender hierarchy. Johnson argues that in Russia the most beneficial foreign intervention that resulted in at least the partial achievement of these global feminist objectives involved alliances of global feminists and large international donors to support local activism in the country. Drawing on the ethnographic methods of participant observation and interviews among other research methods, Johnson assesses different forms of those foreign interventions and local activism that addressed gender violence, relying "on assessing responsiveness of the state and society rather than effectiveness" (Johnson 2009, 10).

Anthropologists have been contributing to studies such as Johnson's in Russia by ethnographically researching how abused women, men and women, and others working on domestic violence at the local level have been receiving, experiencing, interpreting, and integrating feminist and non-feminist foreign and local interventions that attempt to address domestic violence in their communities. Here, I also investigate the changing, multiple ideologies of gender and violence that shape women's subject positions and their subjectivities in Việt Nam. My approach views women's agency as dynamic but constrained by a broader set of cultural meanings and social structures. From this perspective, I can better understand: (1) the options women can access in the face of violence; and (2) the conflicting culturally informed goals to which they aspire. In this respect, my work has also been influenced by Henrietta Moore (see also Merry 2006;

Rydstrøm 2003). Moore's approach to the study of gender violence incorporates the multiple and contradictory discourses on gender in societies including the dominant discourses that construct categories of men and women as "mutually exclusive and hierarchically related" (Moore 1994, 154).

Therefore, while it is important to know if increased state and societal mobilization, awareness, and responsiveness have resulted from global and local feminist interventions and activism focusing on domestic violence (Johnson 2009), how these play out and are experienced and interpreted by people living in local communities must be understood. We need to evaluate their impacts on domestic violence and people's everyday experience of the problem. My research adopts this feminist anthropological approach to studying domestic violence, and depicts the contribution that feminist anthropological perspectives have made to undermining gender inequality in Việt Nam. In addition, by adopting this feminist anthropological approach, my work enhances our understanding of intersecting global and local approaches to preventing gender violence, as well as our understanding of domestic violence cross-culturally. For example, in their edited volume, Jennifer Wies and Hillary Haldane present anthropologically informed ethnographies of frontline workers addressing gender violence in a variety of countries. By investigating the intimate and professional lives of frontline workers, they demonstrate "the ways that workers create meaning, frameworks, and identities in a local context," while simultaneously illustrating ways that global feminism and institutions influence these frontline workers addressing gender violence (Wies and Haldane 2011, 2). Feminist anthropological ethnography of everyday experiences and struggles of frontline workers shows us the intricacies of putting policy and legal reforms influenced by global feminist objectives into practice, the complexities of the lives of these workers, and the plight of women who have experienced gender violence from a different, rather intimate, perspective. In this chapter, in addition to exploring the experiences of abused Vietnamese women, I elucidate encounters between frontline workers and abused women both inside and outside of the workers' institutions in Việt Nam. I also examine the anxiety and strain experienced by women who identify with the subject positions of both women abused by their husbands and frontline workers aiding other abused women, in the context of a society undergoing significant sociocultural change.

In addition, like many feminist scholars, I examine the internationally influenced state social and legal resources battered women may draw upon to escape domestic violence (Hautzinger 2007; Johnson 2009; Lazarus-Black 2007; Merry 2006). Feminist anthropologists' work provides us with significant findings about the domains of the courts, police stations, and other venues associated with the legal system that abused women interact with, in addition to their local communities. For example, Sarah Hautzinger (2007) analyzes domestic violence in Brazil by investigating women's police stations that handle cases of different forms of male violence against women. She shows how the policewomen who are increasingly committed to this gendered social project are contributing to major social transformation toward gender equality in Brazil. In another study, Nia Parson (2013) discusses the changing legal and social system responding to domestic violence in Chile. She argues that social inequalities make recovery from trauma due to domestic violence for abused women more difficult, and stresses the need for addressing both simultaneously. Sally Engle Merry (2006) analyzes the process of "translating international law into local justice." Using a cross-cultural approach, Merry focuses on understanding how legal approaches and principles around women's rights and gender violence operating on a global scale (such as UN cultural practice and law) are translated by local populations and also drawn upon by states to expand state power as they intersect with local cultures and forms of justice. Merry investigates legal processes at the global, national, and local levels, and also explicates the impacts of changing domestic laws and policies on battered women, their families, and social relationships. My analysis draws upon, but also differs from, these important works since I focus particularly on the cultural contradictions and unequal power relations impeding the potentially positive impact of providing accessible legal resources at the community and interpersonal levels, as they intersect with state and global ideologies. These cultural contradictions are visible, even within Vietnamese legal documents, without being recognized as such by many in either leadership positions or the population.

CONDUCTING RESEARCH IN NORTHERN VIỆT NAM

I conducted ethnographic fieldwork during six research periods between 1997 and 2013 in the city of Hà Nội, the former Hà Tây province (now integrated into Hà Nội), and Hòa Bình province, focusing on domestic violence. While engaging in participant observation, I also conducted in-depth interviews with sixty-one women who had been battered by their husbands, and with numerous community members, health and social service providers, government officials and leaders, police, NGO professionals, international organizations personnel, religious leaders, scholars, and others. I also collected books, documents, and information from the media relevant to my research.

Conducting research on a sensitive topic such as domestic violence was challenging, since committing violence against a family member was illegal even at the start of my research (see also Skinner, Hester, and Malos 2005). Domestic violence is also an issue that Vietnamese women and men often feel hesitant about discussing, due to feelings of shame about its occurrence or weakness in defending themselves. Many abused women expressed fear of their husbands' next act of violence against them, enhanced if they revealed to others their husbands' abusive behavior. Nevertheless, many of the women I interviewed had sought help from family members, neighbors, community officials and leaders, among others. During the years of my research, a new conceptualization and interest in domestic violence emerged. These changes were influenced directly or indirectly by international organizations and local NGOs operating in Việt Nam since the 1990s, combined with Vietnamese government officials and professionals' participation in global and regional conferences, meetings, workshops, and other forums that addressed violence against women—though gender violence may not have been the main item on the agenda. This shift has made discussion of domestic violence generally more acceptable among community members, government leaders, and abused women.

CHANGING DEFINITIONS OF DOMESTIC VIOLENCE AND PROBLEMS OF SUPPORT

Feminist anthropologists have argued that domestic violence is a concept that is culturally defined and socially delimited (Cameron and Frazer 1994; Harvey and Gow 1994; Merry 2009). According to my informants, prior to the mid-1980s, the Vietnamese defined a husband's violence against his wife as primarily physical abuse. Following the mid-1980s, the country became reinserted into the global economy through economic and political reforms, referred to as *đổi mới* (Kwiatkowski 2011c). Resulting social changes in Vietnamese society included a new emphasis on the family and household economy with integration in the global market, and the intersection of local innovation and international influences. It was in this context that the domestic violence law was approved. Through these changes, and exposure to the global women's rights movements, the definition of a husband's violence against his wife as a form of "domestic violence" was broadened considerably.

For example, in addition to physical abuse, the Vietnamese domestic violence law states that domestic violence involves "purposeful acts of certain family members that cause or may possibly cause physical, mental, or economic injuries to other family members," including "forced sex" (National Assembly, Socialist Republic of Viet Nam 2007, 1). Many women I interviewed also included adultery in the definition of domestic violence because it causes emotional distress and/or is interpreted to be a form of marital sexual abuse. Adultery has become more common among men as social, political, and economic changes associated with *đổi mới* have occurred (Phinney 2009). The emergence of this addition to the discourse on domestic violence in Vietnamese society was influenced by international agreements, such as the 1993 United Nations Declaration on the Elimination of Violence against Women.

Still, most people continue to consider domestic violence to be a private family issue. The imposition of patriarchal Confucian ideologies of marriage, family, femininity, and masculinity in Việt Nam, particularly during the approximately 1,000 years of Chinese colonialism beginning in the second century B.C.E., interpreted a husband beating his wife as a form of education. Confucian gender ideologies defined women as subordinate to men throughout their lives. Ideologically, if not always in practice, ideal women were to be "submissive, supportive, [and] compliant toward their husbands" (Jamieson 1993, 18). Through the Confucian "four virtues" (*tứ đức*) prescribed for women, they were taught to be hardworking, neat and humble in appearance, soft-spoken and self-controlled in their speech, and filial, loyal, kind, and trustworthy in their behavior (Ngo 2004, 47–48, 50–51).

The Vietnamese state has historically deployed discourses influencing gender ideologies aligned with their changing political and economic needs (Drummond 2004; Kwiatkowski 2011b, 2011c; Pettus 2003). While Confucian patriarchal principles influenced Vietnamese gender ideologies, especially among the Vietnamese elite, not all women strictly obeyed these precepts. By the time of the French colonial period (1859–1954), ideas of gender equality and new family forms had been debated, and drawn upon by socialist-led anti-colonial movements (Bélanger and Barbieri 2009; Jamieson 1993; Marr 1981). But while the Vietnamese Communist Party promoted gender equality in the 1946 Constitution of the Democratic Republic of Việt Nam, Confucian gender ideologies still guided women and men's behavior. The state later promoted a "revolutionary femininity" during the Việt Nam war (1959–1975), which involved American military intervention and is commonly referred to in Việt Nam as the American War, since a strict Confucian femininity and family ideology was unattainable during the conflict (Ngo 2004; Steinberg 1987). Women were drawn into the revolutionary movement through state social mobilization campaigns that promoted gender equality and the "new socialist woman." North Vietnamese women provided labor outside of the home during the American War and the postwar period following reunification. The ideal of femininity constructed for the "new socialist woman" during the 1960s and 1970s combined features of traditional femininity and masculinity, as women were encouraged to be assertive, fearless, vocal, and economically productive (Ngo 2004). Men were enjoined by the state to embrace the egalitarian ideals of socialism, including supporting women's greater political and economic participation in Vietnamese society, and moving away from the family unit toward the socialist collective, in support of the political economic needs of the nation during the war. This weakened, but did not eliminate, the male-centered patrilineal family (Luong 2003). The period of collectivization (1950s–1980s) relied on everyone's combined labor for the success of the agricultural collectives under state control, with household production supplementing the collective economy (Kwiatkowski 2011c; Werner 2002). During this period, women abused by their husbands could expect some public support from the leaders of their collectives, communities, and state-supported unions and groups (Kwiatkowski 2011c). While maintaining Confucian female virtues such as chastity, hard work, and proper behavior and speech, socialist virtues also made women responsible for both the nation and the family, rather than responsible solely for the family (Gammeltoft 2001).

With the dismantling of the collectivization system and the institution of a socialist-led market economy by the mid-1980s, the household economy was resurrected by the state. The traditional Vietnamese family and women's position in it were again emphasized, as the state revived Confucian conceptions of femininity, making women responsible for family happiness, harmony, and unity (Bélanger 2004; Drummond 2004; Gammeltoft 1999; Ngo 2004, 53; Pettus 2003; Werner 2002). With these transformations, combined with anxiety over increasing change and globalization, state discourses on traditional Vietnamese culture, family, and Confucian ideals have reemerged (Bélanger 2004).

In recent years, state-promoted cultural conceptions of femininity have included the intersection of revived historical Confucian ideologies of femininity, and contemporary state and global discourses of gender equality and women's rights (Drummond 2004; Kwiatkowski 2011c; Pettus 2003), creating tensions. These distinct and somewhat contradictory conceptions of femininity complement diverse but separate political and economic goals of the Vietnamese state. They include: reinforcing the family and the family economy as important foundations for the national economy, in part through the revival of Confucian ideologies, while also enhancing Việt Nam's integration into the global economy through the promotion of gender equality, rights discourses, and laws that support these concerns (Bélanger and Barbieri 2009; Kwiatkowski 2011c; Merry 2006; Werner 2002).

As noted earlier, some women reported that community groups or leaders of collectives handled domestic violence occurrences during the collectivization period publicly. However, by the time of the emergence of the neoliberal market system, husbands' abuse of their wives came again to be viewed by the Vietnamese predominantly as a private family matter (Vu et al. 1999). In recent years, though, the influence of the international movement against violence toward women and regional women's movements has begun to shape a new view of domestic violence as a social problem. This occurred through a variety of mechanisms. International organizations sponsored new programs with Vietnamese government agencies, research institutes, and NGOs, including: government health care worker trainings on treating and counseling women affected by domestic violence; community clubs for abused women; discussions of domestic violence during government supported mass organization meetings such as those held by the Women's Union, Farmers' Union, and Youth Union; and the establishment of a Western-style shelter. The media also conveyed new ideas about gender violence, including magazines produced by state agencies or mass organizations such as the Women's Union and the Youth Union, and television, which often airs programs that highlight professionals who work with the new programs addressing domestic abuse. Given this publicity, what had previously been a limited discussion of domestic violence in the public realm became a national dialogue about this form of gender aggression. Greater efforts toward generating prevention programs and intervention activities have resulted. Johnson found that Russia, facing similar economic and social shifts following the breakup of the Soviet Union in 1991, also experienced much foreign intervention to address gender violence, from this time to the mid-2000s. As previously noted, the intervention to address domestic violence mainly took the form of funding from large international donors aligned with global feminists. Johnson states that although awareness of domestic violence and reform in policy and practice addressing violence against women are incomplete in Russia, international funding generated a "women's crisis center movement." During the period of international funding, this movement also generated greater awareness of domestic violence nationally, increased media coverage of domestic violence, mobilized more local feminist activism addressing the problem, enacted some reforms in policy and practices, such as the approval of some regional domestic violence laws, and worked toward undermining the sex/gender system in Russia (Johnson 2009, 150).

In Việt Nam, despite these discursive changes and the implementation of prevention programs, the introduction of a new cultural conception of gender for women, one that posits women's right to freedom from abuse, has not yet entirely superseded the persistent Confucian gender prescription for women to sacrifice for their children and families (Pettus 2003). The latter gender dictum supports the persistence of domestic violence, and influences women who have experienced such abuse, even among those who have been abused by their husbands and provide assistance to other battered women (see later discussion). Many abused women and other women assisting them seem to have deeply internalized the Confucian gender ideology that women should sacrifice their well-being for their family, suffer the consequences of continued violence, and remain in their marriage. Through this influence, which reinforces strong cultural notions of the importance of family harmony and stability, abused women regularly receive direct or indirect social pressure from state organizations and institutions, other abused women, their families, and other community members to remain with their abusive husbands (Rydstrøm 2003). For instance, Kim, an abused woman who is a member of the Women's Union, said, "I have only shared my story [of my husband's abuse toward me] with a woman who is a member of the Women's Union. Just when we talk informally." This woman was being ill-treated by her husband at the time. "We say to each other that now we should just try our best to suffer this and to live for our children. Whatever happened, we were afraid that if we talked back or did something bad to our husbands, our family would be broken. We also thought about living far away, leaving our homes together to go far away. But we thought about our children, and didn't do that."

Divorced women still face social stigma in their communities, since divorce has traditionally been discouraged, with poor women anticipating huge economic difficulties as well. In addition, the state has made divorce difficult to obtain, mandating counseling and encouraging reconciliation by government leaders, before granting a divorce (Bélanger and Barbieri 2009).[5] Reconciliation may be carried out by reconciliation committees, which are composed of government and community leaders such as the head of a commune, the president of a commune People's Committee, leaders of government mass organizations (e.g., the Women's Union, Farmers' Union, Association of the Elderly, and Youth Union), and other respected community members. Police officers and court officials also perform reconciliation. Reconciliation is managed by the Vietnamese state, and implemented through different levels of government, such as the Ministry of Justice, provincial and municipal levels of government, and the courts (National Assembly, Socialist Republic of Viet Nam 2000; Standing Committee of National Assembly, Socialist Republic of Viet Nam 1998).

Under this kind of social pressure, in this case informal but coming from abused women influenced by the Women's Union, many Vietnamese battered women choose to remain with their husbands and children. It is important to recognize, though, that abused Vietnamese women's choices are made within and constrained by the context of broad-based gender and economic inequality in Vietnamese society. As feminist anthropologists have argued, we need to analyze the multiple gendered subject positions and contending voices within a society to understand the complex dynamics of gender and, in this case, gender violence (Moore 1994; Ortner 1995). Another strong contributor to the persistence of domestic violence has been the near absence of economic support for those abused women with low incomes and of programs that could provide emotional, legal, health, and social services, and other support, at the community level.

While at the community level the Women's Union is one of the primary organizations that women turn to for assistance with domestic violence, leaders of the Women's Union have promoted multiple and at times contradictory cultural constructions of femininity and womanhood. For example, this organization has fostered the expectation that a proper wife should meet the needs of her husband and reserve her protests against her husband's anger and violence until a time when he is calm (Kwiatkowski 2011c). At the same time, Women's Union leaders have asserted that women are equal with men, and should not be ill-treated by their husbands (Kwiatkowski 2011c). As previously noted, Women's Union leaders are also members of commune-level, government reconciliation committees that, in cases of domestic violence involving spouses, are tasked specifically to reunite husbands and wives experiencing conflict.

As Women's Union leaders have continuously intervened in husbands' violence against their wives, they have often been invited by international organizations to participate in programs that introduce new discourses about and approaches to domestic violence at the local level. This was the case in the Hà Nội communities in which I conducted research, where, in 2002, two international organizations, a local NGO, and the state jointly worked to establish the first hospital-based women's counseling center and numerous domestic violence community clubs to provide support for abused women (Kwiatkowski 2011a). The counseling center in particular espoused internationally influenced ideas about gender violence, such as women's right to be free of aggression, the need to provide temporary shelter for abused women in crisis, and the prioritizing of abused women's decision making about the domestic violence they face, rather than only promoting reconciliation. While not entirely effective in translating and putting into practice Western conceptions of women's rights and the prioritization of abused women's decision-making ability in local communities, the counseling center had particularly helped abused women feel greater emotional and social support from the counselors and some of the health workers at the hospital, and members of the women's community, particularly through domestic violence community clubs (see Kwiatkowski 2011a for an extended discussion of this program). Unfortunately, the funding for this international organization-sponsored program ended in 2009.

Since then, the hospital-based counseling services for women have continued to function with state funding, but the work of the domestic violence community clubs has been reduced. According to local Women's Union leaders, the latter occurred because of the reduction in funding for activities related to domestic violence. Some of the international/state jointly sponsored clubs had provided a forum for abused women to speak out publicly about their experiences of abuse, to garner emotional and social support from other abused women who shared similar experiences, and to learn about legal, health, counseling, and other resources available to address domestic violence. Although a few community leaders' homes were designated as "reliable, or trusted addresses," which served as local, temporary shelters for women in crisis, they did not offer group meetings for abused women. Since the clubs were no longer in existence by 2013, abused women could not avail themselves of this kind of support. For example, during my fieldwork at a women's counseling center, I observed an abused woman, Nguyệt, who, on two occasions expressed a desire to learn about the experiences of other abused women who happened to be in the counseling center at the same time; she spoke with two abused women during these visits. She later said that this kind of exchange helped her to better understand her own situation. After speaking with another abused woman, Bình, at the counseling center, Nguyệt said,

> I think my community should share in my problem. They don't think about me now, and don't care about my problem. They should care and understand my feelings. I think they should create a club for many people who have experienced domestic violence so that they can exchange information as I and Bình just did. Since I know that domestic violence is very extensive today . . . this problem should be publicized so that many people who are like me can raise their voices. When their calls for assistance are not effective, though, the women stop raising their voices and they think it is their fate [to be abused by their husband]. I want to solve the problem directly, so that the person who is wrong [the abusive husband] will be punished.

Nguyệt's desire for a club for women who have experienced domestic violence, a place where they can share their feelings, difficulties, and information about resources, was shared as well by some of the other abused women I interviewed. The loss of funding has made such clubs impossible, according to Women's Union leaders, and underscores how recent decreases in international funding have diminished services for abused women.

INTERNALIZING AND RESISTING CONTRADICTORY GENDER AND FAMILY IDEOLOGIES

Here I turn to women's experiences of domestic violence in Hà Nội and their expression of agency as they seek assistance, as well as the complex advice and forms of aid they receive from those in their families and communities who make sincere attempts to help them. I suggest that the complexity of the situation stems from the linking of international and state cultural discourses and practices that prioritize women's right to well-being and freedom from violence with contradictory local cultural narratives, also promoted by the Vietnamese state, that continue to emphasize a gendered subject position for women that privileges their familial and marital duties as mothers and wives. Many women's deep internalization of the privileging of their familial and marital duties over their own needs and safety, and the social pressures placed on them to meet these responsibilities, have in some cases circumscribed other female support for battered women's attempts to break free from their abusive husbands.

A Personal Problem

Ly had been physically abused for about five or six years by her husband. Ly said her husband had once thrown a bowl at her, cutting her leg, resulting in her receiving four or five stitches at a private hospital. On another occasion, he hit her and broke her knee. He also tied and pulled her hair on a regular basis, and has at times slammed her head into a wall. Over the previous year, he had also forced her to have sex with him. Ly lamented that when she tells him she does not wish to have sex, he slaps her, and physically forces her to lie down and have intercourse.

Ly said her family is struggling economically, and that she and her mother-in-law are the income earners for their household of six, which includes herself, her husband, parents-in-law, and her two children. Ly works as a tailor. She complained that her family's economic status is "very low, because my husband does not earn much money [repairing bicycles at our home], and then he usually goes out with his friends and spends it." Conflicts between Ly and her husband often arise following his loss of money from gambling, and his adultery. She had spoken with him about her fear that he may have a sexually transmitted disease and refused to have sex with him, but he became angry and hit her. She sought help from many individuals and organizations but has not been able to change her situation. When I met her, she was receiving assistance from the women's counseling center, which advised her to talk with her husband. Bolstered by their advice and the counselors' emotional support, Ly told her husband that spouses are equal now, and even though a wife works outside the home, her husband should also find a job. Her husband became angry and said his unemployment was none of her business. She also told him that since the domestic violence law had recently been implemented in Việt Nam, he should change his abusive behavior toward her because it is illegal. He claimed, however, that there was no such law. She bemoaned the fact that despite her talks with her husband, nothing in her family life had changed.

Ly's mother-in-law suggested that Ly contact the Women's Union leaders in her community for help. Ly's parents have encouraged her to leave her husband, telling her that people's views are different now compared to the past, and assured her that no one will criticize her for leaving him. But others, such as advisors from the women's counseling center and Women's Union leaders, asked her to speak with her husband or offered to give him advice themselves, with Women's Union leaders recommending she try to negotiate with her husband a reduction in the number of times they have sex each week. Women's Union leaders also visited Ly's home and spoke with her husband, advising him to keep calm. They suggested that if he and his wife have a problem, they should talk with each other without using force or hitting each other. Ly related that her husband threw the Women's Union leaders out of their house, asserting that his marriage was none of their business and that he had the right to do anything he wanted in his home. Once Ly called the local security force in her community for help, but her husband locked the door of their home and the security personnel could not enter. The security personnel had come to Ly's house to speak with her husband at other times, as well, but he avoided talking with them. When I asked Ly if she had ever considered divorce, she said, "Yes, but I haven't done it yet because I think of my children. They don't want me to leave him [my husband] because the children don't want to be separated from each other." While not mandated by law, Ly and her two children feared the children would be separated from each other if she acquired a divorce. At the time of our interview, if Ly and her husband could not agree to keep their children together following divorce, the children could express their desire to the court not to be separated because they are over nine years old (her son is seventeen, and her daughter ten years old). While the law stated that the court should assign one parent to rear all of the children, other factors may be taken into account, and the court was only required to take the children's wishes into consideration, making Ly's anxiety legitimate (National Assembly, Socialist Republic of Viet Nam 2000).

Ly said, "I think no one can help me, because this is my problem. Only advice is given to my husband and it's his choice to follow it or not. . . . We have a [domestic violence] law, but my husband locks the door and no one can do anything. . . . The law should state that the police must intervene, even in the house. The police should not do nothing just because of a locked door." The domestic violence law states that individuals present at the scene, "depending on the severity of the acts and their ability," must stop acts of domestic violence and protect the victim (National Assembly, Socialist Republic of Viet Nam 2007, 7). Nevertheless, the social service providers and police personnel with whom I spoke said that both the police and community security personnel perceive the new law to be unclear, and that they do not always know how to appropriately intervene in domestic violence cases. Ly tried to acquire help from government sources, but was unable to gain their support to stop her husband's violence. Following these failed attempts to solve her problem with assistance outside of her family, Ly began to perceive her husband's abuse to be a personal family problem, stating, "I think no one can help me, because this is my problem."

Ly's strategies seem contradictory. On the one hand, she has internalized prevailing gendered ideologies of motherhood that stress the importance of mothers prioritizing their children's needs over their own well-being. This is evidenced by her desire to prevent her children from being separated from each other by remaining married in the face of continuing domestic violence. On the other hand, she has also used legal and community resources to try to resist her husband's violence, but to no avail.

Creating New Happiness

In another case, a wealthy woman named An, who has adult children, was in the process of acquiring a divorce when I first met her. She told me that her husband had a girlfriend with whom he'd had a son, a situation she could not accept. Other women I spoke with said that they perceived An to be experiencing domestic violence, since her husband did not speak with or interact with her much, and he was also having an affair with another woman. These women saw these acts as emotional violence, defining adultery as marital sexual abuse. An said that when she first learned about her husband's infidelity, she was very sad. She subsequently felt relieved because she thought her husband was not a good man and that now she could find a better husband and have a more joyful life. She was relatively financially secure, with a job in a business and some savings that would help her to live on her own if she moved from her husband's home. At the same time, An complained that although her husband is quite wealthy, he had refused to give her any property or money as part of their divorce settlement.

One day, I joined a group of women with whom An was sitting in a restaurant and found she was discussing her marital issues. Two women were supporting her in a calm manner when two other women joined us to drink tea. One, a woman named Mai, had been abused by her husband approximately twenty years earlier, and, according to her friends, had tried to commit suicide during that period. Due to her desire to help other women who face similar situations, Mai, a Women's Union member when we met, had her home designated as a community shelter or "reliable address" for abused women. When addressing An, Mai seemed very agitated and talked openly about her own experiences of domestic violence. She related that even though her husband had beaten her, she did not pay attention to him and instead only focused on the happiness of her children. Mai advised An not to divorce her husband, explaining that in the past she too had wanted to divorce her husband when he was abusive and had affairs with other women. In the end, she did not divorce, and now people admire her.

At a gathering at a friend's home a few weeks later, after An had gotten a divorce from her husband, a woman named Phương addressed An in a commanding manner, admonishing her for getting a divorce. Phương reasoned that a divorce would only allow An's husband to marry his girlfriend and be happy, and also provide the opportunity for the husband's girlfriend to create difficulties for An. Phương, a former Women's Union leader, had assisted abused women in her community as part of her work in this position. Her friends remarked to me at a later time that Phương herself was being physically abused by her husband. Previously, Phương strongly pursued gender equality through Women's Union activities. During the gathering, An replied that she disagreed with Phương's opinion about her divorce, asserting that she would now be able to live a happier life. Yet, An looked crestfallen when confronted with these overt public criticisms of her divorce.

I have presented An's experiences to reveal the social criticism women commonly face when they attempt to divorce their husbands. It is significant that the two women, Mai and Phương, both of whom had decided to remain with their abusive husbands and their families, especially for their children, were the most agitated and directly critical of An's decision to divorce, even though they each had worked to assist other abused women. These conversations reveal the lack of support given abused women by other women when they pursue a divorce, including from women who were themselves abused by their husbands, were Women's Union members, but had deeply internalized the contradictory ideologies of womanhood coexisting in Vietnamese society today. These contradictory gender ideologies are conveyed to Vietnamese women particularly through Women's Union meetings or programs, and other forums, such as popular media (both state agency and more commercial media) (Drummond 2004). Rather than perceiving their assistance as contrary to the concerns of abused women, the Women's Union members seemingly view themselves as looking out for the best interests of the abused women and their children.

As noted earlier, while divorce is an option for Vietnamese (abused) women, the divorce process is fraught with tension and many people have conflicting or negative views of the practice. Nevertheless, the rate of divorce in Việt Nam is increasing, particularly in urban areas, and domestic violence is commonly being named today as a growing cause for divorce (United Nations Viet Nam 2008; *Việt Nam News* 2011). Yet, in spite of the increasing rate of divorce, attitudes toward women who obtain a divorce, even if their husbands have mistreated them, have been slower to change, making it more difficult for them to move out of their abusive marriages.

One young woman named Linh said to me in an exasperated tone that Vietnamese women's views will need to change if women are to divorce their abusive husbands, since many women believe that a woman should not leave her husband even if she is in a bad situation. Linh related that her mother, who has aided abused women, holds this view. She said that in Việt Nam it is not easy for a woman to get divorced, since if a woman "abandons" her family she will be severely criticized. I asked if it would be acceptable for a woman to divorce her husband and still raise her children. Linh said that this would not be easy for a woman unless she had a substantial income and was very self-confident. She went on to say that although people might still be kind to a divorced woman, they would negatively judge her and that it would be very hard for her to live with such opprobrium over a long period of time.

Linh compared the situation of Vietnamese women to the US television show *Desperate Housewives*, which she often viewed. She really admired a female character on the show who was married and had children. When this woman learned that her husband had a son with another woman, she left him and moved to another home with her children. Linh thought this would be an uncommon response among Vietnamese women. Linh also was impressed that an older female neighbor of this woman supported her decision. Returning to her views of changing ideas of gender and marriage in Việt Nam, Linh observed that young women who are economically stable, or perhaps even some college-educated women, may be less likely to think that they have to stay with an abusive husband for the rest of their lives, but that not all young women hold this new view of marriage. These variations in expectations for the longevity of marriage may be due to differences among women's economic status, educational level, prospects for future economic security, degree of internalization of traditional Vietnamese gender ideologies of womanhood, and exposure to cultural conceptions of marriage beyond Việt Nam.

Another woman named Hoa told me that while she actively assists women who are experiencing domestic violence through her work in a government health institution, she has not revealed this activity to her family, explaining that her husband does not accept spousal equality. Hoa said that she developed a desire to help abused women when, as a young girl, she observed a man walking behind his wife, kicking her as they moved along. Several years later, she also learned from a small boy that his father had poured boiling water on his mother. These memories always remained with her, and now she helps women in such situations. Hoa is deeply saddened by the impact of domestic violence on women and children, and aids such women to resist their husbands' abuse, even to the extent of hiding her work from her family. In addition, while Hoa works to assist abused women, her sister revealed to me that even Hoa has internalized the dominant cultural prescription for women to remain in their marriage even if they are experiencing domestic violence. The internalization of this perspective by a health worker who aids abused women underscores the difficulty women may have in escaping the social pressure to remain with an abusive husband, even when they request assistance from government personnel.

CONCLUSION

In trying to understand the persistence of domestic violence in Việt Nam, it is important to take into account the changing cultural definitions of and approaches to such abuse, as well as the guarded and unpredictable government economic and public social support for this new agenda. It is especially vital to understand the dominant gender and family ideologies circulating in this society and the role they have played in perpetuating domestic violence. We must recognize, though, that some women who have suffered aggression from their husbands have deeply internalized and found meaning in the prevailing Confucian ideologies. These abused women may approach the violence in ways that they perceive to be morally powerful, or in many cases, economically advantageous for themselves and their families, but that may not be beneficial for their own well-being. Multiple discourses of gender and gender violence circulate in and intersect with structures of power and economic inequality influencing different women to approach domestic violence in seemingly divergent ways. Many Vietnamese women seem to internalize differing gender ideologies and approaches to domestic violence that lead them to pressure abused women to stay married, while simultaneously actively resisting domestic abuse in their own marriages and in their communities. Still needed, along with new definitions of and approaches to domestic violence, is a fuller understanding of the actual social expectations of women as Việt Nam becomes integrated into global social discourse. Also needed is consistent government support of programs for abused women.

Feminist anthropologists, especially those working in the area of domestic violence, must pay attention to the many contradictions embedded in this kind of research. No matter what approaches are proposed to the problem of domestic violence, the violence often persists. As anthropologists we understand how powerful women's desires to maintain the unity of their families and their own respectability can be, particularly given the prevailing anti-woman cultural ideologies that can exist alongside ideas promoting gender equality. Feminist anthropology has enhanced our understanding of the multiple levels of meanings and economic factors that affect gender violence, and helped elucidate the complexity of influences that shape domestic violence in Việt Nam and elsewhere.

This research offers a major lesson for feminist anthropology. While some feminist anthropologists have conducted comparative ethnographic analyses of domestic violence (e.g., Counts, Brown, and Campbell 1999; Merry 2006) and others have contributed ethnographies of domestic violence in specific societies, more feminist anthropological engagement with this issue can strengthen our knowledge of the efficacy of specific attempts to address domestic and other forms of gender violence. The findings of feminist anthropologists can elucidate the work of international organizations to fully appreciate the powerful cultural forces that complicate their efforts to end gender violence. Cultural transformation is never simply formulaic and linear. My research in Việt Nam demonstrates that feminist organizations, NGOs, and governments will be stymied unless complex cultural mechanisms and structural inequalities that inadvertently perpetuate gender violence are fully taken into account.

ACKNOWLEDGMENTS

I am profoundly grateful to Dr. Le Thi Quy, Dr. Le Thi Nham Tuyet, and Dr. Nguyen Thi Hoai Duc for providing me affiliation with their institutions and excellent assistance in my research. I deeply thank all of the participants in my research in Việt Nam who generously shared their experiences and knowledge with me. I am enormously grateful to Ellen Lewin and Leni M. Silverstein for their thoughtful and invaluable comments, and for editing this volume. Special thanks also to Tom Boellstorff and an anonymous reviewer for their insightful feedback and suggestions on earlier versions of this chapter. For their financial support of my research, I extend sincere thanks to Colorado State University, the Centers for Disease Control and Prevention, the Colorado Injury Control Research Center, and the University of South Alabama. This chapter's contents are solely my responsibility, though, and do not necessarily represent the official views of these institutions.

NOTES

1. I use Vietnamese diacritical marks in my chapter, but the references follow the text of the original publication.
2. All names of people and organizations used in this chapter are pseudonyms, to protect the identity of the participants in my research.
3. The Women's Union is a Communist Party-affiliated mass organization that is supported by the Vietnamese government. It is a sociopolitical organization with a nationwide network concerned with achieving gender equality and women's development, and conveying Party and state policies to the population.
4. The first national study on domestic violence in Việt Nam, conducted in 2009 and 2010, found that the 4,838 women participating in the survey, the majority of whom had been married, reported experiencing the following forms of violence from their husbands in their lifetime: 32 percent experienced physical violence, 10 percent experienced sexual violence, and 54 percent experienced emotional violence (GSO, UN-JPGE, and WHO 2010, 50). Vietnamese men have reported experiencing domestic violence from their wives, but in fewer numbers than women (GSO, UN-JPGE, and WHO 2010, 101).
5. Reconciliation is pressed on women facing domestic violence in other countries as well, such as in Chile, Fiji, Peru, Russia, and Trinidad (Alcalde 2010; Johnson 2009; Lazarus-Black 2007; Merry 2006; Parson 2013).

REFERENCES

Adelman, Madelaine. 2004. "The Battering State: Towards a Political Economy of Domestic Violence." *Journal of Poverty* 8 (3): 45–64.

Alcalde, M. Cristina. 2010. *The Woman in the Violence: Gender, Poverty, and Resistance in Peru.* Nashville, TN: Vanderbilt University Press.

Bélanger, Danièle. 2004. "Single and Childless Women of Vietnam: Contesting and Negotiating Female Identity?" In *Gender Practices in Contemporary Vietnam*, ed. Lisa Drummond and Helle Rydstrøm, 96–116. Singapore: Singapore University Press.

Bélanger, Danièle, and Magali Barbieri. 2009. "Introduction: State, Families, and the Making of Transitions in Vietnam." In *Reconfiguring Families in Contemporary Vietnam*, ed. Magali Barbieri and Danièle Bélanger, 1–44. Stanford, CA: Stanford University Press.

Cameron, Deborah, and Elizabeth Frazer. 1994. "Cultural Difference and the Lust to Kill." In *Sex and Violence: Issues in Representation and Experience*, ed. Penelope Harvey and Peter Gow, 156–171. New York: Routledge.

Counts, Dorothy Ayers, Judith K. Brown, and Jacquelyn C. Campbell, eds. 1999. *To Have and to Hit: Cultural Perspectives on Wife Beating.* 2nd ed. Urbana and Chicago: University of Illinois Press.

Davis, Dana-Ain. 2006. *Battered Black Women and Welfare Reform: Between a Rock and a Hard Place.* Albany: State University of New York Press.

Drummond, Lisa. 2004. "The Modern 'Vietnamese Woman': Socialization and Women's Magazines." In *Gender Practices in Contemporary Vietnam*, ed. Lisa Drummond and Helle Rydstrøm, 158–178. Singapore: Singapore University Press.

Gammeltoft, Tine. 1999. *Women's Bodies, Women's Worries: Health and Family Planning in a Vietnamese Rural Community.* Richmond, Surrey, GB: Curzon Press.

———. 2001. "'Faithful, Heroic, Resourceful.' Changing Images of Women in Vietnam." In *Vietnamese Society in Transition: The Daily Politics of Reform and Change*, ed. John Kleinen, 265–280. Amsterdam: Het Spinhuis.

General Statistics Office of Viet Nam (GSO), United Nations-Government of Viet Nam Joint Programme on Gender Equality (UN-JPGE), and World Health Organization (WHO). 2010. 'Keeping Silent Is Dying.' Results from the National Study on Domestic Violence against Women in Viet Nam. Ha Noi. Unpublished report.

Harvey, Penelope, and Peter Gow, eds. 1994. *Sex and Violence: Issues in Representation and Experience.* New York: Routledge.

Hautzinger, Sarah J. 2007. *Violence in the City of Women: Police and Batterers in Bahia, Brazil.* Berkeley: University of California Press.

Jamieson, Neil L. 1993. *Understanding Vietnam.* Berkeley: University of California Press.

Johnson, Janet Elise. 2009. *Gender Violence in Russia: The Politics of Feminist Intervention.* Bloomington: Indiana University Press.

Kwiatkowski, Lynn. 2011a. "The Cultural Politics of a Global/Local Health Program for Battered Women in Vietnam." In *Anthropology at the Front Lines of Gender-Based Violence*, ed. Jennifer R. Wies and Hillary J. Haldane, 139–164. Nashville, TN: Vanderbilt University Press.

———. 2011b. "Domestic Violence and the 'Happy Family' in Northern Vietnam." *Anthropology Now* 3 (3): 20–28.

———. 2011c. "Prolonging Suffering: Domestic Violence, Political Economy, and the State in Northern Vietnam." *Gendered Perspectives on International Development (GPID) Working Paper No. 299.* East Lansing: Michigan State University.

Lazarus-Black, Mindie. 2007. *Everyday Harm: Domestic Violence, Court Rites, and Cultures of Reconciliation.* Urbana: University of Illinois Press.

Luong, Hy V. 2003. "Gender Relations: Ideologies, Kinship Practices, and Political Economy." In *Postwar Vietnam: Dynamics of a Transforming Society*, ed. Hy V. Luong, 201–223. Lanham, MD: Rowman and Littlefield.

Marr, David G. 1981. *Vietnamese Tradition on Trial, 1920–1945.* Berkeley: University of California Press.

Merry, Sally Engle. 2006. *Human Rights and Gender Violence: Translating International Law into Local Justice.* Chicago: University of Chicago Press.

———. 2009. *Gender Violence: A Cultural Perspective.* Malden, MA: Wiley-Blackwell.

Moore, Henrietta. 1994. "The Problem of Explaining Violence in the Social Sciences." In *Sex and Violence: Issues in Representation and Experience*, ed. Penelope Harvey and Peter Gow, 138–155. New York: Routledge.

National Assembly, Socialist Republic of Viet Nam. 2000. The Marriage and Family Law, Law No. 22/2000/QH10.

———. 2007. Law on Domestic Violence Prevention and Control, Law No. 02/2007/QH12.

Ngo Thi Ngan Binh. 2004. "The Confucian Four Feminine Virtues (*tu duc*): The Old versus the New—*Ke thua* versus *Phat huy*." In *Gender Practices in Contemporary Vietnam*, ed. Lisa Drummond and Helle Rydstrøm, 47–73. Singapore: Singapore University Press.

Ortner, Sherry B. 1995. "Ethnography among the Newark: The Class of '58 of Weequahic High School." In *Naturalizing Power: Essays in Feminist Cultural Analysis*, ed. Sylvia Yanagisako and Carol Delaney, 257–274. New York: Routledge.

Parson, Nia. 2013. *Traumatic States: Gendered Violence, Suffering, and Care in Chile.* Nashville, TN: Vanderbilt University Press.

Pettus, Ashley. 2003. *Between Sacrifice and Desire: National Identity and the Governing of Femininity in Vietnam.* New York: Routledge.

Phinney, Harriet M. 2009. "'Eaten One's Fill and All Stirred Up': *Doi Moi* and the Reconfiguration of Masculine Sexual Risk and Men's Extramarital Sex in Vietnam." In *The Secret: Love, Marriage, and HIV*, ed. Jennifer S. Hirsch, Holly Wardlow, Daniel Jordan Smith, Harriet M. Phinney, Shanti Parikh, and Constance A. Nathanson, 108–135. Nashville, TN: Vanderbilt University Press.

Rydstrøm, Helle. 2003. "Encountering 'Hot' Anger: Domestic Violence in Contemporary Vietnam." *Violence against Women* 9 (6): 676–697.

Skinner, Tina, Marianne Hester, and Ellen Malos, eds. 2005. *Researching Gender Violence: Feminist Methodology in Action.* Cullompton, Devon, UK/Portland, OR: Willan Publishing.

Standing Committee of National Assembly, Socialist Republic of Viet Nam. 1998. Ordinance on the Organization and Activities of Reconciliation at the Grassroots, No: 09/1998/PL-UBTVQH.

Steinberg, David Joel, ed. 1987. *In Search of Southeast Asia: A Modern History.* Rev. ed. Honolulu: University of Hawaii Press.

Thanh Nien News. 2013. "Domestic Violence a Symptom of Family Breakdown." *Thanh Nien News*, Ho Chi Minh City, Vietnam, March 28. http://thanhniennews.com/society/domestic-violence-a-symptom-of-family-breakdown-3024.html.

United Nations Viet Nam. 2008. "Family Undergoing Major Shifts in Viet Nam, Shows First-Ever Nationwide Survey on the Family." Ha Noi: United Nations. June 26. http://www.un.org.vn/en/unicef-agencypresscenter2–89/548-family-undergoing-major-shifts-in-viet-nam-shows-first-ever-nationwide-survey-on-the-family.html.

Việt Nam News. 2011. "Divorce Cases on a Sharp Rise in VN." *Việt Nam News*, Hà Nội, Việt Nam, July 1. http://vietnamnews.vn/society/212894/divorce-cases-on-a-sharp-rise-in-vn.html.

Vu Manh Loi, Vu Tuan Huy, Nguyen Huu Minh, and Jennifer Clement. 1999. *Gender-Based Violence: The Case of Vietnam.* Hanoi: World Bank in Vietnam.

Werner, Jayne. 2002. "Gender, Household, and State: Renovation (*Đổi Mới*) as Social Process in *Việt Nam*." In *Gender, Household, State: Đổi Mới in Việt Nam*, ed. Jayne Werner and Danièle Bélanger, 29–47. Ithaca, NY: Cornell Southeast Asia Program Publications.

Wies, Jennifer R., and Hillary J. Haldane. 2011. "Ethnographic Notes from the Front Lines of Gender-Based Violence." In *Anthropology at the Front Lines of Gender-Based Violence*, ed. Jennifer R. Wies and Hillary J. Haldane, 1–17. Nashville, TN: Vanderbilt University Press.

STUDYING GENDER AND NEOLIBERALISM TRANSNATIONALLY

Implications for Theory and Action

CATHERINE KINGFISHER

Since the mid-twentieth century, feminist anthropology has followed a general trajectory from grand theory to cultural and historical specificity. In the 1970s, efforts focused on articulating grand theoretical explanations for widespread, if not universal, gender asymmetry. Then, emphasis was placed either on asymmetries built into the nature of culture itself (e.g., Ortner 1974, 1996; Rosaldo 1974; Rubin 1975), or on the widespread inequalities resulting from the rise of private property and capitalism, including colonial expansion (e.g., Leacock 1981; Leacock and Safa 1986; Sacks 1975). Later, as scholars moved from the anthropology of women to the anthropology of gender and then to a feminist anthropology (Lewin 2006), theorists and ethnographers, influenced by postmodernism, rejected grand narratives in favor of historical and cultural specificity (MacCormack and Strathern 1980; Mohanty 1991; Rosaldo 1980). This move served to challenge a range of assumptions (about, e.g., the universal category "woman"), and thus (hopefully) to intervene in unreflexive impositions onto other cultures or into the categories of social scientific research itself (Rosaldo 1980; see also Moore 1988, 2006). Although tensions between the grand and the specific have long been recognized in feminist anthropology, for some time now cultural and historical specificity seems to have had the greatest purchase on our analytical imaginations and ethnographic engagements, even in the face of cogent critiques of postmodernism (Mascia-Lees et al. 1989) and ongoing references to large-scale or universal patterns of inequality (e.g., Moore 1994; see also Mohanty 2003; Ortner 1996): it has been *difference* and *specificity* that have garnered the most attention.

In this chapter I ruminate on the tensions between widespread structures of gender oppression and the nuances of specific contexts by means of an analysis of the travel of neoliberal policies of welfare state restructuring, and, in particular, welfare reforms targeting poor single mothers, from Aotearoa/New Zealand[1] to Alberta, Canada (Kingfisher 2013). I make the very simple argument that, rather than favor the specific over the universal *or* vice versa, we need to simultaneously foreground both, since it is in the details of how the conversations between the two play out that patterns as well as possibilities for intervention are placed into relief.

I present my argument by means of two stories: one involving official policy production, and one focused on policy reception. Both stories highlight policy as a key site for the exploration of patterns of similarity and difference. On the one hand, policy grounds the more amorphous phenomena—for example, capitalism, globalization—that many analysts turn to when attempting to locate pervasive patterns of oppression. By the same token, however, policy movement—what happens as policy travels through sites of (official) production and implementation—also provides entry points into the generation of difference, reminding us of the importance of specificity.

I begin with a brief sketch of the basic parameters and history of neoliberalism in Aotearoa/New Zealand and Alberta, Canada, with particular emphasis on the gendered underpinnings of transnational neoliberalism. I then turn to the two stories: one about the emergence of the New Zealand Model of welfare reform and its travel to and indigenization in Alberta; and one about the ways in which poor women in two mid-sized cities, Kingston in Aotearoa/New Zealand and Riverview in Alberta,[2] engaged with the new policies. I conclude with a discussion of the insights the stories provide into universalism and particularism vis-à-vis transnational neoliberalism.

THE GENDERED NATURE OF NEOLIBERAL WELFARE STATE RESTRUCTURING

Neither unique nor aberrant, welfare state restructurings in Aotearoa/New Zealand and Alberta were in keeping with, and contributed to, wider global shifts toward neoliberal forms of governance. Emerging neoliberalisms entailed a radical departure from liberal progressive forms of governance, which conceptualized and responded structurally and collectively to social ills, and toward forms of governance that highlighted individual causalities and decentralized and individualized remedies for social problems (Brodie 2002, 2008). Attacks on the welfare state were a central element of these projects in the advanced capitalist countries of North America, Europe, and the Pacific Rim, where government officials and neoliberal pundits constructed social provisioning as prohibitively expensive in the context of international economic competition, and the receipt of state support as disempowering of recipients in its fostering of dependence (Kingfisher 2002a).

Although seemingly gender neutral, the shift to neoliberalism entails a particular double bind for welfare mothers, who serve as a "litmus test . . . of gendered social rights" (Hobson 1994, 171). In particular, in both Aotearoa/New Zealand and Alberta, welfare state restructuring brought in new rules regarding engagement in paid labor, in the process redefining poor single mothers as potential able-bodied workers—as unemployed rather than unemployable (see, e.g., Kingfisher 2002b; Kingfisher and Goldsmith 2001; Mason 2003), and rendering motherhood a less acceptable reason for reliance on the state. The emphasis on employment, however, did not mean that poor single mothers were relieved of, or adequately supported in, their responsibility for their dependent children. The reforms accordingly placed welfare mothers in a double bind: they were simultaneously mothers and low-paid workers who did not have the resources to pay someone else to look after their children.

It is worth noting that, in contrast to their powerless position as a global force, poor single mothers play a pivotal, albeit unmarked, role in global imaginaries and practices. This may seem counter-intuitive. Globalization has been variously described as: the increasing international interdependence of economic, political, and social forces; the movement of finance, technology, people, and ideas across national borders; the development of circuits of travel for technology, finance, people, and ideas that are outside the control of national states; and the decentering of state and interstate relations as the primary loci of activity. Poor single mothers do not leap to the forefront of any of these frames. They do not figure in the glittery high-speed and high-powered transnational developments applauded by pundits of globalization. Nor do they have a place in either grassroots or above-the-state global social movements: they are not part of anti-globalization efforts; they do not demonstrate at WTO or G20 meetings; there is no welfare rights movement akin to the global indigenous or gay movements.

However, just as the practices of high-powered businessmen are often made possible by the housewives behind the scenes who do the child care, entertaining, and sustaining, so high-powered global finance and technology are made possible by territorially situated armies of low-paid and insecure workers—the metaphorical housewives of globalization who in many cases, and in keeping with gendered constructions of women's "nature" (as, e.g., more docile than men), and of their supposedly marginal material contributions to household maintenance (thus justifying lower rates of remuneration), also happen to be actual women (McDowell 1991; Ong 1987; Sassen 1996, 1998; Sjolander 1996). Poor single mothers, then, are located in one particular space of globalization—that occupied by those who either people the ranks of low paid labor or who are penalized for their inability to do so. The workfare ideologies and programs to which welfare mothers are subjected—enticing/coercing them into being the housewives of a global free market—are accordingly one element of the transnational spread of neoliberal forms of labor market regulation.

Poor single mothers are also one of the ideological keystones of the global travel of neoliberal constructs of the person. *Ideoscapes*, as Arjun Appadurai describes them, are traveling images that are "[o]ften directly political and frequently have to do with the ideologies of states and the counter ideologies of movements explicitly oriented to capturing state power or a piece of it. These ideoscapes are composed of elements of the Enlightenment worldview, which consists of a chain of ideas, terms, and images, including *freedom, welfare, rights, sovereignty, representation, and the master term democracy*" (1996, 36; emphasis in original). Appadurai's focus is on a particularly positive set of keywords, to which I would add the term *individual*, which, in an Enlightenment frame, refers to the *self-possessed* (that is, sovereign) and *self-actualized* bearer of rights and a participant in democracy. This model of the person is closely tied to the idea of *freedom* which, in the context of transnational neoliberalism, concerns the freedom/right to participate in markets without the hindrance of state interference (Clarke 2004; see also Harvey 2005; Kingfisher and Maskovsky 2008; Smith 2007). Roland Robertson (1992) argues in this respect that the increasing global circulation and influence of the definition of persons as self-sufficient, autonomous entities comprises a key feature of the current era of globalization. The force of this ideology is not necessarily revolutionary or liberatory, however; on the contrary, in the case of workfare, it entails the imposition of a particularly pernicious and imprisoning form of "individualism" and "freedom."

Thus, just as an increasingly insecure and poorly paid segment of the labor force provides the foundation for the valorized aspects of economic globalization, so poor single mothers provide the (negative) foundation for the valorized aspects of the (globalized) neoliberal individual. In the context of the increasing movement and spread of free-market forms of social and economic organization, poor single mothers in prereform welfare systems are retrospectively reconstructed as "dependent" on the state, and are, by virtue of that dependence, neither sovereign nor self-actualized. They represent one embodiment of the non-neoliberal subject, the non-enterprising, the non-self-sufficient (Kingfisher 2007a, 2007b); they travel as a negative image (Kingfisher 1999). The simultaneous dissemination of ideas of how to transform welfare mothers into ideal subjects—sovereign, independent, and free—is testimony to both the purchase and the asserted "naturalness" of the neoliberal model of the person, as well as to the labor involved in claiming such naturalness. It also works to undermine notions of collectivity (as manifested, e.g., in welfare rights groups and labor unions)—thus Pierre Bourdieu's (1999, 2003) observation that neoliberal forms of governance are characterized simultaneously by individualization and decollectivization.

Given this, welfare reforms targeting poor single mothers provide a particularly fruitful opportunity to trace the "active society" model, a keystone of neoliberal governance, as it moves, via policy, across sites and through persons. Articulated by the Organization for Economic Co-operation and Development (OECD) in 1990, this approach to state-market-individual relations entailed "fostering economic opportunity and activity for everyone in order to combat poverty, dependency and social exclusion" (OECD 1990, xi, cited in Walters 1997, 224). Whereas the welfare society distinguishes between those who have to engage in paid labor and those who do not, in an active society framework, "the market is the only true source for satisfaction of human desires and needs, just as participation in paid employment is the key to personal fulfillment, self-development and membership in society" (Walters 1997, 224). This represents a shift away from a conception of society in which the market has a place within a larger overall scheme, and toward one in which everything has to be put into market space—in which the market *is* the overall scheme and the economy becomes the organizing frame for society. Governments drawing on this framework accordingly work to alter both the institutional and cultural terrain of action (Larner 2000; Schwartz 1997) in an attempt to write relations among state, market, and society, and to change individual behavior and, by extension, notions of proper personhood and citizenship.

Building on the philosophies of Friedrich Hayek and Milton Friedman, the active society model asserts that "the wellbeing of both political and social existence is to be ensured not by centralized planning and bureaucracy, but through the 'enterprising' activities and choices of autonomous entities—businesses, organizations, persons—each striving to maximize its own advantage by inventing and promoting new projects by means of individual and local calculations of strategies and tactics, costs and benefits" (Rose 1992, 145). The person is here reconfigured as an active, entrepreneurial agent, "highly motivated and energized, competitive, ambitious, goal-setting and strongly oriented towards free market rewards; and underlying all these are the ideas of individual autonomy and independence" (Heelas 1991, 77; see also Dean 2007; Fairclough 1991; Miller and Rose 2008; Rose 1992).

As I have noted elsewhere (Kingfisher 2002a; Kingfisher and Goldsmith 2001), the active society model of the person is profoundly gendered, raced, classed, and historically and culturally specific. Insofar as poor single mothers challenge the supposedly natural and universal status of this construct—as women, as poor persons, and often as either members of racialized minorities or attributed with their constructed negative characteristics—they become targets for reform, for efforts to remake the person. As Paul Heelas (1991, 72) claims, "[r]adical government must surely go to the heart of the matter—character reform." In this sense, regulating and disciplining (Foucault 1995) some, via welfare reform, provides a way of governing the whole; policing those on the margins becomes a powerful mechanism for the construction and assertion of the normative. The 1990 reforms instituted by the New Zealand and Alberta governments—complete with condemnations of parasitic tendencies, rhetorics of responsibilization, work tests, and forms and procedures enabling/coercing welfare recipients to engage in their own self-transformation while simultaneously providing mechanisms for the surveillance of that effort—are thus prime examples of active society approaches to governing the "marginalized," as opposed to the "civilized," who, in contrast, are capable of managing their own risk and therefore do not require policing and intervention (Dean 1995, 580).

TRANSLATING AND ASSEMBLING WELFARE REFORM POLICY: THE NZ MODEL AT HOME AND IN ALBERTA

Until 1984, New Zealand was a cradle-to-grave welfare state, with universal employment, education and health care, state housing, and, since 1973, a welfare program (the Domestic Purposes Benefit) that provided reasonably adequate means for single parents to stay at home with their children until the youngest reached the age of eighteen. The story is, of course, much more complicated than this—Maori were particularly poorly treated—but there was certainly something to lose when the Fourth Labour government came into power and Roger Douglas, the new finance minister, assembled what came to be known as Rogernomics. A keystone of Rogernomics, an approach focused on deregulation and privatization, was the discursive repositioning of citizens as consumers; this served to reconfigure a collectivity into a collection of individuals, each an active agent and expert in making self-interested choices and mitigating risk. The changes Rogernomics inaugurated in turn provided the groundwork for the specific reforms to the welfare system brought in by Ruth Richardson under the more right-leaning National government elected in 1990. Ruthanasia, as it was popularly tagged, included tighter targeting of potential welfare recipients coupled with major cuts to welfare benefits and to a range of cognate services in health and housing. These changes were followed in 1996 by the introduction of work tests requiring beneficiaries to be available for part- and full-time work once their youngest child reached the ages of seven and fourteen years, respectively. The results of Rogernomics and Ruthanasia were dramatic: sky rocketing inflation, a decline in median income, and sharp increases in unemployment, poverty rates, morbidity, and crime (Belgrave 2004; Kelsey 1993, 1995; Waldegrave and Frater 1996).

Neither Douglas nor Richardson backed down from their visions, however; and Douglas, in particular, took an active role in the spread of the NZ Model to other jurisdictions. After being pushed from political office in 1988, he transformed himself into a consultant and became a global proselytizer of neoliberal market ideology. Arguing that governments, less efficient than markets, were an affront to freedom, and that government levels of debt were unsustainable, he called for a comprehensive and immediate, rather than gradual or piecemeal restructuring, including the complete elimination of an interventionist welfare state. In the early 1990s, Douglas, the consultant, made two visits to Alberta where he met with the conservative caucus and gave speeches for the right-wing Alberta Taxpayers Association. His presence in Alberta was highly publicized, and various members of the newly elected Progressive Conservative government of Ralph Klein indicated that he had played a significant role in their decision making regarding the radical restructurings implemented in 1993–1994 (Alberts 1994; Crockatt 1994; Martin 1994).

Although Douglas's message was not unique—neoliberalism was "in the air" at the time, with wide global circulation and purchase—the NZ Model provided a particularly useful external justification for the Klein administration's approach: it conveniently precluded accusations of too close a connection between Alberta and its domineering neighbor to the south, and it provided a perfect so-called "First World" blueprint for how to transform a marginally reasonable welfare state (which was what was in place in Alberta at the time) into a deeply neoliberal and residualist one—that is, minimalist and increasingly narrowly targeted—and fast. "Don't blink," Douglas's highly mobile slogan (Czarniawska and Sevón 2005, 10) that underscored simultaneously the need to act quickly—in the time between blinks—and to stare down one's opponents, had particular resonance in Alberta, articulating easily with what then-Treasurer Jim Dinning described as the province's "cowboy capitalism" (Crockatt 1994). And the government did indeed move quickly and unblinkingly: a year after Douglas's first visit, it stated that, "individuals and families are responsible for meeting their basic needs and for the safety and security of their children" (Government of Alberta 1994, 9–10). Justifying the reforms in Douglasian fashion in terms of debt elimination and global economic competition, the government sought a shift in welfare "from a passive system to an active-re-employment program" (Alberta Family and Social Services 1994, 5), and proceeded, by 1995, to cut welfare benefit levels by 13.4 percent, remove more than half of the welfare population from its rolls, and require recipients to engage in work-related activities when their youngest child reached six months of age (Alberta Family and Social Services 1996, 2–4).

On the one hand, then, welfare state restructurings in New Zealand and Alberta clearly contributed to the establishment of a transnational policy regime characterized by neoliberal forms of governance. Crucial features of the NZ Model, reflective of the foundational aspects of neoliberal approaches to social and economic organization, were taken up and operationalized in Alberta: the foregrounding of debt elimination as the central concern of government; the need to exercise both comprehensiveness and speed in undertaking restructuring; and a vision of a golden past of enterprising, rugged individualism. If we were to conceptualize this global policy regime in traditionally grand theoretical terms, the active society model would be one of its keystones, and the various binary distinctions of 1970s feminist grand theory would here take the form of oppositions between the independent versus the dependent self, or the market self versus the other to the market (Maskovsky 2001). The gendered underpinnings of such dependent/independent binaries are clear (Fraser and Gordon 1994). Also like 1970s grand theory, there is a direct connection with (although not a reduction to) women's roles as child-bearers, and often, by extension, caretakers. We could, then, entertain a combined universal/political economic feminist grand theory of transnational neoliberalism.

On the other hand, once attended to in detail, the New Zealand–Alberta story is more convoluted than this straightforward "transmission" narrative implies. While the New Zealand rhetorics of reform *were* picked up with great zeal by the Alberta government, the specific programs with which those rhetorics were articulated differed markedly in Alberta when compared to how they played out in New Zealand. This was particularly the case with regard to workfare stipulations, which were brutal in Alberta, but relatively light (requiring engagement in part- and full-time work only when the youngest child reached the ages of seven and fourteen, respectively), and very short lived—a mere six years—in New Zealand. The history of gender regimes in Aotearoa/New Zealand and Alberta provides at least a partial explanation for this: while Albertan cultural history is marked by an emphasis on rugged individualism and by the increasing participation of women, and, in particular, married women, in paid labor since World War II (Langford 2011; Palmer and Palmer 1990), Aotearoa/New Zealand history is marked by a strong strand of maternalism that cuts across class lines, such that it continued through most of the twentieth century to have one of the lowest rates of married women's workforce participation in the OECD (OECD 2005). This more historically based maternalist gender regime may have served to mitigate workfare requirements, if not to soften discourses of parasitism and valorization of worker-citizenship. Thus the (re)emergence of the self-sufficient (pioneering) neoliberal individual in the New Zealand reforms was limited, perhaps, by an enduring gender regime in which women were first and foremost mothers.

This gender regime, however, was irrelevant to policy makers in Alberta. While New Zealand discourses of personal responsibility traveled easily to Alberta, the New Zealand practice of allowing welfare mothers to stay at home with their children for extended periods of time did not. Instead, pieces of the NZ Model were selected out and rearticulated with other approaches to workfare that better suited Alberta's prairie rugged individualism. Additional developments in Aotearoa/New Zealand were also ignored, most notably, the negative impacts of Rogernomics and Ruthanasia, and the policy shifts that occurred after the 1999 election of Helen Clark's Labour-Coalition government, which eliminated workfare and introduced enhanced benefit schemes. These patterns and developments were "unfit to fit" (Lendvai and Stubbs 2007, 2009), and so overlooked by members of the Klein administration in favor of those aspects of the NZ Model that aligned with the administration's ideological and practical agendas.

New Zealand and Alberta thus represented "softer" versus "harder" approaches to welfare reform, mirroring Dean's (1999, 161–162) distinction between relatively left-leaning models that "encompass but go beyond participation in the market to include participation in other social spheres," and more right-leaning models that are about the revival and extension of "the norms and values associated with the market." In other words, neoliberalism—as philosophy, as a cultural system, as a model for social organization, and as a mode of governance—takes on different forms and valences in different contexts. This is in keeping with interpretive analyses (e.g., Shore and Wright 2011; Wedel et al. 2005) that highlight the travel of policy across sites and through persons as comprised of processes of translation and assemblage, rather than transmission. Meaning—the valence a policy framework will take on in a particular context—is, in an interpretive framework, not prior to translation, but emerges *in* translation (Freeman 2009, 437), rendering it unstable and subject to alteration as well as to continuity. The work of policy translation, moreover, involves processes of assemblage: understanding something newly emergent in light of what is received; framing an idea from elsewhere in terms of what is known here; and connecting theoretical frames and practices in new ways—all in light of an array of agendas related to making sense of the world, devising programs of action, and asserting power and control. There is thus a great deal of cutting-and-pasting and improvisation involved as policies travel up, down, and sideways. This is not to claim that policy movement is about the freewheeling creativity of sovereign agents in completely open and unconstrained environments populated by unmoored, empty signifiers. Signs and practices can be disarticulated and set off on travels in any number of directions, and policy assemblages can indeed represent cut-and-paste experimentation, but what and how things are translated, cut-and-pasted, and experimented with is not completely arbitrary. There are always parameters, not the least of which is history: in this case, the history of how poverty and poor people have been conceptualized, of how social welfare systems have been structured, of how human nature has been characterized, and of economic practices.

The point of this story is that something that looks universal can become quite variable and nuanced when we look at it in its specific contexts of occurrence. The study of neoliberal transnationalism is not the study of how a monolithic force traverses and colonizes the globe in any kind of totalizing sense. It is, rather, the study of attempted colonizations that end up being quite piecemeal, disjointed, and particularized. So just when we think we can see a seamless pattern, it turns out that we are looking at something characterized perhaps more by disjuncture than uniformity. We therefore cannot take an uninterrupted, smooth, and uniform transnationalism of the "big" players—capitalism, neoliberalism, etc.—as *fait accompli*. There may be attempts to set the parameters of possibility and to impose uniformity across national and cultural space, but such attempts can never usefully be *assumed* to be successful. In other words, transnational neoliberalism is not our starting point, the taken-for-granted terrain on which we explore the impacts of neoliberalism on the lives of, in this case, poor single mothers. Instead, we need to explore the grounds of possibility for—and, in some cases, the shaky grounds of—actually existing neoliberalisms.

WELFARE POLICY AS LIVED EXPERIENCE: THE TRANSLATION AND ASSEMBLAGE WORK OF WELFARE RECIPIENTS

My second story makes the opposite argument by highlighting how the specific, deeply contextualized iterations and experiences of welfare recipients point to some significant commonalities that cut across a range of boundaries. If my first story problematizes taking for granted ostensibly hegemonic forces such as neoliberalism, this story problematizes the privileging of difference and nuance that has emerged from (among other quarters) feminist critiques of the exclusions and erasures that often accompany grand theoretical frameworks.

In contrast to the big policy players who people the first story—government agents and highly paid consultants—this story focuses on the translation and assemblage work that poor single mothers engage in when they encounter welfare policy. The women who people this story are at the bottom of the hierarchy; they are the targets of surveillance, diagnosis, remedial efforts, and of course, usually insufficient distributions of resources. It is on this level—the level of lived experience—that feminist anthropologists have focused in order to highlight the importance of differences related to various positionalities and their intersections.

Before turning to the engagements of the women I worked with in Kingston, Aotearoa/New Zealand, and Riverview, Alberta, it is worth noting the contradictions embedded in the policy shifts outlined earlier, since these, along with specific program requirements, are what the women had to contend with. I want to point in particular to the presence in the reforms of elements of neoconservatism as well as neoliberalism, which produced glaring contradictions in the messages the women received regarding the kinds of persons they should be. On the one hand, in keeping with neoliberal philosophies, they were expected to be independent individuals. On the other hand, reflective of neoconservative "family values," they were told that their primary function was to be mothers and caregivers. On the surface, the former message appeared to be most pronounced in the Alberta reforms, which reconfigured welfare mothers as genderless (and childless) self-sufficient individuals, and required them, accordingly, to behave as autonomous monads; while the latter approach seemed most pronounced in Aotearoa/New Zealand, as reflected in both the weakness of the work requirements in the reforms and the wider context of its maternalist gender regime. Both strands, however, were present in both sites; thus the New Zealand policy was suffused with rhetorics of individual responsibility and self-sufficiency, while in Alberta, the low minimum wage and tax legislation favoring single earner nuclear families served to latently promote traditional nuclear family formation as the solution to poverty (Harder 1996; Harder and Trimble 2005). In addition to inconsistencies within the policies themselves, poor single mothers were also confronted by contradictions both among and between welfare workers and the providers who staffed the various community service agencies they frequented. Not only were they subjected to different messages about what kinds of persons they should be; how they should interact with the welfare system; and how they should run their lives more generally; but they also received conflicting information about welfare requirements and entitlements, such that they were often confused about how to proceed.

In response to these contradictory messages, and in keeping with their own everyday knowledges and survival needs, the women in Kingston and Hamilton produced a unique assemblage of meanings and frameworks for action that cut across the programmatic and cultural differences between the two sites. Significantly, they co-produced these assemblages in group settings; they are thus *collective* representations. On the one hand, the women accepted the neoliberal (and neoconservative) approaches embedded in welfare policy: the need to be enterprising and self-directed, the critical role of employment in self-fulfillment (and the primacy of the idea of self-fulfillment itself), the overriding importance of independence, and the centrality of mothering. Thus, in keeping with neoliberal constructions of the independent individual, they looked down on dependence in adults, condemned irresponsibility, and valued motivation, determination, and persistence, as reflected in their positive approaches to paid labor (as conducive to self-esteem as well as to financial independence), and to the Personal Development and Employment (NZ) and Client Investment (Alberta) Plans they were required to complete by the welfare office. (As one woman in Kingston put it, such plans were good because "it's making you sit down and set goals for yourself to achieve and it's all up to you, so you actually do it, and it's all for you.") In addition, in keeping with neoconservative models, they adopted, as commonsensical, constructions of women as natural mothers and caretakers.

On the other hand, the women's "good" translations of these ideas did not survive their articulations of those ideas with their practical knowledges of undependable and irresponsible men, the inadequacies of welfare provisions, the unreasonable nature of work expectations, the sexist and racist realities of the workplace, and the capriciousness of both the policies themselves and the various providers engaged with them. These knowledges provided the grounds for critical scrutiny, throwing into relief contradictions within and between ideologies, and between the ideal and the real. In response, the women profoundly transformed, in remarkably similar ways, the dominant discourses informing welfare mandates in each site. Most notably, although they universally and strongly favored independence, they were oriented toward independence from men rather than from the state. In their hands, and by means of a reversal of the unarticulated gender relations informing neoliberal models of the person, the very grounds of independence as well as the objects from which persons were ideally independent were radically shifted. Specifically, the women claimed that they, as *women*, and as *mothers* in particular, displayed the traits of self-sufficiency, responsibility, and motivation so valued in neoliberal discourse. *They* were the ideal neoliberal individuals, not men, insofar as they had developed, by means of their specifically gendered roles as mothers, the qualities so valued in neoliberal-inflected discourses. Moreover, the women constructed themselves not only as more responsible and motivated than men, but also as more *adult* than men, who they constructed as childish and immature. In a neoliberal cultural framework, adults are "naturally" utility maximizing, self-sufficient, and enterprising, having experienced dependence and gone through the process of learning to become independent during childhood and adolescence. Children are, in this sense, full-persons-in-the-making. The women accepted this characterization of their children as natural, but were highly critical of this quality in the men they encountered, who were, after all, fully grown and therefore reasonably expected to behave accordingly. The women's constructions of men as childish, then, took on a particular valence: men were not persons-in-the-making, but rather, *failed* persons. Significantly, this description mirrors neoliberal criticisms of welfare recipients as irresponsible, lazy, and specifically unadult in their dependence and inability to defer gratification. Instead of hankering for independence from the state, then (which is what the state told them they should want), the state itself, in the form of welfare programs—even meager postreform ones—became the means by which the women could gain independence from men and fulfill their roles as mothers. Constructing mothers instead of male monads as the embodiment of the responsibility and motivation valorized in neoliberal models of the person, the women made claims against the state for better support. In keeping with neoconservative models of women as mothers, however, they also inserted a temporal delay in their professed desires to pursue fulfillment through employment, which they could take up only once their children were grown. They thus turned both neoliberal and neoconservative models on their heads, deferring and deflecting criticism in ways that allowed them to survive (albeit often barely) both ideologically and materially.

What is most remarkable about this second story is that it illuminates how specific, deeply contextualized experiences can produce a pattern that not only cuts across but also may well be evident beyond Alberta and Aotearoa/New Zealand. In key areas, women in Kingston and Riverview expressed astoundingly similar views in almost identical language. To give just one example from the convergences noted earlier: in their work of constructing men as childish, expressions in Kingston such as "it doesn't help [to be with a man] because then you end up with two child[ren]" were mirrored by phrases such as "I'm tired of raising overgrown kids" uttered by women in Riverview.

This convergence of views and language is simultaneously striking and mundane. Its banality reflects the obvious point that the women shared certain structural locations in cultural contexts characterized by family resemblance: they were all single mothers struggling to care for their children more or less on their own; they were all poor; they were all recipients of stigmatized financial assistance in historical periods marked, in both cases, by radical reconfigurations of the welfare state in social contexts in which neoliberalism (and strands of neoconservatism) had a great deal of purchase; and, as non-ideal persons, they were also all subjects of state interference designed to alter their very selves. The shared discursive patterns I encountered therefore make some sense.

It is precisely the differences in the situations of these two groups of women, however, that renders the convergences in their constructions striking as well as mundane. Regardless of the family resemblances between the two sites, each has its own unique historical, cultural, ethnic, and political compositions and trajectories. The cultural and ethnic diversity within each site was significant: I worked with First Nations and non-Native women in Canada, and with Maori, Pacific Island, and Pakeha (European) women in Aotearoa/New Zealand. Although there were some differences among them that correlated loosely with ethnicity, these differences were not absolute but a matter of degree—and a surprisingly small degree at that. Non-Native and Pakeha women, for example, were slightly—but only slightly—more likely to express career-related desires, while First Nations, Maori, and Pacific Island women were slightly—but again, only slightly—more likely to emphasize the importance of family and community. While I would never claim that these differences were irrelevant, they pale in comparison to the convergences in the women's views that cut across the various ethnic and cultural divides that otherwise separated them. Nor did the differences in the historical trajectories of the two countries or in their welfare programs show up in the women's constructions.

What this second story highlights, then, is not so much widespread structures of gender oppression as widespread forms of resistance. Oppressed in *somewhat* similar ways on the basis of motherhood and poverty—while workfare was a keystone of the reforms in both sites, the differences between the New Zealand and Alberta requirements were significant—the women I worked with responded in *stunningly* similar ways, also on the basis of their roles as mothers. These convergences were in some cases so close that terms and concepts were not just shared, but almost identical in meaning and the uses to which they were put (cf. Freeman 2006, 381). It is precisely this kind of convergence, across a range of differences—geographic, national, cultural, ethnic—that provides the grounds of possibility for transnational feminist solidarity and activism (see, e.g., Moghadam 2005; Mohanty 2003).

CONVERGENCE AND DIVERGENCE; OR, NEOLIBERALISM AND ITS LIMITS

Neoliberalism—as a cultural system, governing practice, or policy regime—doesn't just exist, despite claims of a naturalized inevitability; rather, it is an activity, the outcome of processes of translation and assemblage in specific, already-inhabited contexts, which means that it is always in conversation with other cultural formations. Although it may be characterized by a particular "grammar" (Kingfisher 2002b), this grammar is constantly "disarticulating and rearticulating, disjunctive and contradictory" (Kingfisher and Maskovsky 2008, 120). Neoliberalism's existence thus takes shape only in the fluid and multiple translations on which it depends for its movement, and it accordingly rarely realizes its totalizing desires (Clarke 2004; Kingfisher and Maskovsky 2008). Since various neoliberal assemblages "cannot be analytically reduced to cases of a uniform global condition of 'Neoliberalism' writ large" (Ong 2006, 14; see also Collier and Ong 2005), we are enjoined to attend to concrete specificities—to avoid taking the so-called global neoliberal policy regime for granted, and to instead treat it as something that "needs to be explained in particular places and with reference to particular peoples, territories, states and cultural formations" (Kingfisher and Maskovsky 2008, 123–124). The New Zealand–Alberta connection provides just such an opportunity for the analysis of particular unfoldings and articulations—unfoldings and articulations, moreover, that simultaneously buttress and unsettle ideas and practices of a transnational neoliberal policy regime.

On the one hand, insofar as the policy movements that serve to operationalize neoliberalism entail translation and assemblage, convergence is impossible. The concept of translation, which "attracts attention to the fact that a thing moved from one place to another cannot emerge unchanged"—that "to set something in a new place is to construct it anew" (Czarniawska and Sevón 2005, 8)—enjoins us to recognize policy movement as entailing processes of transformation rather than replication (see also Johnson and Hagström 2011; Lendvai and Stubbs 2007, 175). As Bruno Latour (1986, 268) claims, "tokens"—here, policy mandates—do not "move in the same direction as long as there is no obstacle." Rather, they move through *people*, "who slowly turn . . . [them] into something completely different as they [seek] to achieve *their* own goals" (Latour 1986, 268; emphasis in original). Transmission via diffusion is thus transmuted into transformation via translation and (re)assemblage. On the other hand, in tracing the emergence, travel, and various articulations of the NZ Model in Aotearoa/New Zealand and Alberta, I encountered some remarkable convergences: in the general discursive framings that informed reform policies in both sites, and in how recipients in two small cities on opposite sides of globe translated and assembled knowledges of policy.

It is thus important to situate our analyses in the space of in-betweenness where convergence and divergence are negotiated and produced: in this case, between Aotearoa/New Zealand and Alberta, and between policy mandates, providers, and recipients. This focus draws attention to the ongoing tensions between similarity and difference, providing an opportunity to move beyond binaries that skew our vision. It becomes clear, in this space, that neoliberalism is *both* a blueprint with considerable force, *and only* "found amongst its others, in a state of messy coexistence" (Peck 2013, 8; see also Hall 2011). Thus the result of the articulation of the NZ Model with Albertan cultural formations was both marked difference (most notably in workfare programs) *and* family resemblance (in the realm of discursive frames and programmatic orientations). The power of such family resemblances is revealed in the second story about the engagements of women on welfare: responding to the neoliberal "blueprint," they repurposed (Ferguson 2009)—appropriated, and, in some cases, reversed—neoliberal tenets in order to meet their material and social needs. The nature of their translation and assemblage work provides insight into transnational economic and ideological policy structures as they impinge on women's lives, as well as grounds for theorizing agency and resistance vis-à-vis these structures and patterns cross-culturally. As I noted earlier, the latter is essential to conceptualizations of and engagements in transnational feminist practice (Ferree and Tripp 2006; Moghadam 2005; Mohanty 2004).

In this chapter, I have flipped back and forth between a focus on the grand and a focus on the specific: in telling each story I chose to place the accent on one aspect of what is in reality part of a whole. Transnational phenomena—in this case, transnational policy regimes reflecting neoliberal forms of governance—provide the perfect entry point for analyzing the tensions among the different aspects of this messy conglomeration. There may indeed be a "grammar" informing (attempted) transnational neoliberal policy regimes, but it does not exist outside of particular contexts of occurrence—it may be in "in the air," but it never really floats around unmoored; even its foundational claims about the nature of the person or about the appropriate configuration of state-market relations are only ever articulated *in situ*. But this *in situ-ness*, in turn, cannot occur without reference to some kind of generalized grammar. So the idea that we need to focus on universals *or* specifics, foregrounding one as the context for the other, is problematic, both theoretically and practically. In good old-fashioned feminist parlance, it's not either/or but both/and, and we need to stay in this space of both/and in order to think and act clearly.

ACKOWLEDGMENTS

This chapter contains revised excerpts from my book *A Policy Travelogue: Tracing Welfare Reform in Aotearoa/New Zealand and Canada* (2013). Research for the book was supported by the Wenner-Gren Foundation for Anthropological Research, the Social Science and Humanities Research Council of Canada, and the University of Lethbridge Research Fund. Many thanks to Ellen Lewin, Leni M. Silverstein, and the anonymous reviewers for Rutgers University Press for their contributions to my thinking and writing.

NOTES

1. *Aotearoa/New Zealand* refers to a place and a social system that includes, while simultaneously marking a tension between, both Maori and Pakeha (European) cultural formations, and *New Zealand* refers more narrowly to the state and its practices.
2. Kingston and Riverview are pseudonyms.

REFERENCES

Alberta Family and Social Services. 1994. *Business Plan 1994–95 to 1996–97*. Edmonton: Government of Alberta.

———. 1996. *Alberta Welfare Reforms Progress Report: March 1993–December 1995*. Edmonton: Government of Alberta.

Alberts, Sheldon. 1994. "Protest! Muted So Far, Opposition Has Been More Effective When Aimed at Specific Targets." *Calgary Herald*, May 29.

Appadurai, Arjun. 1996. *Modernity at Large*. Minneapolis: University of Minnesota Press.

Belgrave, Michael. 2004. "Needs and the State: Evolving Social Policy in New Zealand History." In *Past Judgement: Social Policy in New Zealand History*, ed. Bronwyn Dalley and Margaret Tennant, 23–38. Dunedin, New Zealand: University of Otago Press.

Bourdieu, Pierre. 1999. *Acts of Resistance: Against the Tyranny of the Market.* New York: New Press.

———. 2003. *Firing Back: Against the Tyranny of the Market.* New York: New Press.

Brodie, Janine. 2002. "The Great Undoing: State Formation, Gender Politics, and Social Policy in Canada." In *Western Welfare in Decline: Globalization and Women's Poverty*, ed. Catherine Kingfisher, 90–110. Philadelphia: University of Pennsylvania Press.

———. 2008. "The New Social'isms': Individualization and Social Policy Re-form in Canada." In *Contested Individualization: Debates About Contemporary Personhood*, ed. Cosmo Howard, 153–170. London: Routledge.

Clarke, John. 2004. *Changing Welfare, Changing States: New Directions in Social Policy.* London: Sage Publications.

Collier, Stephen J., and Aihwa Ong. 2005. "Global Assemblages, Anthropological Problems." In *Global Assemblages: Technology, Politics, and Ethics and Anthropological Problems*, ed. Aihwa Ong and Stephen J. Collier, 3–21. Malden, MA: Blackwell.

Crockatt, Joan. 1994. "Bedside Reading for Alberta Tories: The Books Behind the Budget." *Edmonton Journal*, March 6.

Czarniawska, Barbara, and Guje Sevón. 2005. "Translation Is a Vehicle Imitation Its Motor, and Fashion Sits at the Wheel." In *Global Ideas: How Ideas, Objects, and Practices Travel in the Global Economy*, ed. Barbara Czarniawska and Guje Sevón, 7–12. Liber and Copenhagen: Business School Press.

Dean, Mitchell. 1995. "Governing the Unemployed Self in an Active Society." *Economy and Society* 24 (4): 559–583.

———. 1999. *Governmentality: Power and Rule in Modern Society.* London: Sage.

———. 2007. *Governing Societies: Political Perspectives on Domestic and International Rule.* Maidenhead, Berkshire, and New York: Open University Press.

Fairclough, Norman. 1991. "What Might We Mean by 'Enterprise Discourse'?" In *Enterprise Culture*, ed. Russell Keat and Nicholas Abercrombie, 38–57. London and New York: Routledge.

Ferguson, James. 2009. "The Uses of Neoliberalism." *Antipode* 41 (S1): 166–184.

Ferree, Myra Marx, and Aili Mari Tripp, eds. 2006. *Global Feminism: Transnational Women's Activism, Organizing, and Human Rights.* New York: New York University Press.

Foucault, Michel. 1995. *Discipline and Punish: The Birth of the Prison.* New York: Vintage.

Fraser, Nancy, and Linda Gordon. 1994. "A Genealogy of *Dependency*: Tracing a Keyword in the U.S. Welfare State." *Signs* 19 (2): 309–336.

Freeman, Richard. 2006. "Learning in Public Policy." In *The Oxford Handbook of Public Policy*, ed. Michael Moan, Martin Rein, and Robert E. Goodin, 367–388. Oxford: Oxford University Press.

———. 2009. "What Is 'Translation'?" *Evidence & Policy* 5 (4): 429–447.

Government of Alberta. 1994. *A Better Way: A Plan for Securing Alberta's Future.* Edmonton: Government of Alberta.

Hall, Stuart. 2011. "The Neo-Liberal Revolution." *Cultural Studies* 25 (6): 705–728.

Harder, Lois. 1996. "Depoliticizing Insurgency: The Politics of the Family in Alberta." *Studies in Political Economy* 50: 37–63.

Harder, Lois, and Linda Trimble. 2005. "The Art of Contradiction: Women in Ralph Klein's Alberta." In *The Return of the Trojan Horse: Alberta and the New World (Dis)Order*, ed. Trevor Harrison, 297–312. Montreal: Black Rose Books.

Harvey, David. 2005. *A Brief History of Neoliberalism*. Oxford and New York: Oxford University Press.

Heelas, Paul. 1991. "Reforming the Self: Enterprise and the Characters of Thatcherism." In *Enterprise Culture*, ed. Russell Keat and Nicholas Abercrombie, 72–90. London and New York: Routledge.

Hobson, Barbara. 1994. "Solo Mothers, Social Policy Regimes, and the Logics of Gender." In *Gendering Welfare States*, ed. Diane Sainsbury, 170–187. London: Sage.

Johnson, Björn, and Bo Hagström. 2005. "The Translation Perspective as an Alternative to the Policy Diffusion Paradigm: The Case of the Swedish Methadone Maintenance Treatment." *Journal of Social Policy* 34 (3): 365–388.

Kelsey, Jane. 1993. *Rolling Back the State: Privatisation of Power in Aotearoa/New Zealand*. Wellington: Bridget Williams Books.

———. 1995. *The New Zealand Experiment: A World Model for Structural Adjustment?* Auckland: Auckland University Press with Bridget Williams Books.

Kingfisher, Catherine. 1999. "Rhetoric of (Female) Savagery: Welfare Reform in the United States and Aotearoa/New Zealand." *National Women's Studies Association Journal* 11 (1): 1–15.

———. 2002a. "Neoliberalism I: Discourses of Personhood and Welfare Reform." In *Western Welfare in Decline: Globalization and Women's Poverty*, ed. Catherine Kingfisher, 1–31. Philadelphia: University of Pennsylvania Press.

———. 2002b. "Where to Next? Against and Beyond Neoliberalism." In *Western Welfare in Decline: Globalization and Women's Poverty*, ed. Catherine Kingfisher, 164–176. Philadelphia: University of Pennsylvania Press.

———. 2007a. "Discursive Constructions of Homelessness in a Small City in the Canadian Prairies: Notes on Destructuration, Individualization, and the Production of (Raced and Gendered) Unmarked Categories." *American Ethnologist* 34 (1): 91–107.

———. 2007b. "Spatializing Neoliberalism: Articulations, Recapitulations, and (a Very Few) Alternatives." In *Neoliberalization: States, Networks, Peoples*, ed. Kim England and Kevin Ward, 195–222. Malden, MA: Blackwell.

———. 2013. *A Policy Travelogue: Tracing Welfare Reform in Aotearoa/New Zealand and Alberta, Canada*. New York and Oxford: Berghahn Books.

Kingfisher, Catherine, and Michael Goldsmith. 2001. "Reforming Women in the United States and Aotearoa/New Zealand: A Comparative Ethnography of Welfare Reform in Global Context." *American Anthropologist* 103 (3): 714–732.

Kingfisher, Catherine, and Jeff Maskovsky. 2008. "Introduction: The Limits of Neoliberalism." *Critique of Anthropology* 28 (2): 115–126.

Langford, Tom. 2011. *Alberta's Day Care Controversy: From 1908 to 2009—And Beyond*. Edmonton: Athabasca University Press.

Larner, Wendy. 2000. "Post-Welfare State Governance: Towards a Code of Social and Family Responsibility." *Social Politics* 7 (2): 244–265.

Latour, Bruno. 1986. "The Powers of Association." In *Power, Action and Belief: A New Sociology of Knowledge?*, ed. John Law, 264–279. London: Routledge and Kegan Paul.

Leacock, Eleanor Burke. 1981. *Myths of Male Dominance: Collected Articles*. New York: Monthly Review Press.

Leacock, Eleanor Burke, and Helen I. Safa, eds. 1986. *Women's Work: Development and the Division of Labor by Gender*. South Hadley, MA: Bergin & Garvey.

Lendvai, Noémi, and Paul Stubbs. 2007. "Policies as Translation: Situating Transnational Social Policies." In *Policy Reconsidered: Meanings, Politics, and Practices*, ed. Susan M. Hodgson and Zoë Irving, 173–189. Bristol: Policy Press.

———. 2009. "Assemblages, Translation, and Intermediaries in South East Europe: Rethinking Transnationalism and Social Policy." *European Societies* 11 (5): 673–695.
Lewin, Ellen. 2006. "Introduction." In *Feminist Anthropology: A Reader*, ed. Ellen Lewin, 1–38. Malden, MA: Blackwell.
MacCormack, Carol, and Marilyn Strathern, eds. 1980. *Nature, Culture, and Gender*. Cambridge: Cambridge University Press.
Martin, Don. 1994. "Alberta Strategies in U.S. Textbook." *Calgary Herald*, March 12.
Mascia-Lees, Frances E., Patricia Sharpe, and Colleen B. Cohen. 1989. "The Post-Modernist Turn in Anthropology: Cautions from a Feminist Perspective." *Signs* 15 (1): 7–33.
Maskovsky, Jeff. 2001. "Afterword: Beyond the Privatist Consensus." In *The New Poverty Studies: The Ethnography of Power, Politics, and Impoverished People in the United States*, ed. Judith Goode and Jeff Maskovsky, 470–482. New York: New York University Press.
Mason, Robin. 2003. "Listening to Lone Mothers: Paid Work, Family Life, and Childcare in Canada." *Journal of Children & Poverty* 9 (1): 41–54.
McDowell, Linda. 1991. "Life without Father and Ford: The New Gender Order of Post-Fordism." *Transactions of the Institute of British Geography* 16: 400–419.
Miller, Peter, and Nikolas Rose. 2008. *Governing the Present: Administering Economic, Social and Personal Life*. Cambridge: Polity.
Moghadam, Valentine M. 2005. *Globalizing Women: Transnational Feminist Networks*. Baltimore, MD: Johns Hopkins University Press.
Mohanty, Chandra Talpade. 1991. "Under Western Eyes: Feminist Scholarship and Colonial Discourses." In *Third World Women and the Politics of Feminism*, ed. Chandra Talpade Mohanty, Ann Russo, and Lourdes Torres, 51–80. Bloomington: Indiana University Press.
———. 2004. *Feminism without Borders: Decolonizing Theory, Practicing Solidarity*. Durham, NC: Duke University Press.
Moore, Henrietta. 1988. *Feminism and Anthropology*. Cambridge: Polity Press.
———. 1994. *A Passion for Difference: Essays in Anthropology and Gender.* Bloomington: Indiana University Press.
———. 2006. "The Future of Gender or the End of a Brilliant Career?" In *Feminist Anthropology: Past, Present, and Future*, ed. Pamela L. Geller and Miranda K. Stockett, 23–42. Philadelphia: University of Pennsylvania Press.
OECD. 2005. *Economic Survey of New Zealand: Raising Female Labour Force Participation.* Paris: OECD.
Ong, Aihwa. 1987. *Spirits of Resistance and Capitalist Discipline: Factory Women in Malaysia.* Albany: State University of New York Press.
———. 2006. *Neoliberalism as Exception: Mutations in Citizenship*. Durham, NC: Duke University Press.
Ortner, Sherry B. 1974. "Is Female to Male as Nature Is to Culture?" In *Woman, Culture, and Society*, ed. Michelle Zimbalist Rosaldo and Louise Lamphere, 67–88. Stanford, CA: Stanford University Press.
———. 1996. "So, *Is* Female to Male as Nature is to Culture?" In *Making Gender: The Politics and Erotics of Culture*, 173–180. Boston: Beacon Press.
Palmer, Howard, and Tamara Palmer. 1990. *Alberta: A New History*. Edmonton: Hurtig Publishers.
Peck, Jamie. 2013. "Explaining (with) Neoliberalism. Territory, Politics, Governance." Taylor & Frances Online. http://dx.doi.org/10.1080/21622671.2013.785365, accessed September 2, 2014.
Robertson, Roland. 1992. *Globalization: Social Theory and Global Culture*. London: Sage.

Rosaldo, Michelle Zimbalist. 1974. "Woman, Culture, and Society: A Theoretical Overview." In *Woman, Culture, and Society*, ed. Michelle Zimbalist Rosaldo and Louise Lamphere, 17–42. Stanford, CA: Stanford University Press.

———. 1980. "The Use and Abuse of Anthropology: Reflections on Cross-Cultural Understanding." *Signs* 5 (3): 389–417.

Rose, Nikolas. 1992. "Governing the Enterprising Self." In *The Values of the Enterprise Culture: The Moral Debate*, ed. Paul Heelas and Paul Morris, 141–164. London and New York: Routledge.

Rubin, Gayle. 1975. "The Traffic in Women: Notes on the 'Political Economy' of Sex." In *Toward an Anthropology of Women*, ed. Rayna Reiter (Rapp), 157–210. New York and London: Monthly Review Press.

Sacks, Karen. 1975. "Engels Revisited: Women, the Organization of Production, and Private Property." In *Woman, Culture, and Society*, ed. Michelle Zimbalist Rosaldo and Louise Lamphere, 207–222. Stanford, CA: Stanford University Press.

Sassen, Saskia. 1996. "Toward a Feminist Analytics of the Global Economy." *Indiana Journal of Global Legal Studies* 4 (1): 7–41.

———. 1998. *Globalization and Its Discontents: Essays on the New Mobility of People and Money*. New York: New Press.

Schwartz, Herman. 1997. "Reinvention and Retrenchment: Lessons from the Application of the New Zealand Model to Alberta, Canada." *Journal of Policy: Analysis of Management* 16 (3): 205–232.

Shore, Cris, and Susan Wright. 2011. "Conceptualising Policy: Technologies of Governance and the Politics of Visibility." In *Policy Worlds: Anthropology and the Analysis of Contemporary Power*, ed. Cris Shore, Susan Wright, and Davide Però, 1–26. New York and Oxford: Berghahn Books.

Sjolander, Claire Turenne. 1996. "The Rhetorics of Globalizations: What's in a Wor(l)d?" *International Journal* 51 (4): 603–616.

Smith, Paul. 2007. *Primitive America: The Ideology of Capitalist Democracy*. Minneapolis: University of Minnesota Press.

Waldegrave, Charles, and Peter Frater. 1996. "New Zealand: A Search for a National Poverty Line." In *Poverty: A Global Review. Handbook on International Poverty Research*, ed. Else Oyen, S. M. Miller, and Sayed Abdus Samad, 16–186. Oslo: Scandinavian University Press; Paris: UNESCO.

Walters, William. 1997. "The Active Society: New Designs for Social Policy." *Policy and Politics* 25 (3): 221–234.

Wedel, Janine R., Cris Shore, Gregory Feldman, and Stacy Lathrop. 2005. "Towards an Anthropology of Public Policy." *Annals of the American Academy of Politics and Social Science* 600: 30–51.

EPILOGUE

TOM BOELLSTORFF

In his short story "On Exactitude in Science," Jorge Luis Borges imagined cartographic masters who created a map the size of the territory it represented. Perfect but without scale, one mile equaling one mile, the map was recognized by subsequent generations as useless: "In the Deserts of the West, still today, there are Tattered Ruins of that Map" (Borges 1998, 325).

Borges's point is simple but profound: while mapmaking is about representation, it always involves omission as well. But there is something else important about maps: they are guides to practice. Maps make lovely wall hangings but are meant to orient travelers in the context of the new. We do not use maps to reach the familiar. As Pierre Bourdieu noted, "it is significant that 'culture' is sometimes described as a map; it is the analogy which occurs to an outsider who has to [use] . . . a model of all possible routes" (1977, 2). Setting aside maps is in a sense the anthropological imperative: the move from etic to emic, from looking in to walking alongside. The best ethnographies might chart the cultural terrain, but ultimately they provide a sense of everyday lifeworlds, where maps stay in the drawer.

These aspects of the fascinating form of knowledge production known as mapmaking are both evident when surveying the rich and varied chapters comprising *Mapping Feminist Anthropology*. The contributors have delved into the diverse histories and contemporary practices of feminist anthropology, and from this context have mapped out key themes, debates, and lines of inquiry. In a sense this epilogue is a "legend," not in the mythical sense but in the sense of a guide to a map's meaning. In other words, I see my goal as highlighting some key insights evident in this volume as a whole. Freed from any pretense of comprehensiveness, I wish simply to trace four promising pathways evident in these chapters—with the hope that you, dear reader, will discover new horizons of feminist anthropological insight as you explore them. These pathways involve intersectionality, difference, power, and collaboration.

As I trace these pathways, I will keep in mind the question of history, an overarching concern of this volume. Robyn Wiegman has spoken of "the difficulty of being in time with feminism, by which I mean the difficulty of sustaining a relationship to a political and intellectual project that is itself historically transforming and transformative" (2004, 163). These chapters explore questions of temporality that link feminism and anthropology in unexpected and productive ways. In addition, I will foreground the specifically anthropological contributions of these chapters. As Tim Ingold has noted, "anthropology is an inquiry into the conditions and possibilities of human life in the world; it is not—as so many scholars in fields of literary criticism would have it—the study of how to write ethnography, or of the reflexive problematics of the shift from observation to description" (2008, 88–89). As part of acknowledging the powerful interdisciplinarity that has shaped feminist work, I thus want to value and highlight the specifically anthropological contributions that feminists have made. These contributions include the fine-grained attention to everyday life provided by ethnographic research, but they also include generalizable, comparative knowledge.

INTERSECTIONALITY

The chapters that make up *Mapping Feminist Anthropology* chart a fascinating set of pathways with regard to intersectionality. This paradigm has been powerfully shaped by feminism and in particular women of color feminism, but also by a long history within anthropology itself. These linked histories are illustrated, for instance, by Sylvia Yanagisako and Carol Delaney's observation that "a productive question is to ask how culturally-specific domains have been dialectically formed and transformed in relation with other cultural domains, how meanings migrate across domain boundaries, and how specific actions are multiply constituted" (1995, 11). Furthermore, they emphasized the danger of a misreading of Michel Foucault that assumes, for instance, that "medical discourse" shapes "medical practice." In contrast to such inaccurate approaches, they asserted that "people think and act at *the intersections of discourses*" (1995, 18, emphasis added).

Various intersectionalities are pivotal to the analyses presented in this volume. Elise Kramer shows how the relationship between language and gender has been an enduring domain of research throughout the history of feminist anthropology, and Frances Mascia-Lees traces how embodiment and affect have shaped feminist anthropological work. Both of these lines of inquiry link up with Margot Weiss's discussion regarding how intersections of gender and sexuality theory demonstrate the theoretical power, relevance, and generosity of feminist thought. Louise Lamphere emphasizes how feminist anthropology's engagement with social movements has acted as a kind of motor of intersectionality, shaping pathbreaking and transformative conversations within and far beyond the academy. Leni Silverstein and Ellen Lewin, and also A. Lynn Bolles, carefully track how intersectional analyses have long characterized the relationship between feminist studies and women's/gender studies. Matthew R. Dudgeon notes how men can see benefits from these dynamics of intersectionality in some respects, even while disadvantaged in other respects. This resonates with Theidon's examination of the intersection of militarism and gender in Peru, as well as Lynn Kwiatkowski's exploration of how in Vietnam, intersectionalities of scale (local, state, global) in regard to gender and domestic violence have nonlinear and emergent consequences for women. Elizabeth Roberts addresses the nature/culture binarism, one of the most significant intersectional interventions of feminist work that has at the same time been an interdisciplinary intervention linking feminist studies and STS. This reflects Catherine Kingfisher's exploration of the transnational reworkings of law.

One of the most powerful lessons we can learn from these feminist explorations of intersectionality is not just how domains intersect, but the prior cultural and political move by which they are construed as separate such that they can later be said to "intersect" at all. For instance, Meena Khandelwal and Kingfisher explore how assumptions of prior separation have informed efforts to decolonize anthropology and forge a truly world anthropology that engages with a transnational range of scholarly communities, languages, and research agendas.

These analyses regarding intersectionality thus underscore the mutual insights anthropology and feminist scholarship can bring to each other. More generally, we see the key role of feminist work in theorizing the multivalence of intersectionality, in the sense that it can be a source of oppression but also a source of resistance and coalition. Feminist anthropologists have been central to demonstrating this insight in the everyday lives of people around the world and in linking these realities to conceptual innovation in anthropology itself.

DIFFERENCE

My second pathway, difference, is (as Silverstein and Lewin note) one of the most fundamental questions of feminist thought, linked to but not identical with intersectionality. In her discussion of the relationship between transnational feminism and anthropology, Khandelwal builds on the work of Marilyn Strathern to discuss how the question of difference has also been central to anthropology, but in varied ways that make the relationship between feminism and anthropology complex and at times vexed. Bolles takes up these themes when discussing the relationship of feminist anthropology to the "transnational," and also its relationship to the women's movement in the United States with regard to race, sexuality, and class. It bears noting that all disciplines have a colonial history that shapes them, acknowledged or not. It is fascinating to set these analyses alongside that of Weiss as she explores debates between feminism and queer studies, particularly with regard to their objects of study.

As Lamphere emphasizes, a particularly important intervention addresses the question of the "Other" as it relates to questions of difference and shapes the positionality of anthropologists themselves. Khandelwal notes how the history of anthropology has been shaped by specific colonial histories that cannot be conflated. I would add that it was the British tradition stretching back to figures like Haddon and Malinowski, and appearing to this day in the work of scholars like Ingold, that has sometimes presumed a Self/Other division as necessary for anthropology: "the objective of ethnography is to describe the lives of people other than ourselves" (Ingold 2008, 69). In contrast, one of the most valuable legacies of the Boasian tradition in the United States is that it "does not rest on a distinction between ethnographic Self and native Other but, instead, draws its analytic leverage from a rigorous historicity that refigures the question of Otherness in terms of temporal rather than cultural alterity" (Bunzl 2004, 437). This United States tradition was far more welcoming to women than the British tradition: for example, Boas along with two of his students who founded the Department of Anthropology at Berkeley (Alfred Kroeber and Robert Lowie) "trained eight of the nine women who received Ph.D. degrees from American universities [in any discipline] before 1929" (Patterson 2001, 65).

More generally, there are important insights in these chapters with regard to the dangers of universalizing in terms of sameness or difference. On the one hand, Kwiatkowski emphasizes how feminist anthropologists have questioned homogenizing frameworks regarding violence against women. Mascia-Lees discusses how this attention to difference has extended to the question of the body and its complicated relationship to women's subordination. As Dudgeon notes, feminist insights have also informed work on hegemonic masculinities, work that both reflects the multiplicity of masculinities in any social context, and the fact that certain forms of masculinity usually hold a dominant position that devalues and subordinates women.

On the other hand, feminist anthropologists have challenged understandings of women's lives predicated on difference taken as self-evident in a manner that leads to "othering" and denies possibilities for coalition and social change. Kramer discusses how feminist anthropological work on language has shifted from questions of how women talk to how different forms of speaking are seen as gendered in the first place. Kimberly Theidon pushes this question into the realm of law when examining the efforts of Peruvian women to secure legal redress for violence, and Roberts moves into the realm of technology when noting how feminist deconstructions of the nature/culture binarism have challenged deterministic accounts of sexuality and race.

As emphasized throughout *Mapping Feminist Anthropology*, questions of difference are also internal to the communities with which feminist anthropologists have collaborated—for instance, with regard to the relationship between pregnancy and selfhood, choice, and life narrative, as Roberts notes. This compels us to consider how intersectionality in a sense produces difference as a set of interlocking oppressions but also as a set of potentialities and resistances that can be tracked through emergent yet historically informed senses of selfhood and community. As Weiss explores in her chapter, such questions of difference have been central to the articulations between feminism and queer studies more broadly. They also recall Kingfisher's observation that while the women she studied in New Zealand and Canada were different in many ways, similar experiences of motherhood and poverty shaped similar responses that could serve as a foundation for transnational alliances. This powerful linkage between experience, theoretical insight, and politics encapsulates one dimension of the contributions that feminist anthropology has to offer, and reminds us as well that to speak of similitude is not automatically to overgeneralize or conflate.

These insights thus raise theoretical issues of cultural holism and change, but also linked political issues of shared identity (or not), of coalition and alliance, of the distinctions between "speaking about" and "speaking for" another. These are crucial insights that have inspired an incredibly broad range of work. They have, for instance, informed my own realization that assumptions about sameness and difference are themselves part of globalization—indeed, can constitute resistances and transformations of globalizing processes. This body of work has helped shape my interest in what I have termed an anthropology of similitude that does not immediately consign sameness to contamination or false consciousness (Boellstorff 2005).

POWER

My third pathway, power, has been a core interest of feminist anthropology since its beginnings and the location of profound theoretical insights and political interventions. As both Bolles and Lamphere discuss at length, the range of approaches to the question of power within feminist anthropology across multiple generations of scholarship is truly staggering. Kwiatkowski puts power center stage when discussing how with regard to domestic abuse and gender violence, Vietnamese women and men work within (and often against) dynamics of power that move across spatial scales and between state and non-state actors. Theidon links sexual violence to acts of war itself, violence that targets both men and women and links sexualized power over bodies with military power. Pre-existing "peacetime" forms of gender inequality and violence can thereby shape forms of political violence during war. Dudgeon notes how the study of power with regard to masculinity has been fundamentally shaped by feminist insights, and Khandelwal explores the complicated power dynamics at play when working in social change projects tied to development discourse. Another set of linkages between everyday inequality and broader cultural formations of sexism is discussed by Kramer with regard to the politics of language, while still another set of linkages is foregrounded in Mascia-Lees's analysis of affect and embodiment as they relate both to individual women's experiences and their place in economies of power.

Indeed, as Silverstein and Lewin emphasize from the outset, one of the great gifts of feminist anthropological thought has been to link attention to everyday questions of power and inequality with forms of structural state power. A more general question in this regard is how the power relations between Euro-American centers and other regions framed as "peripheral" reproduce within anthropology the power relations that shape patriarchal, white-dominant, and heterosexist social dynamics. In other words, geopolitical and social power dynamics of inequality are immanent to each other. These dynamics operate within the academy itself in the reproduction of disciplinarity: as Weiss notes, for instance, the notion of "queer" has had both utopic connotations in terms of new possibilities, yet by definition works within the horizon of the power dynamics from which it emerged. This historicity of "queer" is not just about *longue durée* historical dynamics, but more personal histories of the life course and particularly "agonized conversations about feminism's generational transmission" (Wiegman 2004, 164–165). Particularly given that many queer persons are estranged from their families of origin in both biological and scholarly senses, respecting and learning from queer elders is a crucial imperative, an ideal not always kept. In this regard Bolles and several other contributors to this volume show how feminist anthropology provides an excellent example of an intellectual community attentive to its historical conditions of existence and the innovative work earlier cohorts of scholars have produced.

In terms of my opening comments regarding the importance of not reducing feminist anthropology to feminist ethnography, it is important to underscore Roberts's reminder about the power of comparison to challenge universalist tendencies in some quarters of anthropology. As Kingfisher notes, this recalls longstanding feminist insights regarding the value of addressing both specificities and broader patterns—for instance, with regard to historically and culturally specific articulations of neoliberalism that cannot be predicted in advance. Such feminist anthropological insights provide a way to think about activism that does not predicate social change on a complete overthrow of dominant power structures, emphasizing instead how those power structures are vulnerable to reconfiguration.

COLLABORATION

My fourth pathway may sound a bit odd, but as an analytical thread linking the chapters of *Mapping Feminist Anthropology*, it definitely merits discussion. Collaboration is a helpfully complex term. One can be prosecuted for "collaborating with the enemy," but one also "collaborates" with allies and interlocutors. What I specifically mean by "collaboration" with regard to the discussion at hand is the feminist insight that the world does not divide simplistically into good and evil, right and wrong. Women find themselves caught up in social dynamics and even forms of selfhood that do not stand outside the systems of power that oppress them, and that as Dudgeon notes always include men, directly or indirectly. In intellectual and political work we often find ourselves working within horizons of knowledge and power; often there is no pure constitutive outside, comfortably external to the power we question. Such complexities inform Kramer's insights regarding how the idea that there are discrete forms of men's speech and women's speech masks a much more complicated set of linguistic practices and ideologies that are culturally and historically specific.

Overall, rethinking collaboration is a major insight of feminist anthropological thought. Lamphere shows how "collaboration" can be a way to think about the coalitions and messy entanglements that emerge from ethnographic work and have implications for method, theory, knowledge production, and activism. Khandelwal notes how conversations with interlocutors turned into forms of collaboration, and Kingfisher explores how women can sometimes be presenting themselves in neoliberal terms precisely as a means of challenging neoliberal power. Kwiatkowski, Roberts, and Theidon explore collaborations between individuals, NGOs and forms of urban, state, and transnational law as women seek to be free from violence and access equal life opportunities. Roberts and Mascia-Lees note how collaborations between technology, the body, and the social can shape experiences and practices of reproduction, affect, and selfhood. Bolles and Weiss both closely examine how questions of collaboration extend to the disciplinary aspects of feminist work—for instance, in relationships between "women's studies," "gender studies," "gay/lesbian studies," "queer studies," and "feminist anthropology." Silverstein and Lewin discuss how dynamics of collaboration have informed feminist anthropological interventions into forms of writing, representation, and accountability. As Khandelwal notes, notions of collaboration also shape the question of world anthropologies that decenter Euro-American anthropological canons, methods, and priorities. It is less an issue of resolution or discovering the "perfect fit" between terms, theories, and social realities. It is, rather, an issue of tracing through time forms of alliance that mutually rework social relations and the conceptual frameworks we use to understand those social relations.

CONCLUSION: CARTOGRAPHIES OF FEMINIST FUTURES

We live in a contemporary world shaped by the pretense of cartographic closure. The globe meets up with its other side, every inch of land part of some sovereignty. Even the stars have their maps. But this volume suggests another era, an earlier time of cartographies of wonder. Maps of the uncharted, ending in blank spaces without name. Maps that mark the known but point as well to the unknown, to futures of discovery that are not necessarily of conquest. Maps to orient the lost but that gesture as well to emergent encounters.

In setting out these four pathways of intersectionality, difference, power, and collaboration, I hope to have gestured at just some key insights from *Mapping Feminist Anthropology*. I could have chosen other routes across this incredibly rich collection. As noted from the outset, maps always involve choices of omission. My goal has been to indicate some of the landscapes covered—and in doing so, to show how the contributors to this volume have also provided a guide to future navigation, a means to move forward through the terrain of feminist anthropology to valuable destinations for scholarship and politics.

These chapters also demonstrate the centrality of feminism to anthropology. Feminist concerns shaped the disciplines' beginnings; they are vital to current debates, and they will certainly shape the emergent anthropologies to appear throughout the twenty-first century. From these chapters we can take the message of feminist anthropology as an intervention and even an interruption, but also as an invitation, a powerful conversation that benefits everyone not least because it challenges the either/or thinking that shapes the mistaken belief that one person's gain is inevitably another person's loss.

We can all look forward to the continuing powerful contributions of feminist anthropology to the discipline and to the human journey. Let us set sail!

REFERENCES

Boellstorff, Tom. 2005. *The Gay Archipelago: Sexuality and Nation in Indonesia*. Princeton, NJ: Princeton University Press.

Borges, Jorge Luis. 1998 [1946]. "On Exactitude in Science." In *Collected Fictions*, trans. Andrew Hurley, 325. New York: Penguin.

Bourdieu, Pierre. 1977. *Outline of a Theory of Practice*. Cambridge: Cambridge University Press.

Bunzl, Matti. 2004. "Boas, Foucault, and the 'Native Anthropologist': Notes toward a Neo-Boasian Anthropology." *American Anthropologist* 106 (3): 435–442.

Ingold, Tim. 2008. "Anthropology Is *Not* Ethnography." *Proceedings of the British Academy* 15: 69–92.

Patterson, Thomas C. 2001. *A Social History of Anthropology in the United States.* London: Berg.

Wiegman, Robin. 2004. "On Being in Time with Feminism." *Modern Language Quarterly* 65 (1): 161–176.

Yanagisako, Sylvia, and Carol Delaney. 1995. "Naturalizing Power." In *Naturalizing Power: Essays in Feminist Cultural Analysis,* ed. Sylvia Yanagisako and Carol Delaney, 1–22. New York: Routledge.

NOTES ON CONTRIBUTORS

TOM BOELLSTORFF is a professor in the Department of Anthropology at the University of California, Irvine; from 2007 to 2012 he was editor-in-chief of *American Anthropologist*, the flagship journal of the American Anthropological Association. His publications include *The Gay Archipelago: Sexuality and Nation in Indonesia* (2005), *A Coincidence of Desires: Anthropology, Queer Studies, Indonesia* (2007), *Coming of Age in Second Life: An Anthropologist Explores the Virtually Human* (2008), and (as co-author) *Ethnography and Virtual Worlds: A Handbook of Method* (2012).

A. LYNN BOLLES is professor emerita of women's studies and affiliate faculty in anthropology, African American studies, comparative literature, and American studies at the University of Maryland, College Park. Author of *Sister Jamaica* (1996), *We Paid Our Dues* (1996), *Claiming their Rightful Position* (1992), *My Mother Who Fathered Me and Others* (1988), she was elected to the executive board of the American Anthropological Association (2012–2015) and was an NSF-funded ADVANCE professor (2012–2013) and she won the 2013 Association of Black Anthropologists Legacy Award. Bolles was named 2014 UMD graduate school mentor of the year.

MATTHEW R. DUDGEON completed his MD and PhD at Emory University. His dissertation research examined men's roles in maternal and infant health in two K'iche' Maya communities in western highland Guatemala. Following internship in obstetrics and gynecology at Stanford University, he completed residency in internal medicine at Emory University. He is now an attending physician in internal medicine at Emory University Hospital.

MEENA KHANDELWAL conducted groundbreaking research on Hindu women's religious renunciation in India, the results of which are published in *Women in Ochre Robes* (2004). To highlight a new and growing body of research on female renunciation, she co-edited a volume with Sondra Hausner and Ann Grodzins Gold entitled *Women's Renunciation in South Asia* (2006, 2007). More recently, Khandelwal has turned her attention to transnational studies and has published on various topics, including transnational aspects of Hindu renunciation, Indian diaspora, transnational feminist methodologies, and development.

CATHERINE KINGFISHER is a professor of anthropology at the University of Lethbridge in Alberta, Canada. She is author of *A Policy Travelogue: Tracing*

Welfare Reform in Aotearoa/New Zealand and Canada (2013), and *Women in the American Welfare Trap* (1996); and editor of *Western Welfare in Decline: Globalization and Women's Poverty* (2002). Her current research focuses on governance and happiness/well-being in Japan and Canada.

ELISE KRAMER received her PhD in anthropology from the University of Chicago. Her research focuses on language, politics, and identity in the United States, with particular interests in gender, humor, and Internet sociality. She currently lectures in anthropology at the University of Illinois, Champaign–Urbana.

LYNN KWIATKOWSKI is an associate professor of anthropology at Colorado State University. She is the author of *Struggling with Development: The Politics of Hunger and Gender in the Philippines* (1998). Her current research concerns domestic violence, gender, health, and global health and development in Vietnam.

LOUISE LAMPHERE is distinguished professor of anthropology emerita at the University of New Mexico and past president of the American Anthropological Association. She began her career in feminist anthropology with the publication in 1974 of *Woman, Culture, and Society*, co-edited with Michelle Zimbalist Rosaldo. She has studied issues of women and work for almost forty years, beginning with her study of women workers in Rhode Island industry, *From Working Daughters to Working Mothers* (1977). She also co-authored a study of working women in Albuquerque entitled *Sunbelt Working Mothers: Reconciling Family and Factory* (1993) with Patricia Zavella, Felipe Gonzales, and Peter Evans and co-edited *Situated Lives: Gender and Culture in Everyday Life* (1997) with Helena Ragoné and Patricia Zavella. Her most recent book is a biography of three Navajo women entitled *Weaving Women's Lives: Three Generations in a Navajo Family* (2007).

ELLEN LEWIN is a professor of gender, women's, and sexuality studies, and anthropology at the University of Iowa. Her scholarship has focused on LGBT family formations, with her books *Lesbian Mothers: Accounts of Gender in American Culture*; *Recognizing Ourselves: Lesbian and Gay Ceremonies of Commitment*; and *Gay Fatherhood: Family and Citizenship in America* each concerning a different family- and kinship-related issue. Her current book project concerns a coalition of predominantly African American, LGBT, Pentecostal churches and is titled *Filled with the Spirit*. She has also edited three volumes with William L. Leap on lesbian and gay anthropology (*Out in the Field, Out in Theory, Out in Public)* and other volumes on women's health, lesbians in America, and feminist anthropology.

FRANCES. E. MASCIA-LEES is a professor of anthropology at Rutgers University, where she has served as chair of the Department of Anthropology and dean of social and behavioral sciences. She has been an International Scholar at Sophia University (Bulgaria), University of Prishtina (Kosovo), and Tbilisi State University (Republic of Georgia). Her extensive work on feminist theory, gender/difference, and the body includes the edited collections *A Companion to the Anthropology of the Body and Embodiment* (2011) and *Tattoo, Torture, Mutilation, and Adornment: The Denaturalization of the Body in Culture and Text* (with P. Sharpe, 1992), and the books *Gender and Difference in a Globalizing World: 21st Century Anthropology* (2010), *Taking a Stand in a Post-Feminist World* (with P. Sharpe, 2000), and *Gender and Anthropology* (with N. Black, 2000). She served as editor-in-chief of *American Anthropologist* from 2001 to 2006 and was the recipient of the AAA/Mayfield Award for Excellence in Undergraduate Teaching of Anthropology in 1998.

RAYNA RAPP teaches anthropology at New York University where she is associate chair of the department. The author of over eighty articles on gender and health and the politics of reproduction, she also wrote the prize-winning *Testing Women, Testing the Fetus: The Social Impact of Amniocentesis of America*, and edited/co-edited four books. Currently, she and Faye Ginsburg, with whom she has a longstanding collaboration, are writing a book entitled *Disability, Personhood, and the "New Normal" in 21st Century America.*

ELIZABETH F. S. ROBERTS, a feminist ethnographer of science, medicine, and technology, is an associate professor of anthropology at the University of Michigan. Her work has included research on assisted reproduction in Ecuador (*God's Laboratory: Assisted Reproduction in the Andes*, 2012), reproductive governance in Latin America, transnational medical migrations, and currently environmental health science in Mexico and the United States.

LENI M. SILVERSTEIN, an anthropologist and reproductive health professional, has more than fifteen years of experience creating, managing, and evaluating international development projects focused on health, population, human rights, reproductive rights, and gender advocacy. As the founder of Strategies for Development, a consulting firm, she has worked extensively in South America and Africa on projects affecting reproductive health, HIV/AIDS, child marriage, and women and girls' adolescent health, and has consulted with foundations, government officials, multilateral agencies, and commercial enterprises. She taught the first course on anthropology and gender in Brazil at the National Museum, Rio de Janeiro.

KIMBERLY THEIDON is a medical anthropologist focusing on Latin America. Her research interests include political violence, transitional justice, reconciliation, and the politics of postwar reparations. She is the author of many articles, and *Entre Prójimos: El conflicto armado interno y la política de la reconciliación en el Perú* (1st edition 2004; 2nd edition 2009) and *Intimate Enemies: Violence and Reconciliation in Peru* (2012). *Intimate Enemies* was awarded the 2013 Honorable Mention from the Washington Office on Latin America–Duke University Libraries Book Award for Human Rights in Latin America, and the 2013 Honorable Mention for the Eileen Basker Prize from the Society for Medical Anthropology for research on gender and health. She is the Henry J. Leir Professor of International Humanitarian Studies at the Fletcher School, Tufts University.

MARGOT WEISS is an associate professor of American studies and anthropology at Wesleyan University and the co-chair of the Association for Queer Anthropology. Her scholarship explores intersections of sexual politics and capitalism, primarily in the United States. She is the author of *Techniques of Pleasure: BDSM and the Circuits of Sexuality* (2011), awarded the Ruth Benedict Book Prize and a finalist for the Lambda Literary Award in LGBT Studies. Her current book project, "Visions of Sexual Justice," draws on multi-sited fieldwork with North American queer left activists to explore the possibilities of a radical political imagination at a time of economic precarity.

INDEX

CPSIA information can be obtained
at www.ICGtesting.com
Printed in the USA
BVHW050159030523
663497BV00011B/355

9 780813 574288